Devouring Japan

Devouring Japan

*Global Perspectives on
Japanese Culinary Identity*

Edited by
Nancy K. Stalker

OXFORD
UNIVERSITY PRESS

Oxford University Press is a department of the University of Oxford. It furthers
the University's objective of excellence in research, scholarship, and education
by publishing worldwide. Oxford is a registered trade mark of Oxford University
Press in the UK and certain other countries.

Published in the United States of America by Oxford University Press
198 Madison Avenue, New York, NY 10016, United States of America.

© Oxford University Press 2018

All rights reserved. No part of this publication may be reproduced, stored in
a retrieval system, or transmitted, in any form or by any means, without the
prior permission in writing of Oxford University Press, or as expressly permitted
by law, by license, or under terms agreed with the appropriate reproduction
rights organization. Inquiries concerning reproduction outside the scope of the
above should be sent to the Rights Department, Oxford University Press, at the
address above.

You must not circulate this work in any other form
and you must impose this same condition on any acquirer.

CIP data is on file at the Library of Congress
ISBN 978–0–19–024040–0 (hbk.)
ISBN 978–0–19–024041–7 (pbk.)

9 8 7 6 5 4 3 2 1

Paperback printed by WebCom, Inc., Canada
Hardback printed by Bridgeport National Bindery, Inc., United States of America

Contents

Acknowledgments ix
Contributors xi
Chronology: Japan's Historical Eras xvii

Introduction: Japanese Culinary Capital 1
Nancy K. Stalker

PART I. JAPAN'S CULINARY BRANDS AND IDENTITIES

HISTORICAL CULINARY IDENTITIES 33

1. Japanese Food in the Early Modern European Imagination 35
   Ken Albala

2. Gifting Melons to the Shining Prince: Food in the Late Heian Court Imagination 48
   Takeshi Watanabe

3. Soba, Edo Style: Food, Aesthetics, and Cultural Identity 65
   Lorie Brau

4. The Three Waves (and Ways) of Sake Appreciation in the West 81
   Dick Stegewerns

CULINARY NATIONALISM AND BRANDING 97

5. Washoku, Far and Near: UNESCO, Gastrodiplomacy, and the Cultural Politics of Traditional Japanese Cuisine 99
   Theodore C. Bestor

6. "We Can Taste but Others Cannot": Umami as an Exclusively Japanese Concept 118
   Yoshimi Osawa

7. Rosanjin: The Roots of Japanese Gourmet Nationalism 133
   Nancy K. Stalker

REGIONAL AND INTERNATIONAL VARIATIONS 151

8. Savoring the Kyoto Brand 153
   Greg de St. Maurice

9. *Love! Spam*: Food, Military, and Empire in Post–World War II Okinawa 171
   Mire Koikari

10. Nikkei Cuisine: How Japanese Food Travels and Adapts Abroad 187
    Ayumi Takenaka

PART II. JAPAN'S FOOD-RELATED VALUES

FOOD AND INDIVIDUAL IDENTITY 205

11. Miso Mama: How Meals Make the Mother in Contemporary Japan 207
    Amanda C. Seaman

12. Better Than Sex? Masaoka Shiki's Poems on Food 220
    J. Keith Vincent

13. The Devouring Empire: Food and Memory in Hayashi Fumiko's Wartime Narratives and Naruse Mikio's Films 242
    Noriko J. Horiguchi

FOOD ANXIETIES 259

14. Eating amid Affluence: Kaikō Takeshi's Adventures in Food 261
    Bruce Suttmeier

15. An Anorexic in Miyazaki's Land of Cockaigne: Excess and Abnegation in *Spirited Away* 273
    Susan Napier

16. Discarding Cultures: Social Critiques of Food Waste in an Affluent Japan 287
    Eiko Maruko Siniawer

17. The Unbearable, Endless Anxiety of Eating: Food Consumption in Japan after 3/11 302
    Faye Yuan Kleeman

    Afterword: Foods of Japan, Not Japanese Food 312
    Eric C. Rath

    Glossary 329
    Index 339

Acknowledgments

In 2013, UNESCO recognized Japanese cuisine (washoku) on its List of Intangible Cultural Heritage. To commemorate this award, my UT Austin Japanese Studies colleagues Patricia Machlachlan, Kirsten Cather, and I decided to host a year-long program on Japanese foodways featuring guest lectures, films, and a conference entitled *Devouring Japan: An Interdisciplinary Conference on Japanese Cuisine and Foodways*, held in February 2014. All of these events were made possible though a generous grant from the Japan Foundation's Small Grant Program. We are also grateful for additional support received from other sponsors, including the Northeast Asia Council of the Association for Asian Studies and the Mitsubishi Caterpillar Heavy Industries Endowment. Papers by many of the scholars who participated in the conference became the basis for this volume. We also gratefully acknowledge the contributions of scholars who made presentations at the conference that are not part of the final volume, including Victoria Lyon Bestor, Robert Hellyer, Barak Kushner, Patricia Maclachlan, Amy Bliss Marshall, Robyn Metcalfe, Yoneyuki Sugita, R. Kenji Tierney, and Merry White. Their thoughtful and critical participation helped make the conference a success. We also wish to thank Mark Metzler, Kirsten Cather, Robert Oppenheim, Madeline Hsu, Heather Hindman, and Robyn Metcalfe for chairing panels and offering vital comments and questions for participants. Staff members from UT's Department of Asian Studies, especially Jeannie Cortez and Salcha Parvaiz, provided invaluable assistance in organizing, administering, and overseeing logistics. Nicole Elmer created wonderful graphics and posters for the conference. Erin Newton, a graduate student, organized a troupe of student volunteers, including the members of my Cuisine and Culture in Asia course, and helped manage many conference-related matters. Zachary Long assisted with proofreading and editing the volume. Finally, we offer our deep gratitude to Susan Ferber of Oxford University Press for her interest in and support of this project and to the anonymous Press reviewers who provided helpful and detailed critiques that guided us in the revision process.

Contributors

Ken Albala is Professor of History at the University of the Pacific and Chair of the Food Studies MA program in San Francisco. He has authored or edited twenty-four books on food, including *Eating Right in the Renaissance, Food in Early Modern Europe, Cooking in Europe, 1250–1650, The Banquet, Beans* (winner 2008 IACP Jane Grigson Award), *Pancake, Grow Food, Cook Food, Share Food,* and *Nuts: A Global History*. He was coeditor of the journal *Food, Culture and Society* and has also coedited *The Business of Food, Human Cuisine,* and *Food and Faith* and edited *A Cultural History of Food: The Renaissance* and *The Routledge International Handbook of Food Studies*. Albala was editor of the Food Cultures Around the World series, the four-volume *Food Cultures of the World Encyclopedia*, and the three-volume *Sage Encyclopedia of Food Issues* published in 2015. He is also series editor of Rowman and Littlefield Studies in Food and Gastronomy, for which he wrote *Three World Cuisines* (winner of the Gourmand World Cookbook Awards' best foreign cuisine book in the world for 2012). He has also coauthored two cookbooks: *The Lost Art of Real Cooking* and *The Lost Arts of Hearth and Home*. His latest works are a *Food History Reader* and a translation of the sixteenth-century *Livre fort excellent de cuysine*. His course Food: A Cultural Culinary History is available on DVD from the Great Courses. He is now working on a book about noodle soups.

Theodore C. Bestor is Professor of Social Anthropology and Director of the Reischauer Institute of Japanese Studies at Harvard University. He is the author of *Neighborhood Tokyo* and *Tsukiji: The Fish Market at the Center of the World*, among many other publications. He is the coeditor of *Doing Fieldwork in Japan* and the *Routledge Handbook of Japanese Culture and Society*. Bestor was featured in the documentary *Tsukiji Wonderland* (directed by Naotarō Endō). His current research focuses on the controversial relocation of the Tsukiji marketplace to make way for the 2020 Olympics and on various aspects of Japanese food culture, including perceptions of washoku in Japan and abroad, the concept of umami, and Japanese cuisine outside Japan. Bestor was the founding president of the Society for East Asian Anthropology in 2001–2003, and in 2012–2013 he was President of the Association of Asian Studies.

Lorie Brau is an Associate Professor of Japanese in the Department of Foreign Languages and Literatures at the University of New Mexico. She received her MA in Japanese literature from the University of Michigan and her PhD in performance studies at New York University (1994). To research her book *Rakugo: Performing Comedy and Cultural Heritage in Contemporary Tokyo*, she became a disciple of storyteller Kokontei Engiku and learned to perform Japanese comic storytelling. She is an avid reader and researcher of such culinary manga as *Oishinbo* (The gourmet) and is presently writing a monograph on the discourses of culinary manga titled *Gourmanga: Reading Food in Japanese Comic Books*.

Greg de St. Maurice is a cultural anthropologist whose research is primarily concerned with "place," globalization, foodways, and Japan. He currently serves as the Vice President of the Association for the Study of Food and Society (ASFS). He received his PhD in cultural anthropology from the University of Pittsburgh in 2015. His recent publications include "Kyoto Cuisine Gone Global" (in *Gastronomica*), "Everything but the Taste: Celebrating Kyoto's Shishigatani Squash as Culinary Heritage" (in *Food, Culture, and Society*), and "The Movement to Reinvigorate Local Food Culture in Kyoto, Japan" (in the edited volume *Food Activism*).

Noriko J. Horiguchi (PhD, University of Pennsylvania) is an Associate Professor of Modern Japanese Literature at the University of Tennessee. Her research is at the interface of literary criticism, history, women's studies, and cultural studies. Horiguchi's first monograph, *Women Adrift: The Literature of Japan's Imperial Body*, examines women's paradoxical relationship with the empire of Japan in the first half of the twentieth century. Horiguchi's second book project, on the discourse on food, examines narratives (political, literary, and visual) and memories of food and hunger that negotiated, both materially and metaphorically, the power dynamics among Japan, neighboring Asian nations, and the Western powers (especially the United States) in the prewar, wartime, and postwar periods.

Faye Yuan Kleeman is a Professor of Modern Japanese Literature and Culture at the University of Colorado. She specializes in modern and contemporary Japanese and literature, Japanophone studies, as well as film, gender, (post)colonial theory, and visual culture. Her works include *In Transit, Under an Imperial Sun*, and recent articles "Chain Reactions—Japanese Colonialism and Global Cosmopolitanism in East Asia," "Body (Language) across the Sea: Gender, Ethnicity, and the Embodiment of Post/colonial Modernity," "Body, Identity, and Social Order: Japanese Crime Fiction," and "Exophony and the Locations of (Cultural) Identity in Levy Hideo's Fiction."

Mire Koikari is Professor of Women's Studies at the University of Hawai'i at Mānoa. Her publications include *Cold War Encounters in US-Occupied Okinawa: Women, Militarized Domesticity, and Transnationalism in East Asia* and *Pedagogy of Democracy: Feminism and the Cold War in the U.S. Occupation of Japan*. Her research interests include feminism, militarism, and imperialism in the Asia-Pacific region. She is currently working on a project in which she explores gendered and gendering dynamics of safety and security politics in Japan following the triple disaster of earthquake, tsunami, and nuclear meltdown in 2011.

Susan Napier is the Goldthwaite Professor of Rhetoric at Tufts University. Previously she held the Mitsubishi Heavy Industries Chair at the University of Texas. She attended Harvard University for both undergraduate and graduate degrees, all of which were in East Asian studies. She has also taught at the University of London and been a visiting professor at Harvard, the University of Pennsylvania, and the University of Sydney and a visiting scholar at Keio University in Tokyo. Her first two books were on Japanese literature, and she has since published two books on Japanese animation along with numerous articles and book chapters. Her new book on the Japanese animator Hayao Miyazaki will appear in 2018.

Yoshimi Osawa is an ethnobiologist and an anthropologist of food and the senses. She received her PhD from the University of Kent in the United Kingdom. Dr. Osawa's research centers on understanding of relationship between humans and nature, particularly by looking at food, ecology, and human sensory perceptions. She has published in several key journals including *The Senses and Society* and *Ecology of Food and Nutrition*. She is currently based at

Kyoto University as a University Research Administrator and also serves as Deputy Director of the Kyoto University ASEAN Center in Bangkok.

Eric C. Rath is Professor of Premodern Japanese History at the University of Kansas, where his courses include History of Sushi and Beer, Sake, and Tea: Beverages in Japanese History. A specialist in the history of Japanese dietary cultures, he is the author of *Japan's Cuisines: Food, Place and Identity* and *Food and Fantasy in Early Modern Japan*, and editor with Stephanie Assmann of *Japanese Foodways Past and Present*. He is now writing a history of food in Japan.

Amanda C. Seaman received her PhD in East Asian languages and civilizations from the University of Chicago, and is a Professor of Japanese Language and Literature at the University of Massachusetts, Amherst. In addition to her books *Bodies of Evidence: Women, Society, and Detective Fiction in 1990s Japan* and *Writing Pregnancy in Low-Fertility Japan*, she is the author of numerous articles on contemporary Japanese detective fiction and women's literature, and the translator of works by Matsuo Yumi, Matsuura Rieko, and Takahashi Takako. Her current research focuses upon popular cultural representations of, and reactions to, illness and disease in modern Japan.

Eiko Maruko Siniawer is a Professor of History at Williams College. She is the author of *Ruffians, Yakuza, Nationalists: The Violent Politics of Modern Japan*, which examines issues of political violence and democracy through a focus on violence specialists. Currently, Siniawer is completing a book that examines shifts in what was considered waste and wasteful in Japan from the 1940s through the present. An article on this research has been published in the *Journal of Asian Studies*. Siniawer holds a PhD in history from Harvard University.

Nancy K. Stalker is the Soshitsu Sen XV Distinguished Professor of Traditional Japanese Culture and History at University of Hawai'i at Mānoa. Her research focuses on twentieth-century material culture in Japan, examining the interplay between ideology and market forces in manifestations of traditional culture in modern eras. She received her PhD in East Asian History from Stanford University and is the author of *Japan: History and Culture from Classical to Cool*, *Prophet Motive: Deguchi Onisaburō, Oomoto and the Rise of a New Religion in Imperial Japan*, and numerous articles published in such journals as the *Journal of Japanese Studies*, *Positions: East Asia Cultures Critique*, and *Gastronomica*. She is currently working on a book entitled *Budding Fortunes: Ikebana as Art, Industry, and Cold War Culture* and conducting research on the relationship between culinary identity and masculinity in modern Japan.

Dick Stegewerns is Associate Professor at the University of Oslo and Visiting Professor at Nichibunken, Kyoto. He teaches courses on modern Japanese history, international relations, politics, society, culture, and film. At present he conducts research projects on postwar Japanese war films, a century of democracy in Japan, the visualization of Japanese history in film, manga and anime, the discourse on the dichotomy of Eastern and Western civilization (*Tōzai bunmeiron*), the Japanese film director Naruse Mikio, and a global modern history of the Japanese fermented drink sake. His main publications are *Nationalism and Internationalism in Imperial Japan*, *Adjusting to the New World: Japanese Opinion Leaders of the Taishō Generation and the Outside World*, and *Yoshida Kijū: 50 Years of Avant-Garde Filmmaking in Postwar Japan*. He is also active in introducing some of his interests in Japan to Europe, in the form of film retrospectives, concert tours, and pure sake tastings.

Bruce Suttmeier is Associate Dean of Faculty and Associate Professor of Japanese at Lewis & Clark College. He has published on several postwar writers, including Kaikō Takeshi and Ōe Kenzaburō, as well as on travel writing in the 1960s and on war memory in the postwar period. His recent work includes "Speculations of Murder: Ghostly Dreams, Poisonous Frogs and the Return of Yokoi Shōichi" in *Perversion and Modern Japan: Experiments in Psychoanalysis*, and "On the Road in Olympic-Era Tokyo" in *Cartographic Japan: A History in Maps*.

Ayumi Takenaka currently teaches sociology at Aston University. Her main research interests lie in the global mobility of people and food and their transformations over time and across spaces. She has engaged in research primarily in the areas of immigration, identities, social inequality, and diaspora politics in Japan, the United States, Latin America (mostly Peru), and Europe (Spain and the UK). Her current research projects include the computational analysis of global remigration patterns, immigrants' social mobility in Japan and Spain, and gastrodiplomacy in Peru. She also engages in activities to promote washoku in the UK and Europe.

J. Keith Vincent is Associate Professor of Japanese and Comparative Literature and Chair of World Languages and Literatures at Boston University. He is the author of *Two-Timing Modernity: Homosocial Narrative in Modern Japanese Fiction*. Recent essays include "Takemura Kazuko: On Friendship and the Queering of American and Japanese Studies" in *Rethinking Japanese Feminism*, and "Queer Reading in Japanese Literature," in the *Routledge Handbook of Modern Japanese Literature*. His translation of Okamoto Kanoko's *A Riot of Goldfish* won the 2011 U.S. Japan Friendship Commission Prize for the Translation of

Japanese Literature, and New Directions published his translation of Tanizaki Jun'ichirō's novel *Devils in Daylight*. Together with Alan Tansman and Reiko Abe Auestad, he is currently coediting two collections of essays on the novelist Natsume Sōseki. He is also writing a book on the literary friendship between Sōseki and Masaoka Shiki.

Takeshi Watanabe is an Assistant Professor in the College of East Asian Studies at Wesleyan University. He received his PhD in premodern Japanese literature from Yale University. He has published work in English and Japanese on the sixteenth-century *Illustrated Scroll of the Wine or Rice Debate*. He has also contributed to the tea utensil exhibition catalog *Tea Culture of Japan*. A short essay on Heian court cuisine is forthcoming in *Birth of a Monarch: Selections from Fujiwara no Munetada's Journal "Chūyūki"*. After completing his current manuscript on the eleventh-century historical tale *A Tale of Flowering Fortunes*, he is planning to work on ambivalent representations of food and consumption from ancient to medieval Japan.

Chronology: Japan's Historical Eras

Start Date	End Date	Era Name
?	≈ 250 BCE	Jōmon
≈ 250 BCE	≈ 250 CE	Yayoi
≈ 300	710	Yamato
710	794	Nara
794	1185	Heian
1185	1333	Kamakura
1333	1568	Muromachi (aka Ashikaga)
1568	1600	Azuchi-Momoyama
1600	1868	Edo (aka Tokugawa)
1868	1912	Meiji
1912	1926	Taishō
1926	1989	Shōwa
1989	Present	Heisei

Introduction

Japanese Culinary Capital

Nancy K. Stalker

Why do today's celebrity chefs seem so besotted with Japan? David Chang, subject of the first season of PBS's *The Mind of a Chef*, who named his New York restaurant Momofuku after the inventor of instant ramen, asserts that Tokyo is the world's best food city and that "nothing comes close."[1] Rene Redzepi, founder of Noma, the Copenhagen restaurant voted best in the world for several consecutive years, relocated his entire operation to Tokyo for five weeks in January 2015 to open a "pop-up" at the five-star Mandarin Oriental Hotel, chronicled in the documentary *Ants on a Shrimp* (2016). In an interview Redzepi explained his rationale: "I wanted to get as close as possible to the country's mind-boggling culinary variety and the devotion to craft that fellow chefs from the West speak of in hushed and reverential tones."[2] And the king of food celebrities, Anthony Bourdain, visited Japan more frequently than any other foreign country save France in his TV series *No Reservations* and *Parts Unknown* and even penned a graphic novel, *Get Jiro*, about a "renegade" sushi chef in Los Angeles who beheads a customer for requesting a California roll.[3] What is it about Japanese cuisine that currently attracts the admiration of both celebrity chefs and ordinary diners around the globe? In other words, why is Japan increasingly a source of culinary capital—that is, food-based status and power?[4]

Japanese cuisine has been rising in international esteem since the 1980s, when sushi first began to conquer the West, but in recent years it has reached new heights of global popularity, with the number of Japanese restaurants outside Japan doubling between 2003 and 2013.[5] It increasingly challenges the primacy of French, considered the pinnacle of haute cuisine since the eighteenth century. In 2009, the French were the first to receive UNESCO recognition for their food, when their "gastronomic meal" was named to UNESCO's intangible cultural heritage list, an honor Japan achieved in 2013 (see the Bestor chapter in this volume). Some food critics, however, increasingly view French cuisine as "dull" and "predictable."[6] As early as 1997 Adam Gopnik complained that even French nouvelle cuisine was overly rich and had become formulaic. "The hold of the master sauté pan, and the master sauce, and the thing-in-the-middle-of-the-plate, is still intact."[7]

Research from Krishnendu Ray's recent book *The Ethnic Restaurateur*, which uses *Zagat* guides and major US newspapers to gauge the comparative popularity of ethnic cuisines in the United States, confirms such opinions. Ray graphically demonstrates that interest in French and Continental cuisine (with the exception of Italian) has declined sharply since the 1940s, while interest in, and the price of, Japanese restaurant meals has climbed steadily since the 1980s, surpassing the average cost of a French meal in the mid-2010s.[8] The most expensive meal in New York is generally acknowledged to be at Masa's, a three-Michelin-star, sushi-centric restaurant with a tasting menu of twenty or more courses that runs over five hundred dollars per person, before wine. As the culinary star of the French fades, Japan is the current ingénue of the global gourmet economy, with both its highbrow and its lowbrow cuisines earning accolades and devotees at home and abroad.

On the elite end of the spectrum, Tokyo has more Michelin-starred restaurants than Paris and New York combined. Of the 213 Tokyo restaurants awarded stars in 2016, 141 feature Japanese cuisine. Awardees also include Japanese branches of celebrated French restaurants, from the old-school Tour d'Argent to contemporary establishments by master chefs such as Joel Robuchon, Alain Ducasse, and Paul Bocuse, but the vast majority of the forty-eight French and ten Italian Michelin-starred restaurants are helmed by European-trained Japanese chefs who fuse local ingredients and sensibilities with techniques learned abroad, as illustrated in figure I.1. Among New York's Michelin-starred establishments, Japanese cuisine is usually the most dominant international category.[9]

In terms of lowbrow cuisine, humble ramen noodles have achieved cult status in many American cities, thanks in part to the efforts of David Chang, who first achieved acclaim in 2004 for his Momofuku Noodle Bar and who featured ramen as the theme for the first issue of his hip food quarterly *Lucky Peach*. Ramen and its purveyors in America have been lionized in mainstream publications such as the *New York Times* and *Food & Wine* alongside trendier food media, including *Lucky Peach, Saveur,* and *Roads & Kingdoms*. Its ascent,

FIGURE I.1 Example of Japanese-French plating of grilled squid at chef Shibata Hideyuki's La Clairiere in Tokyo. Photograph by the author.

in both Japan and the United States, took surprising routes. Ramen was first introduced in Japan in the nineteenth century, when it was considered an inexpensive Chinese food for laborers and students. During the post–World War II occupation, a time of dire food shortages, American wheat imports spurred ramen's popularity; the invention of instant ramen in 1958 by Momofuku Ando made the dish a cheap staple for the masses and began the process of changing its national identification to distinctly Japanese. In the 1970s, as Japanese domestic tourism boomed, so did ramen; local variations (e.g., Sapporo's miso-based broth, Fukuoka's thick tonkotsu style, and Iwate's light chicken broth) became available nationwide. Ramen quickly became the most popular object of lowbrow culinary connoisseurship, a trend that expanded even further with the advent of the Internet and social media.[10]

Instant ramen was introduced in the United States in the 1970s as a commodity, fueling college students and jail inmates alike for as little as twenty-five cents per serving. Few could have imagined that this chemical-laden sodium bomb would transform into a gourmet dish. New Yorkers and Los Angelinos became fans of "real" ramen in the early to mid-2000s, as branches of iconic Japanese shops, such as Ippudō and Tsujita, began to appear in these cities. By 2014 a *New Yorker* cartoon portrayed a mother giving advice to her adolescent son: "We could have a lemonade stand, sweetie, but wouldn't you rather do a pop-up ramen shop?"[11] Quality ramen is now even fashionable in Middle America. In Austin, Texas, for example, there are at least four dedicated ramen shops, including the Japanese chain Jinya. Ramen Tatsu-ya, established locally, was named one of *Bon Appetit*'s fifty best new restaurants in 2013 and America's best ramen by *Time Out* in 2016. Hipsters, Japanese expats, and middle-aged professors queue there for an hour or more for a delectable bowl. Whole Foods Market, the upscale grocery chain headquartered in Austin, features a made-to-order ramen counter at many locations. In the United States today, good restaurant ramen represents an affordable, yet exotic and "authentic," gourmet experience.

Before America's ramen craze, Japanese cuisine became chic among elites beginning in the late 1980s, largely through the efforts of maverick chefs traveling global circuits and creating innovative dishes that appealed to cosmopolitan palates. Nobuyuki Matsuhisa, founder of Nobu, was frustrated with the ten-year apprenticeship required of sushi chefs in Japan and so decamped to Peru, where he infused sashimi with local flavors like chili and cilantro for expat Japanese elites, and then to Beverly Hills, where he served it lightly seared with hot oil for Americans unaccustomed to raw fish.[12] His signature miso-marinated black cod and elegant omakase (chef's choice) menus attracted celebrities, such as Robert DeNiro, who became Matsuhisa's partner for the 1994 opening of Nobu in New York. Eschewing traditional decor for cutting-edge style, it soon became a sophisticated global brand, with thirty-three branches on five continents today. Nobu's unconventional route to culinary stardom opened the door for non-Japanese chefs, such as David Chang, Tim Cushman of Boston's Oya, and Austin's Tyson Cole of Uchi and Uchiko, to appropriate and play with Japanese cuisine with minimal in-country training. In a recent volume on the globalization of Asian cuisine, James Farrer refers to this phenomenon as the "deterritorialization of culinary fields, or the delinking of cuisine from place," noting that important innovations in "national" cuisines often occur outside their borders by foreign chefs with a variety of kitchen experience.[13] Unmoored from arduous traditional training and loyalty to the master, such chefs create hybrid cuisines that are, nevertheless, experienced as "authentically Japanese" by many customers.

As Japan's reputation for its cuisine expands abroad, its food and food-related practices are increasingly a source of individual identity, cultural capital, and distinction among a broad range of food producers and consumers around the globe.[14] In their work *Culinary Capital*, Peter Naccarato and Kathleen Lebesco argue that such capital is increasingly valued in contemporary American culture but recognize that "all cultures use food and food practices as a way of conferring cultural authority and circulating dominant ideologies just as their citizens may use them to both reinforce and transgress their culture's norms."[15] They also assert that culinary capital is increasingly considered a geopolitical asset, "separating and stratifying countries based on the extent to which they aspire to particular, favored foodways" in a global gourmet economy.[16] Americans are ever more conscious of food identities and quick to seize upon food fashions, such as ramen, but the Japanese hunger for culinary capital, both individual and national, is equal to if not greater than the American pursuit; in Japan, as in the United States, food is currently an all-consuming matter.

As Naccarato and Lebesco note, culinary capital does not accrue to individuals alone, but also to businesses, public and private institutions, and localities from village to nation. At a national level, cuisine has become one of Japan's most visible and influential cultural "brands" abroad, an important source of soft power in the world. "Place branding," the practice of marketing nations, regions, and cities, promoted by development gurus like Simon Anholt, identifies and promotes aspects of an area's culture to provide it with an appealing personality, affecting its ability to attract media attention, tourism, public and private investment, and even new residents and students.[17] Foods are, of course, popular and widely recognized aspects of most national brands. Within nations, too, regional and city culinary brands are increasingly important aspects of local identity, recognized by both domestic and foreign connoisseurs. Scholarship on Japanese popular culture and its soft power abroad has focused largely on mass media (e.g., manga, anime), giving inadequate attention to food cultures as components of Japan's contemporary nation brand.

Together with manga and anime, pop music, fashion, and "cute" consumer goods, cuisine is part of the "Cool Japan" brand that promotes the country as a new kind of pop cultural superpower, the "Pokémon Hegemon" exporting Hello Kitty, pop idols, animated films, and other forms of popular culture.[18] While the notion of Cool Japan has circulated in the international mass media since the early 2000s, the Japanese government has only recently embraced this reputation, establishing the Creative Industries Promotion Office in the Ministry of Economy, Trade and Industry (METI) in 2010. METI recognized the significance of cuisine for national branding and specified *B-kyū gurume* (second-class gourmet), the celebration of creative and local versions of Japanese comfort foods like fried noodles (yakisoba) and *okonomiyaki* savory pancakes, as a key element of its Cool Japan initiative.[19] Foods can also be marketed by adopting other elements of the Cool Japan brand as seen in the Hello Kitty confections illustrated in figure I.2. Other governmental agencies, including the Ministry of Foreign Affairs (MOFA), the Ministry of Agriculture, Forestry and Fisheries (MAFF), and the Japanese National Tourist Organization (JNTO), are also deeply invested in the idea of Japanese culinary identity as a source of national soft power.

The imagining, branding, and representation of Japanese culinary identity, which tend to highlight purity, seasonality, and aesthetic presentation, do not, however, necessarily conform to historical and social realities. As a whole, this

FIGURE I.2 Hello Kitty bean jam buns (*manjū*) at Tokyu Toyoko department store in Shibuya. Photograph by the author.

volume casts a critical eye toward idealization of Japanese cuisine and culinary values that inadequately consider the actual eating habits and everyday foods consumed by the Japanese. The title *Devouring Japan* allows a transnational perspective whereby Japan can be analyzed as subject or object, the nation that devours or is devoured by others. What does Japanese cuisine (*washoku*) mean to different audiences? What food-related values are imposed or implied by the term? What roles do media, the state, and other social institutions play in shaping notions of national cuisine? What elements of washoku are most visible in Japan's international culinary identity and why? Does the global enthusiasm for Japanese cuisine indicate the decline of Euro-American influence and the ascendance of Asian nations in post–Cold War geopolitics, or, rather, is it a form of orientalist appropriation? Individually, essays from a variety of disciplinary perspectives question how food and foodways have come to represent aspects of a "unique" Japanese identity. They call attention to how cuisine has been used as a foil to assert a culinary identity that contrasts with that of the Euro-American "other" and how cuisine and foodways are infused with official and unofficial ideologies. They reveal how food habits and choices are gendered and scrutinized by the state, mass media, and the public at large. And they examine the thoughts, actions, and motives of those who produce, consume, promote, represent, and work with foods.

The Globalization of Japanese Food

The current popularity of Japanese cuisine might seem surprising from a historical perspective. The premodern traditional diet was bland and monotonous, consisting largely of rough grains like millet and barley, sometimes mixed with rice and local vegetables. The widely held domestic conception of a "traditional Japanese meal" as a bowl of steamed white rice with miso soup, pickles, and three side dishes (*ichijū sansai*) did not become a possibility for most Japanese until well after World War II. That meal was not one particularly coveted by international audiences. Although Ken Albala's chapter points out early modern European admiration for Japanese foodways, foreign travelers to Japan from the nineteenth century through the 1970s often complained that native fare, including raw and fermented foods, was unpalatable for Euro-Americans. In 1878, intrepid Victorian traveler Isabella Bird cautioned would-be visitors to Japan to carry their own food, as "the fishy and vegetable abominations known as 'Japanese food' can only be swallowed and digested by a few, and that after long practice."[20] Through the 1970s, restaurants in Japan catering to Euro-American tourists who wished to sample native cuisine usually offered only a few select dishes, such as Kobe beef steak or sukiyaki, as seen in figure I.3, although meat was rarely consumed by locals. In short, until quite recently, the world paid scant attention to Japanese cuisine.

The globalization of Chinese food, described in a 2002 volume of essays edited by David Wu and Sidney Cheung, provides interesting contrasts to the Japanese case. China boasts four (or more) regional "high cuisines" with distinct ingredients, flavors, and methods of preparation.[21] For decades, international diners have recognized the differences between, for example, spicy Sichuan and more subtle Cantonese styles of cooking.[22] Chinese food spread across the globe with the vast Chinese diaspora, dating back centuries, and was a particularly powerful force in shaping food practices in Southeast Asia, where Chinese merchant classes often dominated local society. In late nineteenth- and early twentieth-century America, Chinese immigrants faced discrimination, but the cheap and tasty dishes they invented, like chop suey, became popular staples among America's laboring classes, while banquet halls in ethnic enclaves produced fine feasts for the immigrant elite.[23] Following World War II, middle-class families across America began to turn to Chinese restaurants and

FIGURE I.3 1963 Foreigners enjoying sukiyaki at Suehiro restaurant in Ginza.

takeout for exotic culinary variety. Within China itself, the rise of the Chinese Communist Party impeded the importation of Euro-American cuisines, which did not fundamentally transform the daily diet of most ordinary Chinese.

By contrast, Japanese regional cuisines are not as distinctive as those of China. Some areas introduce local specialty ingredients (*meibutsu*) into popular dishes like sushi or *okonomiyaki*, but the main flavoring agents—soy sauce, dashi stock, and miso—remain the same. The most noted distinction in regional tastes is between Kantō (eastern Japan, i.e., Tokyo), which favors heavier and more intensive flavors, and Kansai (western, i.e., Kyoto and Osaka), which leans toward light, more complex flavors (see de St. Maurice chapter). The Japanese diaspora is miniscule in comparison to the Chinese and much more recent, dating back only to the mid-nineteenth century, and the food practices immigrants brought to new lands were not very influential, except in Japan's colonized territories and more recently in Peru (see Takenaka chapter). With wartime defeat followed by rapid economic growth in the 1950s and 1960s, the Japanese diet was radically "Americanized," including sharp increases in meats, breads, sugar, and dairy.

Japan's ascendance to the status of economic powerhouse in the early 1980s was accompanied by a "gourmet boom," that is, the elevation of both foreign and domestic cuisines in popular consciousness, abetted by a glut of food-centric TV programming, discussed later in this chapter. Alongside and in reaction to the gourmet boom came the ennoblement of everyday foods, or *B-kyū gurume*—fast, cheap, and tasty comfort foods that satisfied hearty appetites—such as ramen. Many iconic dishes of *B-kyū* cuisine, like the rice omelet (*omuraisu*) and fried pork cutlets (tonkatsu), had foreign origins, but were introduced in the prewar period and subsequently Japanized in terms of taste and ingredients. The domestic demand for sushi also grew to massive proportions in the 1980s and 1990s as low-cost alternatives emerged for what was once seen as an expensive treat. Technological innovation, like conveyor belt sushi (*kaiten zushi*) and the use of precut frozen fish, enabled chain restaurants, takeout shops, and the ubiquitous convenience stores (*konbini*) to offer fast, no-frills sushi.[24]

As business and governmental elites and their families increasingly moved abroad to support Japanese economic interests in the 1970s and 1980s, they were accompanied by purveyors of Japanese goods and services, including restaurants that served sushi, pub (izakaya) fare, or elegant kaiseki meals to expat clientele. Non-Japanese urban cognoscenti developed a taste for sushi available at these new establishments in the 1980s and 1990s, marking the first time Euro-American elites broadly embraced Japanese cuisine. Sushi fit both the growing demand for healthy, less processed foods and the desire for exotic dining adventures; it whetted the Euro-American appetite for more Japanese delicacies. Meanwhile, in small towns and rural hinterlands across America and in other cities throughout the world, inexpensive California rolls, chicken teriyaki bowls, and other "glocalized" dishes were offered in Japanese or pan-Asian restaurants operated largely by Chinese, Vietnamese, and other Asian immigrants who benefited from both the premium charged for fashionable Japanese cuisine and the ethnic capital of "simply looking Asian."[25] By the 2000s, Japanese food had become another common genre on the global menu, with a range of offerings from elite delicacies to cheap fast food purveyed by transnational, multiethnic groups of chefs and entrepreneurs.

Japan's Contemporary Food Environment

As noted, the Japanese gourmet boom began decades earlier than the current US foodie phenomenon. The result of the Japanese boom, a mass advancement of cuisine and culinary values, was a necessary precondition for today's global acclaim of Japanese food culture.

In their insightful study of North American foodies, Johnston and Baumann note that the traditional divide between highbrow and lowbrow cuisine has eroded as "new markers of high-status food have emerged: Quality, rarity, locality, organic, hand-made, creativity, and simplicity all work to signify specific foods as a source of distinction for those with cultural and economic capital."[26] Like their American counterparts, Japanese foodies similarly value the organic, local, and handmade or artisanal. Farmer's markets and organic grocery chains, like Natural House, proliferate across the nation; highway rest stops and "antenna" stores sprout in Tokyo, selling regional produce and food specialties as seen in figure I.5. Restaurants increasingly advertise their use of local products and non-GMO foods, as shown in figure I.4, sometimes offering biographical information about the actual farmers. Craft beers such as the popular Hitachino Nest brand, multiply rapidly; specialty coffee houses like Tokyo's Bear Pond Espresso cater to obsessive java buffs. In short, the global "gourmet-scape," with nodes in major cities in the United States, Japan, and other global capitals, shares many of the same food values, concerns, and trending interests.

American and Japanese foodies also appreciate cooks and chefs who play with established categories and attempt new combinations. Aided by the rise of inexpensive food truck culture, Americans relish clever culinary fusions, such as bulgogi burritos and barbecued brisket sushi. In Japan, fried chicken curry, tofu donuts, and rice burgers, as seen in figure I.6, similarly titillate and

FIGURE I.4 Display for restaurant in Shimokitazawa advertising that it uses Tokyo specialty ingredients. Photograph by the author.

tempt bored diners. In both countries, concocting exciting new combinations can lead to social media stardom for cooks and restaurants. The search for novelty in the everyday acts of cooking and eating can be seen as a tactic that subverts established food categories, granting producers and consumers symbolic status as trendsetters.

American and Japanese foodies also differ in significant ways. Contrasting shapes and color combinations and varieties of texture are more important to the Japanese than to most Americans. Like the fifty Inuit words for snow, there are at least seven onomatopoeic words to describe food textures Americans would simply call crunchy, including the "pari pari" crackly crunch of potato

FIGURE I.5 Antenna store for Wakayama prefecture in Tokyo selling regional produce such as plums. Photograph by the author.

chips or "shaki shaki" juicy crunch of an apple. Japanese food producers and consumers place a higher value on packaging than their American counterparts, demanding artistic containers for gift foods purchased at department stores, as illustrated in figure I.7, and individually packaged servings for many supermarket products.

According to Johnston and Baumann, in terms of demographics and culinary values American foodies are disproportionately white and middle or upper class. They hold "authenticity" and "exoticism" in high esteem, echoing bell hooks's description of "the pleasure to be found in the acknowledgment and enjoyment of racial difference . . . [W]ithin commodity

FIGURE 1.6 Rice burger with vegetable tempura from the fast-food chain Mos Burger. Via Wikimedia Commons.

culture, ethnicity becomes spice, seasoning that can liven up the dull dish that is mainstream white culture."[27] Johnston and Baumann also describe how foodies "negotiate a fundamental ideological tension between democracy and distinction," frowning on snobbery and embracing greasy spoons and down-home diners while underplaying the considerable cultural and economic capital usually required to experience and appreciate culinary exoticism and authenticity. They wish to see themselves as democratically and internationally inclusive, "while they simultaneously work to legitimize and reproduce status distinctions."[28]

Japanese foodies, in contrast, tend to be more geographically and demographically diverse than their American counterparts. In a nation that has long considered itself monolithically middle class, accruing and performing culinary capital is considered an integral part of a middle-class lifestyle and thus very widespread. The foodie designation in Japan is not dominated by young professionals or creative industry types in urban enclaves, as in the United States; it extends to seniors, farmers, and housewives in remote rural towns,

FIGURE 1.7 Artful packaging of rice crackers (*senbei*) using colorful handmade papers at Tokyu Toyoko department store in Shibuya. Photograph by the author.

groups usually disenfranchised by the latest trends in popular culture, as well as blue- and pink-collar workers in urban areas.

Another apparent difference is that most Japanese foodies seem less oriented toward exoticism and less obsessed with issues of cultural authenticity when, in the words of bell hooks, "Eating the Other."[29] Instead, the Japanese are well known for readily adapting and hybridizing foreign foods to suit domestic tastes, from the Portuguese deep-fried foods that became tempura in the sixteenth century to *wafū pasuta*, Japanese-style pasta with ingredients like cod roe, soy sauce, and seaweed, to the "moon-viewing" (*tsukimi*) burger available seasonally at McDonald's. This is not, however, to deny that there are also many Japanese gourmands who prize "authenticity." They can select from a dazzling array of world cuisines offered by immigrants in ethnic restaurants and grocery stores in Japan's major cities, or carefully study and cultivate "authentic" methods and ingredients to produce their variants of food products, some of which eclipse the original, as the case of Suntory's Yamazaki whiskey—voted best in the world in 2014—demonstrates.

Japanese seekers of culinary capital may focus on a single practice or food, either domestic or foreign in origin, in contrast with their American omnivore cousins, for whom "more is more" and who thus seek out authentic and exotic experiences across the broadest possible food spectrums.³⁰ One example of Japanese single-minded pursuit of culinary capital is Speyside Way, a tiny bar in a Tokyo suburb with walls lined with hundreds of different bottles of single malt Scotch whiskeys; a thousand or so additional varieties are in storage. In the same neighborhood, Jiyūgaoka Sweets Forest is a large theme-park restaurant that serves only dainty desserts.³¹ Many Japanese foodies seek out endless instances of one everyday food like gyoza dumplings or udon noodles, consulting and contributing to websites, databases, and guidebooks. There are even connoisseurs of cheap, industrial foodstuffs, such as blogger Ton Tan Tin (Yamamoto Toshio), who has reviewed over five thousand varieties of instant ramen noodles and created hundreds of highly popular video reviews on YouTube.³² It is difficult to imagine such a variety of, or dedication to, instant mac and cheese.

A quintessential example of this relatively narrow focus in connoisseurship is the irascible Ono Jirō, proprietor of Sukibayashi Jirō, the ten-seat sushi bar awarded three Michelin stars and featured in the documentary *Jiro Dreams of Sushi* (2011), seen serving President Obama in figure I.8. In the film, Jirō appears to be a strict and intolerant master of his domain, a Japanese version of *Seinfeld*'s Soup Nazi. Yet the type of dedication he and the single-minded Japanese foodies described above demonstrate is, in part, a result of the

FIGURE I.8 Ono Jirō, President Obama, and Prime Minister Abe at Sukibayashi Jirō in April 2014. Official White House photo by Pete Souza via Wikimedia Commons.

historical development of restaurants in Japan, which evolved from food stalls and small establishments specializing in a single dish (see Brau chapter). From the early modern period until today, chefs (*shokunin*) earned reputations for their particular preparation of popular dishes like yakitori (grilled chicken skewers), unagi (grilled eel), fugu (puffer fish), and tempura, which are all individual categories in Japan's Michelin rankings, alongside sushi and the general category Japanese cuisine. In contrast with French chefs, trained to demonstrate range across a variety of courses, ingredients, and techniques, popular *shokunin* have historically demonstrated extreme depth of knowledge and perfectly honed techniques. Such specialists continue to flourish, alongside an array of Japanese restaurant styles that serve multiple types of dishes and courses, from rowdy izakaya pubs to elegant kaiseki establishments.

Johnston and Bauman also note that Americans foodies are highly influenced by food media and attain culinary capital through individual consumer choices "made within a media-saturated environment that promotes specific food related values and practices."[33] No one could fail to notice how American food media have grown explosively in the past few decades, encompassing dedicated cable networks, dozens of glossy food magazines, thousands of cookbooks in every genre, and innumerable blogs. Nevertheless, the Japanese appear to be even more inundated with food-centric media and entertainment. T. J. M Holden claims that "food is present on virtually every channel every hour, every day of the week throughout the broadcast day" in Japan.[34]

While Japan similarly possesses scores of culinary magazines, books, and cooking shows, food represents a regular theme in other forms of Japanese entertainment to a larger degree than in the United States. Since the gourmet boom, there has been a proliferation of food-centered media entertainment. Itami Jūzō's *Tampopo* (1985) was arguably the first internationally acclaimed gourmet feature film. Hundreds of gourmet manga comic titles have spawned from the successes of the best-selling series *Oishinbo* (1983–2014) and *Cooking Papa* (1985–present). Food TV programming comes in a variety of genres beyond cooking shows, including competitions, such as *Iron Chef* (1993–1999), the progenitor of all battling chef shows; animated series, often based on gourmet manga and designed to appeal to a variety of audiences; and popular food-centric serial TV dramas that air during prime time on every major network.[35] Three key ideological themes often found in TV food programming, especially dramas, resonate with larger social beliefs and values: (1) Ordinary people have the resources to cultivate discerning taste, (2) sincerity is crucial when offering hospitality (*omotenashi*), and (3) one must always try one's hardest in every endeavor (*gambaru* or *isshōkenmei*). Recently, the number of

FIGURE I.9 Recreation of late 1950s cityscape at the Shinyokohama Ramen Museum. Via Wikimedia Commons.

gurume-themed TV programs has spiked even higher, perhaps due to national pride in the UNESCO award.

Food-based entertainment, moreover, extends beyond restaurants and media. Japan hosts a plethora of food-related museums and theme parks, from the elaborate Shin Yokohama Ramen Museum, seen in figure I.9, offering samples of nine famous regional versions, to the food court-like Ikebukuro Gyoza Stadium, providing opportunities to taste a wide variety of dumplings. In Shizuoka prefecture, tourists can taste and learn at the Sushi Museum and World Tea Museum complexes. Another form of Japanese food-based entertainment is the specialty café, blending snacks or drinks with other engaging experiences: maid and butler cafes provide gendered pampering; animal cafes have broadened beyond cats to include communing with goats and owls; "cute" cafés like Tokyo's Kawaii Monster and Pom Pom Purin Café in fashionable Harajuku sell trendy goods alongside twee foods, such as seen in figure I.10, allowing consumers to commemorate their visit.

The wider range and broader dissemination of Japanese food-based entertainment can help deliver messages about national food culture and food-based gender norms more effectively than the more limited American food media, persuading Japanese consumers to cook and consume in ways that fit into

FIGURE 1.10 Banana caramel pancake in the image of Sanrio character Pom Pom Purin at the Pom Pom Purin Café in Harajuku. Photograph by the author.

prevailing attitudes about proper social roles. Japan's ubiquitous food-based entertainment promotes the maintenance and spread of culinary nationalism, the continuity of gendered production and consumption practices, and the idea that food knowledge gleaned from the media provides a source of cultural capital.

The current celebration of Japanese food identity, however, encountered a major setback with the events of March 2011, when an earthquake, tsunami, and subsequent nuclear meltdown in Japan's northeastern Fukushima province took approximately 1,600 lives and caused over $105 billion in damages. These events threw into question the safety of the Japanese food supply, as Fukushima is Japan's fourth-largest farming area and a major provider of fish and seafood (see Kleeman chapter). Government secrecy and obfuscation on the extent of damage and the danger of radiation poisoning, especially acute for children, was compounded by the mass media's complicit self-censorship, leading to a crisis in national food consciousness. Even five years after the disaster, many still remain wary of foodstuffs from the region. These heightened anxieties over food safety coexist uneasily with the orgies of conspicuous food consumption driven by popular culture and entertainment media.

Japanese Food Scholarship

Until recently, there was relatively little academic scholarship—in English or Japanese—critically examining the relationship between food and national identity. In Japan, well-known food scholars such as Ishige Naomichi, Kumakura Isao, and Haga Noboru tended to employ a sweeping approach, examining dietary culture according to received epochs in national history, or to highlight Japanese culinary exceptionality (see Rath chapter).[36] Such scholarship works to establish food as a medium for imagining and constructing national identities based on the shared, everyday practice of eating. Nation-branded foods and practices thus become "banal national symbols" that serve as "constant reminder of the nation." They encourage culinary nationalism through forging an "intimate, indissoluble bond between cuisine and country."[37] In sum, such scholarship rarely uses food as a critical lens to examine social issues, hegemonic ideologies, or entrenched gender biases.

From the late 1980s to 2000s, critical English-language works on Japanese foodways appeared sporadically by scholars including Anne Allison, Emiko Ohnuki-Tierney, Michael Ashkenazi, and Jordan Sand.[38] Following the 2006 publication of Katarcyzna Cwiertka's influential *Modern Japanese Cuisine: Food, Power and National Identity* (London: Reaktion Books, 2006) and in keeping with the expansion of food studies over the last decade, there has been an outpouring of academic work on Japanese foodways across disciplinary fields. In addition to dozens of outstanding journal articles on aspects of Japanese food culture, the last few years have witnessed important monographs by historians Eric C. Rath, Barak Kushner, George Solt, and Jeffrey Alexander; anthropologist Theodore Bestor; sociologist Merry White; and literature scholar Tomoko Aoyama, among others.[39] Rath and Stephanie Assman's edited volume, *Japanese Foodways: Past and Present* (Urbana: University of Illinois Press, 2010) provided new scholarship that spanned early modern, modern, and contemporary food practices. Cwiertka's two-volume *Critical Readings on Food in East Asia* (Leiden: Brill, 2013) brought together reprints of some of the most influential academic writing on Japanese food to date. This mushrooming interdisciplinary field of Japanese food studies is still rife with possibilities for future research. This volume aims to help shape and contribute to this rapidly expanding field, moving beyond engagement with specific foods and food practices to provide an exploration of social, cultural, historical, and geopolitical factors that inform culinary choices.

Food and cuisine are unusual cultural goods, as they are both material and highly symbolic, simultaneously providing bodily sustenance, distinction, markers of social status, and icons of national, regional, religious, gender, and other identities. James Farrer further explains that "Cuisine ... encompasses talking and writing about food, but also eating itself as a form of social communication through sharing tastes."[40] Pierre Bourdieu's work on cultural production helps to delineate Japanese cuisine and foodways in the essays contained here, although most contributors do not explicitly address this connection. Bourdieu was concerned with the production, circulation, and consumption of cultural goods. He sought out the enduring principles that inform practices and perceptions of those goods (termed the *habitus*); the many actors who produce, promote, and consume the goods; and the dynamic relationships between them. For Bourdieu, the actors and their relationships form the "field"; his work situates that field vis-à-vis the dominant power relationships in society and shows the symbolic capital that accrues around cultural goods.[41] In his astute observations on the globalization of Asian cuisine, Farrer asserts that a given cuisine is a culinary field "with its own cultural repertoire, hierarchies of value, established actors, and forms of capital." These actors include "cooks, ... consumers, food writers, scholars, business people, and government officials" who acquire culinary capital through "long socialization in the cognitive schema and habitus particular to the field." Farrer emphasizes the globalization of culinary fields, with "greater importance played by border crossing social media, international businesses ... (and) institutionalized pathways of cross-border mobility," such as culinary schools that train Japanese chefs in Italy or France.[42]

The eclectic and interdisciplinary essays within this volume comment upon key aspects of Japan's culinary field, elaborating upon the roles of Japanese and non-Japanese chefs, eaters, artists, travelers, bureaucrats, and others, interacting domestically or transnationally to forge conceptions of both the material and intangible qualities of Japanese cuisine. Part I, "Japan's Culinary Brands and Identities," contains three sections: "Historical Culinary Identities," "Culinary Nationalism and Branding," and "Regional and International Variations." Ken Albala, one of the world's leading scholars of food history, kicks off the volume by tracing international admiration for Japanese foodways to sixteenth- and seventeenth-century accounts of Japan left by a variety of Europeans, including a Portuguese Jesuit priest, Florentine merchant, and German doctor in the employment of the Dutch East India Company, which held a monopoly on European trade with Japan from the seventeenth to mid-nineteenth centuries. Primary sources left by these early modern travelers express esteem for culinary characteristics such as table etiquette, frugality, precision in production, and quality ingredients. Albala argues that Japanese cuisine has long acted as a foil to Western excess or coarseness in foodways. Many of the foods and foodways noted by the early travelers remain central aspects of Japanese culinary brand identity today.

Literary specialist Takeshi Watanabe's contribution works to solve the mystery of cuisine during the Heian period (794–1185), Japan's classical age, when court literature, poetry, and arts flourished. While literature from the era often addresses the carnal appetites of courtiers, accounts of actual foods and foodways are largely absent. Watanabe innovatively pieces together Heian-era references to food from a variety of sources including Buddhist morality tales, historical anecdotes, and poetry to produce an account of the era's conflicted attitudes toward food as a source of both guilt and pleasure and as an important means of mediating human relationships. Such attitudes are mirrored in the more contemporary accounts of conflict between morality and enjoyment in food values included in Part II of this volume. In contrast with Albala's account of elegance in early modern meals, Watanabe reveals that the foods of classical era courtiers diverged from the contemporary "hallmarks of Japanese cuisine," such as aesthetics and seasonality, relying heavily on preserved and dried foodstuffs and served on plain, round dishes.

Lorie Brau, a literature scholar specializing in traditional storytelling (*rakugo*) and gourmet manga, addresses another historical era strongly associated with Japanese traditional culture, the Edo period (1603–1868), named for the shogunate's capital city (now Tokyo), which eclipsed the imperial capital at Kyoto in cultural production over the course of the era. Brau examines the centrality of soba, or buckwheat noodles, in the culinary identity of Edo commoners who idealized *iki*, an attitude and aesthetic of "cool chic." Mining popular cultural references to soba from kabuki theater, literature, and rakugo storytellers, Brau demonstrates how soba helped dispel culinary inferiority vis-à-vis the imperial capital and became an important symbol of Edo identity. Furthermore, she provides insights on the activities and criteria of soba connoisseurs today.

In the final contribution in this section, Dick Stegewerns provides a transnational perspective on exports of Japan's iconic traditional beverage, sake. In addition to being a historian of modern Japan, Stegewerns is himself a sake importer in Europe and brings keen insights to his account of how sake has been introduced to contemporary Western palates. He identifies three waves: in the first, cheap, mass-produced sake was invariably served hot in an "orientalist" setting; second, in the 1990s, highly polished varieties of sake (*ginjō* or *daiginjō*) with added fruity and floral ingredients were served chilled as novelty drinks in a variety of bars and high-end restaurants and "evangelized" by emerging Western "experts" who propagated romanticized stereotypes but knew little about traditional sake production; finally, since around the turn of the century, "pure sake" (*junmaishu*) made using early modern slow-brew methods without additives has gained ascendance and begun to be incorporated into the world of fine wines as a beverage that can be aged, paired with foods, and served at any temperature. This final wave provides a revealing example of the increased circulation of culinary knowledge in the global gourmet economy, and the shared respect for artisanality and for creative fusions by both Euro-American and Japanese foodies.

The section on culinary nationalism begins with a contribution by Theodore Bestor, a renowned anthropologist of Japanese food culture. Here, Bestor examines the politics of cultural heritage and gastrodiplomacy, or official efforts at "edible nation branding" designed to increase trade, tourism, and national soft power. He explains how and why most Japanese conceive of washoku as a conceptual category in contrast with *yōshoku*, or Euro-American cuisine. Tracing Japan's pursuit of a UNESCO designation for washoku as an intangible cultural treasure, Bestor details how officials sought the award both for foreign recognition and to encourage the domestic public to consume more traditional foodstuffs. He describes how a failed earlier effort to strictly regulate Japanese restaurants abroad, ridiculed as "the sushi police," has led state agencies to adopt softer and more inclusive campaigns to promote washoku, such as the annual World Washoku Challenge, a competition for foreign chefs.

Yoshimi Osawa, a specialist in ethnobiology, interrogates the concept of umami—the fifth "savory" taste recently recognized alongside sweet, sour, salty, and bitter—as a symbol of Japanese culinary, and thus cultural, distinctiveness. Osawa explores earlier usages of this term and its more recent promotion as a key element of Japan's culinary brand in state-sponsored pavilions at international food exhibitions and trade shows. She reveals the popular, nationalistic belief that the Japanese have a superior ability to discern this taste and contextualizes this belief in a larger discourse of national chauvinism that claims, among other things, that the Japanese sensitivity to aesthetic refinement exceeds that of other nations.

Culinary nationalism is also a theme in historian Nancy Stalker's piece on ceramic artist Kitaōji Rosanjin (1883–1959), the most celebrated epicurean of twentieth-century Japan, who has seemingly been raised to the status of culinary saint following the UNESCO award. As a restaurateur, Rosanjin developed a reputation for exacting standards in selecting fresh, local ingredients and for plating his dishes artistically on tableware he often designed himself. His ideals have inspired contemporary chefs and foodies alike and deeply inform idealized conceptions of washoku, such as the one presented by UNESCO. Stalker discusses how Rosanjin attempted to elevate esteem for Japanese cuisine among his countrymen during the 1950s, far before Japanese cuisine was considered internationally desirable, by bombastically claiming its superiority over French and other national cuisines. She further suggests that Rosanjin's insistence on the centrality of aesthetic appeal in Japanese cuisine lays the groundwork for its global appeal in the highly visual world of food media today.

The final section in Part I contains three chapters that introduce regional and international circumstances that mediate national culinary identity. Greg de St. Maurice, an anthropologist of food culture, explains how people in Kyoto city and prefecture crafted appealing identities for their regional foods, now considered an integral aspect of the Kyoto brand, which is considered Japan's most attractive city brand. Using an ethnographic approach, de St. Maurice identifies how stakeholders, from farmers to chefs, have strengthened the local agricultural economy through promoting the heritage, craftsmanship, and provenance of Kyoto food products, especially its famed "traditional vegetables," although these were not identified as such until the 1980s. The efforts of these Kyoto actors have capitalized on current awareness of artisanality, terroir, and small-batch production—all parts of First World foodie consciousness—to invent and promote a "traditional" brand.

Next, sociologist Mire Koikari, an expert on gender in US-Japan postwar relations, delivers a complex tale of Okinawan identity through a surprising medium, Spam, the gelatinous pink lunchmeat that accompanied the American military in its imperialist expansion across the Pacific. Spam and similar competitors were welcomed by Okinawans as luxuries following the exigencies of the war and were soon adapted and indigenized as an ingredient in popular local dishes like *pōku tamago* (pork and eggs) and *chanpurū* (mixed stir-fry). Koikari reveals how luncheon meat created a powerful narrative space to express discordant emotions and attitudes: memories of war and militarized occupation, gendered nostalgia for "home cooking," and feelings of distinction from, and marginalization by, mainlanders. She points out how the domestic and domesticating dynamics of empire, in both Japanese and American varieties, work to obscure and soften the raw power of militarization.

Ayumi Takenaka, a scholar of food and immigration, describes the emergence and popularization of Nikkei cuisine, a fusion of Japanese and Peruvian championed by celebrity chefs such as Gaston Acurio and Nobu Matsuhisa, in the final piece in this section. Characteristically combining Japanese-style preparations of fish and seafood with Peruvian spices, especially aji peppers, typical Nikkei dishes include *tiradito*, a raw fish ceviche in a piquant sauce, and *maki acevichada*, a ceviche-based sushi roll. Takenaka contextualizes the ascent of Nikkei cuisine within state policy to boost seafood consumption and the new affluence from overseas remittances received from migrant workers in Japan, among other factors. She argues that the promotion of Nikkei cuisine has been orchestrated in a top-down manner by political, media, and culinary elites who seek to construct a marketable vision of ethnic diversity within national unity, but points out that, although the Japanese-Peruvian community has benefited from the elevation of Nikkei within the nation, the indigenous underclasses, whose staple grains like quinoa and amaranth are marketed to international gourmets, have not.

Part II of this volume, "Japan's Food-Related Values," addresses principles or dispositions that underlie acts of production and consumption and generate food-related practices and perceptions. Some of these principles are made visible through analyzing media discourse and cultural products such as film and literature, while others appear in the physical bodies of those subjected to group-based food norms. The chapters included here describe how individuals and institutions use food practices and representations to forge, symbolize, and sustain identities that conform to or contest social norms or other ideals. Norms often reflect shared "national" values valorizing, for example, self-discipline, prescribed gender roles, and belief in Japanese uniqueness while decrying waste, self-indulgence, and blind consumerism. Such values are inculcated beginning in early childhood via the family and the educational system, among other social institutions. Moralistic food values, however, exist in tandem and in tension with their opposites, food-related values that celebrate excess consumption, luxury, style, and connoisseurship, often inspired and promoted by both popular and elite culture and the mass media. Many of the chapters in this part speak to the tension between duty—whether as national citizen, family, or group member—and desire, the bodily cravings for, in this case, different foods. This tension has a long history in Japanese literature and culture as a central dynamic in many narrative forms—from early mythology to kabuki and puppet theater to contemporary films—and is usually described as the conflict between *giri*, or social obligation, and *ninjō*, human emotions and desires.

The first section of Part II, "Food and Individual Identity," contains three chapters that discuss how food practices and beliefs shape or express the identities of given individuals or groups. Literature specialist Amanda Seaman examines how pregnancy manuals and literature, from the Edo period until present day, advocate strict weight management and a restrictive dietary regime for the mother, warning that maternal and fetal well-being are dependent upon the mother's ability to control her appetite and engage in self-sacrifice. Seaman notes the increasing association between the maternal and national body with the advent of modernity. Despite the medicalization of birth practices in the Meiji era (1868–1912), folk wisdom restrictions on pregnancy foods remains unchanged; traditional Japanese foods, such as brown rice, tofu, and fish, are considered the proper diet for the pregnant body, while "foreign foods" endanger maternal and fetal health. Postwar "Westernization" of dietary practices led to even greater concerns over pregnancy weight gain. Nevertheless, in contrast to strict medical advice manuals, popular women's magazines advocate small indulgences, such as occasional desserts. Tensions between maternal duty and bodily desire are illustrated in the autobiographies of three actresses that reveal how food anxieties shaped their pregnancies.

Next, literary scholar J. Keith Vincent interrogates the food passions of Meiji-era poet and inventor of the modern haiku, Masaoka Shiki (1867–1902). Bedridden for his final five years, he continued to obsessively consume and write about choice morsels he demanded from his family and disciples although his body was no longer capable of digesting them. Vincent reveals the deceptive simplicity in Masaoka's poetry and prose on food, how his use of descriptive minimalism, lists, and personification worked to impart the "essences" of food and the (homo)social relationships evoked by eating. Vincent uses the phrase "the cooking show paradox" to describe how any medium dedicated to conveying the pleasures of eating is incapable of fully doing so since it has only audio and visual signs at its disposal. He suggests that Masaoka employed minimalism because language was insufficient to wholly convey one individual's sensual experience to another.

Finally, Noriko Horiguchi, another scholar of literature, examines the impact of war, empire, and gender identity in shaping one's food values via the depictions of food and hunger in the works of famed novelist and poet Hayashi Fumiko (1903–1951). Horiguchi argues that food and the act of eating serve as metaphors for the colonial and imperial relationships between Japan, its occupied territories, and its own occupation by US forces. Hayashi's attitudes toward national and imperial identity shift between her works: in *Diary of a Vagabond* (1929), the hungry heroine defies and critiques normative gender roles and middle-class values in her pursuits of work and food; as a war correspondent in 1938, however, Hayashi expressed patriotic attitudes in response to food scarcity and appeared to embrace prescribed gender roles. Finally, in *Floating Clouds* (a 1949 novel and 1955 film adaptation), the heroine moves from a position of colonial privilege in Indochina, dining luxuriously in the formerly French territory, to one of abjection in occupied Japan, selling sexual favors to American military men for chocolate and other rations.

The second half of Part II, "Food Anxieties," demonstrates how modern food worries are represented in mass media and literature. Literature scholar Bruce Suttmeier examines the tensions between the pleasures and discomforts of indulgence in the 1960s and 1970s, an era of growing affluence and consumption, through the work of writer Kaikō Takeshi (1930–1989), who frequently waxed rhapsodically and nostalgically about favorite foods in essays and novels. In his satiric 1972 serial *A New Star*, a middle-aged bureaucrat is ordered to literally eat his ministry's budget surplus through lavish meals and regional excursions to consume local delicacies. Caught in this escalating spiral of extravagant expense and consumption, the narrator's body finally rebels in an excremental explosion of every item consumed, minutely cataloged in the novel's final pages. Suttmeier observes that, while the novel can be read as a critique of consumption and government waste, there is also a nostalgic tone to Kaikō's final inventory of dishes that suggests both the pleasure and pain of overconsumption and thus reflects the complex relationship between duty and desire.

Copious excretion and vomit also feature in popular animator Miyazaki Hayao's Academy Award–winning feature *Spirited Away* (2001). Susan Napier, a renowned scholar of Japanese literature and anime, reads these bodily eruptions as critiques of rampant consumer capitalism in contemporary Japan. Set in a carnivalesque world revolving around a luxurious bathhouse for gods of all shapes and sizes, the film repeatedly portrays scenes of food excess, denial, and expulsion, which Napier, following Susan Bordo, interprets as anorexia and bulimia. Napier identifies how the world depicted resembles the medieval European utopia of Cockaigne in its bottomless service of delicious food and offering of healing springs. She sees the eating frenzies depicted as Miyazaki's metaphor for materialistic overconsumption and interprets the strong work ethic and self-denial that bring about the protagonist Sen's salvation, along with the nostalgic bathhouse setting, as Miyazaki's call for a return to traditional values, which might here be interpreted as the director Miyazaki's prioritization of duty over desire.

Historian Eiko Siniawer continues the analysis of Japanese social critique of overconsumption in her account of how the issue of food waste was linked to broader concerns, such as environmental degradation and the low rate of national food self-sufficiency, from the 1980s to 2000s. She describes how bureaucrats, citizens, corporations, and social critics mobilized to dissuade the consuming public from its tastes for convenience and disposability. Using examples from didactic materials, such as the conservationist cartoons of High Moon and children's books, Siniawer reveals national anxieties around food issues and the recourse to nostalgia as a solution for contemporary waste. Critics sought to imbue consumers with the spirit of earlier times, when food was cherished because it was in short supply and when consumers respected whole foods, produced through the sweat of farmers and prepared with motherly love, rather than relying on processed convenience foods.

Finally, literature scholar Faye Kleeman discusses the "endless anxiety" over food safety caused by the March 11, 2011, earthquake and tsunami, when concerns over issues such as food waste and self-sufficiency were quickly superseded by worries about food contamination. For the public, the tragedy symbolized Japan's loss of economic advantage and problem-solving ability, capping decades of economic recession. Efforts to downplay the contamination of the food supply through, for example, ad campaigns urging citizens to ignore safety concerns and support Fukushima agriculture by eating its products were one factor in the public's increased distrust of government and media. Kleeman presents two popular works that address emerging food values post 3/11: Hatanaka Mieko's critique of contemporary food practices as fashion driven, akin to consuming a form of popular culture, and Yūki Masumi's examination of the ecological impact of eating via essays and conversations with other writers.

Devouring Japan concludes with an afterword by historian Eric C. Rath, a specialist in Japanese food studies, who begins by reflecting on the transformation of international attitudes toward Japanese food from 1946, when postwar tourists were warned against native fare like sashimi and pickles, to the present, when it can even be encountered in the unlikeliest of places, such as remote regions of Tibet. The main thrust of this piece, however, is a call for new approaches and chronologies of Japanese food history, attentive to factors including changes in technology and staple foods and reflecting the full diversity of what people actually ate, rather than the existing models of "national cuisine" that largely reflect only the diets of historical elites. Rath reveals how state intervention in promoting ideological models of national cuisine both domestically and abroad, such as with the UNESCO effort, rely on faulty perceptions of the deterioration of home cooking and traditional dietary culture. He thus reminds us that the idealized representations of Japanese culinary identity, ingested by a global population of Japanese food lovers from celebrity chefs to ramen wannabes, does not really conform to historical or contemporary realities. They are pretty fictions, ideological paradigms designed to enhance state power and presence in the competitive global gourmet economy.

While the chapters presented here can only address a small subset of issues in the vast and complex world of Japanese food culture(s), the authors hope they will inspire additional scholarship and provide a bridge between the field of food studies, which tends to focus on ethnic American or European subjects, and that of Japanese studies, a narrower audience that sometimes has difficulty relating and translating to other areas of the academy. Anyone who enjoys devouring Japanese cuisine will hopefully find something to savor in *Devouring Japan*.

NOTES

1. David Chang, "Why Tokyo Is the World's Best Food City," *Lucky Peach* 18 (Spring 2016). http://luckypeach.com/why-tokyo-is-the-worlds-best-food-city-david-chang/.

2. Rene Redzepi, "Why We're in Japan," *Saveur* 171 (January 27, 2015). http://www.saveur.com/article/food/rene-redzepi-why-were-in-japan.

3. Anthony Bourdain and Joel Rose (writers), Langdon Foss (artist), *Get Jiro* (New York: Vertigo Comics, 2012); Anthony Bourdain and Joel Rose (writers), Ale Garza (artist), *Get Jiro: Blood and Sushi* (New York: Vertigo Comics, 2016). The inaugural title in Bourdain's elegant new book series on food travel extols Japanese regional food cultures.

4. Peter Naccarato and Kathleen Lebesco, *Culinary Capital* (London: Berg, 2012), 3.

5. In 2013, this number reached 55,000. David L. Wank and James Farrer, "Chinese Immigrants and Japanese Cuisine in the United States: A Case of Culinary Glocalization," in *The Globalization of Asian Cuisines: Transnational Networks and Culinary Contact Zones*, ed. James Farrer (New York: Palgrave Macmillan, 2015), 79.

6. Michael Steinberger, "Who Can Save French Food," *New York Times*, March 28, 2014; and Josée Johnston and Shyon Baumann, "The Fall of the French: A Historical Perspective," in *Foodies: Democracy and Distinction in the Gourmet Foodscape* (New York: Routledge, 2010), 5–14.

7. Adam Gopnik, "Is There a Crisis in French Cooking?," *New Yorker*, April 28, 1997.

8. Krishnendu Ray, *The Ethnic Restaurateur* (London: Bloomsbury Academic, 2016), 77–87.

9. In 2016 rankings, of the 213 Michelin starred restaurants in Tokyo, 13 have three-star ratings; of these, 11 serve Japanese cuisine, 2 serve French. New York has 74 starred restaurants, including 6 three-star ratings, with 3 American nouvelle, 2 French, and 1 Japanese in this category, but among the one- and two-star restaurants, Japanese is the most frequent non-American category; Paris has 100 starred restaurants, all 10 three-star are French, and there are 6 one-star Japanese restaurants in Paris. https://www.finedininglovers.com/blog/news-trends/michelin-guide-tokyo-2016-the-full-list/ ; http://www.grubstreet.com/2015/09/michelin-stars-2016-new-york-city.html; https://www.viamichelin.com accessed 8/22/2106.

10. For more on ramen history see Barak Kushner, *Slurp! A Social and Culinary History of Ramen—Japan's Favorite Noodle Soup* (Leiden: Global Oriental, 2012); and George Solt, *The Untold History of Ramen: How Political Crisis in Japan Spawned a Global Food Craze* (Berkeley: University of California Press, 2014).

11. *New Yorker* (September 29, 2014), 44.

12. Sasha Issenberg, *The Sushi Economy: Globalization and the Making of a Modern Delicacy* (New York: Gotham Books, 2007), 109–123.

13. Farrer, *Globalization of Asian Cuisines*, 7.

14. On food and individual identity, see Warren Belasco, *Food: The Key Concepts* (Oxford: Berg, 2008), 15–33; and Isabelle de Solier, *Food and the Self: Consumption, Production and Material Culture* (London: Bloomsbury, 2013).

15. Naccarato and Lebesco, *Culinary Capital*, 12.
16. Naccarato and Lebesco, *Culinary Capital*, 14.
17. See, for example, Simon Anholt, *Competitive Identity: The New Brand Management for Nations, Cities and Regions* (New York: Palgrave Macmillan, 2007) and *Places: Identity, Image and Reputation* (New York: Palgrave Macmillan, 2009).
18. Margaret Talbot, "Pokémon Hegemon," *New York Times*, December 15, 2002.
19. http://www.meti.go.jp/policy/mono_info_service/mono/creative/.
20. Isabella L. Bird, *Unbeaten Tracks in Japan* (London: Kegan Paul, 2013), 19.
21. Jack Goody, "The High and the Low: Culinary Culture in Asia and Europe," in *Cooking Cuisine and Class: A Study in Comparative Sociology* (Cambridge: Cambridge University Press, 1982), 97–153.
22. The four "great traditions" of Chinese cuisine also include Huaiyang and Shandong. Other approaches, however, define six or eight great regional cuisines.
23. Andrew Coe, *Chop Suey: A Cultural History of Chinese Food in the United States* (Oxford: Oxford University Press, 2009); Yong Chen, *Chop Suey U.S.A.: The Story of Chinese Food in America* (New York: Columbia University Press, 2014).
24. Theodore C. Bestor, "Kaiten-zushi and Konbini: Japanese Food Culture in the Age of Mechanical Reproduction," in *Fast Food / Slow Food: The Cultural Economy of the Global Food System*, ed. James Wilk (New York: Rowman & Littlefield, 2006), 115–130.
25. Farrer, *Globalization of Asian Cuisines*, 6; Wank and Farrer, "Chinese Immigrants."
26. Johnston and Baumann, *Foodies*, 3.
27. bell hooks, "Eating the Other: Desire and Resistance," in *Eating Culture*, ed. Ron Scapp and Brian Seitz (Albany: State University of New York Press, 1998), 181. Originally published in *Black Looks: Race and Representation* (Boston: South End Press, 1993).
28. Johnston and Baumann, *Foodies*, 37.
29. hooks, "Eating the Other," 181.
30. Johnston and Baumann, *Foodies*, 104–126. Naccarato and Lebesco claim about Americans that "those who seek out the greatest variety of tastes and who are open to the broadest range of experiences emerge as the most culturally capitalized." *Culinary Capital*, 9.
31. See http://www.sweets-forest.com/index2.php.
32. Frederick Errington, Tatsuro Fujikura, and Deborah Gewertz, *The Noodle Narratives: The Global Rise of an Industrial Food in the Twenty-First Century* (Berkeley: University of California Press, 2013), 33–37.
33. Naccarato and Lebesco, *Culinary Capital*, 15.
34. T. J. M. Holden, "The Overcooked and Underdone: Masculinities in Japanese Food Programming," in *Food and Culture: A Reader*, ed. Carole Counihan and Penny Van Esterik (New York: Routledge, 2012), 119–136. Originally published in *Food & Foodways* 13.1 (2005): 39–65.
35. See Nancy Stalker, "Gourmet Samurai: Changing Gender Norms in Japanese Food TV," *Gastronomica* 16 (November 2016), 78–90.
36. See for example, Ishige Naomichi, *Shoku no bunka o kataru* (Tokyo: Domesu shuppan, 2009); Kumakura Isao, *Nihon no shokuji bunka* (Tokyo: Ajinomoto shoku no

bunka sentā, 1999); Haga Noboru, *Zenshū Nihon no shokubunka* (Tokyo: Yūzankaku, 1996–1999).

37. Atsuko Ichijo and Ronald Ranta, *Food, National Identity and Nationalism: From Everyday to Global Political* (New York: Palgrave Macmillan, 2016), 3–5; Priscilla Ferguson, *Accounting for Taste: The Triumph of French Cuisine* (Chicago: University of Chicago Press, 2004), 81.

38. Anne Allison, "Japanese Mothers and Obentōs: The Lunch-Box as Ideological State Apparatus," *Anthropological Quarterly* 64 (1991): 195–208; Emiko Ohnuki-Tierney, *Rice as Self: Japanese Identities through Time* (Princeton, NJ: Princeton University Press, 1993); Michael Ashkenazi and Jeanne Jacob, *The Essence of Japanese Cuisine* (Philadelphia: University of Pennsylvania Press, 2000); Jordan Sand, "A Short History of MSG: Good Science, Bad Science, and Taste Cultures," *Gastronomica* 12.3 (2012), 38–49.

39. Kushner, *Slurp!*; Solt, *Untold History of Ramen*; Eric C. Rath, *Food and Fantasy in Early Modern Japan* (Berkeley: University of California Press, 2010); Jeffrey W. Alexander, *Brewed in Japan: The Evolution of the Japanese Beer Industry* (Honolulu: University of Hawaii Press, 2014); Theodore C. Bestor, *Tsukiji: The Fish Market at the Center of the World* (Berkeley: University of California Press, 2004); Merry I. White, *Coffee Life in Japan* (Berkeley: University of California Press, 2012); Tomoko Aoyama, *Reading Food in Modern Japanese Literature* (Honolulu: University of Hawaii Press, 2008).

40. Farrer, *Globalization of Asian Cuisines*, 4–5.

41. Pierre Bourdieu, *The Field of Cultural Production*, ed. Randal Johnson (New York: Columbia University Press, 1992).

42. Farrer, *Globalization of Asian Cuisines*, 4–5.

PART I

Japan's Culinary Brands and Identities

Historical Culinary Identities

1

Japanese Food in the Early Modern European Imagination

Ken Albala

It would be fairly easy to trace the influence of Japanese cuisine on the West in the last fifty years. Not only has there been a proliferation of sushi bars and teppanyaki restaurants and a much greater appreciation for and availability of Japanese ingredients and kitchen utensils, not to mention popular media representations in movies like *Tampopo* and *Iron Chef*, but the overall Japanese aesthetic has dramatically influenced Western cuisine, especially in the plating of food since the nouvelle cuisine era. But this modern phenomenon did not spring from nowhere; it has roots in a particular attitude toward this cuisine that springs from the very first encounters. Rather than examine the appeal of Japanese cuisine today, an examination of the first three centuries of Western contact will be productive, in order to make some sense of how foreign visitors looked at the food they tasted and the customs they witnessed. Why did Westerners find Japanese food appealing from the very start? Why were they interested in Japanese food processing and ingredients like miso, soy, and sake, long before these products would be exported?

These early accounts also provide evidence that despite the current branding and codification of particular features of Japanese cuisine as a commodity in the West, there has been a remarkable consistency over the past five centuries in the ingredients, modes of presentation, overall aesthetic, and practice of hospitality that we have come to associate with Japanese dining.

Our initial assumption might be that this fascination with Japan sprung primarily from curiosity with the unfamiliar and exotic. Because it was virtually closed off until the 1860s, the allure of Japan in preceding eras was primarily in its being unattainable and for the most part unknown. But the appeal appears to go deeper than this. And at a fundamental level, the entire Japanese culinary aesthetic functions as a foil to Western culinary arts in periods of decadence and excess. That is, when a particular style becomes overly ornate, fussy, or excessively decorative, the perceived simplicity and pristine elegance as well as the functionality of Japanese food and utensils serve as a corrective, an antithesis, if you will, that leads to a revamping of Western aesthetics with a strong nod, if not bow, to the east. This was clearly the case with French chefs in the 1970s like Paul Bocuse, the Troisgros Brothers, and Alain Chapel. Suddenly the excessive complexity and butter-laden sauces gave way to focus on fresh ingredients, especially vegetables, prepared simply and presented in ways directly influenced by Japanese plating and even modes of service.

This was not an isolated fad; Japanese cuisine has often at some level served as a positive corrective for Western culinary frivolity. From the very start, the idea that a people could live a frugal abstemious life primarily on rice, fish, and vegetables has always been a convenient counterbalance to Western culinary excess, devotion to large cuts of meat, and techniques that seek to disguise the main ingredients. Japanese manners and decorum, even cleanliness, also consistently provide a contrast with European customs.

From the start there was a certain appreciation for the craftsmanship that went into Japanese cuisine, much the same kind of admiration we know prevailed among the Arts and Crafts Movement of the late nineteenth century and in the style of Japonisme among the impressionists, or among architects like Frank Lloyd Wright. Painters and especially potters (such as Bernard Leach) were attracted to Japanese arts precisely because they were diametrically opposed aesthetically to the Victorian mass-produced gaudy frou-frou. Exactly the same appeal held true in the culinary arts, and this same attitude of appreciation for Japanese cuisine existed from the earliest accounts in the sixteenth century.

In fact among the earliest encounters of the Portuguese with Japan in the sixteenth century, illustrated in the three-panel screen painting in figure 1.1, there is already a fascinating reference to Japanese foodways as a foil to European. In the *Peregrinations* of Fernão Mendes Pinto, about his trip to Japan in 1546, there are some interesting descriptions of the food. It is mostly about the generosity of the people, who on many occasions bring fruits, rice, boiled fish. But toward the end of the book, on a return voyage to "Tanixumaa" (Tanegashima), he and his four companions are invited to a feast by the "king

FIGURE 1.1 Portuguese priests and merchants arriving in Japan. Kanō Sanraku, *Nanban byōbu*, seventeenth century. Suntory Museum of Art, Tokyo, via Wikimedia Commons.

of Bungo," that is, the ruling daimyo of Bungo province in Kyushu, who at this point is an old friend. The king decides to use the occasion to have a good laugh by requesting that the Portuguese eat according to their own manner.

> Whereas we were then at a Treasurer's house of his, where we were appointed to lodge, he sent for us all five and entreated us that we should eat in his presence in the manner of our Country, adding that the Queen did infinitely desire it. Then having caused a table to bee covered for us, and on it placed store of excellent good meat and well drest, which was served up by fair women, we fell to eating after our own manner, of all that was set before us, whilst the jeasts which the Ladies broke upon us, in seeing us feed so with our hands, gave more delight to the kind and Queen, then all the comedies that could have been presented before them: for those people being accustomed to feed with two little sticks, as I have declared elsewhere, they hold it for a great incivilitie, to touch the meat with ones hand, as we do.[1]

And then the Japanese took the jest a little too far, with a skit in which some merchants come in with bundles, and when they open them, out pour handfuls of wooden arms with hands, and they say since your hands always smell of fish or meat or whatever you're eating, you should try using these. The Portuguese clearly become angry over being made fun of at this point, but things are patched up. But the more interesting point to be made about this little encounter is that the author telling the story clearly begins to realize that eating with your hands is kind of disgusting, and there's a glimmer of envy over the Japanese using chopsticks. It's very clearly the more elegant and refined way to eat, in Pinto's mind. Japanese table manners are indeed superior to the Portuguese.

There is probably no better-known account than the description of Japan by the Jesuit João Rodrigues, who was there through the late sixteenth century until 1610. The author gives the fullest early account by a Westerner of the tea ceremony, and was clearly struck by the beauty and elegance of the entire event. "Far from being excessive and abundant, the banquet is very sober and moderate; each guest eats and drinks soberly as much as he pleases without having to be persuaded. Nor do the guests converse among themselves while eating, but they say only what is necessary in a low voice. Great modesty and tranquility are observed in everything."[2] The direct implication for readers is that this ceremony is completely different from European banquets of the era, where there would be a great deal of noise, people would be induced to drink too much, and the food would indeed be excessive and abundant. In fact later in the century the *Arte de Cozhina* by the Portuguese Domingos Rodrigues (no relation as far as I know) attests to European banquets being exactly that: the menus are stupendously excessive with dozens of plates festooned with various meats, fowl, pastries, and confections enticing the eye and mouth to gluttony.

In Japan there is "no pomp or splendor involved," as João explains. The intention is to contemplate nature. Thus the setting is simple and rustic, the utensils of clay or iron rather than precious metals. But the real marvel for Rodrigues, again I think in contrast to European custom, is the cleanliness. "Above all else they pay more attention that can be easily imagined to the cleanliness of everything, however small it may be, in this rustic and ancient setting." He also marvels how the Japanese deeply appreciate and pay enormous sums of money for the simplest of earthenware vessels, much as to this day a raku bowl can cost several thousand dollars and a potter can be designated a living national treasure. It is the appreciation for craft here that provides a contrast to the Western aesthetic.

Rodrigues also appears to have become quite an aficionado of tea himself and believed it perfectly suited for maintaining health, improving the digestion, and stimulating the mind—it even promotes chastity because it restrains and cools the kidneys. One poor peasant even thought he should give up tea when he decided to get married. But Rodrigues is clearly promoting tea drinking as the sober alternative to wine, which according to humoral theory is highly nutritious, does heat the body, and does stimulate the libido. Conceptually, this ordained priest admires tea as a national beverage, in contrast to the drink of choice among his own countrymen. "The purpose of this art of cha, then, is courtesy, good breeding, modesty, and moderation in exterior actions, peace and quiet of body and soul, exterior modesty without any pride, arrogance, fleeing from all exterior ostentation, pomp, display, and splendor of social life."³ In other words, it is exactly the opposite of a European meal.

Of the food, especially a banquet before serving tea, it is once again quality and simplicity rather than abundance and ostentation that are desired. "The banquets before the cha consist of a few but excellent and substantial dishes of costly things which they greatly esteem, sometimes a fresh crane is served in the shiru [soup] and will cost up to sixty cruzados. Then they serve other prized and expensive birds, the best and choicest fish, and various other things." He discusses how tables are set and mentions the highly sought-after raw fish cut into small pieces, with dishes containing a tart sauce (presumably soy based) or one that burns like mustard (probably wasabi). Though the name is not used, this appears to be sashimi little different from that served today. Rodrigues also discusses the craft aesthetic in a way that rings true to this day: above all else it is naturalness that is sought rather than artifice, which leads to tedium and boredom. Objects that are symmetrical, or strictly ordered, offer much less aesthetically than those that are haphazard, as nature would arrange things, with all its imperfections. Rodrigues is describing precisely what Yanagi Soetsu discusses in *The Unknown Craftsman* several centuries later concerning mingei (folk art), and especially how nature suggests the form, which art merely accentuates or liberates. For example, flames in a kiln are allowed to roam freely across the surface of a tea bowl, creating random charring. In the same way the natural essence of the ingredients is the focal point, which Rodrigues seems to understand.

About the same time Rodrigues was writing, the English also attempted to open up trade with the Japanese. The most famous accounts come from the letters of William Adams, on whose life James Clavell's novel *Shogun* was based. Adams was not much interested in describing food, unless there wasn't any, but there is a fascinating passage in his letters where he mentions three thousand Japanese soldiers marching through villages and being openly welcomed with food, because the villagers understood that the soldiers would pay for everything. The direct implication is that European soldiers pillage on their way through the countryside and peasants try to hide everything they can from them. His comments also attest to a thriving hospitality industry, again in contrast to Europe, "every towne and village upon the way being well fitted with cookes and victualling houses, where they might at an instant have what they needed, and dyet themselves from a pennie English a meal, to two shillings a meal." In other words everyone from the poorest to the wealthiest person can find a meal to suit his or her budget.⁴

Japanese generosity also contrasts starkly with European selfishness. "Fish, rootes and rice are their common junkets, and if they chance to kill a hen, ducke or pigge, which is but seldome, they will not like churles eat it alone; but their friends shall be surely partakers of it." A diet primarily of fish also appears to have fascinated Europeans, who of course were forced to eat fish as penitence during Lent. Surprised, one English account says, "Indeed they delighte not much in fleshe, but they lyve for the most part with hearbes, fyshe, barley and ryce, which thinges are their cheoffe nowrishments. Their ordinary drinke is water and that is made most times hot in the same pot where they seethe their ryce that so it may receive some thicnesse and substance from the ryce."[5]

Francesco Carletti was a Florentine merchant in the late sixteenth century who traveled all around the world, including Japan, where he too commented on the foodways with admiration. Carletti visited Nagasaki in 1597 and wrote in his *Ragionamenti del mio viaggio intorno al mondo* (Memoirs of my trip around the world):

> They prepare various sorts of dishes from fish, which they flavor with a certain sauce of theirs which they call *misol*. It is made of a sort of bean that abounds in various localities, and which—cooked and mashed and mixed with a little of that rice from which they make the wine already mentioned, and then left to stand as packed into a tub—turns sour and all but decays, taking on a very sharp, piquant flavor. Using this a little at a time, they give flavor to their foods, and they call *shiro* what we would call a potage or gravy. They make this as I have said, of vegetables and fruit and fish all mixed together, and even some game, and then eat it with rice, which serves them as bread and is cooked simply in water and served in certain wooden bowls lacquered with red lacquer, eating it very cleanly and never toughing it with their hands.[6]

Although Carletti's descriptions are fairly straightforward, he clearly liked much of what he tasted in Japan. For example, he marvels at the "radishes of such marvelous size that three or four of them weight a man down (and I have seen displayed, and have taken into my hands, some of them that were as thick as a man's thigh), and these are of a very sweet flavor and tender. They make salads by breaking them up and by cutting them lengthwise very carefully. And they are very tasteful to eat." Presumably he had seen a daikon cut into long ribbons and then tiny match sticks. He also describes salted vegetables: "With these they prepare both fresh and dried fish, their common and usual food. And fish are so abundant as to be worth almost nothing, and they often eat them raw, passing them through vinegar first." Fascinatingly, it is anything but disgust that this early encounter with sashimi elicits.

Not everyone loved Japanese food from the start, but even the detractors were forced to admit the beauty and cleanliness of the cuisine. Bernardino de Avila Giron, a Spanish merchant in Japan from 1597 to 1598, wrote, "I will not praise Japanese food for it is not good, albeit it is pleasing to the eye, but instead I will describe the clean and particular way in which it is served."[7]

The Portuguese were expelled in 1614 and the *nanban* (i.e., "barbarian" European) trade came to an end. The Dutch, of course, took their place, though after 1638, they were isolated on the artificial island of Deshima outside Nagasaki. Before that isolation François Caron wrote a description of Japan in 1636, which was later translated into English by Roger Manley in 1663 as *A True Description of the Mighty Kingdoms of Japan and Siam*.[8] Caron was of Huguenot extraction and worked for the VOC (Dutch East India Company), starting in 1619 as a cook's mate and rising to chief officer. He stayed in Japan over twenty years, taking a Japanese concubine and raising a family with her in Hirado. The most interesting comments, again in contrast to Europeans, are about hospitality and drinking.

> The Jappanners are very hospitable and civil to such as visit them, they treat them with Tobacco and with Tsia, and if the friend be more then ordinary, with Wine; They cause them first to sit down, and setting a Lack bowl before them, will not suffer them to depart before they have tasted of it; they sing, they pipe, and play upon such stringed instruments as they have, to rejoyce their Guests, omitting no manner of carouses and kindnesses to testifie their welcome, and the value they put upon their conversation. They never quarrel in their debauches, but he that is first drunk retires and sleeps until the fumes of the wine be evaporated.

Here Caron is clearly contrasting the Japanese custom with typical European carousing in taverns; of course he could very easily imagine a typical Dutch tavern painting with people drinking, fondling each other, and smoking amid broken pottery and general mayhem. Moreover Caron says: "There is no such thing as a Tavern or publick drinking House in all the Countrie; they eat, drink and are merry, but all in their own houses, not refusing lodging and refreshment for the traveller and stranger."[9] This naturally is completely different from Holland, where drinking is public and a moneymaking business.

In the latter seventeenth century, a few food products from Asia began to arrive in Europe, gaining popularity. The word *soy* and the English name for the bean both come from the Japanese sauce—*shōyu*. Its first appearance in English is credited to the philosopher John Locke, who in 1679 mentioned in his journal that "mango and saio are two sorts of sauces brought from the East Indies."[10] It was about this time that ketchup also became popular in England.

A noticeable change also happens at this time and into the eighteenth century; the focus shifts largely to scientific or ethnographic accounts by the very few people who were allowed to set foot on Japanese soil. The Enlightenment also marks the point when European powers embarked on a new phase of imperialism that included justifying their actions with assumptions about the inferiority of those they attempted to subjugate. This makes their admiration for this culture all the more remarkable, and the technical descriptions betray a deep respect for Japanese food artisanship. The German botanist Engelbert Kaempfer was among the very few allowed to travel through Japan in the 1690s, and his account, the *Amoenitatum exoticarum*, was published 1712 and included the illustration of Japanese tea implements seen in figure 1.2.

Kaempfer's description of soy and the techniques used to transform it are remarkably detailed and seem to show a deep respect for the complex processing.

> The place of legume in Japanese cooking could fill the page; Indeed from it is made: a porridge called Miso, which is added to dishes for consistency in the place of butter, for butter is an unknown thing to

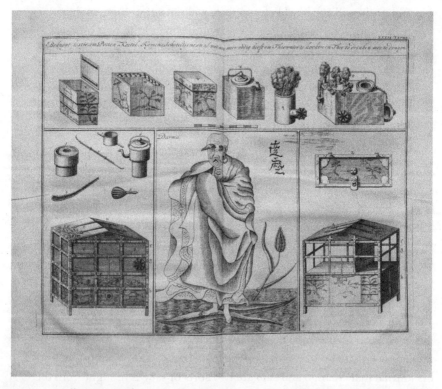

FIGURE 1.2 Illustration of Japanese tea boxes, cups, and kettle by Engelbert Kaempfer. From Dutch translation of *The History of Japan* (1727) via Wikimedia Commons.

these skies; then Sooju which the celebrated sauce is called, which is poured on, if not all dishes, then certainly fried and roasted ones. The way of making both I will describe:

For preparing Miso, they take one measure of Máme or Daidsu beans which are thoroughly cooked until soft in water for a long time, which they pound into a smooth paste. To the paste, while continually pounding, is mixed common Salt, four measures in summer, in winter three; for less salt added makes the process quicker, but less durable. Then in quantity equal to the beans is added, while repeatedly pounding, Koos, i.e. hulled rice which has been partially steamed with pure water and then cooled, in a warm storeroom, one or two days and nights, and left to rest until it contracts. This mixture (which is the consistency of porridge or a poultice) is placed into a wooden vessel which had once contained the beer popularly called Sacki, and before use, one or two months it remains undisturbed. Koos gives the paste a pleasant taste, and preparing it, like porridge of the Germans, requires the expert hand of a master; On account of which those who work in making it are in a unique position and sell it prepared.

To make Sooju they take the same beans cooked to the same softness; Muggi, i.e. grain, either barley or wheat (with wheat the product is darker) coarsely ground; and common Salt in equal parts, or a single measure of each. The beans are mixed with the crushed grain and in a hot place the mixture is left for a day and night so that it ferments. Then in a clay pot salt is added to the mass and stirred while pouring water, commonly two and a half measures: which being done, the mass is well covered and the next day and following days stirred at least once (better twice or thrice) with a shovel. This work continues two or three months, the mass is pressed and drained, and the liquid is kept in wooden vessels; the older it is, the clearer and better. Water is again added to the drained mass to moisten, it is stirred a few days and pressed.[11]

Among the Dutch accounts of this period the fullest are those written by Isaac Titsingh, who wrote an entire book on the festivals and wedding and funeral ceremonies of the Japanese. He was the *Opperhooft*, or chief agent, for the VOC in the 1780s. Titsingh describes the traditional festivals with almost poetic admiration, one in particular being the Obon festival of the lanterns, which honors deceased relatives:

Green mats, made of the grass kaya, are previously spread out, on the two sides of which are put ears of rice and millet, culinary vegetables, and raw fruits as beans, figs, pears, chest-nuts, hazel-nuts, horse-radish, and the earliest autumnal fruits. In the middle is set a small vase, in which are burned pastils and other perfumes. Before this vase are placed, on the one hand a jug full of pure water, and on the other a jug with a green leaf of the rose-colored water lily, on which are put a little raw rice and small square pieces of a species of turnip.

These, according to Titsingh, are later replaced with cups of tea and rice with other food, set out for the morning and evening meal. And there are dainties presented between them, "laksak, cakes, stewed mansi, sugar loaves, etc." Eventually all the food is packed up into little straw boats, set alight, and launched on the water to dismiss the souls of the dead.

> This festival produced a highly picturesque effect: outside the town the view of it from the island of Desima is one of the most beautiful. The spectator would almost imagine he beheld a torrent of fire pouring from the hill, owing to the immense number of small boats that are carried to the shore, to be turned adrift on the sea. In the middle of the night and when there is a brisk wind, the agitation of the water causing all these lights to dance to and fro, produces an enchanting scene.[12]

Titsingh also offers a detailed description of the production of sake in a short essay written for the Batavian Academy of Sciences.[13] The measurements are in Japanese gantings, which approximate a kilo. In this case there is an admiration not exactly for any particular aesthetic approach in the cuisine, but rather the scale and precision of the procedure, which rivals anything in alcohol production in Europe.

> A usual brewery consists of 80 kilos of the best white rice that is cooked and then allowed to cool, 32 kilos of moldy rice and 96 kilos of fresh water, which they mix together and divide into 8 [containers]. They are stirred five or six times a day for 25 days in order to let it ferment. They then store it in a big pot for 14 or 15 days it develops a sort of mold, and is transferred to a big vat. The following day they mix together 160 kilos of cooked white rice at bloodwarm temperature, 64 kilos of moldy rice, and 150 kilos of fresh water. After letting it rest a day, the mixture from the previous day is removed from the vat and divided into 3 parts to the new mixture and put into vats that are five feet high and five feet in diameter and left to stand for 3 days, meanwhile from time to time they stir into it

with a wooden spoon into another 240 kilos of white rice that is just below blood temperature, 96 kilos moldy rice, and 180 kilos of water. This mixture they divide again into 3 parts in bigger tubs, let it stand for a day and then mix in one more time 320 kilos of cold rice, 128 kilos of moldy rice, and 240 kilos of water as preparation for its final fermentation.

After four days of letting it stand, they stir it and taste it and if they consider it to be good, then they let it stand for 15 days, after which it is poured into linen sacks and pressed out into a large cask . . . they make sure there is no debris remaining and carefully fill the cask with the sacks until it is filled. They measure four thumbs from the bottom and insert a tap, which allows men in usual establishments to tap the contents. When the cask is filled with 1100 kilos of fresh, clear saki it is ready to be sold, but the breweries much be careful there is no contamination of the saki, or else the brewery will be ruined.

The last line seems to recognize the high standards of quality demanded by Japanese consumers, which in his mind probably contrasted with much of the cheap adulterated gin popular in Europe at the same time.

Another account comes from Carl Pieter Thunberg, a Swedish botanist who had studied under Linnaeus and came to Japan with the VOC in 1775. He visited Edo with Titsingh and left some of the most detailed accounts of Japanese cuisine up to that time. Notice that at this time in Europe, service a la Française would have demanded everything in a course appear at once and be proportioned at the table. He seems to like that the cutting and plating all happens in the kitchen, a much tidier solution.

All their meals are cut into small morsels, and furnished with delicious sauces. Thus the master of the house doesn't have to trouble himself with cutting meat and serving it to his guests. Each person sits on a square mat with a little table in front of him and the servants put a plate on each table, in which is a portion all prepared in the kitchen and dressed in a vessel of porcelain or lacquered wood. These types of plates or shallow bowls have a covering. . . . The first course consists of fish and soups of fish. One drinks the soup from these shallow bowls and eats the fish with the varnished sticks, which they manage so adroitly with the right hand that they can pick up the tiniest grain of rice. These sticks take the place of forks and spoons.

People eat three times a day and at each meal, miso soup is made with fish and leeks. . . . Miso or soy sauce constitutes the principal nourishment of the Japanese.... And here is how they make it: you cook the beans just until they are a little soft. Then it is mixed with an equal quantity of barley or wheat, and then let this mixture ferment 24 hours in a warm place. Then mix the same quantity of salt and two and a half times the amount of water, then one stores the whole thing in an earthen pot well sealed for two and a half months, stirring it for the first few days. After the necessary time, you press out the liquor and save it in a barrel. The inhabitants of some provinces make much better soy than others.[14]

Again, the last line implies serious connoisseurship. Thunberg also describes the many types of fish and the vegetables they eat, and he marvels at a kind of macaroni made from a black grain, which is called *sobakiri* (i.e., buckwheat soba), which he says is very nourishing and of an excellent taste. He also remarks that while they make sake and enjoy tea, they haven't taken to the perfidious distilled liquors of the Dutch. Sake on the other hand he finds infinitely agreeable.

I'm not sure if it's by pure chance that practically nothing negative is mentioned about Japanese food by any visitors prior to the modern era, unless I've overlooked something. Nor do I think these accounts romanticize or caricature Japanese cuisine the way it so easily could be in the latter nineteenth and twentieth centuries. In either case, the reports of Japanese food are entirely different from almost all other reports of European merchants and colonials around the world, because they are always written with admiration, appreciation for the beauty of the settings and manners, and a keen interest in the technological sophistication of manufacturing products like soy and sake. Accordingly, Japan provided a perfect foil for much that was seen either as uncouth in Europe (like eating with your hands in the early accounts) or later on as a corrective to the excessively fussy and overwrought baroque and rococo cuisine. It was precisely this aesthetic of simple formality, elegance, and craftsmanship that would also appeal so powerfully to Europeans of the industrial era, once again in contrast to their own culinary style in the nineteenth and twentieth centuries.

NOTES

1. *The voyages and adventures of Ferdinand Mendez Pinto, a Portugal: During his travels for the space of one and twenty years . . .* , trans. H.C. (Henry Cogan) (London: Printed for Richard Bently, Jacob Tonson, Francis Saunders, and Tho. Bennet, 1692).

2. Joao Rodrigues, *This Island of Japon*, trans. Michael Cooper (Tokyo: Kodansha International, 1973), 263.

3. Rodrigues, *This Island of Japon*, 274.

4. Thomas Rundall, ed., *Memorials of the Empire of Japan* (London: Printed for the Hakluyt Society, 1850), 63.

5. Rundall, *Memorials*, 5–6.

6. Francesco Carletti, *My Voyage around the World*, trans. Herbert Weinstock (New York Pantheon, 1964), 110.

7. Michael Cooper, ed., *They Came to Japan* (Ann Arbor: Michigan Classics in Japanese Studies, 1995), 194.

8. François Caron, *A True Description of the Mighty Kingdoms of Japan and Siam by Caron and Schouten*, trans. Roger Manley, ed. C. R. Boxer (Amsterdam: N. Israel, 1971).

9. Caron, *A True Description*, 47.

10. John Locke, *Journal*, ed. Lord King (1829), 133–134.

11. Engelbert Kaempfer, *Amoenitatum Exoticarum* (Lemgo: Heinrich Wilhelm Meyer, 1712). Passage translated by Ken Albala.

12. Isaac Titsingh, *Illustrations of Japan* (London: R. Ackerman, 1822), 143.

13. Isaac Titsingh, "Bereiding van de Sacki," in *Verhandelingen van het Bataviaasch Genootschap*, vol. 3 (Rotterdam: Arrenberg, 1787). Passage translated by Ken Albala and Kris Alexanderson.

14. Carl Peter Thunberg, *Voyages de C. P. Thunberg au Japon* (Paris: Benoit d'André, 1796), 276.

2

Gifting Melons to the Shining Prince

Food in the Late Heian Court Imagination

Takeshi Watanabe

"Hazy spring moon," "dew on the stones," "wind in the pines"—such poetic names abound in the colorful cases of Japanese confectionaries.[1] Many of these sweets, as in figure 2.1, allude (verbally and visually) to classical literature, such as *The Tale of Genji* (c. 1000), a masterpiece that is a touchstone of Japanese sensibilities. As Greg de St. Maurice's chapter shows, Kyoto's heritage, established in the Heian period (ninth through twelfth centuries), continues to propel its powerful branding. Whether in the names of sweets, kaiseki menus, or decorative motifs on ceramics, the Kyoto seasons continue to resonate in the culinary landscape. Yet if one were to ask a reader today what the Shining Prince ate, the answer might be, beyond rice, a blank. In contrast to other eras, the Heian period presents a gap in knowledge of Japanese cuisine.[2] This lacuna is all the more notable since its legacy has otherwise been profound, underpinning perceptions of what is quintessentially Japanese. But it is precisely the reticence of these canonical works on food that leaves readers in the dark about what those courtiers ate.

The historian Higuchi Kiyoyuki presents one provocative theory to explain this absence of eating: "I believe that Heian men and women did not write about their appetites, though they may have detailed their sexual desires, because they led lives in which they felt no joy in eating. Heian cuisine tasted awful, and food was not something to be enjoyed." He goes on to claim that the aristocracy was malnourished, a chronic state of depression that led to the rise of the

GIFTING MELONS TO THE SHINING PRINCE 49

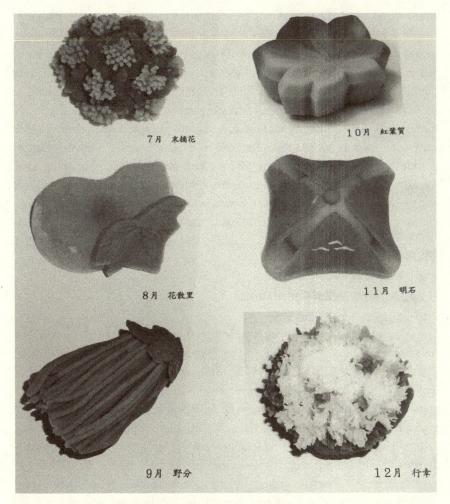

FIGURE 2.1 Sweets inspired by *The Tale of Genji*, named after its chapter titles, and tied to the months of the year. Courtesy of Tsuruya Yoshinobu.

enervated sentimentality characteristic of how Heian court culture was later viewed.[3] He, among others, also contends that the plump beauty of nobles, as depicted in art, was an aesthetic that served to mask their unhealthy, bloated condition by valorizing it.[4]

Whether or not Higuchi's argument is accepted, the role of diet in Heian culture has not been adequately discussed. While foods made in Kyoto often evoke the court mystique, there is little reflection on their actual history and the allusion's relevance. In fact, even the meals of the upper class differed from what people today consider to be Japanese. Not only did the cuisine's aesthetics, flavors, and dining practices diverge, but also the attitude itself.[5] This chapter uses overlooked accounts to describe not so much the actual dishes or customs, but the perception of food. Questioning the reputation of the Heian period as one of the seminal origins of native culture, it aims to uncover some of the continuities and ruptures in the Japanese relationship with food from the eleventh century to today. Victuals remained in the shadows, it contends, because of negative connotations that were anchored in its indispensable nature: food was essential not just for survival, but for social interactions, which were not always as pure as the romances evoke. Discussion of cuisine balances the idealized, lyrical vision of the Heian court, one that its authors cultivated. As Warren Belasco declares, "To eat is to distinguish and discriminate, include and exclude. Food choices establish boundaries and borders."[6] Heian aristocrats likewise maintained their identity by excluding food from high literature, while negotiating its tensions through moralizing and aestheticizing representations.

How Bad Were Heian Court Meals?

Considering the intense gastronomic interests of today's Japanese consumers, the absence of food in the masterpieces comes as a surprise. Even in such an expansive work as *The Pillow Book*, Sei Shōnagon mentions only a handful of dishes, such as shaved ice in a silver bowl—hardly meaty stuff. Indeed, despite the pervasive connection between food and sex, Sei (at least) objects to giving food to men on nocturnal visits, finding them repulsive to look at while eating.[7] Higuchi thus describes Heian texts as "a literature in which no appetite appears."[8] What might explain this lack of references?

It is true that, because of practical limitations and serving practices, court cooking could not have been very appetizing. While Japanese cuisine today emphasizes the taste of seasonal, fresh ingredients, because of capital city's location, most of the seafood, meats, and some produce came to the palace kitchen preserved—salted, fermented, dried, or partly cooked. Such handling can heighten flavors, namely umami—as seen in the essential dashi (broth) ingredients of bonito and kelp—but the preponderance of dried goods, even reconstituted, must have tested the jaw muscles.[9]

On the Japanese table of today, the annual cycle comes to the fore in the presentation. Here, too, Heian cuisine diverged. Rather than small, beautifully arranged portions in various wares, banquets featured mounds of cold food served on circular, plain dishes, set atop lacquer tables with chairs, as in figure 2.2.[10] For his formal meals, the emperor sat in a chair at a table with silver dishes, silver chopsticks, and a spoon. These details depart from what

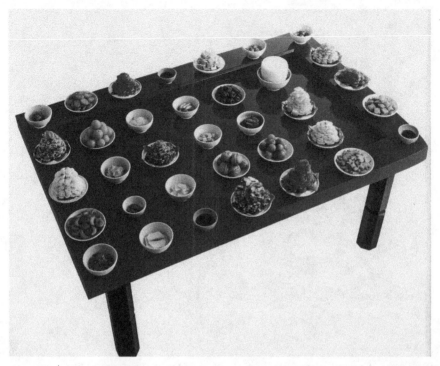

FIGURE 2.2 An emperor's banquet table. Courtesy of the Costume Museum (Fūzoku Hakubutsukan, Kyoto).

many today around the world consider to be the hallmarks of Japanese cuisine. Indeed, the historian Satō Masatoshi demonstrates that courtiers understood these ceremonial sittings to be Chinese, especially in contrast to the newer domestic settings that arose during the tenth century.[11]

This duality in the court cuisine places it alongside the era's other cultural productions that operated within the Chinese-Japanese dialectic. This binary facilitated the later establishment of a "Japanese" identity, yet as in the realms of literature or art, this distinction remained relative. The emperor's domestic-style mealtimes featured wooden utensils, sitting on floors, and serving attendants with Japanese hairstyles.[12] A typical setting for the aristocracy is illustrated in figure 2.3. The "Chinese" repasts were, though, continental mostly in form and in the Heian imagination. In fact, contemporaneous Chinese fare featured more cooking techniques, such as stewing and frying, that made for more exciting menus.[13] From today's vantage point, Heian cuisine was neither Japanese nor Chinese. What makes it seem so awful, and not worth writing about, lies in its departures from the present ideals.

FIGURE 2.3 A typical aristocratic meal. Courtesy of Mukō City Cultural Museum (Mukō-shi Bunka Shiryōkan).

Buddhist Guilt

Dreadful foods can elicit more words than the mundane, as any cursory look at online forums reveals. Still, the opinionated Sei Shōnagon, who might have otherwise flourished in this selfie age, has little to say about her own meals. Beyond taste, there must be other factors that underlie this Heian reticence. For one, Buddhism has been blamed for promoting a sense of guilt toward eating, a belief that a good appetite demonstrates an unhealthy attachment to the vulgar world.[14] The impact of Buddhism on the Japanese diet has mostly been discussed through the prohibitions on the eating of meat. This connection has, however, been downplayed by scholars, who have noted the continuation of under-the-table meat consumption in premodern Japan.[15] But even if Buddhism was not effective in persuading people to give up what they wanted (drinking and sex being some of the other proscribed activities), that did not prevent its values from coloring the discourse about food. In fact, Buddhism's ambivalence about consumption led to an intensification of anecdotes (*setsuwa*) about food during the late Heian period, as people grappled with the moral tensions in the guilty pleasure of eating. The disappearance of food in high court literature then points neither to the dreadfulness of Heian cuisine nor to lack of interest. Like eating, writing was a practice that straddled both public and private and afforded an ostensibly open glimpse into the self. Just as foodies today use local, organic heirloom tomatoes as part "of the story they tell themselves and others about who they are," Heian writers shaped their identity by their transcendence over food.[16] While meals punctuated everyday life, they were pushed under the table in aristocratic writing, which instead attempted to carve out an idealized space and identity that banished such physical, mundane affairs.

There are in fact a number of stories that feature eating. Since many of them come from a more popular, oral tradition, it is not surprising that they would display an earthiness uncharacteristic of court literature. The *Uji shūi monogatari* (*A Collection of Tales from Uji*, compiled c. 1221) contains several episodes that advocate vegetarianism by describing the cruelty of slaughter (tale 59) and the frightening possibility that one might be eating loved ones in their reincarnated states (tales 167 and 168). Tale 19, "About the Supernatural Powers of the Holy Man Seitoku," provides another view into perceptions about eating's problematic nature.[17]

Seitoku's holiness is seen in how he undertakes his mother's funeral. For three years, he circumambulates her coffin while chanting. He never stops to rest, sleep, eat, or drink. In a dream he learns that she has attained Buddhahood. He then conducts the final services. Seitoku's suppression of all his bodily functions underlines his superhuman quality. Yet the human body is not rejected outright. While Seitoku forgoes somatic needs, he still requires his body to chant, to circumambulate, and to undertake the funeral. Unlike Western Enlightenment attitudes of mind over body, Buddhist views emphasize the interdependence of the two. That his mother's corpse requires her son's purifying ministrations points, though, to how women needed to, according to the era's values, transcend their particularly polluted corporeality.[18] This difference in gender perception explains why almost all depictions of eating come from writings associated more with male discourse, such as the *setsuwa*. Since women's writings dominated the later reception of Heian court culture, their characteristics have prevailed, masking some of the alimentary landscape visible in other texts.

The story follows Seitoku to the capital, where, famished after three years of fasting, he encounters paddies filled with pondweed (*nagi*, Latin: *Monochoria korsakowii*). He proceeds to devour seven acres' worth. News of his voracious appetite spreads, capturing the interest of Minister of the Right Morosuke (908–960), who offers Seitoku fifty bushels of rice, which he also wolfs down. Having special powers, Morosuke can see that hungry ghosts (*gaki*) surround

Seitoku, although they are invisible to others. Seitoku's copious ingestion of a weed-like plant growing out of mud (not unlike the lotus), it turns out, was not for feeding himself, but for helping those suffering creatures. This tale thus turns the problematic act of overconsumption into a selfless act of compassion.

However, the story does not end there. The ghosts were so reborn because of excessive desires in their previous lives that condemned them to unending hunger. Seitoku alleviates their suffering for that moment. Ultimately, though, they will never be satiated. Gluttony remains a vice. The episode concludes with the shocking image of Seitoku and his entourage defecating, turning a lane black as ink. Even if one is as holy as Seitoku, overeating has odious consequences, condemning one to being perennially famished in the next life.

The Appetite for Food and Power

Another story from this collection emphasizes the problematic nature of unbridled appetites. "The Third Avenue Middle Counselor and Watered Rice" (tale 7:3) presents Fujiwara no Asahira (917–974) and his struggles with obesity. In fact, he is so obese that the strain forces him to call a doctor, who recommends, "You must eat watered rice, with hot water in the winter, and cold in the summer."[19] While this prescription may not match diet trends today, the logic is evident. Asahira agrees to try it, but he later complains that it is not working and has the doctor observe his dining protocol.

> There were about ten, three-inch sliced pieces of white dried melons. Also, layered with their heads and tails overlapping were about thirty large, pressed preserved ayu sweetfish. . . . He first had some melon, eating five or six slices in three bites at most. Then he had five or six of the fish in two bites or so. Next he pulled the rice to him and with two or three twirls of his chopsticks, it was gone. "Fill it up again," he said, and passed the bowl. After two or three helpings, the rice container was empty. . . . At this point, the doctor Shigehira commented, "It's all very well to make a point of eating watered rice, but you won't get your weight down if you eat as much as that."[20]

The story derives its energy through the comical description. The narrator's numerical repetition gives the impression of adding up sums, emphasizing Asahira's insuppressible appetite. Its bantering tone suggests a lighthearted story about a silly, fat man, but he was a historical figure with a fearsome reputation. In the *Ōkagami* (*The Great Mirror*, a historical tale from the twelfth century), he is featured in a political battle with Fujiwara no Koremasa (924–972).

The *Ōkagami* account is historically inaccurate. But in the story, Asahira loses this contest, their relationship sours, and when he attempts to reconcile, he ends up being humiliatingly left waiting outside of Koremasa's gate. Falling ill from the heat and his anger, he vows on his deathbed to haunt his rival's family.[21] These stories illustrate his reputation: a man of voracious appetite for food and power. Pay heed, though, to the narrator's bias. Being plump could be charming, but Asahira is simply fat and made to look morally unfit.[22] The story simultaneously erases his reappearance as a vengeful specter, using comedy to overwrite this threatening possibility. Moreover, by poking fun at sloppy eaters, such anecdotes allowed the elite to revel virtually in victuals. Problematic desires and acts could be attributed to unworthy, disgraced people, who, in their gorging, allowed themselves to be consumed as fodder to alleviate readers' anxieties, while fulfilling some taboo fantasies.

Food and Desire

Court literature avoids graphic descriptions of ingestion and excretion, but in comparison to later court works of the eleventh century, the *Utsuho monogatari* (Tale of the hollow tree, tenth century) contains more references to dining. Still, the narrator does not elaborate on the food, instead paying closer attention to the entertainment, the fashion, and the furnishings. This focus might again suggest that eating elicited little enthusiasm. Whether the dishes tasted good or not, an episode in the tale shows the negativity surrounding copious eating and makes explicit links to sexual desire.

In "Tadakoso" (book 3), the evil, elderly widow of the Minister of the Left attempts to seduce Tachibana no Chikage. She relies on her wealth to engage his interest and plies him with "clothing for winter and summer" and "many kinds of foods for morning and evening."[23] On those rare visits from Chikage, she sets out "seven or eight dishes of delicacies that he did not even touch with his chopsticks, and brocade clothing that he did not even bother to try."[24] The stated number of dishes is exorbitant. In the twelfth century, a regular meal for aristocrats is believed to have consisted of rice, one soup, and three side dishes. This assumption is based on illustrations such as the scene of the man with a toothache in the *Yamai no zōshi* (Scroll of diseases and afflictions, twelfth century, figure 2.4). However, the art historian Yamamoto Satomi contends that, given the work's context, the man's ailment should be seen as retribution for his greediness, which is exemplified by the amount of food.[25] If three side dishes were considered abundant, seven or eight would be, by any measure, extravagant, signaling the widow's decadence and her preoccupation with corporeal pleasures.[26]

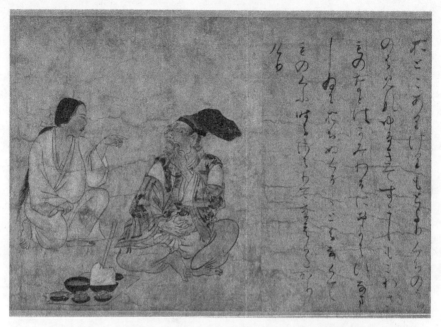

FIGURE 2.4 "Man with a Toothache" from *The Illustrated Scroll of Illnesses* (*Yamai no zōshi*). Courtesy of the Kyoto National Museum (Kyoto Kokuritsu Hakubutsukan).

On the other hand, Chikage is not at all tempted. He begins to feel ill and escapes. Back at home, enjoying a relaxing meal with his son, he remarks: "My appetite has strangely returned. At Ichijō [the widow's place], everything left a bad taste in my mouth. . . . Empty in the House of Jewels—that's what being at Ichijō leaves you feeling."[27] For him, the enjoyment of food does not depend on its amount or its attributed quality, but the affective context. Unlike the hedonistic widow, he derives emotional satisfaction from the company of his beloved son. Indeed, at many of the described court banquets, the emphasis may appear to be on luxury. However, the enjoyment of the music, dance, or poetry is a matter of taste and reserved for select, discerning people. This episode demonstrates how food and its partaking had negative, carnal connotations that could be overcome through affect, character, and context. In the dictates of social class, then and today, those in the know who possess "culinary capital" exhibit what Pierre Bourdieu termed an "aesthetic disposition" that downplayed practical functions of things such as food, while highlighting its aesthetic values.[28] It is not surprising then that, as Ted Bestor discusses in this volume, Japan's recent UNESCO application for washoku likewise skirted ingredients or techniques to celebrate instead appreciation of the environment and communal customs.

Dining Etiquette

Beyond such narratives, there are some other kinds of texts that manifest the "aesthetic disposition." The *Fukego* (Stories of Lord Fuke, twelfth century) consists of 258 short anecdotes as told by Fujiwara no Tadazane (Lord Fuke, 1078–1162). Nineteen of them deal with practices related to food. Many of them are prescriptive, providing directions for protocol. For example, one of the shortest entries (number 154) sounds like an admonishment any parent would utter: "Lord Fuke stated: 'When eating at a public, formal venue, one should not take big mouthfuls of food.' "[29] A longer record contains more instructions.

> Lord Fuke stated, "When being served, first the mounded salt and such will come out, next the rice. Then the various soups and dishes will be served. Thereupon start eating. . . . At public events, do not reach for faraway items by leaning while sitting. Do not drag a clay dish closer with your chopsticks. Do not shovel the food down. . . . If rice is sticking to your chopsticks, pull it off inside your mouth; do not lick it off."[30]

This etiquette elevates one of the most primal of human behaviors into refined ritual. When to start eating, how to handle certain fares, what uncouth behaviors to avoid: such knowledge—which Tadazane sought to pass down to his descendants through such records—turns dining into a display of cultural capital that demarcates the right to rule, especially in the face of new warrior dominance. The samurai may be brawny, but lack finesse: the nobility's condemnation that resonated with some samurai, who hence sought aristocratic ties or tutelage. Because of the negativity surrounding copious consumption, and limitations in what one could eat in twelfth-century Kyoto, the aristocracy had to rely more on how they ate, rather than how much or what they ate, to distinguish themselves.

The rarefying of ingestion through protocol does not mean, however, that the pleasures of food vanished. Toward the end of *Fukego*, two entries center on melons. In the first one, Tadazane counsels not to eat the fruit all the way to the rind, as one would then appear to be gluttonous. He follows: "When melon is served with other foods, and one has not yet touched it, first stick one's chopsticks upright into the melon, and eat it later. This act wards off evil."[31] Like marketing today that converts commodities into identities, such customs channel foods' significance away from consumption into production, whether of myth, values, or identities. Melons have a history in Japanese mythology that attributes to them special powers.[32] But the account that follows underlines the satisfaction of eating, as it seeks to retrieve precious memories through shared experience.

> Tadazane stated: "Morozane stated, 'In the summer, when I visited my father Yorimichi, I was served melon. Because it was hot, I ate a lot of it. Until that point, Yorimichi had seemed to be in a foul mood and short tempered, but seeing me eat the melons, he brightened, and said, "Look at how you're gulping them down!" Yorimichi did not have any melon himself.' "[33]

Morozane (1042–1101) was Tadazane's grandfather as well as adoptive father. This passage thus provides an intimate portrayal of august figures of the Fujiwara pantheon. Far from rankling the irritable Yorimichi, Morozane's enthusiasm for melons evokes mirth and creates a moment through which both of them can be remembered afterward. The fact that Yorimichi does not partake of any allows the movement to transcend the act of eating to achieve a personal bond, not only between the two, but also with the readers of later generations, who could share virtually the sensations of a juicy melon on a hot day.

Eating can be a solitary affair, but it is one all must do, making it vital to social interactions. Neither bad taste nor Buddhist attitudes alone can explain the absence of food in Heian court literature. As the Tadazane's melons demonstrate, the role of food in noble residences was substantial, even if minimized or transfigured in literature. Indeed, its very rootedness in worldly affairs made it unattractive as a part of an idealized discourse.

Poems on Food

Whereas the *Man'yōshū* (Collection of ten thousand leaves; compiled in the late eighth century) features many types of foodstuffs, the *Kokin wakashū* (Collection of ancient and modern poems; early tenth century) does not. This fact confirms the late Heian avoidance of food in lyrical expression, but such verses were recited at banquets that staged the sovereign's consumption of his realm's bounty.[34] More explicit mentions of food can be found in poems of less exalted settings. For example, delicacies and staples were given as gifts or rewards, and not surprisingly, they came with notes that included poems. While they are not exemplars of Heian poetry, they show how the constructed canon promotes certain poetic activity over others. Later in this volume, Keith Vincent's study of Masaoka Shiki's poems demonstrates that the treatment of food in Japanese poetry remained idiosyncratic, hence all the more powerful in its discomfiting originality.

This discussion of food poems relies on episodes from the *Kokon chomonjū* (Notable tales old and new, compiled by Tachibana no Norisue in 1254), a collection of anecdotes that spans the Heian and Kamakura periods. Norisue organized the roughly 720 entries into twenty books based on disparate topics such as love, games, and animals, as well as eating and drinking. Book 18 on dining contains thirty-three stories. The preface to this section begins: "Eating is the source of a person."[35] This pithy declaration sounds like a thirteenth-century Japanese version of "You are what you eat." But the contents do not correspond to such a notion of nutrients, however abstract. Rather, the preface continues by noting food's centrality to governance and to play. The accounts, too, focus on how food mediates human relationships, allowing the reader to connect with people of the past, even if she never gets to eat that described piece of melon. In other words, *shoku* (eating) here points less to ingestion than to the social act. The statement suggests that identity is constituted by the relationships cultivated through the exchange and consumption of food.

Of the section's thirty-three anecdotes, fifteen contain poems. The poets encompass nobility and clergy, some unknown, others famous for their way with words, such as Minamoto no Toshiyori (1055–1129). They show that, contrary to assumptions, versification took place in mundane circumstances. Poets could be inspired by such everyday things as miso (entry 622), buckwheat (616), and melons (617, 633, and 637).

In episode 637, four poems by the monk Taikaku (latter half of the twelfth century) are presented. The account begins:

> Fujiwara no Suetsune sent melons to Taikaku, stating "In exchange for these melons, please copy the Daihannya-kyō (Prajna Paramita Sutra)." He also sent one or two rolls of paper. In response, Taikaku composed this poem:
> The five-colored melons I had—
> but once I saw the yellow-dyed paper, their taste turned bitter.[36]

Taikaku's poem is propelled by the implied pun, "five-colored" (*goshiki*), which can also signify "melon." This allusion to colors allows him to segue into the "yellow-dyed paper," which was produced by using the bark of the plant *kihada* (phellodendron), a bitter medicine as well as a dye. Taikaku's poem tastefully articulates his displeasure in the transaction. Like food instead of money, verse instead of prose mitigates the harshness of the exchange by making it seem more personal. One has to keep in mind, however, that at this time, coinage was not widespread, so some foods, such as rice, had more direct monetary connotations than they do today.

In the next poem, Taikaku complains about a help's cooking skills.

When a person turned regular, cooked rice into grains, Taikaku composed:
> People all steam rice to prepare it as a dish,
> yet this cook turned the cooked into the uncooked.³⁷

Since it is impossible to reverse the cooking process, the cook may have been attempting to prepare rice into dried rice (*hoshi ii*), which was done to supply travel fare. Since complaints about cooking are rare in classical poetry that dwells on love, sorrow, or other emotions through comparisons to nature, this poem provides a unique example of the varied settings and uses in which poetic discourse could be deployed.

So the question becomes whether such poetry was simply forgotten, or whether Taikaku's verses were the exception. The episodes in the *Kokon chomonjū* suggest that, just like food, poetry was enmeshed into everyday life with its dilemmas and its aspirations. People then could, if adept as Taikaku in versification, tap into this discourse for utilitarian ends such as chastising annoying clients or reprimanding household staff. In this respect, however, poems diverged in the collective memory, with prosperity remembering those that fit the court taste for elevated pathos, moving imagery, or verbal virtuosity. Those on food receded, as they were consumed in their uttered moments to chide, to express some banal concern, albeit with some grace. This division in the level of discourse further removed food as a suitable topic of high literature. In the coming centuries, it may very well be the case that many expressions of Japanese contemporary gastronomy vanish, presenting a different vision of culinary life on the archipelago.

Coda

The English translation of the bestselling manga series *Oishinbo* contains a brief commentary by the author, Kariya Tetsu, writing from the vantage point of his residence in Australia. Just as Heian Japan had "China," Kariya evokes Australia (from where Japan imports much of its agricultural products) as a foil to address the question: what is Japanese cuisine? In the end, he concludes that "Japaneseness" has little to do with the origin of ingredients, preparation, or even taste, but is encapsulated in the term *washoku*: "a cuisine that brings people together in harmony and brings them pleasure."³⁸

Oishinbo covers a wide range of delectable foods from delicacies out of reach for most people to the simple pleasures of a hot cup of tea. But in this variety, there is a tension that spans its publication history from 1983 (near the commencement of Japan's bubble years) until 2014, when controversies over the series' critical depiction of the Fukushima nuclear disaster's continuing impacts on the environment forced the current suspension of its publication. As in the Heian period, feelings about food in post–World War II affluent Japan, as seen in *Oishinbo*, Kaikō Takeshi's *A New Star* (see Bruce Suttmeier's study in this volume), or Miyazaki Hayao's *Spirited Away* (see Susan Napier's study in this volume), straddle an uncomfortable spectrum. On the one hand, chefs on television dazzle viewers with rare ingredients prepared with special expertise. In this multimedia age, foods have to capture not only the taste buds, but the eyes and the imagination, in what Lisa Heldke has described as the foodie's colonialist bent that seeks the explorer's thrills for adventure.[39] On the other, the trend for organic, wholesome living signals an anxiety about consumerist excesses, waste, and commodification. Instead of extravagance, quantity, or convenience, the heart is key. In the same volume of *Oishinbo*, Kariya presents the character of Ian Nakazato, a Japanese American senator who returns to Japan, where he had spent his childhood during World War II. He is feted with extravagant spreads, but is only fulfilled when the protagonist presents him with green tea served in an idyllic, traditional Japanese house with a thatched roof. "I've just had a taste of real Japan," the senator sighs with satisfaction.[40] Despite the irony that such buildings require prohibitively expensive maintenance and that gyokuro tea would be a luxury for many people, the message is clear: true washoku facilitates communitas and harks back to a Japan uncorrupted by Western consumerism. This nostalgia remains pronounced in the context of the Fukushima nuclear disaster that ravaged rural Tōhoku, the agricultural homeland that is often sought in the imagination, if not in real life.

Where should one turn for the roots of Japan? Contrary to popular belief, the "Japan" of the Heian period would be alien to most Japanese today. Most would find its cuisine wanting. As we have seen, the ambivalence toward food reverberates both then and now. For the Heian period did not usher in just the age of glorious cultural flowering, but the degenerate age of *mappō*, when Buddha's teachings were believed to become all but inaccessible. War, famine, disease: such ominous disasters marked the end of the world. People turned all the more to religion. Not surprisingly, the heroes of twentieth-century organic movements, such as Fukuoka Masanobu (1913–2008), a farmer who devised and advocated a "do nothing" practice of agriculture, tap into a discourse laden with Eastern philosophies as a foil to Western modernity.[41] *Oishinbo* does not turn to religion as such, but to longing for a Japan that cherished nature (and, by extension, food), human bonds, hard work, and time-honored customs.

This Japan is a fantasy—a constructed brand in this age of consumerism. Still, such negotiations of the tensions inherent in food as a symbol have had a long history. While the dishes themselves have and will continue to change, perhaps this ambivalence and its response present one constant in the Japanese relationship with food.

NOTES

1. These sweets are just a few that are in Sen Wakako, *Chaseki de wadai no meika* (Tokyo: Sekaibunkasha, 2001).

2. This gap stems in part from a relative lack of sources dating to this era. In contrast, excavations at the Heijō Palace site have yielded records that have energized scholarship about Nara-period cuisine (see Watanabe Akihiro, *Heijō-kyō sensanbyakunen zenkenshō Nara nomiyako o mokkan kara yomi toku* [Tokyo: Kashiwa shobō, 2010]). As for the Kamakura period and beyond, the rise of warriors and merchants led to more diverse records of trade and banquets that paint a more colorful vision (see Kumakura Isao, *Nihon ryōri bunkashi: Kaiseki o chūshin ni* [Kyoto: Jinbun shoin, 2002]; Eric Rath, *Food and Fantasy in Early Modern Japan* [Berkeley: University of California Press, 2010]).

3. Higuchi is referring to *mono no aware* ("the pathos of things") that lamented, as well as celebrated, the fleeting nature of this world. The term was coined by the influential eighteenth-century scholar Motoori Norinaga (1730–1801), but has come to describe the Heian court sensibility. Higuchi Kiyoyuki, *Taberu Nihon shi* (Tokyo: Asahi shinbunsha, 1996), p. 89. See also Wayne Farris, *Japan to 1600: A Social and Economic History* (Honolulu: University of Hawai'i Press, 2009), p. 73.

4. Watanabe Minoru, *Nihon Shokuseikatsu shi* (Tokyo: Yoshikawa kōbunkan, 1964), pp. 108–10, 113; Higuchi, *Taberu Nihon shi*, 100–105.

5. For an introduction to the Heian court diet, see Takeshi Watanabe, "What Did Munetada Eat?" in Christina Laffin, ed., *Birth and Death in the Royal House: Selections from Fujiwara no Munetada's Journal "Chūyūki"* (Ithaca, NY: Cornell University Press, forthcoming).

6. Warren Belasco, "Food Matters: Perspectives on an Emerging Field," in *Food Nations: Selling Taste in Consumer Societies*, ed. Warren Belasco and Philip Scranton (New York: Routledge, 2002), p. 2.

7. *The Pillow Book of Sei Shōnagon*, trans. Ivan Morris (New York: Columbia University Press, 1967), 49, 257–258. Other notable mentions include square dumplings called *heidan* (136) and the uncouth dining manners of carpenters (259–260).

8. Higuchi, *Taberu Nihon shi*, 90.

9. The long history of these ingredients presents one of the few continuities in Japanese cuisine. Yet their usage varied from later techniques in that they were eaten, rather than used for their extracts in broths. As Yoshimi Osawa's chapter in this volume shows, the discourse surrounding umami has recently been central to identifying the purportedly unique characteristics of Japanese cuisine.

10. *Nenjū gyōji emaki*, ed. Komatsu Shigemi (Tokyo: Chūō kōronsha, 1987), 31–32. For illustrations of the table settings and furniture, see *Ruiju zatsuyōshō sashizukan*, ed. Kawamoto Shigeo and Koizumi Kazuko (Tokyo: Chūō kōron bijutsu shuppan, 1998).

11. Satō Masatoshi, "Kodai tennō no shokuji to nie," in *Heian jidai no tennō to kanryōsei* (Tokyo: Tokyo Daigaku Shuppankai, 2008). Satō discusses the *asagarei gozen*, informal, meals that the emperor ate. Another setting was the *on [no] za*, a postbanquet "relaxed seating," in which courtiers enjoyed food with poetry recitations, dance, and music. For information about the *onza*, see Kumakura, *Nihon ryōri no rekishi*, 16–18. A scene from the *Nenjū gyōji emaki* illustrates the *onza* (28).

12. Satō, "Kodai tennō no shokuji to nie," 337–339.

13. Ishige Naomichi, *The History and Culture of Japanese Food* (London: Kegan Paul, 2001), 72–75.

14. Higuchi, *Taberu Nihon shi*, 89.

15. Ishige, *History and Culture*, 52–58; Akira Shimizu, "Meat-Eating in the Kōjimachi District of Edo," in *Japanese Foodways Past and Present*, ed. Eric Rath and Stephanie Assmann (Champaign: University of Illinois Press, 2010).

16. Josée Johnston and Shyon Baumann, *Foodies: Democracy and Distinction in the Gourmet Foodscape* (New York: Routledge, 2015), 2.

17. *Uji shūi monogatari*, ed. Ōshima Tatehiko (Tokyo: Shinchōsha, 1985), 65–66; *A Collection of Tales from Uji: A Study and Translation of "Uji Shūi Monogatari"*, trans. D. E. Mills (Cambridge: Cambridge University Press, 1970), 161–164.

18. In the *Lotus Sutra*, the Dragon Girl must first be reborn as a man before she can achieve Buddhahood.

19. *Uji shūi monogatari*, 256; *Collection of Tales from Uji*, 275.

20. *Uji shūi monogatari*, 256–57; *Collection of Tales from Uji*, 275–276.

21. *Ōkagami*, ed. Tachibana Kenji (Tokyo: Shōgakukan, 1974), 198–202; *Ōkagami, the Great Mirror: Fujiwara Michinaga and His Times*, trans. Helen McCullough (Princeton, NJ: Princeton University Press, 1980), 145–146.

22. See descriptions of court women in *Murasaki Shikibu nikki*, ed. Nakano Kōichi (Tokyo: Shōgakukan, 1971), 224–228; *The Diary of Murasaki Shikibu*, trans. Richard Bowring (London: Penguin, 1996), 47–48.

23. *Utsuho monogatari*, ed. Nakano Kōichi (Tokyo: Shōgakkan, 1999), 1:215.

24. *Utsuho monogatari*, 1:216.

25. Yamamoto Satomi, "Food for Good or Evil: Buddhist Precepts and Food as Depicted in Medieval Japanese Paintings," *Kyōritsu Joshi Daigaku bungeigakubu kiyō* 58 (2013): 6.

26. *Ruiju zatsuyōshō sashizukan*, 4.

27. *Utsuho monogatari*, 1:221.

28. Peter Naccarato and Kathleen LeBesco, *Culinary Capital* (New York: Berg, 2012); Pierre Bourdieu, *Distinction: A Social Critique of the Judgment of Taste*, trans. Richard Nice (Cambridge, MA: Harvard University Press, 1984), 54.

29. *Fukego*, ed. Kawamoto Shigeo and Koizumi Kazuko (Tokyo: Iwanami Shoten, 1997), 431.

30. *Fukego*, 454–455.

31. *Fukego*, 470–471.

32. Hollow interiors of plants or fruits sometimes gave magical birth to creatures or gifts from the numinous world. Ryūsawa Aya, "Mastering Visions of the Borderlands: Claiming Sovereignty through Myth," paper presented in the panel "Visualizing Stories of Heian Japan: Go-Shirakawa-in's Image Repository," at the Annual Meeting of the Association for Asian Studies, San Diego, California, March 2013.

33. *Fukego*, 471.

34. For a chart of the vegetables in the *Man'yōshū*, see Toriimoto Yukiyo, *Shōjin ryōri to Nihonjin* (Tokyo: Shunjūsha, 2006), 28–29. Gustav Heldt describes the connection between the *Kokinshū* and the sovereign's symbolic consumption of his subjects and their production: *The Pursuit of Harmony: Poetry and Power in Early Heian Japan* (Ithaca, NY: East Asian Program, Cornell University, 2008), 142–144.

35. *Shoku ha hito no moto nari. Kokon chomonjū*, ed. Nishio Kōichi and Kobayashi Yasuharu (Tokyo: Shinchōsha, 1986), 2:303.

36. *Kokon chomonjū*, 322.

37. *Kokon chomonjū*, 322.

38. Tetsu Kariya and Akira Hanasaki, *Oishinbo: Japanese Cuisine* (San Francisco: Viz Media: 2009 [2006]), 114.

39. Lisa Heldke, *Exotic Appetites: Ruminations of a Food Adventurer* (London: Routledge, 2003).

40. *Oishinbo*, 259.

41. Fukuoka Masanobu, *The One-Straw Revolution: An Introduction to Natural Farming* (New York: New York Review Books Classics, 2009 [1975]).

3

Soba, Edo Style

Food, Aesthetics, and Cultural Identity

Lorie Brau

Japan is infatuated with noodles, as seen by the prevalence not only of such traditional domestic varieties as sōmen, udon, and soba, but also Western or "ethnic" noodles, from spaghetti to pad thai. In terms of popularity and quantity consumed, ramen wins the title of Japan's "national noodle" hands down, coming in third place overall in one recent Japanese online survey as a favorite food.[1] But soba (buckwheat noodles), seen in figure 3.1, also makes the list. One woman commented, "There are lots of kinds of noodles, but I think that only Japan has soba." A man described soba as *nihonteki*, "typically Japanese," and praised its texture, which he claimed is not found in foreign noodle dishes.[2]

Sometimes referred to as "Nihon (Japanese) soba" to distinguish them from Chinese "soba," that is, ramen, buckwheat noodles are eaten all over Japan. Commuters and travelers slurp them at stands on train platforms. Numerous regions—Izumo on the Japan Sea and Iwate in the north, for example—promote their style of preparing soba as a local specialty (*meibutsu*). The mountainous Nagano region, formerly called Shinshū, is associated with excellent soba, in particular, its *kiri no shita soba* (under-the-mist buckwheat) grown at high altitude; the daily wide range in temperature and superior water produce a high-quality crop.[3] The prefecture's promotional material sometimes capitalizes on the fact that soba noodles are said to have originated at a Nagano temple (see below). Shinshū soba is advertised to tourists as a local specialty. Nagano's dried soba noodles are sold throughout Japan.

FIGURE 3.1 Zaru soba, i.e., cold soba noodles eaten with a dipping sauce. Via Wikimedia Commons.

While Kyoto is noted for *nishin soba*, soba noodles in soup topped with simmered herring, the western Kansai region (encompassing Kyoto, Osaka, Nara, Hyōgo, Mie, Wakayama, and Shiga prefectures) is considered udon country. The rivalry between these thick, white wheat noodles and soba noodles dates to the Edo period (see below). Devotees of udon or soba still debate their noodle preferences in Internet discussion groups.[4] Given the increased mobility of the Japanese populace and the homogenizing effects of mass media, the divide between the two noodle camps has blurred. Tokyo now boasts more udon specialty restaurants, for example. Although some Osakans, strongly identified as udon eaters, may substitute udon for soba in the New Year's noodle-eating ritual (*toshi koshi soba*), most Japanese close out the old year with a bowl of soba noodles. Soba's prominence in this national practice confirms its importance as a "Japanese" food.[5]

Rather than cite the many sites of soba production and consumption as evidence for soba's status as Japan's "national noodle," this chapter focuses on the soba tradition of the city of Edo (now Tokyo), inquiring into how buckwheat noodles in the Edo period (1603–1867) and later contribute not only to a local, but also to a national, Japanese gastronomic identity. It examines contemporary discourse and summarizes research on soba's place in the culture of the Edokko, the "children of Edo," that is, merchants, craftspeople, and their descendants who since the eighteenth century have taken pride in their identity as the true natives of the city and creators of its urban culture. After tracing how soba came to be one of Edo's most popular "fast foods," the chapter considers the role of such traditional performance genres as kabuki and *rakugo* storytelling in enhancing soba's status as a food that embodies the aesthetic of *iki*, or Edo "chic." It concludes with an examination of more recent discourse on soba as a food that evokes the Edo past.

In "The Invention of Edo," historian Carol Gluck argues that since the Meiji period (1868–1912), the Japanese have come to view the Edo period as "tradition," "the way we (Japanese) once were."[6] Among the uses to which "Edo as tradition" has been put is the "commodification of nostalgia," which has engendered a heritage industry.[7] The construct of "Edo as Japanese tradition" has precipitated a number of "Edo booms," some initiated by government policies or mass media.[8] For example, the four hundredth anniversary of the 1603 opening of the shogun's government in Edo was commemorated in Tokyo with a number of events throughout 2003, including a festival celebrating four hundred years of Edo food culture.[9] Much of the mass-media discourse on the Edo period originates in Tokyo and centers on the city's past. While the transformation of Tokyo into a "world city" has obliterated most physical traces of the old city, its past has been reincarnated today as "heritage."[10]

Soba figures in some of this heritage production and has itself enjoyed a boom for the last twenty years or so. Television coverage, magazine articles, soba fan websites, manga, and a plethora of recently published popular books on soba, from how to make and eat it to soba chefs' memoirs and restaurant guides, attest to a lively interest in the noodle.[11] Soba academies, as well as organizations offering soba-making experiences as a form of tourism, have sprung up throughout Japan.[12] Japanese food booms tend to respond to a hunger for something new, but the soba boom also embodies nostalgia for an imagined past. In a foodscape dominated by convenience foods, soba enthusiasts appreciate the freshness and taste to be had in the handmade, artisanal product offered at an old Edo-style *sobaya* (soba restaurant). By partaking of the iconic food of the Edokko, they accrue culinary capital as they display their knowledge of Edo style.

From Buckwheat to Buckwheat Noodles

Before it came to refer to noodles, soba meant "buckwheat," a crop related to rhubarb, whose seed was hulled and eaten as porridge or ground into flour for dumplings in Japan. The earliest written evidence of buckwheat used as a food in Japan dates to the Nara period (710–794).[13] The easily cultivated buckwheat served as a contingency food, providing sustenance in years of poor rice or wheat harvests.

The first written reference to soba in noodle form dates to 1574 and is found in the records of the Jōshōji temple in Kiso, in what is now Nagano prefecture.[14] A plaque in Osaka marks the spot where the sobaya Sunaba was first opened in 1583, at the sand pit (*sunaba*) where Toyotomi Hideyoshi was building Osaka Castle.[15] In spite of their later association with Edo and the Edo period, buckwheat noodles and noodle shops seem to have originated elsewhere and earlier.

The term *sobakiri* (soba dough cut into noodles) began to appear in Edo accounts in the seventeenth century.[16] A work from 1664 mentions "kendon udon sobakiri" as being eaten by the lower classes.[17] "Kendon" noodle shops serving both the thick wheat udon noodles and soba, which first appeared in the pleasure quarters, were named after low-priced prostitutes (*kendon jorō*). These restaurants were cheap places to grab a quick bite, as opposed to places to drink and socialize. A proclamation issued by the Tokugawa government in 1686 prohibiting yatai (food stalls, illustrated in figure 3.2) that sold udon and soba after dark suggests that soba was among street vendors' offerings. Selling cooked food from carts or stalls in the evening was forbidden because of fear of fire. In spite of frequent bans, these food stalls, and soba, proliferated.[18]

Soba and the Edokko (Children of Edo)

In addition to technical improvements in the milling of buckwheat flour and experimentation with various methods of increasing the viscosity of the dough with such fillers as egg white, mountain yam, and wheat flour, it was the Edokko, soba scholar Iwasaki Shin'ya argues, who boosted soba's popularity.[19] The association of Edokko with soba continues to dominate soba discourse today. One commentator on a YouTube travelogue called soba the Edokkos' "soul food" (using English).[20] Another soba fan writes, "Edokko to ieba, soba," "For Edokko, it's soba."[21]

Nishiyama Matsunosuke, a leading scholar of Edo culture who has written extensively on the Edokko, defined them as families who had lived in Edo since the city's early days, acquiring wealth by running fish markets or working as rice brokers or lumber dealers, for example.[22] The later Edokko, who achieved critical mass in the early nineteenth century, were a more diverse and less wealthy group than the earlier Edo-identified natives.[23] A good number of them originally came from the neighboring countryside to work in construction, a much-needed trade in a city famous for its devastating fires. These men typically relied on food carts or soba shops to tide themselves over with a snack until the end of their workday. Along with tempura, sushi, and grilled eel, soba became one of Edo's top four "fast foods."[24] One encyclopedia of Edo life,

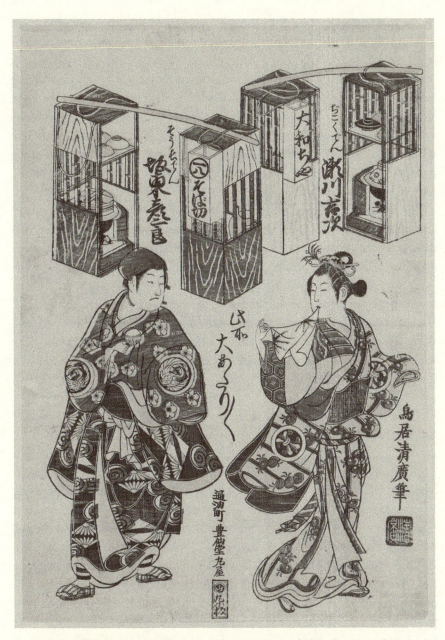

FIGURE 3.2 Torii Kiyohiro, *Edo meibutsu soba ga* (Picture of Edo's famous sobas), eighteenth century, illustrating portable soba vendor equipment in background. Via Wikimedia Commons.

Morisada Mankō (Morisada's sketches: A history of the manners of the Edo period) (1837), noted that there were soba restaurants on nearly every block of Edo.[25]

While Edokko promoted soba, soba also played a role in constructing Edokko identity and helped to dispel Edo's inferiority complex toward the more advanced culinary culture of Kamigata (Osaka and Kyoto).[26] Kamigata soy sauce and sake, deemed superior, were exported to Edo.[27] Feisty Edokko took soba noodles, made from buckwheat, a foodstuff that had been a staple of the poor, and made them stylish in order to declare their independence from the high culture of Osaka and Kyoto.[28]

A 1776 satiric picture book (*kibyōshi*), *Udon soba bakemono Ōeyama* (Udon and Soba, monster of Mount Ōe), demonstrates how soba symbolized Edo in opposition to the udon of Kamigata. In this parody, based on the story of Minamoto Raikō's triumph over the demon Shuten Dōji on Mount Ōe, Minamoto no Sobako (soba flour), aided by his four great warriors (all soba condiments parodying the original characters' names), Usui no Daikon (radish), Urabe no Katsuobushi (bonito flakes), Sakata no Tōgarashi (chili pepper), and Watanabe no Chinpi (dried tangerine peel) slay the demon, Udon Dōji.[29] The work suggests that whether or not soba beat out udon as a favorite noodle on the street, by 1776 it had come to symbolize Edokko pride.

Iki: The Edokko Style

Santo Kyōden (1761–1816), a popular writer of comic fiction and Edo native, listed five characteristics of an Edokko.[30] The last concerned temperament: the Edokko expressed *hari* (strength of character) and iki, which Nishiyama explains was "an aesthetic of the metropolis, where men and women entered into relations subtly tensed with hari, bitai (charm) and akanuke (a cool, unassuming character)."[31] This aesthetic spread from the pleasure quarters, where it had typified the coquetry inherent in the ideal relationship between a geisha or prostitute and her client. A discerning client who patronized and appreciated geisha as an embodiment of iki might be referred to as a *tsū*, a connoisseur. Iki became a symbol for the character of merchants and the lifestyle of a whole social class.[32] In her discussion of iki as a form of "coolness," Elena Giannoulis writes that the lower classes practiced iki to set themselves apart from their rulers, the samurai; iki thus "functioned as a self-protective mechanism in the face of humiliation and expropriations by the authorities."[33]

The code of iki not only shaped manners and fashion, but also how and what one ate. Kasai Toshiya conceptualizes soba and iki as being in a synergistic relationship.³⁴ He elaborates, for example, on the qualities of Edo *ni-hachi soba* (noodles made with 80 percent soba flour and 20 percent wheat flour) that render it iki.³⁵ Edokko preferred their soba noodles thin. The thinness demonstrates the skill of the soba craftsman and enables the eater to swallow with fewer chews. Indeed the connoisseur barely chews Edo soba, enjoying the *nodogoshi*, the sensation of the noodles sliding down the throat. The sound that one makes as one sucks in air and slurps them down, "tsurutsuru," enhances enjoyment of their aroma and cools them off when they are eaten hot. Kasai maintains that soba is even iki in terms of color. In the Edo period, tans and grays were fashionably iki colors; the color of Edo soba ranges from creamy white to a grayish tan.³⁶

Kasai's assessment of soba's intrinsic iki qualities may owe something to philosopher Kuki Shūzō, who raised the aesthetic of iki to the level of a national Japanese philosophy in his 1930 work, *Iki no kōzō (The Structure of Iki)*. In a footnote, Kuki summarizes what constitutes iki in the realm of cuisine and gives a few examples. "In short," Kuki writes, "iki taste is light and well modulated; it stimulates several bodily senses at once—smell and touch as well as the palate."³⁷ Kuki seems to be describing what Kyoto chefs might refer to as *hin*, "restrained elegance" (see the de St. Maurice chapter in this volume). Soba's light taste and the fact that eating it engages all the senses suggest that it would likely meet Kuki's requirements for an iki food.

Soba Style on Stage

In addition to the pleasure quarters, Edokko and their Tokyoite descendants have looked to kabuki for entertainment and to its actors as models of iki. Insofar as many plays depicted everyday life in Edo, soba often makes an appearance. In the iconic Edo kabuki play, *Sukeroku: The Flower of Edo* (1713), Sukeroku dumps a tray of cold soba on the head of one of his enemies. One of the most famous scenes featuring soba in the kabuki repertoire is "The Soba Shop Scene" in "A Narrow Road in Iriya on a Snowy Evening" (*Yuki no yūbe Iriya no azemichi*).³⁸ Naojirō, a samurai turned bandit who is on the lam, stops into a sobaya on a snowy night for a bowl of hot noodles. In one of the few scenes in kabuki that feature real food, Naojirō slurps up the soba in true Edokko fashion.³⁹ On the other hand, the spies on Naojirō's tail consume their soba silently, thereby revealing their non-Edo origins.

One might also read in this soba shop scene an overtone of resignation (*akirame*), that is part of the iki aesthetic. Naojirō is on his way to see his lover, whom he knows that he will likely never meet again after that night. The soba that Naojirō eats before this last visit symbolizes their separation.

Soba's tendency to break easily, due to its lack of gluten (which adds viscosity), renders it an apt symbol for parting.[40] It similarly conveys resignation to fate and farewells in *Kanadehon Chūshingura* (The treasury of forty-seven loyal retainers) celebrated as perhaps the most iconic and beloved Japanese tale of samurai loyalty. Under the rubric of "*Uchiiri soba*" (Soba of the raid), legends have circulated about how the loyal retainers shared a light meal of soba on the second floor of a sobaya before carrying out their vendetta.[41]

Edo dwellers who had neither the time nor money to enjoy kabuki flocked to their neighborhood storytelling house (*yose*) to take in a variety of acts, including rakugo storytelling. While no real food appears on stage in rakugo, some pieces involve miming the eating of noodles, sweets, and other foods. The custom of making sounds as one eats noodles, hilariously parodied in the spaghetti-eating etiquette scene in Itami Jūzō's film *Tampopo* (1985), provides rakugo storytellers (*hanashika*) with great opportunities to connect with their audience. These days their slurping performances typically bring applause. Perhaps these rakugo performances foster an imagined Japanese community around soba, as this manner of demonstrating gustatory pleasure is a part of Japanese gastronomic identity.

In one of the most well-known rakugo stories, "Toki soba" (Time noodles), a foolish protagonist overhears a man cheat a soba street vendor by distracting him with flattery and asking him the time as he counts out sixteen coins to pay for his bowl of noodles. To confuse the cook, the con man holds forth at length on the ideal bowl of soba. He notes that the chopsticks should be disposable, illustrating the Japanese emphasis on purity and avoidance of others' "dirt,"[42] and comments that the bowl in which the noodles are served must be attractive, because one eats with one's eyes first. He adds that soba should be served quickly, and that the noodles should be thin and not mushy. If "Toki soba" spells out the rules that define an excellent bowl of soba, in his rakugoesque novel, *I Am a Cat* (*Wagahai wa neko de aru*, 1905), Natsume Sōseki lampoons the rules for proper consumption of soba through his "aesthete" character, Meitei Sensei.[43] Meitei explains that, having grabbed a few long strands on one's chopsticks, one should dip no more than a third of the noodles into the sauce, swallow them in one gulp without chewing, savor the feeling in the throat, and eat the entire serving in no more than three and a half or four bites.[44] Meitei Sensei's instructions overstate it, but the stereotypical Edokko does not like to dawdle, and does indeed eat cold soba quickly and dips lightly. Rakugo storyteller Kingentei Bashō made fun of this Edokko habit in a prologue to a performance of the rakugo *Sobasei*: "One of the last words heard on the deathbed of an Edokko: Just once before I died, I would have liked to have eaten soba drenched in sauce."[45]

Reviving Soba Cool in Contemporary Japan

For some decades of the twentieth century, soba was not as popular as it is today. Murase Tadatarō, author of *Soba Connoisseur* (*Soba tsū*), expressed apprehension about soba's future in 1930. He wrote that with the introduction of machines to make soba, people no longer acknowledged the skill of the soba artisan. Soba makers had become careless about their training. Much of this soba tasted awful, he lamented.[46] Uehara Rorō's 1972 *Soba Encyclopedia* (*Soba jiten*) expressed similar concern about the waning popularity of soba.[47]

Since the Edo boom, however, downtown Edokko culture has been reinvented as "cultural heritage" at the *yose* where rakugo is performed, on television, and in other digital and electronic media. This reinvention of "Edo" has given rise to such phenomena as the Edo Sobalier Society, founded in 2003, a nonprofit organization that sponsors a certified course for the purpose of "learning about Edo soba and becoming stylish (iki) soba connoisseurs."[48] Like other Japanese foodies, soba aficionados tend to seek distinction by focusing their energy on the pursuit of connoisseurship of one food associated with one region, in this case, the Edo tradition of soba. The Edo Sobalier Society invites Edo soba aficionados to immerse themselves in soba culture from numerous perspectives and develop the techniques to prepare it themselves, with the aim of becoming certified as a *sobarie* (sobalier, a sommelier of soba).

The course curriculum is divided into four parts: learning by ear (lectures), with the hands (lessons in making soba noodles), the tongue (eating at a variety of sobaya), and brain (presenting a research report on soba). The "learning by tongue" segment of the curriculum fosters students' appreciation for the skills of the soba artisan. In their tasting notes, they are instructed to pay attention to such things as the origin of the soba flour used, whether or not the noodles are hand cut, and the noodles' aroma, sheen, and springiness. This concern with the fine points of soba making and with terroir replicates the discourse of many foodies in Europe and the United States, as well as Japan. Students who complete the advanced course earn the credential, "Edo *sobarie* (sobalier)—Le chic," an impressive title that borrows its prestige from French with its reference to "sommelier" and "chic," and bestows culinary capital.

The Edo Sobalier Society also articulates international aims, for example, to further the development of Japanese food culture and, through soba, to make healthy Japanese food and food culture known throughout the world.[49] UNESCO has given this goal a boost by recognizing Japanese cuisine as "intangible cultural heritage" (see the Bestor chapter in this volume). This development was the lead of Alexandra Woodruff's NPR story on Sonoko Sakai, who runs soba-making classes in California. Woodruff mentioned the recent UNESCO decision and noted that many consider soba "the humble jewel of Japanese cuisine."[50] The "humble jewel" that is Edo soba embodies three salient themes as culinary heritage: (1) the way of the artisan; (2) the significance that the Japanese ascribe to knowledge of form (*kata*); and (3) iki and Japanese identity.

Artisanality, the notion of work ethic and pride in one's craft, suffuses both soba discourse and that of Japan as a whole, as seen in the branding of Kyoto taste (see the de St. Maurice chapter). Becoming a soba chef requires strict training (*shugyō*), a period of hardship and sacrifice that is positively valued in Japanese culture. A sentimental ballad entitled "Kantō Edo sobakiri no michi" (The way of the Kantō Edo soba cutter) celebrates these hardships: "Gazing at my damaged hands, I think, how fast these ten years have flown, the artisan training that I endured without shedding a tear. The pride of Edo, imbued with bushido [the way of the samurai]—that spirit shines and takes on a beautiful luster."[51] In this song, equating the soba craftsman with the samurai enhances such artisan traits as stoicism, perseverance, and wholehearted commitment, that is, giving one's all (*isshōkenmei*).

Edo soba discourse not only emphasizes the importance of knowing the proper forms for producing artisanal soba, but also stresses mastery of the forms of soba eating. Sōseki's Meitei Sensei takes this preoccupation too far, but some believe that to be able to call oneself a real connoisseur, one must know how to eat soba "correctly," however that may be defined, and understand how to comport oneself at a sobaya. Books such as *Sobaya no shikitari* (The customs of the soba shop) explain what one needs to know.[52]

If sentimental songs romanticize the way of the artisan, such culinary manga as *Sobamon: Nippon soba angya* (The gate of soba: Japanese soba pilgrimage, 2009–present) emphasize the vast stock of knowledge that generations of soba chefs have acquired and applied in their mastery of the arts of kneading, rolling, and cutting buckwheat flour dough.[53] *Sobamon* features an itinerant protagonist who trained at an old Tokyo soba restaurant. He compares to the wandering masterless samurai in films, the outsider who arrives on the scene to set things right. This soba master imparts insider knowledge, corrects people's misconceptions about soba that have arisen as a result of the information glut produced by media, and equips would-be soba connoisseurs (tsū) with the knowledge to augment their culinary capital.

In one episode, the manga informs readers about what makes a soba tsū. The path to becoming a connoisseur, as also emphasized by the Sobalier Society, requires that one eat at various sobaya. One chooses the best of these restaurants and frequents it for some time. After losing interest in that place, one chooses another establishment and becomes a regular there for a while. In this manner, one can develop a good sense of personal preference and an understanding of the styles of soba offered by different restaurants. Only after developing one's palate for soba can one become a connoisseur; otherwise one is eating with one's head, not one's tongue. Eating with one's head is characteristic of the half-baked *hankatsū* (e.g., Meitei Sensei), someone who talks about what's good without really understanding it.[54]

Uehara Rorō's definition of tsū embraces the ideals of cleanliness and concern for others' comfort that often figure in representations of Japanese cultural identity. He defines the soba tsū as someone who does not leave a messy pile of noodles on the plate, dirty one's chopsticks, or slosh the noodles around in the cup of dipping sauce. It is important not to be an eyesore or otherwise disturb other diners.[55]

Though following the rules implies conformity, some Japanese rules of soba eating could almost be construed as rebellious in a global context. What is considered poor manners in much of the West, such as making noise as one eats noodles, is regarded in Edo soba culture as a demonstration of enjoyment. The Edo Sobalier website essay "Edo sobalier no kokoro" (The spirit of the Edo sobalier) identifies soba itself as a kind of outsider in the Japanese food world in that it is not included among the "five grains" (wheat, rice, beans, and two kinds of millet, *awa* and *kibi*). "That may be why the independent Edokko loved soba," the author concludes.[56]

"The Spirit of the Edo Sobalier" posits the "uniquely Japanese" aesthetics of *ga* (elegance), *mono no aware* (the pathos of things), *yūgen* (mystery and depth), and the ethics of *isshōkenmei* (giving one's all) and *dōri* (truth, reason) as products of Japan's aristocratic and samurai culture. The author adds that the townspeople of Edo developed their own ethos of chivalry and that the aesthetic of iki and tsū and juxtaposes this proud Edo townsman culture against the samurai/aristocratic cultural hegemony. Edo townsman culture, with its copious attention to worldly pleasures, including food, in fiction, drama, and woodblock prints, contrasts the world of the Heian period aristocrat, whose literary productions omitted any mention of food (see the Watanabe chapter in the volume).

With its reference to broad cultural values and aesthetics, "The Spirit of the Edo Sobalier" resembles Kuki Shūzō's 1930 monograph, *Iki no kōzō* (*The Structure of Iki*). Kuki, who studied in Europe for many years, aimed to abstract iki and to express it using Western terminology in order to construct a Japanese aesthetic that "would enable the Japanese to develop a national consciousness of their own."[57]

One behavior associated with iki—eating lightly—seems particularly appropriate to recession-era Japan after decades of overconsumption, the Westernization of the Japanese diet, and recent concerns with obesity. As illustrated by the expressions *hara hachibun me* or *hara hachibu* (belly 80 percent full), a concept of Confucian origin that has even gained traction in the Western health media, the Japanese consider it prudent to stop eating short of complete satiation. One might add that it is also iki to do so. One website notes that the expression, *edobara* (Edo belly) refers to a small appetite.[58] The founder of one of Tokyo's old sobaya used to say that Edokko believed that one should not inflate one's belly on sushi or soba.[59] And noted Edo tsū and manga artist Sugiura Hinako humorously remarked about the small portions of soba served at restaurants, "An Edokko wouldn't say, 'I'm hungry—let's go stuff ourselves with soba.'"[60]

If one is concerned about looking attractively slim, an iki ideal, soba may be prescribed: it has acquired a reputation as a diet food. A recent Japanese Google search with the terms "soba" and "diet" yielded about 454,000 hits. One website notes that despite being a carbohydrate (a word that often evokes negative associations in Japanese diet discourse as well as Western), soba flour is lower on the glycemic index than is wheat.[61] After decades of a "devouring Japan" that has overconsumed, if not quantity, certainly a variety of foods from all over the world, Edo soba's healthiness and its evocation of iki render it a proud symbol to express Japanese cultural identity.

Epilogue

This study has focused on Edo soba's associations with the culture of Edo, Edo chic (iki), and the proud, spirited Edokko, who stood up both to the hegemonic cultural and political authority of their samurai superiors and to the older, udon-eating Kamigata culinary culture. Edo's "fast" food, such as noodles, tempura, and nigiri sushi, evolved into some of contemporary Japan's "favorite foods." These Japanese dishes have found fans all over the world. Soba remains largely uncharted territory for Japanese foodies, but it is gaining more attention abroad. The vast majority of Western recipes using soba, however, either mask or ignore its earthy, buckwheat flavor with other ingredients, suggesting that its flavor has yet to be universally accepted.[62] The small portions and the rules for eating soba, at least in many traditional sobaya, may make it a more challenging (and less satisfying) meal for some non-Japanese.

However, it might be argued that connoisseurship of soba culture endows the non-Japanese with culinary capital as well. In June 2015, Dave Conklin, an American food writer resident in Japan, took me to a small sobaya in east

Ginza. We were initially refused entry; the restaurant had recently instituted a "members only" policy. Though Dave had been there many times, he had not been officially invited to join. After we explained that he was writing a book on soba and that I too was a soba researcher, the chef relented and offered us seats at the counter. Perhaps more than his food writer credentials, however, what really seemed to clinch Dave's membership was the elegant, "iki" manner in which he ate his soba. Even the chef commented on how skillfully Dave slurped the noodles. It was Dave's mastery of the form, as well as his extensive knowledge, that secured him the Japanese culinary capital to earn a membership to this exclusive sobaya. One doesn't have to be Japanese to love soba, or even to be a soba tsū.

NOTES

1. Lifemedia, http://kuchikomi.lifemedia.jp/entertainment/jpn50_3.php. When originally accessed (July 23, 2013), soba came in at number 60. The most popular food was sushi, followed by curry rice.

2. Lifemedia.

3. "Kirishita soba wa donna soba?" *Soba jiten*. Nikkoku Seifun Corp., August 2004, accessed July 17, 2016. http://www.nikkoku.co.jp/entertainment/sobajiten/026.php.

4. For example, "Kantō ga soba, Kansai ga udon . . . ?" *Hatsugen komachi*. May 19, 2014, accessed July 11, 2016. http:/komachi.yomiuri.co.jp/t/2014/0519/659053.htm.

5. *Toshikoshi soba*, a custom associated with the New Year's holiday, is said to have originated in the Edo period. Its origins are unclear, but the most common reason given for eating soba on the symbolically important last night of the year is that soba noodles are stretched long and fine and thus express a desire for a long life and a long stretch of luck. Another reason cites the fact that soba noodles break easily, symbolizing the cutting of ties with any suffering, calamities, or debts from the previous year. Iwasaki Shin'ya, "Toshikoshi soba," Nihon Menruigyō Dantai Rengokai, accessed July 7, 2016. http://www.nichimen.or.jp/zatsugaku/21_01.html.

6. Carol Gluck, "The Invention of Edo," in *Mirror of Modernity: Invented Traditions of Japan*, ed. Stephen Vlastos (Berkeley: University of California Press, 1998), 262.

7. Gluck, "Invention of Edo," 264.

8. Gluck, "Invention of Edo," 273.

9. http://www.asahi-net.or.jp/~UK5T-SHR/kawaraban*.html.

10. Jordan Sand, "Monumentalizing the Everyday: The Edo-Tokyo Museum," *Critical Asian Studies* 33.3 (2001): 352.

11. These include Kasai Toshiya, *Soba to Edo bunka: Nihachi soba no nazo* (Tokyo: Yūzankaku Shuppan, 1998); Fujimura Kazuo, *Edo sobatsū e no michi* (Tokyo: Nippon hōsō shuppan kyōkai, 2009); and Yoshida Etsuko and Kanda Zatsugaku Daigaku, *Edo sobarie—Soba o kiwameru soba no somurie ofisharu handobukku* (Tokyo: Makino Shuppan, 2004).

12. For example, Asobiyū (Asoview), a leisure information website, has links to soba-making workshops throughout Japan. http://www.asoview.com/soba/. Edo Tokyo Soba no kai (Association for Edo Tokyo Soba) includes courses for professionals as well as amateur soba makers. http://www.edotokyosoba.com/exp.html.

13. Suzuki Ken'ichi, *Fūryū Edo no soba: Kū, kaku, yomu* (Tokyo: Chūkō Shinsho, 2010), iii.

14. http://www10.ocn.ne.jp/~sobakiri/1-2.html.

15. Mutsu Ken, "Edo sandai soba 'Sunaba' no hasshōchi o hakken!," *All About, Inc.*, accessed August 10, 2016. http://allabout.co.jp/gm/gc/15161/. Iwasaki Shin'ya discusses the Osaka origin of Sunaba in *Sobaya no keizu* (Tokyo: Kōbunsha chie no mori bunko, 2011), 76–78.

16. Uehara Rorō dates Edo soba to the Kan'ei period (1624–1644). *Soba jiten: Kaitei shinpan* (Tokyo: Tōkyōdō Shuppan 2002), 39. Ōkubo Hiroko cites *Jishō nikki* (1614) as the oldest record in *Edo no fasuto fūdo* (Tokyo: Kodansha 1998), 47.

17. Nisshinsha Yūkyōshi, *Gendaigo yaku: Soba zensho den*, ed. Niijima Shigeru and Fujimura Kazuo (Tokyo: Hāto Shuppan, 2006), 164–165.

18. Iwasaki Shin'ya, *Edokko wa naze soba na no ka* (Tokyo: Kobunsha, 2007), 21.

19. Iwasaki, *Edokko*, 42.

20. Hayashiya Unpei, narrator, JCN Channel, accessed January 22, 2014. http://www.youtube.com/watch?v=c74f4g1WJXU.

21. Sada Morihiro, "Edokko to ieba soba" (1), July 20, 1998, accessed March 10, 2012. http://homepage3.nifty.com/m_sada/TEAROOM/SOBA01.html.

22. Nishiyama Matsunosuke, *Edo Culture: Daily Life and Diversions in Urban Japan, 1600–1868*, trans. Gerald Groemer (Honolulu: University of Hawai'i Press, 1997), 42.

23. While Nishiyama calls these later self-professed "Edokko" "mediocre," he asserts that Edokko culture was created through the interaction of the wealthy, more established Edokko, the samurai living in Edo, and the provincial townsman "outsiders," some of whom assumed the identity of "Edokko" for themselves (*Edo Culture*, 43).

24. Ōkubo Hiroko, *Edo no fāsuto fūdo* (Tokyo: Kodansha, 1998), 81.

25. Nishiyama, *Edo Culture*, 174.

26. Iwasaki, *Edokko*, 42; Kasai Toshiya, *Soba: Edo no shokubunka* (Tokyo: Iwanami, 2001), 207.

27. Iwasaki, *Edokko*, 38–39.

28. Iwasaki, *Edokko*, 38–39.

29. Suzuki Ken'ichi summarizes the story in *Fūryū Edo no soba: Kuu egaku yomu* (Tokyo: Chūō Koron Shinsha, 2010), 127–154.

30. Nishiyama, *Edo Culture*, 42.

31. Nishiyamam *Edo Culture*, 55.

32. Elena Giannoulis, "Iki: A Japanese Concept of Coolness?," in *The Cultural Career of Coolness: Discourse and Practices of Affect Control in European Antiquity, the United States and Japan*, ed. Ulla Hasselstein et al. (Lanham, MD: Lexington Books, 2013), 217.

33. Giannoulis, "Iki," 220.
34. Kasai, *Soba*, 206–207.
35. Two theories on the origin of the expression *ni hachi soba* predominate. The price of a plain portion of soba, cold or hot, at least at the end of the Edo period, was set at 16 (2 × 8) *mon*. The second theory derives from the idea that soba noodles were usually made of 20 percent wheat flour and 80 percent buckwheat. Iwasaki, *Edokko*, 107.
36. Kasai, *Soba*, 209.
37. Nara Hiroshi, *The Structure of Detachment: The Aesthetic Vision of Kuki Shūzō* (Honolulu: University of Hawai'i Press, 2004), 71–72.
38. The author is Kawatake Mokuami. Samuel Leiter, trans., *Naozamurai*, in *The Art of Kabuki: Five Famous Plays*, 2nd ed. (New York: Dover, 1999 [1979]), 205–253.
39. "Kabukiza no soba no ohanashi" *Kabukibito*, Shochiku Co., Ltd., accessed March 15, 2013. http://www.kabuki-bito.jp/special/secom/40/.
40. Kasai, *Soba*, 213.
41. Suzuki, *Fūryū Edo no soba*, 5–29.
42. See Emiko Ohnuki-Tierney, "Japanese Germs," in *Illness and Culture in Contemporary Japan: An Anthropological View* (Cambridge: Cambridge University Press, 1984), 21–49, for one interpretation of concepts of purity and pollution in Japanese culture.
43. "Waverhouse," in the Itō Aiko and Graeme Wilson translation, *I Am a Cat* (North Clarendon, VT: Tuttle, 2002 [1972]).
44. Natsume Sōseki, *Wagahai wa neko de aru* (Tokyo: Shinchō Bunko, 1961 [1905]), 229–231.
45. ". . . Shinu mae ni ichido, tsuyu o tappuri tsukete soba o tabetakatta." *Big Globe Nandemmo Sōdan shitsu*, Accessed August 10, 2016. http://soudan1.biglobe.ne.jp/qa7455758.html.
46. Murase Tadatarō, *Soba tsū* (Tokyo: Kosaido Shuppan, 2011), 19.
47. Nakamura Ayako, "Kaitei shinpan in atatte," in Uehara Rorō, *Soba jiten* (Tokyo: Tokyodo Shuppan, 2002), n.p.
48. Yoshida Etsuko, *Edo sobarie* (Tokyo: Makino Shuppan, 2004), 10.
49. "Edo sobalier no susume" (The promotion of Edo sobalier), accessed August 10, 2016. http://www.edosobalier-kyokai.jp/susume.html.
50. Alexandra Woodruff, "Soba: More Than Just Noodles, It's a Cultural Heritage . . . and an Art Form," *Morning Edition*, NPR, January 21, 2014, accessed August 10, 2016. http://www.npr.org/sections/thesalt/2014/01/21/264399896/why-soba-is-more-than-just-food-its-an-art-form.
51. "Itanda wagate o mitsumete omoi, haya jūnen, namida dasezu shokunin shugyō, bushido tsūjiru Edo kishitu, konjō kagayaki, tsuya to nari." Otani Shigeru (composer) and Okumura Hideo (lyricist), Suzuna (cover artist), "Kantō Edo kiri soba no michi," http://www.youtube.com/watch?v=raIYwE-G2BI.
52. Fujimura Kazuo, *Sobaya no shikitari* (Tokyo: Nihon hōsō shuppan kyōkai, 2001). The introduction on Amazon's website promises that this book will teach the reader the iki manners of the sobaya that would make any man proud.

53. Yamamoto Osamu, *Sobamon: Nippon soba angya* (Tokyo: Shogakukan, 2009–).
54. Yamamoto Osamu, *Sobamon*, vol. 4, no. 30 (2010), 161–164.
55. Uehara, *Soba jiten*, 161.
56. *Edo Sobalier no kokoro*, accessed August 14, 2016. http://www.edosobalier-kyokai.jp/kokoro.html.
57. Giannoulis, "Iki," 220.
58. "Tabetara oishikatta." Accessed January 4, 2014. http://wiseowl.air-nifty.com/foodculture/2007/01/post_915a.html. Of course, just because soba often comes in small portions does not mean that one has to restrict oneself to one serving: it is common to see numerous trays stacked on top of one another, suggesting that the diner ordered a few portions. The rakugo story *Sobasei* tells of a competitive eater who took a bet that he could eat fifty portions of soba.
59. "Ima demo mane dekiru mise ga nai hodo senshinteki datta shodai Horita Katsuzō san no ishiki" (The consciousness of [Namiki Yabu Soba] founder Horita Katsuzō, who was so advanced that, even today, there are no sobaya who can imitate him), accessed August 14, 2016. http://sobaweb.com/magazine/200989/20090814173241.html.
60. Sugiura Hinako, "Sugiura Hinako no Edojuku." *Keiei konsarutanto Guromakon,* Builder story, Inc. 2010, accessed August 14, 2016. http://www.glomaconj.com/joho/edojuku1.htm.
61. "Tansuikabutsu na no ni yaseru?! Soba daietto no miryokuteki na mittsu no tokuchō" ("You lose weight even though it's a carbohydrate?! The three delightful characteristics of the soba diet"). *Daietto de Yasetai*, accessed July 14, 2016, http://diet-de-yasetai.jp/food/soba. See also "Soba daietto de risō no karada to kenkō o te in ireyō" (Let's achieve an ideal body and ideal health with a soba diet), *Koibita*, accessed July 17, 2016. http://za-sh.com/buckwheat-diet-7327.html.
62. For example, most of the recipes in this April 2, 2014 *Huffing Post* article, "The Soba Recipes That Will Compete with Ramen for Your Love," use strong flavors like peanut and garlic. Accessed July 20, 2016. http://www.huffingtonpost.com/2014/04/02/soba-recipes_n_5069282.html.

4

The Three Waves (and Ways) of Sake Appreciation in the West

Dick Stegewerns

Sake, the Japanese "rice wine" with a unique brewing method that results in fermented drink with the world's highest alcohol percentage, has recently become a mainstay in the West, found in cutting-edge Michelin-star restaurants and on the shelves of local supermarkets.[1] It has finally reached a status no longer fully dependent on its traditional Japanese image or on Japanese trade networks. And all markers seem to point to a growing market for sake overseas, which is good news for Japanese brewers, for decades confronted with ever-decreasing consumption in their own country.

Why did it take so long for sake to reach the status of a world-class drink that can be included amongst wine accompaniments to a course menu at a top restaurant? And how could this happen while sake in Japan itself is not a very popular drink, notwithstanding the recent naming of sake as Japan's "national alcoholic drink"? This chapter argues that the delay was, to a large extent, due to the self-imposed limitations and confusion caused by three different waves introducing sake to the Western world. Although all three waves used the term "sake," they each brought completely different products and different ways of drinking sake. Moreover, they were brought to the West by different types of importers who catered to different audiences.

The First Wave: Hot *Atsukan* Orientalism (1970s to the Present)

In the beginning—at least in Western Europe—there was Fukumusume, a rather undistinguished brand of sake from Japan's number one sake-production center, Nada, between present-day Kobe and Osaka. Nada was the major production center of sake in the early modern period, based on its strategic location and reputation for having the best water for sake brewing. In sharp contrast to most other regions, the breweries from this area boasted a solid interregional market, to a large extent aimed at the consumption center of Edo, the world's biggest metropolis during the early modern period.[2] From the Meiji period onward, Fushimi, in the southern part of Kyoto City, developed into the second biggest brewing center, partly because of its strategic location on the newly constructed Tōkaidō railway, the prewar main route of transport between Tokyo and Osaka. Breweries in Japan's western Kansai region flourished, accumulating considerable capital that allowed them to turn their breweries into factories in the postwar period.[3] Today, Kansai's Kobe and Kyoto prefectures produce 28 percent and 15.2 percent of the national amount of sake, occupying almost half of the total sake market.[4]

Today, sake factories are almost completely computer controlled, so that the winter conditions required by a brewery can be simulated year-round. These factories have predominantly focused on continuing the wartime necessity of making as much liquor out of as few rice grains as possible and using many additives. Additives or, in other words, elements that are not part of the natural brewing process, are not necessarily mentioned on sake labels. Just as in the case of wine, the producers of industrial sake containing many additives are supported by a trade organization and related lobby groups, who to the chagrin of pure sake makers have reached an agreement with the government not to bother customers with the details of "modern sake-making." Sake with no additives apart from yeast, which is added for 99.99 percent of all sake and need not be listed as an ingredient, carries the term "pure rice sake" (*junmaishu*) on the label. Sake with other additives does not present itself as such prominently and often goes by the legal term "clear sake" (*seishu*), but might better be described as "processed" or "impure" sake.

Gekkeikan, Shōchikubai, Kizakura, Hakutsuru, Hakushika, Kikumasamune, Hakutaka, and Ōzeki are the most prominent sake brands, all from the Fushimi and Nada brewing centers, but regrettably they primarily produce industrial sake that adds alcohol and other external elements. These are the sakes that have flooded the market and are available nationwide. Their position was further reinforced when the sake market was liberalized in the early 1990s, allowing big retail outlets, supermarkets, and convenience stores to start selling liquor. Liberalization meant the final blow to many small local breweries that lacked economies of scale. Whereas in 1970 there were still more than 3,500 breweries, in 2015 the number was 1,627.[5] This number, however, indicates establishments still holding a brewing license; the number actually continuing the brewing profession is around 1,200. Many breweries that lacked a strong brand name lost out in their traditional local markets, unable to compete with "the big producers" (ōte meekaa) in terms of price and quantity, let alone advertising budgets. The reputations of these factory-made sakes with additives, however, is a long way away from those Nada and Fushimi breweries enjoyed during the early modern and prewar periods. A very high share of the sake produced is cheap "milk-carton sake" (pakku sake) that comes in cardboard containers, the kind of product drunk to become intoxicated relatively cheaply, rather than to enjoy profoundly. Today, sake is often negatively associated with drunk elderly men, making younger generations shy away from it, decimating rates of consumption. In 1935, sake represented 70 percent of all alcoholic drinks. By 1970, this had dropped to 27 percent and by 2015 to a dismal 6.1 percent.[6]

Mass-produced sake with additives was the first type of sake exported to Europe and other places. The industry did not make efforts to introduce sake to the outside world as a rich and varied product that could compete with other fermented alcoholic drinks such as wine. Fukumusume, Gekkeikan, Hakushika, and most other major brands are all relatively dry, alcohol-added, pasteurized, filtered, and diluted sakes, lacking a pronounced taste, aroma, and body. The chefs of Japanese restaurants ironically regarded these bland non-outspoken products as "food sake" (shokuchūshu). Within the Asian culinary tradition of having many dishes on the table simultaneously, the notion of pairing one dish with one drink to bring about a *marriage* of taste is almost absent. Although sake is considered Japan's "national alcoholic drink" (kokushu), food professionals have little or no training in or deep knowledge of it. Their criterion for selecting a sake is a negative one; it should "not disturb the food." In the case of multiple dishes on the table, this leads to the choice of indistinct, watery sake. Accordingly, in many Japanese restaurants the menu will often list sake and the related price, rather than include information such as the type, maker, and brand.

The concept of sake as Japan's national alcoholic drink is relatively recent. It seems to have only been adopted by the Japan Sake and Shochu Makers Association (Nihon Shuzō Kumiai Chūōkai) in the wake of the successful 2013 campaign to include Japanese cuisine on the UNESCO list of intangible cultural practices considered world treasures (see the Bestor chapter in this volume). This is notwithstanding the awkward fact that sake in Japan is no longer a popular drink, that the majority of present-day sake is worlds apart from the pure rice-in-your-face sake of the prewar era, and that the purveyors of Japanese cuisine have hardly any knowledge of sake.[7]

In the West the uniformity of the relatively few sake brands imported was further increased by the way they were served. In Japan one is served sake cold or at room temperature if one does not specifically ask for heated sake (*kan de* or *atsukan de*), but in the West, all sake was served hot, no matter the climate, season, weather, accompanying dish(es), or individual preference. In keeping with the overall heterogeneous experience provided by early Japanese restaurants in the West, sake was served in an orientalist setting by women in kimono, from Asian-style ceramic carafes (*tokuri*) in tiny ceramic cups (*choko*), and enjoyed at a high temperature, in sum, a completely different experience from wine. There was not much culinary sense in heating the sake. The major merit of increasing the drinking temperature is that the aroma is enhanced, but this does not work with industrial sakes with limited, uninteresting aromas. Often the sake was served very hot, between 120° and 130° F. This destroys the taste spectrum of the sake, making most sake taste identical. Moreover, the steam rising from the hot sake will knock out one's sense of smell. One can still enjoy an alcoholic experience, but no longer taste what one is drinking. This style was first introduced by the few traditional Japanese restaurants in the West, further propagated by the wave of American Benihana-style teppanyaki restaurants beginning in the early 1980s, and continued by the deluge of Chinese-managed sushi restaurants from the late 1990s onward. It is often said that many such restaurants heat sake thoroughly to hide the fact that they are serving a cheap and inferior product. In any case, whether the strategy was to provide a complete heterogeneous, new, and exotic experience or to sell cheap booze for a high price (or both), the message was the same. Sake is uniform and lacks all variety, and all sake is consumed hot.

This first wave of sake introduced to the West seriously hampered the appreciation of sake in foreign markets.[8] The strong message of uniformity and interchangeability conveyed by this kind of *atsukan* orientalism caused many foreigners, after having tasted nondistinct sake once, to say that they did not like sake at all. One might have expected a more intricate strategy from an industry coping with a shrinking and aging domestic customer base. On the other hand, those actually working with sake on the Western market lacked knowledge of the variety of the product and in many cases lacked enthusiasm for sake themselves. It was just another element to complete the orientalist experience. The overwhelming emphasis on the Japanese setting meant that the consumption of sake was limited to Japanese restaurants and homemade Japanese dinners, and that sake was mainly sold at Asian food stores, in its cheapest incarnation, from the US factory branch of Gekkeikan. Liquor stores that happened to stock this one brand of sake tended to group it together with other exotic alcohols, which were usually distilled liquors, thus creating the mistaken impression that sake is not a fermented but a distilled drink.

The Second Wave: West Coast Taste "Cool Japan"
(Mid1990s to the Present)

The second wave of Western imports of sake was almost a complete negation of the first, presenting a uniform product and consumed hot. The wave did not emanate directly from Japan, but rather made its way around the world via the United States, more specifically originating on the American West Coast. Japanese restaurants were hardly instrumental in bringing about the new developments of the second wave, and instead found themselves objects to be reformed by it.

In the mid-1990s sake was first introduced outside the circuit of Japanese restaurants when it popped up as a novelty drink in bars, clubs, and fusion restaurants. Its Japanese roots and characteristics were a secondary element to taste and novelty. The types of sake suddenly making a splash on Californian terraces were relatively recent varieties distant from the rice wine roots of sake, trying to a considerable extent to be like wines. The overwhelming majority of these sake were *ginjō* or *daiginjō* varieties, meaning that they are made with rice grains that have been more than 40 and 50 percent polished off, respectively. These new types of sake became possible due to the postwar spread of machine vertical polishing, a process where the rice grains are circulated vertically through a huge polishing machine for up to three days. In this way the rice grains can be polished off to an incredible extent—the present record being 87 percent taken off—without the grain breaking. However, since the taste, aroma, and color of the rice are predominantly concentrated in the outer layers of the rice grain, while ginjō or daiginjō are still sake, they are hardly rice wine anymore. Instead, by means of special yeast strains, fruity and flowery tastes and aromas, hitherto unknown among sakes, are added to the otherwise rather bland and neutral character of the starch nucleus of the rice grain. The original motivation clearly was to upgrade sake by making it closer to wine, a European symbol of high culture, which the Japanese have the general tendency to venerate. One example of trying to sell sake in this way to both domestic and foreign markets is an ad that asked, "Ginjoshu offers the fruitiness of white wine with the body of a red wine. Why not pair this elegant sake with French cuisine?"[9] And if one added sugar or gas to make for bubbles, you could even call it sake champagne!

At first these relatively expensive sakes were made in very limited quantity, in many cases only as contest sake (*shuppinshu*) for entry in annual competitions. However, in 1990 the Japanese government introduced a new system of dividing sake into eight "designated categories" (*tokutei meishōshu*) alongside a remainder category of "plain sake" (*futsūshu*). This made it possible to create a product with a distinct profile as a special brand sake with a special price.[10] The more polished types of sake were produced in greater quantity and widely introduced on the Japanese market, creating a ginjō boom, which later spilled over to California. From there the new novelty drink conquered New York, then crossed the Atlantic Ocean, first to London, and later to the European continent. The dissemination of sake was still limited, as prices were relatively high, and it was mainly the top chefs, having discovered the new sakes in trend-setting New York and London restaurants, who served these in their expensive Michelin-star establishments.

The second wave saw the rise of sake gurus, most prominently the Americans John Gauntner and Beau Timken. The influence of the self-proclaimed "sake evangelist" Gauntner is especially widespread. Through his books and articles on sake in English, his seminars, brewery tours, and consultancy for a whole range of sake-related institutions, he created cohorts of faithful disciples in many Western countries dedicated to spreading the sake message in the same way as their teacher. Generalizations are dangerous, but it is relatively safe to categorize many of these disciples as newly born Japanophiles who tended to lack deep knowledge of the Japanese language and culture. In spite of this—or, maybe rather, due to this—they shared a strong urge to emphasize the quintessential Japaneseness of sake, even characterizing sake as the embodiment of Japanese traditional culture. Blinded by their genuine love for sake, they fell into traps of exotic fantasy, paralleling the temples and cherry blossoms trap set by the Japan Travel Bureau or the geisha- and samurai-populated orientalist wet dream of Japan promoted by Hollywood.

In addition, the Japan Sake Brewers Association also effectively exoticized the product and industry, disseminating images of wrinkled-skin brewer craftsmen in the romantic setting of an all-wooden brewery engulfed in snow, accompanied by texts such as the following:

> Rice is itself respected by the Japanese and *Nihonshu* [sake] is a precious part of daily life and Japanese culture. Knowing *Nihonshu* means connecting with Japanese culture. Through *Nihonshu* we see the wisdom of our forefathers in traditional brewing techniques. . . .

In fact, sake is such an integral part of the Japanese diet that having some knowledge of it can add to one's understanding of Japanese history, culture, and society, as well as of the social environment in Japan today.[11]

The romantic stereotype of Japan and the misleading messages of interest groups conceal the facts that there is not one uniform, traditional Japanese culture but hundreds of very different, mostly nontraditional Japanese cultures, that sake is a relatively unpopular drink in Japan, and that the ginjō sakes they adore are furthest away from the true rice-like roots of sake. Nevertheless, the force, energy, and influence of these sake aficionados transformed the second wave, which started as an appreciation for a novelty drink regardless of its national origin, into a quest to understand and appreciate the true nature of an enigmatic and exotic culture.

However, the major problem of this wave was that it defined sake in terms of the preferences of its "discoverers" and once again obstructed the introduction of all of sake's variety and potential to the outside world. The California climate seemed to determine local tastes, prioritizing the refreshing and fruity qualities of ginjō and daiginjō sake. Gauntner and Timken have a strong tendency to use the term "premium sake" rather than just "sake" or "good sake," and it is clear that this term is their translation of *ginjōshu*. Accordingly, the polishing rate of the rice used for the sake becomes the most important criterion of quality, that is, the more polished the rice grain, the better the sake.[12] Timothy Sullivan, an American sake fan who runs the website UrbanSake.com, is quoted in the influential magazine *Wine Spectator* as saying: "There is a really strong correlation between price and quality because of the rice milling. If you want to try something better, unfortunately you have to pay a little more, but you are universally rewarded."[13] In the same magazine's list of "Recommended Japanese Sake" more than 80 percent are ginjō varieties, and only sakes in the ginjō categories receive the highest evaluation of "outstanding."[14]

A majority of the thoroughly polished ginjō sakes tend to be relatively sweet and fruity, and become overly sweet in our sensation when heated. Moreover, who needs hot sake with California temperatures outside? In short, the message that was conveyed by the second wave was good sake = ginjō sake = relatively expensive = no longer rice wine but closer to grape wine = sweet, fruity, aromatic = should be served cold. The European culinary elite and the trend-watchers confronted with "the new sake" in California or New York restaurants thus received the message that "real sake" was fruity and should be enjoyed cold. Based on their newly acquired knowledge, they looked down upon those who were still drinking their sake heated. In 2003 Timken opened the first

American sake store in San Francisco under the name "True Sake," seemingly emphasizing that everything that had been on the US market previously was "not real sake" or "inferior sake."[15]

The Third Wave: Pure, at Any Temperature (2008 to the Present)

The third wave is not a complete negation of the previous two waves of sake appreciation in the West. It is rather a change of direction, namely a trip down memory lane to the prewar and earlier days, although with a distinctly modern mindset. It is a very recent phenomenon, since the first importing company strictly dealing in pure sake was only founded in 2008. "Pure sake" is a translation of the Japanese *junmaishu*, defined as 100 percent pure rice wine without any additions of alcohol, sugar, or taste-, color- or aroma-enhancing elements (although, in sharp contrast to natural wine, added yeast is not defined as an impure element). Before the war almost all sake was junmaishu, although the term did not exist at that time because brewers did not add elements that had nothing to do with the natural process of fermentation. However, after the wartime economy dictated adulteration and dilution to the sake industry, before long, all pure sake had vanished.[16] As mentioned, these wartime requirements continued to completely dominate production in the first postwar decades. Even today sake containing added alcohol or other external elements comprises more than 70 percent of annual production.[17]

The pure sake movement, which gained clout beginning with the start of this century, linked with other forces in Japanese society, such as the increasing demand for natural and honest products, especially stimulated by consumer cooperatives.[18] Premodern brewing techniques met such demands: they contain no chemical fertilizers and pesticides (*shizenshu, munōyaku*); are handmade (*tezukuri*); use local ingredients (*jizake*); are unpasteurized (*namazake*), unfiltered (*muroka*), and/or undiluted (*genshu*); and represent slow-food ideals (using the premodern slow-brew techniques of *kimoto* and *yamahai*). Such terms have become buzzwords in a contemporary culinary mindset that values pure, natural, real, honest, hands-off, slow, and healthy foods. This movement has resulted in an ever-expanding infrastructure in Japan of junmaishu-only breweries, shops, restaurants, bars, and exporters. Pure sake increasingly has taken on the image of real, true, superior sake, and in the Japanese method of categorizing sake on the basis of the polishing percentage, *junmai* categories are generally ranked above alcohol-added categories. The overall mood in support of pure sake is also clear from the numbers. Even if we confine ourselves to the top eight "designated categories," the share of the four alcohol-added categories in total annual sake production decreased from 24.6 percent in 1998 to 16.0 percent in 2015, while the four pure sake categories increased from 12.1 percent to 26.9 percent.[19] So although more than half of the sake produced is industrial bulk sake, pure sake now comprises almost 65 percent of the "designated categories" sake.

It was only a matter of time before the West tuned into this new current in Japan, especially when one considers the European roots of the slow-food movement and the strong awareness and influence of organic and natural products in many Western markets. In 2008 the first 100 percent pure-sake-only importer was established in the Netherlands, serving the whole of Europe, and in the following years companies with an identical policy were started in Australia, the United States, Canada, and France.[20]

It is important to note that this pure sake wave has been embraced by the nascent natural wine world, itself very much a child of the last decade. "Natural wine" is a relatively new concept, which is distinctly different from so-called organic wines or bio-wines. Whereas in the case of the latter types, wineries often intervene by adding a high amount of sulfites to compensate for the risks taken in the vineyard, the making of natural wines is about minimal intervention both in the vineyard and in the winery and no or minimal addition of sulfites.[21] The cross-fertilization between natural wine and pure sake is especially true for Europe, the cradle of the natural wine movement. In Norway, Sweden, Finland, Denmark, England, Belgium, France, Italy, Germany, Poland, Austria, Croatia, and Slovenia importers and distributers of natural wines have introduced a pure sake division among their offerings. As further proof of the cross-fertilization between pure sake and natural wine, in the Netherlands—probably because of the relatively underdeveloped situation of the natural wine market—there is the unique case of a pure sake distributer venturing into the import and distribution of natural wine.

As there is hardly an autonomous sake infrastructure in Europe, it is not strange that pure sake has ended up making use of the ever-growing niche market of natural wine.[22] They share a common focus on purity, although natural wine emphasizes no use of chemical fertilizers and pesticides and no addition of sulfites, while pure sake stresses no addition of alcohol. The natural wine world, with its preference for a hands-off approach to wine production, has also proven a fertile ground for types of sake without additions of lacto-acid to the starter, or those with hardly any postproduction after the brewing process. The early-modern slow-brew starter types of *kimoto* and *yamahai* sake, and unpasteurized (*namazake*), unfiltered (*muroka*), and undiluted (*genshu*) sake were often completely ignored by sake importers during the first and second wave. However, these types easily make up more than 70 percent of the offerings of pure sake importers, and it are exactly these types that are in most demand by distributers, retailers, and consumers with a natural wine background. In this way, even in southern European wine bastion countries, such as Italy and Spain, with distinctive culinary cultures that contain both robust regional cuisines and regional wines, we see pure sake making inroads along with natural wines.

With pure sake being incorporated in the fine wine and natural wine worlds, it has begun to shed its Japanese skin. In the promotion of pure sake within the portfolios of natural wine distributers there is hardly any stress on its Japanese origin, let alone its Japanese essence or its function as a gateway to understanding Japanese culture. Sake is treated in an equal way and on par with other wines; the stress is on variety and taste.[23] In order to stress the variety of sake and to encourage Western audiences to consume sake in the same way they would wine—or port, whisky, and cognac—some pure sake importers have stopped the Japanese method of categorizing sake on the basis of the polishing rate, since this does not tell much about the taste, the drinking order, or the options for food pairings. Instead they have implemented wine categories (aperitif, sparkling, fruity, sake nouveau, full body, dry, long matured, digestive, etc.), and some others in case these proved insufficient (cloudy, superpolished, liquid rice, cask sake, seawater sake, etc.).

Within this third wave of Western sake appreciation, purity is the primary and objectively determinable quality criterion. Secondary—and more subjective—criteria are full taste, aroma, and body, based on the Western culinary notion that a drink should contribute to the dish it accompanies. The origin of the sake and its polishing rate, let alone its link with a special culture, are of little or no importance. And for the first time there are no strong commands regarding the serving temperature.[24] Pure sake advocates do not claim a special link between quality and drinking temperature, and hardly provide more than the loose general guidelines "Don't heat sweet sake" and "Don't chill long-matured sake." Rather, drinking temperature is influenced or determined by factors including the climate, season, weather, accompanying dish, the aromatic potential, individual taste, or sommelier recommendations.

Conclusion: Lost in Transition?

So where does sake consumption stand in the West following these three waves? First of all, the consumption of sake has risen in the West. Whereas Japan's first colony, Taiwan, which remained relatively pro-Japanese after the demise of Japan's empire, used to be sake's most sizable export market, the

United States took over this position around 2000 and still holds the top position, although Asia—especially South Korea and Hong Kong—is catching up.[25] The European market is growing, but still relatively underdeveloped. The volume imported into the UK, the Netherlands, and Germany is biggest. One might posit a dividing line between "Protestant" countries lacking strongly established culinary cultures in which foreign cuisines and ingredients have been welcomed over the last two decades and many culinary innovations have come about, and "Catholic" countries, with strongly established culinary and wine cultures.[26] The Netherlands is by far the biggest European sake market per capita. Most likely it is the only country where one can easily find sake in three-star restaurants, liquor stores, and supermarkets.[27]

On the other hand, the three waves, although analyzed chronologically above, have not replaced one another but coexist. Fukumusume, the first sake to be exported in the 1970s, is no longer available on the European market due to a lack of demand.[28] However, this merely means that it has been pushed out of the market by cheaper industrial brands made in the United States. Japanese restaurants and Asian food stores, usually managed by Chinese, Thai, and other non-Japanese, still focus on these "buy-cheap serve-hot" types of sake. Disinformation, such as labeling sake as a distilled rather than fermented alcohol, continues to emanate from such places.[29]

Amongst many second-wave aficionados the tendency to advocate their preferences as if these are generally accepted rules in the sake world prevails. For instance, in the magazine *Sake Today*, launched recently by Gauntner, two of the three rules on "How to Choose Sake" are "Drink something with 'ginjo' embedded somewhere on the label" and "Drink it slightly chilled."[30] The message still comes down to "buy expensive, don't heat, don't mature, drink immediately," thus doing away with many of the advantages sake has over wine.

Pure sake advocates, often on the basis of experience in home-maturation of sake, do not treat the headbrewers (*tōji*) as an absolute source of veneration. They are aware that quality is not always the decisive factor on the producer's side, and that the majority of the sake leaves the brewery in too young and stiff a condition, because of rather practical factors such as money and storage space. Pure sake importers' collections include many varieties of minimally polished sake, sakes that have been matured for decades, or are best enjoyed warm because of the enhanced aroma. In comparison to the many dictates emanating from the second wave, their approach is void of any clear rules, basically asserting that "as long as the sake is pure, do what you like." However, because of the strong contradictions with information from previous waves, this approach has led to questions in the eyes of the consumers.

In essence, the sake market seems to be in a stage of transition, with many contradictory influences and messages, which is not an ideal situation for further proliferating the appreciation and consumption of sake in the West. To a considerable extent the same situation exists in Japan as well. It has left consumers in a state of confusion; they do not always know what to do with their sake. Do we show ourselves culinary barbarians when we drink it hot? When in the shop, should we focus on the word "ginjō" or rather "junmai"? Should we buy the relatively expensive wine-size bottle, since some say that you should drink sake as soon as possible? Or should we buy a relatively cheap 1.8-liter bottle, because this is the standard size in Japan and the Japanese themselves should know best? Do Japanese put up with all those huge sake bottles in their fridge, or do they just put them in the basement? Can we still drink that bottle of sake we received five years ago, and is it wise to buy a bottle of long-matured sake? Should we get ourselves a ceramic sake set, or will our wine glasses suffice? There are many different opinions, and this state of confusion will most likely last for a considerable time, until more people have enjoyed a wider variety of sake, experimented with temperature and maturation at home, and come up with their own individual answers to these questions. Or until the revitalizing sake industry is able to regroup under one united banner and will send out a univocal message to the rest of the world.[31]

NOTES

1. Rice will not ferment spontaneously; you first have to make sugar, by transforming the starch in the rice grain to glucose, by means of adding the *kōji* mold to steamed rice. During alcohol fermentation the *kōji* remains active and continues to produce sugar, thus providing the raw material for more alcohol production. Moreover, sake yeasts can endure a considerably higher alcoholic environment than wine yeasts, so fermentation can continue much longer. For a detailed description of the unique sake brewing method, see the two books by the Englishman Philip Harper, the only foreign *tōji* (headbrewer) in Japan. Philip Harper, *The Insider's Guide to Sake*, Kodansha International, 1998, 39–53 and Philip Harper, *The Book of Sake*, Kodansha International, 2006, 79–90.

2. The phenomenal rise of the production and the reputation of sake from the Nada region is a relatively late development, only from the mid-eighteenth century onward. The geographical conditions beneficial to the introduction of rice-polishing by water mills, its strategical location on the Inland Sea route to Edo, and the discovery of the famed *miyamizu* brewing water in 1840 made Nada outdo all other production centers. The medieval sake production center of Kyoto fell on hard times during the Edo period, but Fushimi rose spectacularly in the Meiji period. Sakaguchi Kinichirō and Katō Benzaburō, eds., *Nihon no sake no rekishi* (Tokyo: Kenseisha, 1977), 239–255; Morimoto Takao and Yagura Shintarō, eds., *Tenkanki no Nihonshu meekaa—Nada go-gō*

wo chūshin to shite (Tokyo: Moriyama Shoten, 1998); Yoshida Hajime, *Kyō no sake-gaku* (Kyoto: Rinzen Shoten, 2016), 189–195.

3. Yoshida Hajime, *Kindai Nihon no sakezukuri* (Tokyo: Iwanami Shoten, 2013), 169–170.

4. On the basis of the 2013 numbers on volume of production by prefecture from Japan's tax office. At http://todo-ran.com/t/kiji/18867.

5. *Shurui-tō seizō menkyojō-sū no suii*, part of Japan's tax office annual report *Sake no shiori* on sake production, taxation, and consumption. Available at https://www.nta.go.jp/shiraberu/senmonjoho/sake/shiori-gaikyo/shiori/2017/pdf/007.pdf-page=1.https://www.nta.go.jp/shiraberu/senmonjoho/sake/shiori-gaikyo/shiori/2017/pdf/007.pdf#.

6. Average calculated on the basis of *Shurui seisei sūryō no suii*, *Shurui kazei sūryō no suii* (*Kokuzeikyoku-bun oyobi zeikanbun no gōkei*), and *Shurui hanbai (shōhi) sūryō no suii*. Also available at https://www.nta.go.jp/shiraberu/senmonjoho/sake/shiori-gaikyo/shiori/2017/index.htm. The numbers are from the 2017 report, including data up until fiscal 2015. Although there is a sake boom going on in Japan at this very moment, which has made younger generations aware of the quality and variety of present-day sake, we do not yet have the official numbers to be able to tell whether there is a substantial upturn in the consumption and production of sake.

7. Beginning with its March 2014 brochure *Sake and Japanese Culture*, available in Japanese and English, the brewers' association emphasizes the link between sake and Japanese culture above all. For a detailed analysis of the recent government project to promote sake as Japan's national alcoholic drink, see my "Deconstructing 'Kokushu': The Promotion of Sake as Japan's National Alcoholic Drink in Times of Crisis in the Sake Industry," in *Feeding Japan: The Cultural and Political Issues of Dependency and Risk*, ed. Andreas Niehaus and Tine Walravens (New York: Palgrave Macmillan, 2017), 141–165.

8. For export numbers, see the somewhat outdated *Seishu no aitekoku-betsu yushutsu jisseki no suii (sūryō)* at the Japan Sake and Shochu Makers Association's website (quantity) http://www.japansake.or.jp/sake/about/data/01.html or *Shurui no yushutsu kingaku sūryō no suii* at Japan's tax office website (both value and quantity) https://www.nta.go.jp/shiraberu/senmonjoho/sake/shiori-gaikyo/shiori/2017/pdf/018.pdf#page=3.

9. From Tomoda Akiko's partially Japanese, partially English publication *Sekai ni hokoru—Hinkaku no meishu / The Sake Selection—Brands of Distinction* (Tokyo: Gap Japan, 2009), 9.

10. The new system introduced eight designated categories of sake (*tokutei meishōshu*) including four pure sake categories, *junmai daiginjōshu, junmai ginjōshu, tokubetsu junmaishu,* and *junmaishu,* and four alcohol-added categories, *daiginjōshu, ginjōshu, tokubetsu honjōzōshu,* and *honjōzōshu*. On the alcohol-added side, all sake with less than 30 percent polishing was called "plain sake" (*futsūshu*). The former system, abolished in 1992, divided sake in the three taxing categories—"special rank," "first rank," and "second rank"—independent of the purity of the sake and the polishing rate of the sake rice.

11. Excerpts from the English voice-over from the promotional DVD *Nihonshu ga dekiru made*, produced by the Japan Sake Brewers Association, now known as Japan Sake and Shochu Makers Association.

12. The polishing rate gives the percentage of the rice grain left after polishing. Thus a polishing rate of 90 percent means that 10 percent of the rice grain was polished off.

13. Kim Marcus, "Cracking the Sake Code," *Wine Spectator* 38.2 (May 2013): 71.

14. *Wine Spectator* 38.2 (May 2013): 74.

15. On the True Sake website, Timken tells how he reached sake enlightenment when drinking his first glass of "premium ginjo" in the mid-1990s in a sushi restaurant in South Africa, and understood that all sake he had been drinking previously were in fact "inferior sake."

16. Sakaguchi and Katō, *Nihon no sake no rekishi*, 282–292; Yoshida, *Kindai Nihon no sakezukuri*, 119–129. The terms for the various types of "impure sake" are *gōseishu* (synthetic sake, made chemically with almost or no rice), *arutenshu* (alcohol-added sake), and *sanzōshu* (triple sake, sake where from the usual amount of rice three times more sake is made). There is also the unofficial term *kingyozake* (goldfish sake) for sake that has been diluted to the extent that fish could live in it.

17. Based on data for fiscal 2015 the share of the pure sake categories in the total production has increased to 26.9 percent, and that in taxation to 19.1 percent. *Tokuteimeishō no seishu no taipu-betsu seisei sūryō no suii-hyō* (production) and *Tokuteimeishō no seishu no taipu-betsu kazei ishutsu sūryō no suii-hyō (kokuzeikyoku-bun)* (taxation) at https://www.nta.go.jp/shiraberu/senmonjoho/sake/shiori-gaikyo/shiori/2017/index.htm.

18. In the late 1960s the harbinger of the junmai movement, Uehara Hiroshi (1924–2006), convinced some breweries in Tottori prefecture to experiment with brewing sake without adding alcohol. His pioneering efforts were crucial but relatively limited. In 1987 Ogawahara Yoshimasa (b. 1946), turned his family brewery Shinkame Shuzō into the first "100 percent pure sake brewery" (*zenryō junmai kura*) and established three important organizations promoting production and export of pure sake over the following decades. In 1985 a leader of the natural sake (*shizenshu*) movement, Terada Keisuke (1948–2012) was the first to use 100 percent organic rice, natural *kōji*, natural yeast, and medieval or early modern brewing techniques. Other important figures are Ukai Hiroaki (1948–), whose family sake store Ukai Shōten in Kyoto was the first to go completely junmai around 1988; manga writer Oze Akira (b. 1947) whose manga on junmaishu, *Natsuko no Sake*, was serialized in the weekly *Morning* from 1988 to 1991 and turned into a TV series in 1994; and Yoram Ofer (b. 1962), the world's authority on matured sake, who started the first junmaishu-only sake bar Yoramu in Kyoto in 2002 and became the first junmaishu-only exporter in 2007. See Uehara Hiroshi, *Junmaishu wo kiwameru* (Tokyo: Kōbunsha, 2002); Ueno Toshihiko, *Tatakau Junmaishu—Shinkame Hikomago monogatari* (Tokyo: Heibonsha, 2006); Terada Keisuke, *Hakkōdō* (Tokyo: Kawade Shubo Shinsha, 2007); Ukai Hiroaki, *Shuzō Hōmonki-shū*, two parts (self-published, 2005 and 2013).

19. In terms of taxation the share of the junmai designated categories increased from 9.4 percent in 2002 to 19.1 percent in 2015, while that of the alcohol-added designated categories decreased from 16.4 percent to 13.3 percent. See *Tokuteimeishō no seishu no taipu-betsu kazei ishutsu sūryō no suii-hyō (kokuzekyoku-bun)* at https://www.nta.go.jp/shiraberu/senmonjoho/sake/shiori-gaikyo/shiori/2017/index.htm.

20. These are respectively Yoigokochi Sake Importers, Black Market Sake, The Floating World, PureSake 4U, and Shinkame Europe, of which the first three are related to Ofer and the last two to Ogawahara (see note 19).

21. See Alice Feiring, *Naked Wine* (Cambridge, MA: Da Capo Press, 2011); and Isabelle Legeron, *Natural Wine* (New York: CICO Books, 2014).

22. Pure sake has been introduced at the most prominent European natural wine fairs such as London's RAW and Real Wine Fairs, Saumur's, La Dive Bouteille, and Verona's Villa Favorita since 2012, in contrast with the majority of bio-wines, denied entrance on the grounds of too much postproduction and intervention. As yet there are only two locally organized sake fairs in Europe, namely the Salon Du Sake in Paris and the La Via del Sake in Milan.

23. The Italian national distributor Velier SpA includes pure sake in its natural wine Triple A lineup; French national distributor La Maison Du Whisky plans to open a store in Paris stocking only natural wine and pure sake.

24. In Japan there is a tendency among many all-junmai breweries, especially those linked to Shinkame Shuzō, to promote warm sake. Based on Uehara Hiroshi's motto of *Sake wa junmai, kan nara nao yoshi* (Sake should be pure, and is even better when heated), they established an association to promote the drinking of warm sake. However, their message has not found fertile ground among Western pure sake importers, and most Western restaurants find serving warm sake a nuisance.

25. The United States received 25.9 percent of sake volume exported in 2016 and 33.3 percent of the value of the export market. Korea was second in volume at 18.7 percent; Hong Kong second in value at 16.9 percent. The first year that the total value of sake export exceeded ten billion yen was 2013. The Japanese government has set a goal of sixty billion yen by 2020. *Seishu shōchū no omo na yushutsusaki (Heisei 25-nen)* and *Seishu shōchū no omo na yushutsusaki (Heisei 28-nen)* at https://www.nta.go.jp/shiraberu/senmonjoho/sake/shiori-gaikyo/shiori/2014/index.htm and https://www.nta.go.jp/shiraberu/senmonjoho/sake/shiori-gaikyo/shiori/2017/index.html. On government objectives, see Eric Pfanner and Zhihi Yang, "In Sake, Japan Sees a Potential Stimulus," *New York Times*, February 22, 2013, 1–2.

26. After the UK, the Netherlands, and Germany, France comes in fourth in volume of imports, although it surpasses Germany in terms of value. However, one should be aware that Rotterdam and Hamburg also function as a harbor for other European countries than their own. *Ōshū e no Nihonshu no yushutsu tōkei (yushutsuryō yushutsugaku)* in Nihon Bōeki Shinkō Kikō (JETRO) Pari Jimusho, *Furansu e no Nihonshu no yushutsu gaidobukku*, March 2014.

27. There was a specialized sake store in Paris, Cave Fuji, from 1991 until 2003. A new sake store-cum-restaurant was opened in Paris in 2016. Amsterdam, London,

Paris, Milan, Rome, Lisbon, and Barcelona now also have specialized sake stores, bars, or restaurants.

28. Telephone interview with the sales department of Fukumusume Shuzō on February 17, 2014.

29. For instance, Shabu-Shabu, the biggest and most successful all-you-can-eat Japanese restaurant chain in the Netherlands (managed by Chinese, and rather oddly not serving *shabushabu*), is selling merely one kind of alcohol-added cheap sake in the category "distilled."

30. John Gauntner, "How to Choose Sake: Three Rules," in the inaugural issue of *Sake Today*, Autumn 2013, 17–18.

31. In collaboration with the Japan Sake and Shochu Makers Association, the Wine and Spirits Education Trust (WSET), the world's most authoritative institution providing wine and spirits related education, incorporated a three-level sake course into its program in 2014. The aim is not merely to provide the world outside Japan with qualified sake specialists but also to unify and authorize information about sake.

Culinary Nationalism and Branding

5

Washoku, Far and Near

UNESCO, Gastrodiplomacy, and the Cultural Politics of Traditional Japanese Cuisine

Theodore C. Bestor

Sushi in Tashkent, ramen in Melbourne, wasabi mashed potatoes everywhere, and edamame already at a salad bar near you! Umami ("the fifth flavor") is no doubt on your radar, or will be soon!

Japanese food has been globally appealing for at least a generation or two. Over the past two decades, the Japanese government and the Japanese culinary establishment have together engaged in efforts to vigorously promote traditional Japanese cuisine (under the general rubric of washoku) worldwide, as well as within Japan.

For many people outside Japan, the pinnacles of Japanese culinary accomplishment are savored in sushi and sashimi, but within Japan—or at least in the elite circles of Japanese culinary expertise—the sine qua non of Japanese cuisine is *kaiseki ryōri*. This is the style of cuisine associated with Kyoto, the old imperial capital, and the city's history of extremely rarified patterns of cultured consumption. This cuisine emphasizes seasonality through the presentation of an exquisite progression of dishes, each featuring a particular ingredient and a special cooking technique. In this meal—banquet is a better term—one's palate is exposed to a full range of culinary artistry applied to the ingredients of the season.

For purists, this is Japanese cuisine—washoku—and this ideal of Japanese culinary artistry was at the heart of Japan's application to UNESCO for recognition of washoku as an item of intangible cultural heritage, which was granted in December 2013.

Japan's UNESCO application is an example of "gastrodiplomacy." I explore how washoku is defined both conceptually and in everyday terms, by or for several different audiences: the bureaucratic communities of Japanese officials concerned with food, agriculture, cultural heritage, and diplomacy; the world of elite professional chefs, both in Japan and elsewhere; the food industry generally; foreign fans (perhaps connoisseurs) of Japanese food, particularly tourists visiting Japan; and ordinary Japanese consumers.

The journal *Public Diplomacy* devoted a special issue to gastrodiplomacy, which it defined as

> the practice of sharing a country's cultural heritage through food. Countries such as South Korea, Peru, Thailand, and Malaysia have recognized the seductive qualities food can have, and are leveraging this unique medium of cultural diplomacy to increase trade, economic investment, and tourism, as well as to enhance soft power. Gastrodiplomacy offers foreign publics the opportunity to engage with other cultures through food, often from a distance. This form of edible nation branding is a growing trend in public diplomacy.[1]

As Japanese cuisine has grown in popularity across the globe, why would the Japanese government and other elements of Japan's "food establishment" feel the necessity to promote washoku, or "traditional Japanese cuisine," vigorously? What's to promote, protect, or prove? Hasn't Japanese cuisine already established itself everywhere?

Anxiety over "authenticity" (figure 5.1), the anthropologist Arjun Appadurai argues, becomes an issue as cultures (and cuisines) encounter globalization directly. "Doubt [about culinary authenticity] . . . is rarely part of the discourse of an undisturbed cuisine."[2] If so, what are the "disturbed" (or disturbing) culinary trends addressed by Japanese gastrodiplomacy?

One reason for such concerns may be fusion (or confusion) in the global cafeteria: what really *is* Japanese cuisine? Outside of Japan, what are the expectations of foreign diners, and what are their standards of quality? (And critically, at least to Japanese officials and elite chefs within Japan, what standards might one expect of or impute to non-Japanese chefs who are preparing "Japanese cuisine" outside of Japan?) How can, or should, Japan, as a state or as a society, attempt to control or shape what is served in the name of Japanese cuisine beyond its shores?

An equally important concern may be reinforcing—at home (within Japan) and at home (around the domestic dining table)—significant conceptual distinctions between washoku as the culinary essence of the national diet and other "non-Japanese" foods, which are probably consumed on a daily basis as much or more than washoku itself (strictly defined).

FIGURE 5.1 Concern over culinary authenticity: Door of sushi restaurant, Leicester Square, London, September 2014. Photograph by the author.

Assertions of a distinctively "Japanese" cuisine appeal on the basis of assumed historical continuity and cultural heritage.[3] Japan's gastrodiplomacy takes shape through idioms of cultural heritage that promote, protect, and prove the essence of culinary authenticity, internationally and domestically, at a time when anxiety or precarity is rampant in Japan. Perhaps washoku is home cooking to soothe Japan's soul and assuage uncertainty about its standing in the world.

What Is Washoku?

To parse the term, *wa* indicates something is considered specifically, ethnically, and traditionally Japanese. *Shoku* means "food, meal, or cuisine." Thus, *washoku* refers to cuisine, meals, menus, and dishes that are considered to be intrinsically Japanese. In a broad sense, the term *washoku* means "traditional Japanese cuisine," more-or-less synonymous with terms such as *Nihon ryōri* or *Nihonshoku* (Japanese cuisine or Japanese food, respectively). *Washoku*, however, is the term that Japan promoted in its UNESCO application.

Wa suggests an essentialized or primordial quality of Japanese-ness, in part because *wa* can refer to the Yamato state (the earliest centralized Japanese polity, which existed from roughly mid-third to early eighth centuries CE), a period of history before Japanese culture had been heavily influenced by China. *Wa* alludes to the origins of Japanese culture and society, hence a period of seemingly autonomous Japanese culture. This notion of an age of "pure" Japanese culture is, of course, pure historical fantasy, but it has implicit purchase on popular consciousness of Japan's cultural history. The character for *wa* also generally indicates "harmony," a virtue that is highly regarded in contemporary Japan as indicative of Japanese national personality.

Today, *wa* is a prefix that indicates the Japaneseness of an object, activity, or realm of meaning, most commonly as a direct antonym to Westernness, indicated by the prefix *yō*. As such, washoku is thus contrasted to *yōshoku* (Western, Euro-American cuisine). This opposition between *wa* and *yō* can be found in many other cultural realms as well, including *wagashi*—Japanese sweets (for tea ceremony); *wagyū*—Japanese beef; *washi*—Japanese rice paper; or *wafū*—Japonesque or Japanese-style (in general).

However, yōshoku itself has very specific meanings, based in the selective historical adoption of Western culture in the late nineteenth century. It generally identifies Euro-American dishes that were introduced to Japan (and extensively adapted) during the Meiji period (1868–1912). Beef stew, tonkatsu (breaded pork cutlet), potato croquettes, and many other dishes entered the Japanese diet in the late decades of the nineteenth century and the first half of the twentieth century. The food historian Katarzyna Cwiertka documents that this includes dishes the Japanese military adopted from the British navy during this period.[4] Today, many of these dishes are so common in the ordinary diet of Japanese that yōshoku itself is not usually subject of much discussion in the everyday world of food consumption.

Of course, before there was yōshoku, there would have been little reason to specify washoku as anything in particular. Without a contrast to washoku, as a broad category, sociolinguistic and cultural classifications of culinary forms would have focused on regional specialties, of which there was and is an abundance of well-known varieties, generically referred to as *kyōdo ryōri* (regional cuisine, with a primordial connotation), or particular genre of cuisine defined by such characteristics as ingredients, ritual connotations, or cooking techniques. Washoku could only have been a category that came into existence *after* Japan encountered some radically different cuisines. Across the entire range of material culture, social ideas, and expectations of change, during the Meiji period, cuisine no doubt occupied only one part of the spectrum of transformations that ordinary Japanese encountered.[5]

Along with a binary conceptual distinction between washoku and yōshoku, a tripartite distinction among Japanese, Western, and Chinese cuisines began to form during the Meiji period. China had influenced Japanese foodways for millennia, but Chinese cuisine per se had not been a widely recognizable culinary category until the late nineteenth century, except perhaps in the port of Nagasaki, through which foreign trade passed. Japanese imperial expansion during the late Meiji period and beyond fueled consumption and adaptation of many varieties of Chinese cuisine into customary items in Japan.

Nihon Kokugo Daijiten (Great dictionary of the Japanese national language), an authoritative dictionary of Japanese usage and etymologies, reports the first recorded print appearance of the term *yōshoku* in 1872, in a Japanese-language newspaper in Yokohama.[6] By way of comparison, the first record of *washoku* in print occurred over fifty years later, in the 1929 drama *Ushiyama Hotei* by Kishida Kunio. Prior synonyms such as *Nihon ryōri* and *Nihonshoku* appeared, respectively, in 1881 and 1907. So yōshoku gained linguistic recognition first, and among the terms for Japanese, as opposed to Western cuisine, washoku arrived last.[7] No doubt people distinguished between the two culinary categories earlier, but this suggests that contemporary distinctions between washoku and yōshoku, and articulations of the exemplary characteristics of washoku, took quite a lot of time in the context of cultural and culinary history.

Based on my own experiences studying Japanese in Tokyo in the 1970s and conducting research there during the 1980s and 1990s, including in the massive Tsukiji seafood market, *washoku* did not stand out as a commonly used term. For example, if people were discussing where to have lunch or a casual dinner after work, in my memory, no one would have suggested, "Today, let's go for washoku!" Rather, such questions were framed within particular subgenres of Japanese culinary classification: "Hey, how about tonkatsu?"—or unagi, ramen, soba, sushi, yakitori, *donburi*, and so forth. Or someone in the group might have proposed Chinese, Korean, Indian, Italian, or Thai cuisine. That is, the answers to "What will we eat for lunch?" were not a choice between Japanese (washoku or *Nihon ryōri* or *Nihonshoku*) and a unitary foreign "Western" cuisine, but among a multitude of genres of cooking and cuisine, ranging across styles of Japanese cuisine (many of them originating from foreign culinary adaptations) and an array of foreign cuisines, many of which have only become much more prominent on the Japanese culinary landscape in the past couple of decades. *Wa* versus *yō* is no longer the fundamental distinction, at least in everyday culinary choices.

Japan's Cultural Heritage and UNESCO

The Japan was a global pioneer in formulating and implementing policies for protecting cultural heritage. Legislation in 1950 recognized so-called national cultural treasures, including tangible artistic and architectural masterpieces, as well as individuals (popularly known as "living national treasures") who sustain intangible traditions of artisanship and performance.[8] This legislation and the subsequent successes of Japanese cultural heritage policy were globally important as early and influential examples of cultural policymaking and institutionalizing criteria, standards, and practices for recognizing and preserving heritage sites.

In 1972, UNESCO adopted the Convention Concerning the Protection of the World Cultural and Natural Heritage.[9] During the almost half-century since, UNESCO's designations of cultural and natural heritage sites have become widely recognized and increasingly significant in many nations' strivings for status and prestige, as well as tourist revenue. As of July 2017, UNESCO had designated 1,073 World Heritage Sites across the globe, 21 of which are in Japan.[10]

In 2003, UNESCO promulgated an additional agreement, the Convention for the Safeguarding of Intangible Cultural Heritage.[11] Japan played a very active role promoting this convention, and as Noriko Aikawa-Faure, a former official of UNESCO, has noted, the new concept of intangible heritage reflected an "Asian turn" in UNESCO's policies.[12] That is, the vast bulk of UNESCO sites are European, and the list of heritage items leans toward durable physical monumentality. What she calls the Asian turn is the hard-won recognition that cultural heritage preservation and promotion should include less durable monuments built of perishable materials (e.g., wood, not just stone; requiring periodic renewal) and the multiple ways in which heritage is preserved and handed down via oral tradition, rituals, musical performance, and many other kinds of intangible cultural practices.

The first examples of intangible cultural heritage were recognized in 2008, following UNESCO's definition of "intangible cultural heritage" as

> traditions or living expressions inherited from our ancestors and passed on to our descendants, such as oral traditions, performing arts, social practices, rituals, festive events, knowledge and practices

concerning nature and the universe or the knowledge and skills to produce traditional crafts.[13]

As of the end of 2016, UNESCO had recognized 429 items of intangible cultural heritage worldwide, 21 of which are Japanese.[14] Examples of Japan's intangible cultural heritage include classical theatrical forms (kabuki, bunraku, and Noh), Ainu dance, the craft of making washi or rice paper, traditional Okinawan music, and Kyoto's annual Gion Festival.[15]

In 2010, UNESCO opened new vistas for national cultural aspiration when it recognized French cuisine as intangible cultural heritage (officially "Gastronomic Meal of the French"), as well as "traditional Mexican cuisine—ancestral, ongoing community culture, the Michoacán paradigm," and "gingerbread craft from Northern Croatia."[16]

UNESCO and Washoku

After 2010, a growing queue of countries including Japan also sought culinary honors. On December 5, 2013, UNESCO announced its recognition of Japanese cuisine as intangible cultural heritage.[17] The official designation in English is "washoku, traditional dietary cultures of the Japanese, notably for the celebration of New Year."

The Japanese application defined washoku in sociocultural terms, as sets of practices and values that link foodways to social relationships, affirm connections to the environment and appreciation of nature and seasons, and express deep cultural affinities for rituals and patterns of communal life. The group that framed this application was a government-appointed advisory committee that included officials from relevant national agencies: the Ministry of Foreign Affairs; the Ministry of Agriculture, Forestry and Fisheries (MAFF); the Agency for Cultural Affairs (Bunkachō); the Japanese National Tourism Organization; regional government representatives (e.g., from Kyoto, to put weight behind their culinary and other claims of cultural centrality); officials of national agricultural cooperatives and trade groups of chefs, restaurants, and other organizations; representatives of major food manufacturing corporations (e.g., the Kikkoman soy sauce company); directors of culinary academies; and culinary historians and food critics.

Japan's application said relatively little about ingredients, foodstuffs, flavors, dishes, culinary techniques, menus, terroir, regional styles and local specialties, or many other gastronomic attributes customarily associated with discussions of cuisine and food culture.

This was not an oversight. UNESCO criteria are closely tied to the social and cultural ubiquity of food as lived experience within a particular social/cultural context. The designation of French food culture does not focus on haute cuisine, nor on great chefs with Michelin stars, but rather on the ways in which food preparation and consumption hold particularly important places in the daily fabric of French culture and social life, on the integrative quality of cuisine. Japan's proposal successfully emulated this approach; one Japanese official referred to it as an homage to France.

Japan's application was also framed by a negative example. In 2012, the Republic of Korea, a neighbor and in many respects a fierce rival of Japan, was asked by UNESCO to withdraw its proposal, which focused on the cuisine of its former royal court. The Japanese team interpreted this rejection as UNESCO's stance against proposals that focused narrowly on elite and rarified aspects of cuisine rather than on more populist and inclusive versions of culinary experience. Therefore, despite initial efforts to focus Japan's bid on Kyoto's elite cuisine of *kaiseki ryōri*, promoted by prominent chefs and others, Japanese bureaucrats broadened the scope of Japan's proposal when Korea's UNESCO application failed.

Officials in the Ministry of Foreign Affairs and MAFF told me that their application was ultimately framed to define washoku to encompass many styles of cuisine, across a range of regional and socioeconomic patterns of consumption. Voltaire Cang, a visiting researcher affiliated with MAFF, observed and analyzed meetings among government officials and culinary experts charged with drawing up the proposal for UNESCO. He describes difficult deliberations caught between the allure of the French application, from which the Japanese team borrowed extensively, and the sudden shock when the framers learned that the South Korean proposal had been rejected. Cang argues attention to both the successful French proposal and the apparent perils of the South Korean one shaped the ultimate scope of washoku's definition and the last-minute substitution of washoku in place of *kaiseki ryōri* in the title of Japan's application.[18]

Washoku for Whom?

The UNESCO application clearly was embedded in broad agendas of cultural diplomacy and global projections of Japanese culture, as many of the government officials I interviewed made clear. UNESCO recognition was anticipated to have both international and domestic impact.

Internationally, many officials saw the application explicitly in terms of Japan's projection of "soft power" as a key to maintaining Japan's standing in the world. The political scientist Joseph Nye deployed the twin concepts of "hard power" and "soft power" to describe different modes of nations' conduct of international relations. He defines soft power as "the ability to get what you want through attraction rather than coercion or payments," the latter being instances of hard power.[19] Clearly, for government officials celebrating Japan's soft power diplomacy, promoting cuisine (along with popular culture, fashion, architectural design, and so forth) is highly desirable.[20]

More specifically, officials linked the UNESCO application to the concept of "Cool Japan."[21] This key phrase refers to the economic (and soft power) clout (and coolness) of Japan's so-called content industries (whose products range from manga and anime such as Pokémon, to digital media, music, fashion, architecture, visual arts and design, and cuisine). The global successes of Japanese content industries sharply contrast with the flagging fortunes of formerly mighty industries: automobiles, consumer electronics, and heavy industrial machinery.

The products of content industries are "cool," which appeals to relatively upscale consumers around the globe (and also drives tourism). Japanese cuisine itself has long since joined the product array of Cool Japan as a global icon of sophisticated urban consumption.[22]

Officials also hoped that UNESCO culinary recognition would neatly mesh with other dimensions of cultural projection that the government had been working toward for some time. In June 2013, UNESCO recognized Mount Fuji as a World Cultural Heritage site. In September 2013, Tokyo was awarded the 2020 Olympics. UNESCO's washoku recognition completed a triple crown for Japan's international self-presentation. Domestically, Mount Fuji, the Olympics, and washoku were being promoted to bolster Japanese morale battered by the long recession and the disasters of 2011, and to provide reassurance that Japan is not falling behind internationally, even as it may feel eclipsed or threatened by its neighbors. MAFF officials told me many times about their serious concerns about foreign bans on imports of Japanese food products (especially from Fukushima) in the aftermath of the March 2011 disasters. They were acutely aware of the need to garner foreign recognition of the positive features of Japanese cuisine, something that also weighed on the minds of the Japanese washoku committee.[23]

Washoku at Home

UNESCO's imprimatur bolsters Japanese cuisine both internationally and domestically. MAFF lauds UNESCO recognition to encourage Japanese agricultural and fisheries exports, and to promote domestic production and consumption. It is a matter of both economic and cultural concern that the ordinary diet in Japan increasingly consists of "nontraditional" (and often imported) foodstuffs, at the expense of domestic products. As a matter of national policy, agriculture and fisheries are heavily subsidized, which is a major source of friction with Japan's trading partners.

Domestic promotion of washoku by MAFF in collaboration with many other actors takes many forms. For example, MAFF cooperates closely with the Ministry of Education to encourage Japanese to value their culinary heritage and to eat traditional foodstuffs (which indirectly sustains domestic food producers and processors).

School lunches (*kyūshoku*) are a significant aspect of Japan's educational system; the program serves high-quality meals to all public elementary and junior high school students. These lunch programs involve a high degree of hands-on participation by students—serving, sometimes cooking, cleaning up, and planting and harvesting vegetables in school gardens. As Alexis Agliano Sanborn and others have observed, school lunches come with large servings of lessons about etiquette, nutrition, sociality, and food history.[24] The program reinforces awareness of distinctive aspects of Japanese food culture among schoolchildren.

Encouraging children to eat local foods and enjoy a traditional diet are important goals of *shokuiku* ("food education"), incorporated into Japan's elementary and secondary school curricula since the 1990s (figure 5.2). *Shokuiku* highlights food, body, nutrition, communal consumption (family, school, community, etc.), and connections among agriculture/fisheries, environment, and society. Its values clearly mirror, and are mirrored in, the washoku proposal.

Several elite Kyoto chefs I interviewed in 2017 were themselves active in *shokuiku* projects. They told me of their experiences in classrooms, relating ideas about food and flavor to foster appreciation for washoku itself—careful attention to seasons, the use of different cooking techniques, the visual appeal of foods, the appreciation of food through all the senses (sight, hearing, smell, taste, tactile sensations), the pairings of ingredients and flavors, the social aspects of eating with families and friends, and so forth.[25] Many interviewees explained a nutritional mnemonic used in *shokuiku* to help students remember the elements of a properly balanced traditional washoku diet, *mago ni wa yasashii* ("affection toward grandchildren"):

ma = *mame* (beans)
go = *goma* (sesame)
ni = *niku* (meat)

FIGURE 5.2 Banner celebrating *shokuiku*, School of Agriculture, Ryukoku University, Otsu, June 2017. Photograph by the author.

   wa = *wakame* (sea vegetables)
   ya = *yasai* (vegetables)
   sa = *sakana* (fish)
   shi = *shiitake* (mushrooms)
   i = *imo* (potatoes)

Hard Power or Soft: The Sushi Police

An earlier effort to simultaneously promote and patrol washoku abroad, derisively criticized as the "sushi police," may help account for the state's softer and more expansive conception of washoku in the UNESCO campaign. In the mid-2000s, Minister of Agriculture, Forestry and Fisheries Matsuoka Toshikatsu complained about "inauthentic" Japanese restaurants after visiting a Colorado emporium that featured both sushi and Korean barbecue on its menu. In response, he advocated a system of certification to be applied to restaurants outside of Japan that represent themselves as serving genuine Japanese cuisine. Japanese inspectors were to be deployed to examine them and issue government certificates of approval to those that met standards of "authentic Japanese" cuisine. Matsuoka explained:

> What people need to understand is that real Japanese food is a highly developed art. It involves all the senses; it should be beautifully presented, use genuine ingredients and be made by a trained chef.... What we are seeing now are restaurants that pretend to offer Japanese cooking but are really Korean, Chinese or Filipino. We must protect our food culture.[26]

The proposal was ridiculed in the Japanese press, as well as in government circles; the project came to naught. Nonetheless, the notion of "sushi police" was picked up by the Japanese media and has remained in popular consciousness, perhaps as shorthand for referring to officious gatekeeping of what is and what isn't actually Japanese cuisine. Indicative of such popular derision is a 2016 Japanese television anime series entitled *Sushi Police* (*Sushi Porisu*), consisting of thirteen three-minute segments. It portrays bumbling Japanese officials, accompanied by a robot powered by soy sauce, pursuing inauthentic sushi in the United States, Mexico, China, France, Germany, and elsewhere. Their slogan is "Sushi Police Washoku." One of their recurring adversaries is Sarah, a European woman who espouses "Free Sushi!" or sushi liberated from Japanese dictates.

This sendup of international culinary politics is summarized on the Anime News Network website:

> In order to deal with all the bastardized sushi out there, the Japanese Government's urgent response is to team up with other ruling powers around the world to establish the WFCO (World Food-culture Conservation Organization) to protect and promote authentic local cuisine. And so the [WFCO] deploys its 9th Division to oversee Japanese cuisine abroad. The 9th Division, a.k.a. Sushi Police, is notorious for their aggressive conduct and they hassle anyone serving unauthentic Japanese food.... They will resort to any means necessary to eliminate bad sushi. Soon they are despised by restaurant proprietors around the world.[27]

Undoubtedly the hysterical theatrics and the absurdly absolutist stance of the Sushi Police are satire, but the series does reflect a popular awareness of issues of culinary authenticity in a globalizing world. Hence, I argue this anime speaks to some implicit public reaction to—comedic critique of—the issues the Japanese government and the culinary establishment addressed (and addresses) by promoting washoku through UNESCO recognition and continuing efforts to expand the appeal of washoku (at home and abroad). In my view, these efforts aim to ensure some stable core of meaning to underlying culinary practices, perspectives not necessarily shared by the general public in their food preferences today.

The Sushi Police are a caricature of hard power run amok (and unsuccessful to boot) and perhaps a parodic slam at UNESCO and other international efforts to define and regulate culture. But in the real world, MAFF and its allies have fully embraced a soft-power approach to the promotion of washoku.

MAFF officials in 2015 laid out for me detailed plans linking Japan's participation in Expo 2015 in Milan, Italy (the so-called Food Expo) to the 2016 Olympic Games in Rio de Janeiro, Brazil, and to the 2020 Olympic Games in Tokyo. Japan's pavilion at the Milan fair would kick off a promotion of Japanese ingredients to a largely European audience; food events would be scheduled alongside the Rio Olympics; and major culinary presentations are being planned to coincide with the Tokyo Olympics themselves.

Japan's pavilion at Milan attracted long lines of visitors, with waiting times often stretching well over an hour. The sophisticated electronic exhibits within the pavilion focused on interrelationships among traditional agriculture, especially rice cultivation, the environment, and the cultural practices and symbolism that surround food production and consumption. Virtual tabletops gave visitors views of washoku meals, accompanied by a throbbing techno beat.

Prominent Japanese chefs were invited to Milan to open pop-up restaurants at the Japan pavilion, providing cooking demonstrations for the culinary press and visitors from the European food industry. Of course, Japanese chefs already have extensive relationships with prominent Italian, French, and Spanish chefs—through the now-common global circulation of kitchen staffs—and so the networking possibilities for visiting chefs were enormous.

For the 2016 Olympics, major Japanese food companies sent ingredients and chefs to Rio, with two missions. The most highly publicized effort, at least within Japan, was to support Japanese athletes with the finest Japanese cuisine possible to boost their morale and their nutritional fitness. An equally important goal was to promote Japanese cuisine to the international audience attending the Olympics as part of the general effort to heighten global awareness of washoku.

When the 2020 Olympic games were awarded to Tokyo in 2013, foreign tourists coming to Japan totaled 10.4 million. The Japanese government announced a goal of raising that to 20 million by 2020. By 2016, the number had already exceeded 24 million.[28] Japanese cuisine looms large in establishing the country as a tourist destination; food is a central element of what the distinguished Japanese anthropologist and former commissioner of the Agency for Cultural Affairs, Aoki Tamotsu, refers to as a "national cultural brand."[29]

Rising foreign interest in traditional Japanese cuisine and the increasing numbers of foreign tourists to Japan are closely interrelated. Is Japanese cuisine itself a major lure for the foreign tourist? That is what MAFF planners hope and what the Ministry of Foreign Affairs expects from its promotions of "Cool Japan," which regularly feature succulent depictions of the finest sushi and artfully arranged dishes of *kaiseki ryōri*.

One small indication that Japanese cuisine and its UNESCO recognition motivate some travelers can be found in a 2014 London advertising supplement. The headline was "UNESCO Dining," and it noted (inaccurately) that Japanese cuisine is only the second national cuisine to be designated by UNESCO, "recognized for its centuries-old techniques and seasonal ingredients." A twelve-day tour was offered for £2,385.[30] (Caveat emptor: only three meals were included in the package!)

More conclusive evidence for the touristic appeal of Japanese cuisine can be gleaned from exit surveys of foreign visitors by the Japanese National Tourism Organization asking what aspects of Japan appealed to them or motivated their trip to Japan. In the 2010 survey respondents selected choices to fill in the phrase "the most impressive experience is . . ." "Eating Japanese cuisine" (*Nihon ryōri o taberu*) was the choice of 61 percent, second only to "[viewing] traditional Japanese architecture." JNTO's report notes that "eating Japanese cuisine" had topped the lists for the previous three years. In 2009 and 2010, the tenth-ranked choice was "visiting a fish market" (*uoichiba kengaku*), another culinary-themed activity.[31] Later versions of the survey continue to reflect these general trends. In the second quarter of 2017, 68.4 percent came with anticipation to "eat Japanese food" (phrased in this survey as *Nihonshoku o taberu*); in this survey, fish markets were not an option.[32] Note: the tourism surveys do not use the term *washoku*!

Other forms of global outreach include the World Washoku Challenge, a competition for foreign chefs, first held in Kyoto in 2013, sponsored by MAFF and by an advisory organization made up of food industry leaders, major chefs, and other culinary experts. The Challenge was timed to coincide with the official announcement of UNESCO's recognition of washoku. The initial mission statement states its rationale:

> It is currently estimated that some 80–90% of Japanese restaurants overseas are run by non-Japanese. . . . When the foods or culinary culture of a country are brought to other places, it is essential that

> the fare be adapted to suit the tastes of the locality—that is[,] to popularize such restaurants to appeal to a general audience.
>
> .... Washoku World Challenge 2013 supports these [foreign] missionaries of Japanese culinary culture: by discovering men and women who are working around the world to improve their skills and offer more and more delicious food to as many people as possible—that is[,] making people happy with Japanese food.[33]

The winner of the 2013 competition was a Singaporean chef, Li Kwok Wing, who triumphed with an original dish of steamed pumpkin and chestnuts. Winners in subsequent competitions were chefs from Thailand, Mexico, and Malaysia.[34] Many similar competitions and activities are sponsored worldwide by Japanese culinary organizations with the aim of promoting washoku culinary ideas, ideals, and techniques to foreign chefs and people in the food industry, to sustain the continued growth of interest in Japanese cuisine overseas.

Defining and defending "cultural heritage" seems on the surface to be simple, straightforward, and transparent. Looking at Japan's UNESCO washoku campaign, however, a complicated mix of state actors, international organizations, trade groups, mass media, and consumers (both in Japan and abroad) are variously involved in framing definitions of culinary cultural heritage for a variety of purposes.

The protection and promotion of cultural heritage transforms loosely coordinated cultural features—reflecting aesthetics, historical allusions, daily life and practice, regional identities, social ritual, and social hierarchy—into matters of official definition and government policy, as well as into objects of extensive attention in the mass media. Diverse cultural and social practices are moved out of the realm of relatively unselfconscious daily life into reified categories of distinction and differentiation. In the case of UNESCO recognition, these categories are defined in terms of distinct national assemblages, projected upon a global screen of cultural identities. External cultural politics for (inter)national recognition complexly intertwines with efforts to promote domestic goals of cultural identity formation.

The editors of *Public Diplomacy* refer to gastrodiplomacy as "edible national branding." Washoku clearly is an example of this.[35] Aoki Tamotsu urges attention to the elements of cultural identity—based on exemplary icons as well as on recognizable elements of ordinary, everyday life—that become the basis for "national cultural brands."[36] His point is that as various nations (cultures, societies) project their own representations of fundamental identities onto the world stage, each nation depends in large part on the assemblage of images—some preexisting, some only recently brought to wide attention—that mutually support one another in creating a coherent identity, or "brand" for the culture/nation in question. Some national cultural brands are well saturated with clearly recognizable elements of identity (France: haute cuisine, Eiffel Tower, Edith Piaf, Michelin stars, impressionism, Offenbach, Versailles; Japan: sushi, architecture Genji, woodblock prints, Zen, Mount Fuji, Shinkansen, manga and anime, etc.). Aoki argues that a rich national cultural brand is a form of cultural capital that a nation can utilize as the basis for exerting soft power in global relationships, promoting exports, encouraging tourism, attracting emulation, and positively influencing foreign opinion.

In the case of washoku, I argue that this "brand consciousness" is as much for domestic as for international consumption. The international appeal and domestic appeal of the culinary identity, the "edible cultural brand," are intertwined. The message to an international audience is not necessarily the same as the message to a domestic audience, and the domestic impact is amplified by the cachet of international recognition.

This highlights a fundamental paradox of UNESCO recognition of intangible cultural heritage: in the mission of promoting cultural heritage and preserving diversity as a global effort, UNESCO both promotes national cultural brands and depends on reifying nationalist definitions of culture.

Acknowledgments

In 2015, I was privileged to receive a Fulbright Senior Researcher Fellowship from the Japan-U.S. Educational Commission, which enabled four months of research on washoku while I was a visiting scholar at the Institute of Comparative Culture, Sophia University. The Reischauer Institute of Japanese Studies, Harvard University, also generously provided travel and research support during the summers of 2011–2017.

I am extremely grateful to the many officials of the Agency for Cultural Affairs, the Ministry of Agriculture, Forestry and Fisheries, and the Ministry of Foreign Affairs who allowed me to interview them on Japanese gastrodiplomacy during the summers of 2011, 2012, 2013, 2014, and 2015. Ambassador Kondo Seiichi provided especially valuable information and contacts, as did Aoki Tamotsu and Matsunobu Yōhei.

This project also draws on my previous research on the Japanese seafood industry and food culture (Theodore C. Bestor, "How Sushi Went Global," *Foreign Policy* 121 [2000]: 54–63; Theodore C. Bestor, *Tsukiji the Fish Market at the Center of the World* [Berkeley: University of California Press, 2004]; Theodore C.

Bestor, "Cuisine and Identity in Contemporary Japan," in *Routledge Handbook of Japanese Culture and Society*, ed. Victoria Lyon Bestor, Theodore C. Bestor, and Akiko Yamagata [New York: Routledge, 2011], 273–285).

Ikeda Keiko, Matsunobu Yōhei, and David Slater offered rich commentaries on my research. Victoria Lyon Bestor, Susan Ferber, and Nancy Stalker made many useful comments on the manuscript, and Hannah Perry provided great assistance in preparing the final version. I also thank Enomoto Yuko, Maya Hauser, Hirohara Yukari, and Myeonghee Grace Song for their work as research assistants in Tokyo at various times, and Sarah Berlow, Sara Kang, Stacie Matsumoto, Kuniko McVey, Sakaguchi Kazuko, and Yukari Swanson at Harvard for their very important assistance on many aspects of my research.

NOTES

1. Shannon Haugh et al., eds., "Letter from the Editor," *Public Diplomacy* 11 (2014): 9.
2. Arjun Appadurai, "On Culinary Authenticity," *Anthropology Today* 2 (1986): 25.
3. Theodore C. Bestor, "Cuisine and Identity in Contemporary Japan," in *Routledge Handbook of Japanese Culture and Society*, ed. Victoria Lyon Bestor, Theodore C. Bestor, and Akiko Yamagata (New York: Routledge, 2011), 273–285.
4. Katarzyna Cwiertka, *Modern Japanese Cuisine: Food, Power and National Identity* (London: Reaktion, 2006).
5. Makiko Nakamura's *Makiko's Diary: A Merchant Wife in 1910 Kyoto*, trans. Kazuko Smith (Stanford, CA: Stanford University Press, 1995) was written by a young housewife learning to cook according to the dictates of strict family tradition. She refers extensively but tentatively to novel Western ingredients, dishes, and cooking techniques that were only beginning to enter the experiences or consciousness of well-off but very traditional Kyoto housewives at the time.
6. *Nihon Kokugo Daijiten*, accessed July 17, 2017, "Yōshoku" http://japanknowledge.com.ezp-prod1.hul.harvard.edu/lib/display/?lid=2002044ee061ZSYJATnH.
7. *Nihon Kokugo Daijiten*, accessed July 17, 2017, "Washoku," http://japanknowledge.com.ezp-prod1.hul.harvard.edu/lib/display/?lid=20020480c27f8jW8V1Dz.
"Nihon ryōri," http://japanknowledge.com.ezp-prod1.hul.harvard.edu/lib/display/?lid=20020337026bfikhgHL7.
"Nihonshoku" http://japanknowledge.com.ezp-prod1.hul.harvard.edu/lib/display/?lid=20020336b654dbd8T59Q.
8. The 1950 national legislation Bunkazai Hogo-hō (Law for the Protection of Cultural Properties) drew on laws and regulations about cultural heritage protection that Japan instituted as early as 1897. The 1950 law put designation and protection of cultural properties in the hands of what is now the Bunkachō (Agency for Cultural Affairs), part of the current Ministry of Education, Culture, Sports, Science and

Technology (MEXT). The Bunkachō and the Ministry of Foreign Affairs collaborate in representing Japan to UNESCO's cultural heritage programs.

9. Convention Concerning the Protection of the World Cultural and Natural Heritage, UNESCO World Heritage Centre, accessed December 15, 2013, http://whc.unesco.org/en/conventiontext/.

10. "UNESCO World Heritage List," accessed July 17, 2017, http://whc.unesco.org/en/list/.

11. "Lists of Intangible Cultural Heritage and Register of Best Safeguarding Practices," UNESCO Intangible Cultural Heritage, accessed December 15, 2013, http://ich.unesco.org/en/lists.

12. Noriko Aikawa-Faure, "The UNESCO Convention for the Safeguarding of the Intangible Cultural Heritage: The Roles Played by China, Japan and the Republic of Korea in the 'Asian Turn,'" paper presented at the Association for Asian Studies AAS-in-ASIA Conference, Singapore, July 17–19, 2014.

13. "What Is Intangible Cultural Heritage?," accessed July 17, 2017, http://ich.unesco.org/en/what-is-intangible-heritage-00003.

14. "Lists of Intangible Cultural Heritage," accessed March 28, 2017.

15. "Lists of Intangible Cultural Heritage (filtered for Japan)," accessed September 17, 2016. http://ich.unesco.org/en/lists?display=default&text=&inscription=0&country=00112&multinational=3&type=0&domain=0&display1=inscriptionID#tabs.

16. "Lists of Intangible Cultural Heritage (filtered for Japan)."

17. Yusuke Fuji, "UNESCO Designates 'Washoku' Intangible Cultural Heritage Asset," *Asahi Shimbun*, December 5, 2013.

18. Voltaire Cang, "Unmaking Japanese Food: Washoku and Intangible Heritage Designation," *Food Studies* 4.3 (2015): 49–58.

19. Joseph S. Nye Jr., *Soft Power: The Means to Success in World Politics* (New York: Public Affairs, 2004).

20. Seiichi Kondo, "Japan's Soft Power in Asia and the World," seminar presentation for the Program on U.S.-Japan Relations, Harvard University, October 11, 2016.

21. Douglas McGray, "Japan's Gross National Cool," *Foreign Policy* 130 (2002): 44–54.

22. Bestor, "Cuisine and Identity."

23. Cang, "Unmaking Japanese Food," 51.

24. Alexis Agliano Sanborn, "More Than a Meal: School Lunch in Japan," *Education about Asia* 22.1 (2017): 45–49.

25. *Tsukiji Wonderland*, directed by Naotarō Endō (2016; Tokyo: Shochiku Co., 2017), DVD. The later segments depict *shokuiku* in the classroom, showing children delighted to learn about seafood, deboning fish with chopsticks, and so forth.

26. Anthony Faiola, "Putting the Bite on Pseudo Sushi and Other Insults," *Washington Post*, November 24, 2006, accessed August 20, 2016, http://www.washingtonpost.com/wp-dyn/content/article/2006/11/23/AR2006112301158.html.

27. "Sushi Police," Anime News Network, accessed August 15, 2016, http://www.animenewsnetwork.com/encyclopedia/anime.php?id=17960.

28. "Japan-Bound Statistics," JTB Tourism Research & Consulting Co., accessed May 28, 2017, http://www.tourism.jp/en/tourism-database/stats/inbound/.

29. Aoki Tamotsu, "Toward Multilayered Strength in the 'Cool' Culture," *Gaikō Forum* 4.2 (2004): 8–16.

30. *I*, October 1, 2014.

31. "TIC riyō gaikokujin ryokōsha no hōnichi ryokō jitai chōsa hōkokusho," Japan National Tourism Organization, accessed October 15, 2016, http://www.jnto.go.jp/jpn/downloads/101124_tic_attachment.pdf.

32. "Hōnichi gaikokujin no shōhi dōkō," Japan Tourism Agency, accessed August 5, 2017. http://www.mlit.go.jp/kankocho/siryou/toukei/syouhityousa.html.

33. "Washoku World Challenge 2013," Washoku World Challenge Executive Committee, accessed July 18, 2017, http://washoku-worldchallenge.jp/2013/en/.

34. "Washoku World Challenge 2013."

35. Haugh et al., "Letter from the Editor.".

36. Aoki, "Toward Multilayered Strength."

6

"We Can Taste but Others Cannot"

Umami as an Exclusively Japanese Concept

Yoshimi Osawa

In early 2013, NHK's (Japan Broadcasting Corporation) two popular television shows, *Close-up Gendai* and *Asa-ichi* devoted their entire programs to umami, the savory or meaty taste often identified as the fifth taste, after sweet, sour, salty, and bitter.[1] Both shows emphasized that umami has gained the attention of foreign chefs, including those from top restaurants, and that Japanese chefs have been teaching the foreign chefs who have interests in umami. The shows also explained what umami is and how it has been recognized as a universal fifth taste after the discovery of an umami taste receptor. They further introduced various positive functions of umami in medical science, including helping cancer patients with dry-mouth and taste disorders.

Why did Japanese national television devote two programs to umami in such a short period? Close investigation of the programs demonstrates various attempts to include Japanese cuisine (washoku) on the UNESCO intangible cultural heritage list, discussed in the previous chapter. But what is washoku? How "washoku" should be defined was one of the main discussion points during the four official meetings held by the Ministry of Agriculture and Fisheries in order to discuss the UNESCO washoku registration. What Japan was trying to promote was umami, the so-called fifth taste. The concept of umami was often explained and used by the meeting committees in order to define washoku. For instance, "Most countries form their cuisine centering around oil and fat, but it is only our country that forms our cuisine centering around umami," said a committee member, a chef of Kyoto cuisine. "Culture of umami and dashi (soup stock) is one of the biggest features of Japanese food culture," opined the head of the committee, Kumakura Isao, a history professor.[2]

Kumakura was a guest speaker for one of the TV shows mentioned above, and he commented that "though we had thought that umami could be understood only by Japanese, it is not. It is a great thing that umami has been recognized globally as a universal fifth taste. Parallel to the fact that Japanese food is being accepted in the world, the meanings of umami, which has been creating Japanese taste, has been understood (in the world)." In the context of washoku as UNESCO world heritage, umami has been used as a gustatory instrument to embody the image of Japanese food for promotional purposes. Umami is thus a key element of Japan's culinary brand that is becoming increasingly prominent in Japanese representations of its cuisine abroad. Increasing international acceptance of Japanese food is one of the key factors explaining how umami has become a culinary phenomenon both inside and outside of Japan. Based on fieldwork conducted in Japan and the United Kingdom, this chapter examines the current umami phenomenon and how and why umami has become a symbol of Japanese cultural distinctiveness.

Invention or Tradition?

Close-up Gendai referred to umami as the "home of Japanese people's taste" (*Nihonjin no aji no furusato*).[3] Other media describe umami as "a key to Japanese food" (*Nihonshoku no kagi*) and "the soul/essence of Japanese food" (*Nihonshoku no shinzui*). Why do they need to explain and promote umami in Japan if it is already the basis of Japanese food?

In 1908 the chemical basis of umami was discovered by a Japanese scholar, Professor Ikeda Kikunae (1864–1936) of Tokyo Imperial University.[4] Ikeda extracted crystals of glutamate from a broth made of *konbu* (*Saccharina japonica* and other species of the Laminariaceae family of seaweed), a type of sea kelp often used in Japanese cuisine. He found that the glutamate had a distinctive taste, different from the four "basic" tastes of sweet, sour, bitter, and salty, and he described it using the Japanese word *umami*. There is no exact English equivalent word for this sensation, although some words such as "savory," "meaty," and "brothy" could be considered. Biochemically, there are three main substances that provide umami taste: monosodium glutamate (MSG), disodium 5'-guanylate (GMP), and disodium 5'-inosinate (IMP).[5]

While these umami substances exist naturally in many foods, including seaweeds, vegetables, seafood, mushrooms, meat, and cheese, there are also manufactured umami substances in the form of seasonings and other food additives, such as Ajinomoto, patented by Ikeda in 1909 and marketed in other countries as Accent. The popular seasoning launched the Ajinomoto corporation into a major food manufacturer, worth over $12 billion today. Figure 6.1 illustrates some recent Ajinomoto packaging. Since 2000, when a modified glutamate receptor was identified by a team of scientists from the University of Miami, umami has been recognized as a fifth taste scientifically, although there remain disputes about the definition of "basic tastes."[6]

It should be emphasized that it was Ikeda who first gave the name *umami* to the taste of sodium glutamate. When he claimed that there is one additional taste besides the four basic tastes, he clearly proposed to call that taste *umami* for convenience. *Umai* is a masculine variant adjective of *oishii* (good tasting)

FIGURE 6.1 Ajinomoto (MSG or umami seasoning) in panda bottle and "Do you know Umami?" pamphlet produced by Ajinomoto Co. Photograph by the author.

FIGURE 6.2 Bonito flakes (katsuobushi). Photograph by the author.

driving the noun, *umami*, as some other Japanese adjectives drive nouns using the *mi* form.[7]

The word *umami* is polysemous, defined in Japanese dictionaries variously as (1) a delicious taste and its level of deliciousness, (2) a skillful thing to relish, especially techniques in art, (3) profit that is easily gained in business and so on.[8] In addition to these meanings, the *Daijirin* dictionary describes umami as "a taste of dashi stock which is delivered from *katsuobushi* [dried flakes of skipjack tuna, illustrated in figures 6.2 and 6.3], *konbu*, shiitake mushrooms etc." This taste of dashi reflects exactly the scientific discussion of umami as a fifth taste. However, only one dictionary among the many consulted provides this definition.

The use of the word *umami* by Japanese people is not simply as a term indicating the new fifth taste. I had an opportunity to talk with a former Japanese television presenter about her understanding of the use of *umami* as a term. She had worked for cookery programs, and there were many occasions when she was required to eat food and talk about its taste to viewing audiences. For her, *umami* was a useful term to express how she felt about the food she tasted. She remarked, "To be honest, *umami* is a convenient expression. If I cannot find an appropriate expression to describe the taste of food, I sometimes used *umami* instead of just saying *oishii* [tasty]." Her comment indicates that umami has positive connections while also being ambiguous.

FIGURE 6.3 *Goya chanpurū* (bitter melon stir-fry dish originally from Okinawa) with bonito flakes on top. Photograph by the author.

Figure 6.4 illustrates the dramatic increase in the mentions of the word *umami* in two Japanese newspapers, *Yomiuri* and *Asahi*. The number of articles citing the term *umami* has gradually increased since the late 1990s and then rapidly after 2000. I have also tracked how the term is used by examining its appearance in the title of articles in the *Asahi* between 1945 and 2009. *Umami* as a taste term did not really appear until 1972, and until the late 1990s there were only a few articles citing *umami* in their titles. Between 1945 and 1994 there were ninety-two articles citing the term *umami* in their titles. However only nineteen out of these used *umami* as a taste description. The other seventy-three articles cited *umami* in the sense of "benefit" rather than referring to taste explicitly. In contrast, between 1995 and 2009, there were 416 articles that mentioned *umami* in their titles, and 365 out of the 416 articles used *umami* as a taste descriptor.

Thus, *umami* in the context of taste began to appear more often from the late 1990s and thereafter rapidly increased, particularly after 2000. It is, therefore, not unreasonable to assume that the discovery of the "umami" receptor in 2000 was the trigger. The frequent use of the term in such media and in marketing has doubtless influenced the increasing awareness of umami among Japanese consumers. Despite its short history and its ambiguous folk definition, umami is now regarded by many as exclusively distinctive of Japanese food not just in Japan but globally.

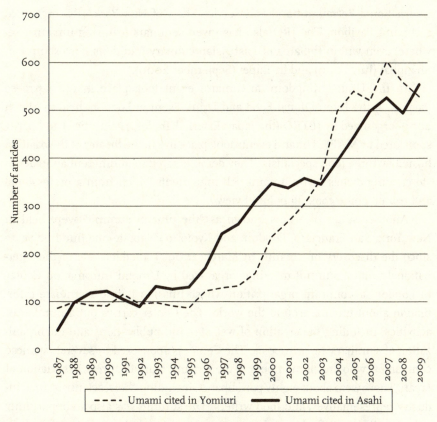

FIGURE 6.4 Number of articles mentioning the term *umami* published in the newspapers *Yomiuri* and *Asahi* between 1987 and 2009. Sources: Yomidasu Bunshokan, Yomiuri Online database and Asahi.com Perfect online database.

Umami as a Gustatory Instrument

Whether it is tradition or not, umami is used as a concept to promote Japanese food overseas by various government and business bodies. It should not be forgotten that what appears to have motivated these actions at a national policy level is the potential economic value of Japanese food. For example, in United States, the JRO (Organization to Promote Japanese Restaurants Abroad), in cooperation with the Japanese Ministry of Agriculture, Forestry and Fisheries of Japan (MAFF), has been exhibiting at the National Restaurant Association (NRA) show, America's largest restaurant show. The JRO contributed a "Japan pavilion," the main theme of which was Japanese taste, umami, and dashi. Umami was introduced as a distinctive and essential quality of Japanese food, and the concept of umami was the device used to introduce Japanese food and ingredients through cooking demonstrations. More recently in 2014, at the

International Restaurant and Foodservice Show of New York, JRO organized a Umami Pavilion. The JRO also has given seminars featuring umami elsewhere, even within the area of East Asian culinary traditions, for example in Shanghai (July 2009) and in Taipei (September 2009).

In the United Kingdom, an umami event took place in the Japanese Pavilion at the International Food and Drink Event in London, held in March 2009, organized by JETRO (the Japan External Trade Organization) and partly sponsored by MAFF. Umami events took place live in the theater of the pavilion hosted by three food specialists. They demonstrated their different approaches "to creating dishes using umami-rich ingredients," both from a professional and from a home cooking point of view.

Another series of events known as "the umami summit" were held in New York, San Francisco, London, and Kyoto to celebrate one hundred years since the discovery of umami. In March 2009, I attended one of the international umami summit meetings organized by Umami Information Center in London, a nonprofit organization whose mission is to disseminate information about umami around the world. The Center carries out a number of activities, including the creation of websites and publications and the organization of seminars and symposia. The Center is sponsored by several Japanese companies, who are all members of the Umami Manufacturers Association of Japan. There were about eighty participants, including chefs, scientists, food industry representatives, and food writers. The summit was also an opportunity to launch the book *Dashi and Umami*.[9] The event included demonstrations on umami and dashi by four well-known Japanese chefs, with two chef panelists from Michelin-starred restaurants in the United Kingdom. The purpose of the event was to take a detailed look at dashi as the very core of Japanese cuisine. In the venue, different types of dashi ingredients were displayed. After the demonstrations by the chefs, the umami dishes that they had created were served to participants in the style of a bento box. The keynote speaker, chef Kunio Tokuoka from Kitcho Arashiyama, a three-starred Michelin restaurant in Kyoto, made and interesting comment: "I was a child when I first became aware of umami, but I have acquired a lot of information about umami by meeting people from the Umami Information Center and professors at the universities." It was surprising to know that even a well-known Japanese chef had learned about umami from the umami organization.

Thus, umami was central to introducing and promoting Japanese food culture in high-profile commercial and trade events, and from this level it has been able to diffuse into other media and contexts in which ordinary consumers encounter Japanese food. It is not surprising for anyone to see soy sauce with the brand name Umami in a supermarket in Bangkok, a Japanese restaurant named Umami in the Netherlands, or Umami dressing for sale in

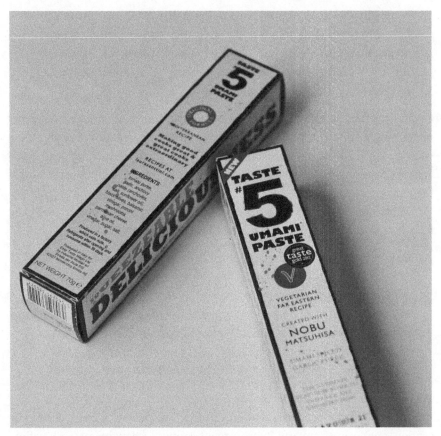

FIGURE 6.5 Taste No5 Umami Paste sold in England. Photograph by the author.

London these days. Figure 6.5 illustrates a product for adding umami flavoring endorsed by the globally famous chef Nobu Matsuhisa.

Umami and Cultural Nationalism

Not only is umami treated as an item to represent a distinctive feature of Japanese culture and food in the global market, but umami also has a strong link to Japanese identity. Some food specialists have theorized that there are strong links between umami and Japaneseness that go beyond food culture itself and make questionable claims in the realm of folk anthropology that seem hardly substantiated by the science. Kiyomi Mikuni, a renowned chef of French cuisine in Japan, gave a talk at the Food Education Forum organized by MAFF in 2006. For Mikuni:

> There are four basic tastes: sweet, sour, salty, and bitter. In addition to these, we Japanese have the fifth taste, umami. Japanese are the only

people in the world who are able to detect this taste.... Japanese have developed great robots and low-emission and economical cars, and can build a house without using nails. By having the sense of umami, we have a great intellectual property.... I think that we, as Japanese, ourselves are a world brand.[10]

Similarly, a food scientist at a university in Japan has claimed that umami has not only established its position as a basic taste after several umami substances were discovered by Japanese scientists in the twentieth century, but also that it is a new taste concept that was discovered because of the "exquisite tongue" of the Japanese.[11]

I obtained a strong opinion about how umami and Japaneseness are linked from a Japanese chef working for a Japanese restaurant in London.

Gaijin [non-Japanese] chefs say that they do not understand umami. They studied [umami], but cannot understand. Umami is something that Japanese have known for long time, like [the use of] *konbu* from the Edo period.... Japanese understand [about umami] better than Westerners. It might be an inborn thing rather than something to understand. We are born with the tongue [that understands umami], so it is difficult to say if Westerners can understand it as we do.

It is not only food specialists and government officials who connect the perception and use of umami to resurgent cultural chauvinism and nationalist sentiment. During my interviews with ordinary Japanese consumers, the assumption of a link between umami and Japaneseness was common. Consider, for example, the following statements:

Japanese can distinguish umami from sweet, salty, hot, etc. I have heard it on TV or something like that. I recently talked about umami with my husband. I do not think that Americans can understand umami. Taste/flavor is too strong in America.... I don't think they can understand as subtle of a taste as umami. (A woman in her thirties who lived in the United States for four years)

Umami is something that we can be proud of.... The delicate taste and balance are unique in Japan. I am not sure if people from other countries can understand it. (Male, forty-seven years old)

Is there umami in overseas cuisines? Can gaijin taste and understand umami? (Female, sixty years old)

By contrasting themselves with others who supposedly cannot understand this taste, Japanese now commonly assert that umami is a taste recognized only by Japanese or that the Japanese understand umami better than foreigners. With the emphasis on its cultural distinctiveness, umami is used as a foil to assert a culinary identity. Thus, umami provides a basis for culinary nationalism. There are at least three technical reasons why these claims exist: (1) all three umami substances (MSG, IMP, and GMP) were discovered by Japanese scientists, (2) Japanese is one of only a few languages to have a word to describe the umami type of taste, and (3) the existence of umami as a fifth taste was not believed outside of Japan until the discovery of the umami receptor in 2000. These facts, as well as the way umami is represented through different media in discourses about what is distinctive in Japanese culture, partly through industrial marketing and government policy, reconfirm some people's beliefs that umami is a strictly Japanese sensation, but we have very little scientific or anthropological evidence.

Besides these three points to explain why Japanese express cultural ownership over umami, the claim must be carefully assessed in the context of sociocultural changes in Japanese society from the Westernization of the diet in postwar Japan and the more recent globalization of foodways. Many scholars have examined how globalization has re-established and strengthened national or local identities.[12] Revival and (re)invention of national and local cuisine due to globalization, as well as the recreation or protections of foodways at the national and local levels, have been examined by many scholars who have focused on the significant role of food in emphasizing and maintaining identities.[13]

Umami and Japanese Identity

The connection between umami and Japanese identity and how Japanese claim cultural ownership of umami can be analyzed in the context of *Nihonjinron* (the theory of Japaneseness), which can be defined as a body of texts featuring "an active concern with national distinctiveness" so as better to organize "significant difference between us and them."[14] Allegedly distinctive cultural features of Japanese people are often claimed in *Nihonjinron*, such as the notions that Japanese are hardworking. Japanese sensitivity (*kansei* or *sensai-sa*) is also central to this idea. Beyond cultural aspects, distinctive biological features of Japanese are also claimed, such as that Japanese have longer intestines than Westerners because Japanese people traditionally had diets based on grains and vegetables, while Western diets were based on meats.

During my fieldwork in Japan between 2008 and 2009, I often heard different phrases used to express the "Japanese palate," such as *Nihonjin no kuchi* (Japanese mouth), *Nihonjin no shita* (Japanese tongue), or *Nihonjin no mikaku* (Japanese sense of taste). These expressions are often used with the verb *au* (fit, suit), for instance, *Nihonjin no shita ni au*, meaning "to suit the Japanese tongue." I observed that such expressions were used at several ethnic restaurants (i.e., Taiwanese, Korean, Thai) to suggest that their foods are cooked to suit the Japanese palate. The emphasis on the adaptation to a local Japanese palate in many cases works better in attracting Japanese customers than some appeal to the "authenticity" of their foods.

Although there is no biological or logical explanation of what the Japanese mouth, tongue, or sense of taste is, such phrases are used to differentiate the Japanese palate from "others" in particular by claiming that the Japanese palate is more exquisite than others. One specialist informant, a manager of a high-end Japanese restaurant in London told me, "There is no way [for non-Japanese people] to understand delicate things and tastes (*sensai na mono ya aji*) such as of *nimono* (Japanese stew) and *katsuo dashi* (bonito broth) . . . although I think, more [non-Japanese] people [have been able to] understand it recently." Another chef at a different Japanese restaurant in London told me that "the Japanese sense of taste (*nihonjin no mikaku*) is the best in the world. It is exquisite (*sensai*), and it can spot the subtle things." Thus, these understandings are linked to the notion that the Japanese tongue is so sensitive that while Japanese can taste umami, non-Japanese people cannot and that maybe the exquisite Japanese sense of taste led to the discovery of umami, as umami represents the sensitivity of the Japanese palate.

The supposed sensitivities of the Japanese, such as sensitivity to nature or the seasons, have featured in *Nihonjinron*, and are often connected to a general aesthetic sense. One of the bestselling books in Japan in 2006, *Kokka no Hinkaku* (The dignity of the nation), which had sold more than 2.65 million copies between November 2005 and May 2006, is a good example of this.[15] The book is introduced by the publisher as a work of *Nihonjinron* "to give pride and confidence to Japanese." The author, Fujiwara, criticizes Western rationalism and emphasizes the importance of Japanese values such as *jōcho* (emotion or feeling) over [Western] logic, and bushido (samurai spirit) over [Western] democracy. In the book, Fujiwara uses his experience with an American professor to demonstrate that the Japanese have a refined sensitivity and how important *jōcho* is to the Japanese. It was autumn when the American professor visited Fujiwara's house and they heard crickets. The professor asked Fujiwara, "What is that noise?" Fujiwara notes that for the professor, the sound of the insect was simply noise. Fujiwara remembered how his grandmother said, "It is already autumn" and cried when she heard the sound of the insects. "How we could have lost a war to such people as the professor?" he wondered. Through this extreme logic, Fujiwara connects the crickets with Japan's defeat in the war, implying the superiority of the Japanese by claiming that they are more sensitive to nature and the seasons. For non-Japanese, the sound of insects is merely noise; therefore they cannot feel or imagine the aesthetic of nature and seasonal change from hearing the sound. According to Yoshino, in *Nihonjinron*, the Japanese find "aesthetic refinement" in nonlogical, empathetic, and nonverbal communication.[16]

The claim that only Japanese can understand umami needs to be analyzed on two levels. First, can non-Japanese perceive the taste umami? And second, can they recognize it as umami? In the case of umami, there is no biological difference in umami perception between Japanese and non-Japanese, as has been demonstrated in various studies.[17] The point is that the umami concept cannot be easily translated into other languages. A common manner of exploring Japanese uniqueness in the *Nihonjinron* is "to infer a uniquely Japanese mode of thinking from Japanese words and phrases that supposedly defy translation."[18] While umami has now gained a universal, scientific, and logical definition as the fifth taste, umami as a sensuous experience is still obscure, and the term is used in other ways in daily discourse. Promoting umami as an abstract sensation that can only be understood through a sensuous yet ambiguous experience encourages this claim.

Conclusion

The discovery of umami by Japanese scientists is an understandable matter of national pride. In 1985, the Japanese Patent Office selected ten great Japanese inventors in order to celebrate a century of the system of industrial rights in Japan. Ikeda was selected as one of these for his discovery of umami. A plaque with his portrait has been displayed at the Japan Patent Office since 1985, along with those of nine other inventors, to commemorate their achievements and introduce them to the Japanese people. In a similar manner, umami was selected in 2009 as an "Important Historical Material of Science and Technology" (*Jyuyō kagaku gijyutsushi shiryo*) by the National Museum of Nature and Science in Tokyo.

In 1971, Den Fujita, the founder of McDonald's Japan, declared at the opening of its first food outlet in Japan that the "the reason Japanese people are so short and have yellow skin is because they have eaten nothing but fish and rice for two thousand years. . . . If we eat McDonald's hamburgers and potatoes for a thousand years we will become taller, our skin white and our hair blonde."[19] Fast food, as typified by McDonald's, was an evocation of the West, and more particularly of the United States in Asia, while meat diets in general have also evoked the West for many Japanese.[20]

This sort of dietary self-criticism goes some way in explaining the shift in Japanese food habits following the aftermath of World War II, and perhaps also helps us to understand the more recent self-conscious revival of distinctive Japanese food values. The postwar nutritional transition shows how Japan, through copying a Western diet, responded to the trauma of defeat in the war, in the same way that rapid industrial recovery was enabled through adopting certain Western features.

However, as the Japanese economy became affluent, the situation changed. The nutritional change reached its peak during "the gourmet boom" of the economic bubble in 1980s. For instance, the intake of both fat and animal protein was a declining trend in the late 1990s.[21] It is now commonly realized that the traditional prewar Japanese diet was healthier and carried less risk of various health issues that emerged after adoption of the Western diet, including obesity, hyperlipidemia, and diabetes mellitus, all of which are becoming common in contemporary Japan. At present, the traditional Japanese diet, characterized by high consumption of rice, millet, vegetables, and fish, is often described as an ideal dietary balance, both inside and outside of Japan. The re-evaluation of the Japanese traditional diet emphatically contrasts with what Japanese society experienced for a few decades after World War II.

So what has this got to do with umami? In considering the revival of washoku as a general cultural trend, we can better understand the context in which umami works as a "traditional" Japanese concept, as well as how umami is used as a branding tool to promote Japanese food. Umami as a distinctive element and symbol of traditional Japanese food, both in the way Japanese culture is perceived by the rest of the world and how it is represented within Japan, is utilized by the industry and by the government. Due to the westernization of diet as well as the more recent globalization of foodways, waves of imported food cultures and food ingredients have impacted the Japanese market and stomach. The revival of washoku is a reaction to these changes, and within this context umami is the abstract sensation that embodies a distinctive identity of Japaneseness.

Umami as the fifth taste is a relatively new concept, and the term in its strict sense as a primary taste descriptor only dates back a little more than a century. The definition and concept of umami is still developing and remains unclear. However, many Japanese have taken cultural ownership of this abstract sensation, and it is now regarded by many as a taste distinctive of, and exclusively associated with, Japanese cuisine. As umami is a Japanese expression and concept, it is reasoned that non-Japanese cannot understand it. While umami as the universal fifth taste has appealed to some industries or media, it is also claimed that umami is a particular element of Japanese identity due to its cultural distinctiveness. The concept of umami has attained its iconic position for Japanese food culture by underpinning contemporary notions of "Japaneseness" through taste. Japanese culinary identity, therefore, is in part defined through a taste, umami, and in the context of the globalization of Japanese foodways, umami has become a symbol of Japaneseness and of Japanese culture on a global level.

NOTES

1. *Close-Up Gendai* is an evening social affair show and *Asa-ichi* is a morning general (life) information program.

2. For the relationship between umami perceptions and dashi, see Yoshimi Osawa, "Glutamate Perception, Soup Stock and the Concept of Umami: The Ethnography, Food Ecology and History of Dashi in Japan," *Ecology of Food and Nutrition* 51.4 (2012): 329–345.

3. For the concept of *furusato*, see Jennifer Robertson, "Furusato Japan: The Culture and Politics of Nostalgia," *International Journal of Politics, Culture and Society* 1.4 (1988): 494–518.

4. Kikunae Ikeda, "Shin Chomiryo Ni Tsuite," *Tokyo Kagaku Kaishi* 30.8 (1909): 820–836; Kikunae Ikeda, "New Seasonings," *Chemical Senses* 27.9 (2002): 847–849.

5. Yojiro Kawamura and Morley Kare, *Umami: A Basic Taste* (New York: Marcel Dekker, 1987).

6. Nirupa Chaudhari, Ana Marie Landin, and Stephan Roper, "A Metabotropic Glutamate Receptor Variant Functions as a Taste Receptor," *Nature Neuroscience* 3.2 (2000): 113–119; Kumiko Ninomiya, "Umami: A Universal Taste," *Food Reviews International* 18.1 (2002): 23–38; Bruce Halpern, "What's in a Name? Are MSG and Umami the Same?," *Chemical Senses* 27.9 (2002): 845–846.

7. Anthony Backhouse, *The Lexical Field of Taste: A Semantic Study of Japanese Taste Terms* (Cambridge: Cambridge University Press, 1994).

8. Akira Matsumura, *Daijirin* (Tokyo: Sanseido, 2006); Izuru Shinmura, ed., *Kojien* (Tokyo: Iwanami Shoten, 1998).

9. Cross Media, ed., *Dashi and Umami* (London: Cross Media, 2009).

10. "Kodomo no mikaku wo sodateru," Norinsuisansho, accessed November 22, 2014, http://www.maff.go.jp/kanto/syo_an/seikatsu/shokuiku/ibennto/18forum_lec.html.

11. "Umami no Himitsu," Mizkan Group Corporation, accessed November 22, 2015, http://www.mizkan.co.jp/company/newsrelease/2008news/080514-00.html.

12. E.g., Arjun Appadurai, *Modernity at Large: Cultural Dimensions of Globalization* (Minneapolis: University of Minnesota Press, 1996); Rob Wilson and Dissanayake

Wimal, *Global/Local: Cultural Production and theTransnational Imaginary* (Durham, NC: Duke University Press, 1996); Sheila Croucher, *Globalization and Belonging: The Politics of Identity in a Changing World* (Oxford: Rowman & Littlefield, 2004); Gordon Mathews, *Global Culture / Individual Identity: Searching for Home in the Cultural Supermarket* (New York: Routledge, 2000).

13. E.g., Katarzyna Cwiertka and Boudewijn Walraven, *Asian Food: the Global and the Local* (London: Curzon Press, 2002); David Howes, *Cross-Cultural Consumption: Global Markets, Local Realities* (New York: Routledge, 1996); Richard Wilk, "Food and Nationalism: The Origins of Belizean Food," in *Food Nations: Selling Taste in Consumer Societies*, ed. Belasco Warren and Philip Scranton (New York: Routledge, 2002).

14. Kosaku Yoshino, "Culturalism, Racialism, and Internationalism in the Discourse on Japanese Identity," in *Making Majorities: Constituting the Nation in Japan, Korea, China, Malaysia, Fiji, Turkey, and the United States*, ed. Dru Gladney (Stanford, CA: Stanford University Press, 1998), 13–30.

15. Masahiko Fujiwara, *Kokka no Hinkaku* (Tokyo: Shinchosha, 2005).

16. Kosaku Yoshino, *Cultural Nationalism in Contemporary Japan: A Sociological Enquiry* (New York: Routledge, 1992), 12.

17. E.g., Michael O'Mahony and Rie Ishii, "A Comparison of English and Japanese Taste Languages: Taste Descriptive Methodology, Codability and the Umami Taste," *British Journal of Psychology* 77 (1986): 161–174.

18. Yoshino, *Cultural Nationalism*, 21.

19. Josh Ozersky, *The Hamburger: A History (Icons of America)* (New Haven: Yale University Press, 2009).

20. Emiko Ohnuki-Tierney, *Rice as Self: Japanese Identities through Time* (Princeton, NJ: Princeton University Press, 1994); Toyoyuki Sabata, *Nikushoku No Shisou* (Tokyo: Chuou Kouron Shinsho, 1966).

21. Yoshimi Osawa, "The Perception and Representation of Umami: A Study of the Relationship between Taste Sensation, Food Types and Cultural Categories," (PhD diss., University of Kent, 2011).

7

Rosanjin

The Roots of Japanese Gourmet Nationalism

Nancy K. Stalker

The world of gourmet cuisines exist along a continuum; according to food historian Paul Freeman, one pole lies at "simplicity," the other at "magnificence."[1] In contemporary international cuisine, magnificence is represented by the realm of molecular gastronomy with chefs such as Ferran Adria of Spain's (now closed) El Bulli who used chemicals, additives, and high tech to change food textures and intensify flavors, creating optical marvels such as inside-out eggs, caviar made of olive oil, and cocktails served in gel form. The roots of such gastronomical magic lie in the creations of French chefs such as Marie-Antoine Careme (1784–1833), who encouraged ostentation and "grand visual effects," and Georges Auguste Escoffier (1846–1935), who codified the five rich "mother sauces" that douse meat and vegetable alike in classical French cuisine.[2] The other end of the spectrum, simplicity, is characterized by highlighting the quality, purity, and locality of foodstuffs, leaving ingredients to speak as much as possible for themselves. These characteristics are prevalent among chefs such as Rene Redzepi of Noma, the "new Nordic" restaurant in Copenhagen known for its use of foraged ingredients, and Ono Jirō, the Spartan master of a ten-seat sushi bar with three Michelin stars, featured in the US documentary *Jiro Dreams of Sushi* (2011). Simplicity in gourmet cuisines is epitomized by fresh, seasonal dishes with a clean, "Zen"-like aesthetic, as seen in figure 7.1, a course from Noma featuring a single fresh clam. The style is largely derived from hegemonic notions of Japanese cuisine associating it with seasonality, highly aesthetic presentation that often incorporates natural elements, and a kind of purity and integrity of both flavor and ingredients. The 2013

FIGURE 7.1 "One-hundred-year-old clam" course at Noma restaurant in Copenhagen. Photograph by the author.

UNESCO recognition of Japanese cuisine as an intangible cultural treasure, in fact, listed these characteristics, rather than any particular foods or dishes, as constitutive of washoku (see the Bestor chapter in this volume).

Actual Japanese food practices, however, do not necessarily conform to these ideals. Katarzyna Cwiertka, a historian of East Asian cuisine, has convincingly argued that modern washoku is best described as a blend of Western, Chinese, and Japanese cuisines, illustrated by everyday foods like curry, ramen, tonkatsu (deep-fried pork cutlets), *gyūdon* (sweet simmered beef over rice), and *korokke* (deep-fried potato croquettes).[3] Furthermore, Eric Rath has demonstrated that premodern Japanese haute cuisine featured dishes on the magnificent end of the spectrum, fantastic and metaphorical creations meant for "conspicuous nonconsumption."[4] Nevertheless, prevalent images of "culinary Japaneseness" emphasize seemingly simple preparations presented in a visually striking manner, best represented in kaiseki, an elite, formalized cuisine consisting of a succession of small dishes served on exquisite tableware in a traditional Japanese setting. While loosely rooted in seventeenth-century tea ceremonies, the term kaiseki was not in general use until the late nineteenth century, when it was associated with an extravagant and flamboyant sequence of dishes.[5]

The contemporary ideal of kaiseki as a unified aesthetic experience tastefully harmonizing food, tableware, season, and surroundings is, however, largely a twentieth-century invention largely associated with artist Kitaōji Rosanjin (1883–1959), the most conspicuous epicurean of Japan's modern age, who has been elevated to near sainthood following UNESCO's designation of washoku as a world treasure. Rosanjin has been the subject of more retrospective exhibitions domestically and abroad than any other Japanese artist, including a 2015 blockbuster at the National Museum of Modern Art in Kyoto, "The Beauty of Rosanjin, Genius of Japanese Cuisine" (*Rosanjin no bi, washoku no tensai*) in commemoration of the UNESCO award, advertised in figure 7.2.[6] At Expo Milano 2015, which highlighted national food cultures under the theme "Feeding the Planet, Energy for Life!," the Japan Pavilion featured the works and words of Rosanjin in numerous exhibitions throughout the hall.

Although Rosanjin was not formally trained as a chef and never established his own restaurant or culinary school, he serves as the symbol of Japanese gourmet identity today because of his exacting standards for ingredients and freshness and for his emphasis on presenting foods beautifully, all of which have become characteristics for internationally hegemonic notions about Japanese cuisine. Furthermore, he possessed abundant personal charisma and self-promotional skills that gave him an unusual prominence in the Japanese culinary world. Rosanjin himself noted "the importance of personality—even in cooking."[7] His culinary philosophies have been transmitted through some of Japan's celebrated chefs, whom he helped train, including Teiichi Yuki (b. 1930), founder of Kyoto's famed Kitcho kaiseiki restaurant, and Tsuji Shizuo (1933–1993), founder of the Tsuji Culinary Institute in 1960 (*Tsuji rishi senmon gakko*) and author of the acclaimed *Japanese Cookery: A Simple Art*.[8] Beloved food writer M. F. K. Fisher provided the text's introduction, in which she claimed she would "never again eat as subtly and exquisitely" as she had during her two weeks with Tsuji in Osaka.[9] Tsūji himself called Japanese cuisine "deceptively simple," with dashi stock and soy sauce as the two key ingredients, and echoed his mentor Rosanjin in his assertion that its two key requirements were "pristine freshness and beauty of presentation."[10]

This chapter introduces Rosanjin and his epicurean standards, arguing that they have deeply shaped conceptions of Japanese culinary identity both domestically and abroad and have helped to crystallize culinary nationalism in contemporary Japan. Past studies of everyday nationalism have often neglected to address how food "builds and sustains a particular relationship between the individual and the nation" but with the burgeoning of food studies, this oversight is changing.[11] Works by Arjun Appadurai, Jeffrey Pilcher, Priscilla Parkhurst Ferguson, Lara Anderson, and Thomas Parker, among others, have

FIGURE 7.2 Poster of 2015 Rosanjin exhibition. Courtesy of the National Museum of Modern Art, Kyoto.

begun addressing the relationship between nation building and the construction of national culinary cultures in countries such as France, Mexico, Spain, and India.[12] Rosanjin's chauvinistic attitudes about the superiority of his own national cuisine, especially in terms of ingredients and presentation, offer a building block for helping to fathom Japanese culinary nationalism and to understand the current international embrace of washoku.

Rosanjin: A Food-Centered Biography

Rosanjin was a famously eccentric and cantankerous personality, married five times, and was a prodigious drinker of beer. He was a self-taught artist of multiple genres, beginning as an engraver of artists' seals before becoming a restaurateur and ceramicist. Though primarily known as a potter, with a remarkably prolific estimated lifetime output of 200,000 pieces, he was also a noted calligrapher, wood-carver, and painter.[13] Rosanjin's petulance and bad temper were well known. For one, he refused the designation of living national treasure (*ningen kokuho*) twice, reportedly because his former helper, Arakawa Toyozu, a master of Shino pottery, had received the award before him.[14] In his meeting with Pablo Picasso, Rosanjin gave the artist a piece of his pottery presented in the traditional signed paulownia box. As Picasso admired the beauty of the container, Rosanjin reportedly scolded impatiently, "Not the box, not the box, you simple child! What I made is inside the box!"[15]

The epicurean's young life was tragic and impoverished. He was born Kitaōji Fusajirō to a family of priests at Kyoto's Kamigamo shrine, but after learning that the infant was the result of his wife's infidelities, the head priest committed suicide and the mother left Fusajirō with a series of foster families, including that of Fukuda Takeizō, an engraver of seals who loved gambling and good food. The boy began learning both Fukuda's trade and his culinary standards, beginning to cook at the age of six.[16] As he reported later, his childhood passion for food was "abnormally intense."[17]

In 1908, at age twenty-five, he arrived in Tokyo to study under artist and poet Okamoto Katei, father-in-law of writer Okamoto Kanoko and grandfather to Okamoto Tarō, the avant-garde artist known best for his iconic sculptures at Osaka's Expo 70. Kanoko's posthumously published short story "Shokuma," translated as "The Food Demon" by J. Keith Vincent, appears closely based on her friend Rosanjin, depicting an overbearing yet insecure young chef with appetites beyond his means, who was "always arrogant to others and tyrannical towards his own family. But when he was working with food he was innocent and childlike."[18] Lacking other foodstuffs, the protagonist prepares a four-course gourmet meal with a single daikon radish.

Rosanjin also served as the model for Kaibara Yūzan, the protagonist's gastronome father in the long-running gourmet manga *Oishinbo*.[19] Like Rosanjin, the Kaibara character established a private, gourmet dining club, and his explosive, intolerant temperament alienated many, but his epicurean sensibilities were unsurpassable. Kaibara, however, is drawn as an elegantly handsome man garbed traditionally in kimono, in contrast to the moon-faced Rosanjin, who favored Western fashion: cashmere coats, a gold-headed cane, and stylish round eyeglasses.

Rosanjin reunited with his mother around 1909 and they spent two years in colonial Korea, where he worked for the government's Printing Bureau. During his tenure in the colony, Rosanjin traveled through Manchuria and China, taking advantage of imperial Japanese privilege by studying and collecting antiquities, calligraphy, and, likely, recipes. Upon his return to Tokyo he found a patron in Nakai Seibei, a wealthy cotton merchant and bon vivant who allowed Rosanjin to indulge his tastes for good food and antiques and further instilled the notion of cuisine as art in the young man.

While best known as an artist, especially abroad, Rosanjin claimed that his ceramics were "mere garnishes to my epicurean pursuits."[20] One of his most famous aphorisms was "Tableware is the kimono of food" (*shokki wa ryōri no kimono*).[21] In fact, he initially produced tableware for his restaurant, discussed below, because he could not find or afford the types of antique tableware he believed would best highlight and harmonize with the dishes he served. Rosanjin is widely acclaimed as the first to raise modern Japanese cooking to an art that valued presentation, scenery, decor, and especially tableware as much as actual cooking technique.[22] Thus, he is the key figure for promoting visuality as a primary characteristic of national cuisine in modern Japan.

Rosanjin's experience as restaurateur earned him national fame and a reputation for an extravagant yet meticulous approach to food. The 1920s and 1930s, a time of ferment in Japanese cuisine, witnessed both the rapid spread of Chinese- and Western-inspired cuisine in urban centers and a new interest in epicureanism.[23] The first real arena for appreciating Rosanjin's cuisine was not a restaurant, but his antique arts shop, the Daigadō, operated with fellow connoisseur and business partner Nakamura Takeshirō. Daigadō acquired a reputation both for its expert collections of calligraphy, Buddhist art, and pottery, and for being a source of amusing conversations with like-minded connoisseurs.[24] As the aesthetes gathered, Rosanjin prepared simple, elegant fare for his guests, served on the shop's antique wares. Soon so many dropped by for lunch that he needed to begin collecting payments.[25] By 1921, he opened a members-only restaurant in the shop, dubbing it Bishoku Kurabu (Gourmet Club) in homage to the 1919 Tanizaki Jun'ichirō novella of the same name, a tale of gluttony featuring exoticized (and eroticized) Chinese cuisine (see the Suttmeier chapter in this volume). Members of Rosanjin's club were required to pay in advance for the year at a rate of two to three yen per month. Initially, members could simply drop in between 11:00 a.m. and 8:00 p.m., but the club became so popular that it was forced to institute a reservation system.[26] After the Great Kanto earthquake of 1923 destroyed the restaurant and shop, Rosanjin set up a temporary restaurant called Hana no Chaya in Shiba Park, garnering rave reviews and further building his following. At Hana no Chaya, he refined his ideals of perfection in cuisine, setting, and service.

Later that year, Rosanjin received the opportunity to take over the operation of Hoshigaoka saryō, an elite tea salon-cum-restaurant (ryōtei) frequented by the nobility, located on the grounds of Hie Shrine in the Akasaka area of Tokyo. Rosanjin's partner Nakamura would act as president, but Rosanjin would preside over matters of kitchen and table. The new restaurant was to meet his exacting standards in all things, "from the fixtures to the method of serving customers."[27] Refusing to use the specialized employment agencies that managed Tokyo's skilled chefs, Rosanjin instead placed advertisements and groomed his own staff from entry level, training them in traditional arts that complemented the ryōtei atmosphere, such as flower arrangement (ikebana) and tea ceremony, in addition to culinary and service skills.[28] In one advertisement for a cook Rosanjin demanded that qualified applicants "attend with scrupulous care to what is good and not good in all he eats, and use his daily meals as his lifetime training ground" to the extent that he "must have been labeled eccentric for the intensity of devotion to good food."[29] Qualifications further specified affinities for painting, sculpture, architecture, handicrafts, and other arts. As a test of skill, potential cooks were brought to his home in Kamakura, where they were given the head and bony parts of a fish, told to forage for vegetables, and ordered to prepare a dish with these ingredients using only a simple charcoal grill.[30]

Under Rosanjin, Hoshigaoka employed twenty waitresses and fourteen to fifteen cooks. The kitchen was organized by course, with one chef responsible for each section: appetizers, sashimi, simmered dishes, grilled dishes, fried dishes, sushi, and pickled items. Tofu and soba noodles were made freshly in-house. The kitchen used ten times the number of ingredients found in similar restaurants, and Rosanjin went to great lengths to obtain the best, procuring his vegetables from Kyoto (see the de St. Maurice chapter in this volume) and special varieties of duck and crab from Japan's far north. For sweetfish (ayu), he sent a truck to procure live specimens from the Katsura River in the Kansai region four hundred miles from Tokyo, with instructions to periodically pour fresh water into the large tanks so the fish would survive the journey. Rosanjin opined that a dish was 90 percent dependent on the freshness and quality of its ingredients and only 10 percent dependent on cooking technique.[31] He is celebrated as the first well-known restaurateur in Japan to put such emphasis on obtaining the finest ingredients at any cost or effort.[32]

Rosanjin was also known for surprising his guests, combining traditional elegant dishes with elements of home-style or Chinese cooking not seen in other *ryōtei* establishments. He also incorporated Japanese regional cuisines into his menus by apprenticing the sons of chefs from famous regional restaurants, who prepared celebrated local dishes.[33] He was said be the first to provide appetizers as a kaiseki course, a practice he probably adopted from Chinese restaurants, which, as noted, were gaining in quality and popularity during the Taisho period.[34] Hoshigaoka's starters were often artfully constructed from leftover bits, such as the leaves of daikon.[35] Rosanjin is also believed to be the first to serve kaiseki courses in sequence, one dish at a time, allowing for service at optimum temperature, rather than serving many or all at once, as exemplified in the bento box or New Year's traditional Osechi meal, which could contain only room temperature foods.[36]

The restaurant soon gained national fame; members of the imperial family, influential politicians, and titans of business became regulars.[37] Seating expanded from ten to eighty guests.[38] In 1935, Rosanjin established a journal called *Hoshigaoka*, which further contributed to the restaurant's reputation, and in 1936 he opened a second branch in Osaka.[39] Because of his fame and his restaurant's reputation, Rosanjin dared to challenge the norms of Japan's elite restaurant culture. *Ryōtei* that catered to the wealthy and powerful tended to focus on elaborate presentation and provided entertainment by singing and dancing geisha, whom Rosanjin prohibited. Furthermore, waitresses were not allowed to pour alcohol for guests, so geisha had to be specially hired separately if diners desired this customary service. Tipping was forbidden, in contrast with the practices of many cafes and restaurants, where it constituted the majority of waitresses' income. When a former prime minister asked to stay beyond the normal closing time of 9:00 p.m., Rosanjin politely refused.[40] He also refused a request for bread from an American guest of a distinguished Japanese baron, sending the table a note suggesting the American return to the Imperial Hotel, where he belonged and where bread was served.[41]

Tableware was a central element of Rosanjin's sense of culinary identity. He believed his food should be plated on ceramics of the highest quality and favored Chinese antiques but could not acquire enough of what he considered suitable, so he personally made or designed all of Hoshigaoka's table and serving ware. His designs drew upon the ceramics in his collection, which he referred to as his mentors, and pieces illustrated in antiques catalogs. His intention to reproduce the finest ceramic wares required Rosanjin to appropriate styles from different regions of Japan, making his own versions of Bizen (unglazed, wood-fired), Oribe (green and copper glaze with bold designs), and other famous styles of regional pottery. Other craftsmen usually made the basic pieces, with Rosanjin adding drawings, overglazes, or other finishing flourishes. His approach was the very antithesis of traditional Japanese craft, in which masters typically spent entire careers perfecting one style, associated with a particular region. His friend, the Japanese-American sculptor Isamu Noguchi, said, "He is a dilettante, though a superb one. His success is predicated entirely on a dream of Old Japan."[42] Noguchi's comment points out a paradox—Rosanjin became an ultimate arbiter of Japaneseness in culinary culture only by violating the norms of Japanese traditions in art and cuisine.[43]

Rosanjin paid close attention to the arrangement of food, carefully harmonizing fare with appropriate tableware. Indeed, ceramics scholar Yoshida Kōzō claims that the "charm" of Rosanjin's pieces is "particularly evident when they are in actual use."[44] He advised putting plainer-looking foods, like dried fish or sardines, on red dishes or on plates with colorful designs and placing more visually arresting foods like large red prawns or bright vegetables on dishes with a more rustic (*wabi*) character like Shigaraki or Bizen wares. Rosanjin's plating philosophies were intuitive, but have been confirmed by recent research findings that demonstrate that the shape and color of a plate can alter the consumers' perception of the taste of the food.[45] His manner of arranging food appeared artless and casual, but, as attested to by his disciples, it was calculated and painstakingly composed to look entirely natural.[46]

Hoshigaoka's scenic location and decor were also key aspects of its dining experience. Situated on a hill surrounded by woods, it offered guests a simultaneous experience of the scenic setting, sounds, tastes, and aromas of the season. Decor also evidenced Rosanjin's meticulous attention to detail, offering different dining room styles. The Japanese "country house" contained sixteenth-century pillars, an antique hearth, charred bamboo roof, Buddhist and Shinto altars, and antique farm implements. The "Western room" featured a fireplace with a fifteenth-century gothic mantelpiece and handmade chairs imported from England.[47]

In sum, at Hoshigaoka, Rosanjin offered "Japanese cuisine as a comprehensive artistic experience . . . (*sōgō geijutsu toshite no nihon ryōri*) serving seasonal

FIGURE 7.3 Example of the soup course in a kaiseki meal at Umi no Hoshi restaurant in Naoshima. Photograph by the author.

meals with the spirit of the tea ceremony." This has become the de facto understanding of kaiseki. Rosanjin's culinary philosophy, embodied at the restaurant, reflected two primary maxims: the importance of fresh, natural flavor and the need for aesthetically pleasing presentation. Neither of these themes was original within Japanese food culture. Thus, Rosanjin did not represent a qualitative difference in his approach to Japanese cuisine, but rather a difference in degree of quality, an insistence on the finest ingredients prepared in the most fitting manner. Fresh, natural flavors and beautiful presentation were the essential secrets of Rosanjin's success, but to execute to his specification required extensive knowledge of each ingredient. Grated white daikon radish (*daikon oroshi*), for example, an accompaniment to many Japanese dishes, was no simple matter. One had to understand how the flavor of the radish subtly changed with the seasons, sweeter in the winter but more bitter in the summer. To bring out the true taste of the radish, Rosanjin insisted that every part, including the skin and hairs, be used.[48] The daikon's flavor also changed quickly after grating, so it had to be prepared only directly before serving, using a soft grating technique on the finest apertures of a large grater. If done with too much strength or on the wrong size grater, it was unacceptable.[49]

FIGURE 7.4 Example of a Rosanjin-style plating for small dried fish.

Rosanjin's Culinary Nationalism

Rosanjin's high standards for Japanese cuisine were mirrored by his disdain for the cuisine of other countries. His culinary values were part of a larger, ongoing ideology of exceptionalism asserting Japan's cultural superiority over Euro-American industrialized nations. An oft-repeated story encapsulates his culinary arrogance. In a visit to Paris's renowned Tour d'Argent, famous for pressed duck, Rosanjin asked that his duck be served raw. He consumed it with wasabi and soy sauce that he had brought along himself to use as condiments. His Japanese disciples were simultaneously delighted at Rosanjin's gutsiness and mortified by the breach of etiquette.[50]

The trip to Paris was part of a 1954 exhibition tour of the United States and Europe arranged around an invitation by the Rockefeller Foundation to exhibit his ceramics at the Museum of Modern Art in New York. Before embarking he laid out his intentions to use his finely honed senses to "test the value of European cuisine," which he believed was overrated because of preconceived ideas about Western superiority. Rosanjin expressed low expectations for Western cuisines, predicting that available ingredients, including seafoods, meats, and vegetables, would taste bad (*mazui*) and that presentation would be unappealing: "Even if your mouth becomes accustomed (to the taste), your eyes will complain. I cannot even hope for the type of beautiful cuisine that gladdens the spirit."[51] He dismissed American cuisine altogether; it was "not even necessary to try."

In contrast with other nations, Japan, he claimed, was "blessed with food," "brimming with delicacies from mountain and ocean, filled with the riches of innumerable ingredients" like dozens of varieties of clams.[52] He acknowledged that European civilizations had been diligent in devising cooking methods, but claimed Japanese cuisine required no such techniques to delight the senses. In short, cuisine was an area in which Rosanjin believed Japan could claim clear superiority over the West, a surprising view given Japan's food situation over the previous decade, with wartime rationing, occupation-era starvation, and the rapid rise in consumption of foods considered Western, such as bread, dairy, and meat. He was not the first to claim that such imports were inferior to traditional Japanese cuisine. Georges Ohsawa, the "inventor" of macrobiotics, based his dietary philosophies on the works of Meiji-era military doctors Mori Ōgai and Ishizuka Sagen, who advocated a return to traditional eating patterns, centered on brown rice, other whole grains, native sea vegetables, and beans, to achieve optimal health.[53]

For Rosanjin, however, Japan's culinary preeminence was especially clear in terms of aesthetics, rather than health. "The beauty of tableware, the design of food arrangement, the beauty of the dining room are without comparison in the world. Europe and America cannot possibly deny this."[54]

During his 1954 journey Rosanjin reported his food experiences in letters to his assistant Kojima Masahirō. Despite his wholesale rejection of American cuisine, he was surprisingly pleased with his first meal during a layover in Honolulu—frog legs fried in olive oil.[55] Moving on to the mainland, the reviews were mixed. In San Francisco, he dined at The Grotto on Fisherman's Wharf and admitted that the prawns and salad were "better than I imagined." The tableware and manner of arranging food, however, were dreadful.

> Even first-class restaurants use boring tableware and pay no attention to the arrangement of food. They're fine with plopping it onto a dish straight from a pot or frying pan. I was completely surprised at the insensitivity to a sense of eye appeal.... Americans have no vision beyond ensuring that the restaurant looks nice and that everything appears hygienic.[56]

A cafeteria in New York robbed him even of this impression of hygiene. He found the arrays of meats and salads lacked "vitality and freshness"; overall, the luncheonette emitted "an unsanitary feeling" that ridded him of all desire to eat.[57] When taken to Miyako, a Manhattan Japanese restaurant, Rosanjin was appalled by the careless preparation of the beef sukiyaki, equating the dish with *chanko nabe*, the jumbled stew eaten by sumo wrestlers. Learning that the owner and cook was a country yokel who had never even visited either Tokyo or Kyoto, Rosanjin decided to instruct him on the correct preparation of this dish, one of the Japan's most famous abroad as it was among the first to suit foreign palates, in order to better represent national culinary honor.

During brief trips around Europe, Finnish shrimp and Danish beer met with Rosanjin's approval, but he was generally dissatisfied with both food and service, upbraiding a waitress in Venice for opening his beloved beer between her thighs.[58] He saved his sharpest criticisms, however, for the French, whom he found "full of self-praise and a sense of their own prestige" in the culinary world. Upon returning to Japan he declared, "We have little to learn from French cuisine," which he deemed "absurdly infantile" and "mere child's play."[59] Rosanjin argued that ambiguity in the sense of taste, both subjective and highly differentiated among individuals, was responsible for the "appeal and glamour" of French cuisine and its "excessively glorified international reputation." Those with the finest palates, like himself, could harshly scrutinize French food, while those who weren't particularly picky would simply accept the ingrained idea of French culinary supremacy.

His primary critiques lay in his two familiar themes, ingredients and tableware. French proteins and produce were judged of poor quality, which was why their chefs often used "questionable contrivances" to disguise low-quality provisions, covering bitter or bad flavors with heavy sauces or olive oil. Rosanjin claimed that such culinary trickery represented the essence of French culinary identity. Furthermore, he was astounded that Paris so lacked pure, high-quality water, essential to good cuisine, that Parisians actually drank bottled water! The complexity and unwholesomeness of French cooking contrasted with his ideological conception of Japanese cuisine as elegantly pure, simple, and sincere. In Rosanjin's view, in addition to utilizing poor ingredients, French cuisine also suffered from unappealing presentations that lacked aesthetic connections between a dish and the food it held. He found the French table "a truly lonely sight" where "the beauty of cuisine that delights the eye is absolutely missing."[60]

Rosanjin deeply lamented his countrymen's tendency to blindly accept French cuisine as the best in the world, berating Japanese Francophiles, from inexperienced young cooks studying in Paris to ambassadorial elites, who "recklessly and exaggeratedly proselytize French cuisine . . . without first understanding Japanese cuisine." He exhorted them to appreciate the true values of their own cuisine, complaining that the Japanese could now expertly cook steaks and Western soups, but no longer knew how to boil tofu properly or make a good miso soup.[61] Condemning French cuisine while elevating his own nation's culinary identity, Rosanjin asserted that it was Japan and not France that deserved to occupy the top rank in the hierarchy of world food cultures. His flamboyant rejection of French cuisine turned the tables on the French, emulating their own culinary snobbery and performing the role they had originated of "epicurean extraordinaire."

Conclusion

Rosanjin's travels abroad occurred in the immediate postoccupation era, when the Japanese government, media, and other institutions attempted to lead the public in redefining Japan as a "country of culture" (*bunka kokka*) following its devastating defeat as an imperialist and militarist power. Its emerging identity as the junior partner in a Cold War alliance with the United States cast the nation as feminized and traditional in contrast with masculine, industrial, and military character of America. Rosanjin's conception of washoku, emphasizing beauty and pristine freshness, diverged from the everyday eating habits of most of his countrymen, but resonated with emerging stereotypes of the Japanese, held both domestically and internationally, as a nation both highly aestheticized and "close to nature." Koji Taihō described his friend Rosanjin as someone who was "proud of being Japanese and loved Japanese culture when, after defeat, Japanese culture was questioned and challenged."[62] His desire to reassert national pride and Japanese cultural superiority was expressed in the idiom of food, and, from the start of his travels, the purpose of testing other cuisines was not driven by curiosity or desire to experience the Other, but rather was an exercise to prove Japan's culinary superiority and his own powers of discernment.

From the 1950s to the 1970s, Americans came to know and appreciate Rosanjin's art, but paid little heed to his gastronomy, probably because "authentic" Japanese cuisine included raw fish and fermented foodstuffs, considered inedible by most Americans at that time. It was not until the 1980s and 1990s, thirty years after his death, with Japan's economic bubble and the simultaneous advent of its "gourmet boom," that Rosanjin's wish for his nation to embrace its dietary supremacy would materialize. As affluence was accompanied by a surge of neonationalism, the elevation of Japanese gourmet consciousness included not only the proliferation of French and Italian restaurants and increased imports of expensive delicacies like foie gras, but celebration of traditional cuisine. TV audiences came to know Rosanjin through the popular *Iron Chef* series (1992–1999), which featured Hirano Masaaki, introduced as "a scholar of Rosanjin," among a roster of movie stars, politicians, and cooking instructors who regularly acted as judges, and through televised documentaries of his life on multiple channels.[63]

At that moment in time, Rosanjin's extravagant, elitist demands for the freshest and finest ingredients and for meticulous aesthetic presentation were perfectly supported in an economic environment of consumerist luxury and an ideological environment of rising cultural nationalism. The simultaneous treasure (*otakara*) boom, with Japanese rushing to buy valuable objects, including ceramic tableware, also renewed interest in Rosanjin's work.[64] An outpouring of media on culinary connoisseurship, including *Iron Chef*, Itami Jūzō's film *Tampopo* (1985), and the emergence of popular gourmet manga comics such as *Oishinbo*, further disseminated Rosanjin's ideals to the general public, empowering and inspiring a nation of would-be gourmets. In turn, growing global acclaim for Japanese cuisine, especially sushi, beginning in the late 1980s, fed Japanese culinary nationalism.

In the twenty-first century, the globally interconnected world of food media—dedicated food TV channels, glossy magazines, blogs, and other social media—have raised the visual aspects of cuisine, rather than its gustatory or aromatic qualities, to unprecedented importance. Washoku's superior visual appeal, extolled by Rosanjin, has helped it procure a multitude of Michelin stars, UNESCO recognition, and the devotion of celebrity chefs around the globe. Six decades after Rosanjin insisted that Japan led the world in the art of the plate, the world's culinary authorities and experts have finally come to agree.

NOTES

1. Paul Freeman, ed., *Food: The History of Taste* (Berkeley: University of California Press, 2007), 18.
2. Yi-Fu Tuan, "Pleasures of the Proximate Senses: Eating, Taste and Culture," in *Passing Strange and Wonderful: Aesthetics, Nature and Culture* (Washington, DC: Shearwater Books, 1993), reprinted in Carolyn Korsmeyer, ed., *The Taste Culture Reader* (New York: Bloomsbury, 2005), 227–230. The sauces are béchamel, velouté, espagnole, hollandaise, and tomato.
3. See Katarzyna J. Cwiertka, *Modern Japanese Cuisine: Food, Power and National Identity* (London: Reaktion, 2007).
4. See Eric C. Rath, *Food and Fantasy in Early Modern Japan* (Berkeley: University of California Press, 2010).
5. Cwiertka, *Modern Japanese Cuisine*, 104–108.
6. The exhibition's official English title was Kitaoji Rosanjin, a Revolutionary in the Art of Japanese Cuisine.

7. Kitaōji Rosanjin, *Rosanjin no ryōri ōkoku*, ed. Kitaōji Kazuko and Shirashu Reiko (Tokyo: Bunka Shuppansha, 1980), 25.

8. Tsūji Shizuo, *Japanese Cooking: A Simple Art*, 25th anniversary ed. (New York: Kodansha, 2012). Originally published as *Japanese Cookery: A Simple Art* (Tokyo: Kodansha, 1980).

9. Tsūji, *Japanese Cooking*, 17.

10. Tsūji, *Japanese Cooking*, 26.

11. Atsuko Ichijo and Ronald Ranta, *Food, National Identity and Nationalism: From Everyday to Global Politics* (New York: Palgrave Macmillan, 2016), 2–3.

12. See Arjun Appadurai, "How to Make a National Cuisine: Cookbooks in Contemporary India," *Comparative Studies in Society and History* 30.1 (1988): 3–24; Jeffrey M. Pilcher, *Que Vivan los Tamales! Food and the Making of Mexican Identity* (Albuquerque: University of New Mexico Press, 1998); Priscilla Parkhurst Ferguson, *Accounting for Taste: The Triumph of French Cuisine* (Chicago: University of Chicago Press, 2004); Lara Anderson, *Cooking up the Nation: Spanish Culinary Texts and Culinary Nationalization in the Late 19th and Early 20th Centuries* (Suffolk, UK: Boydell & Brewer, 2014); Thomas Parker, *Tasting French Terroir: The History of an Idea* (Berkeley: University of California Press, 2015).

13. Shirasaki Hideo, *Kitaōji Rosanjin* (Tokyo: Bungei Shunju, 1971), 205.

14. Shirasaki, *Kitaōji Rosanjin*, 314–315.

15. Sidney Cardoza, *The Art of Rosanjin* (Tokyo: Kodansha, 1987), 10.

16. Shirasaki, *Kitaōji Rosanjin*, 37.

17. Kitaōji, *Rosanjin no ryōri ōkoku*, 132.

18. Okamoto Kanoko, *A Riot of Goldfish*, trans. J. Keith Vincent (London: Hesperus Worldwide, 2010),70.

19. Lorie Brau, "Oishinbo's Adventures in Eating: Food, Communication, and Culture in Japanese Comics," *Gastronomica* 4.4 (Fall 2004): 34–45.

20. Sidney Cardoza, *Rosanjin: 20th Century Master Potter of Japan* (New York: Japan Society, 1972), 17.

21. It is likely that Rosanjin did not coin this phrase but borrowed it from an unidentified Edo-period writer.

22. Masuda Akifumi, "Botsu go 50 nen: Bi to shoku no kyojin, Kitaōji Rosanjin ga nokoshita mono," *Shūkan shinchō* 54.3 (2009): 130–133.

23. George Solt, *The Untold History of Ramen: How Political Crisis in Japan Spawned a Global Food Craze* (Berkeley: University of California Press, 2014), 25–28.

24. Kuroda Kusaomi, *Bishoku Tensai Rosanjin Art Box* (Tokyo: Kodansha, 200), 56–57.

25. "Zadankai," *Taiyō* 41 (Spring 1983): 39–47.

26. "Zadankai," 42.

27. Kuroda, *Bishoku Tensai Rosanjin Art Box*, 78.

28. "Zadankai," 39–47.

29. Sidney Cardoza, *Uncommon Clay* (Tokyo: Kodansha, 1998), 101–102.

30. "Zadankai," 39–46; also see "Rosanjin's Views on Cookery," accessed July 14, 2015, http://www.tsuji.ac.jp/hp/jpn/jp_e/kanazawa/5.htm.

31. Kitaōji, *Rosanjin no ryōri ōkoku*, 35.
32. Shirasaki, *Kitaōji Rosanjin*, 121–123. Unfortunately, Hoshigaoka's owners did appreciate Rosanjin's extravagant expenditures and he was eventually dismissed. He would never again act as a professional restaurateur.
33. Hirano Masaaki, "Rosanjin midō: Hoshigaoka saryō," *Taiyō* 41 (Spring 1983): 7–10.
34. Harada Nobuo, *Washoku to Nihon Bunka* (Tokyo: Shogakkan 2005), 190–200.
35. Shirasaki, *Kitaōji Rosanjin*, 123.
36. Masuda, "Botsu go 50 nen," 132.
37. Shirasaki, *Kitaōji Rosanjin*, 143.
38. "Zadankai," 39–46.
39. Shirasaki, *Kitaōji Rosanjin*, 188.
40. "Zadankai," 39–46.
41. Cardoza, *Rosanjin: 20th Century Master*, 9.
42. Cardoza, *The Art of Rosanjin*.
43. An anonymous reviewer of this chapter notes that Mitsuhiro Yoshimoto has made similar observations on the career of filmmaker Akira Kurosawa. See Mitsuhiro Yoshimoto, *Kurosawa: Film Studies and Japanese Cinema* (Durham, NC: Duke University Press, 2000).
44. *Shinkenchiku*, February 1964.
45. Nicola Twilley, "Accounting for Taste: How Packaging Can Make Food More Flavorful," *New Yorker*, November 2, 2015, 50–55.
46. Tsūji Yoshikazu, *Rosanjin: Utsuwa to Ryōri* (Tokyo: Ribun shuppan, 1999), 91–93.
47. Kuroda, *Bishoku Tensai Rosanjin Art Box*, 80–82.
48. Masuda, "Botsu go 50 nen," 130–133.
49. Tsūji, *Rosanjin*, 86.
50. Tsūji, *Rosanjin*, 102.
51. Kitaōji, *Rosanjin no ryōri ōkoku*, 263–265.
52. Kitaōji, *Rosanjin no ryōri ōkoku*, 263–265.
53. Nancy Stalker, "The Globalisation of Macrobiotics as Culinary Tourism and Culinary Nostalgia," *Asian Medicine* 5.1 (2009): 1–18.
54. Kitaōji, *Rosanjin no ryōri ōkoku*, 263–265.
55. Kitaōji, *Rosanjin no ryōri ōkoku*, 269–271.
56. Kitaōji, *Rosanjin no ryōri ōkoku*, 269–271.
57. Kitaōji, *Rosanjin no ryōri ōkoku*, 269–271.
58. Shirasaki, *Kitaōji Rosanjin*, 314–315.
59. Kitaōji Rosanjin, *Chosakushū* (Tokyo: Gogatsu Shoten, 1980), 237–240.
60. Kitaōji, *Chosakushū*, 237–240.
61. Kitaōji Rosanjin, "Bimi kyūshin," *Kaizō* 36.1 (1955): 193.
62. "Rosanjin to watashi," *Taiyō* 41 (Spring 1983): 122–126.
63. Hirano has produced eighteen books on Rosanjin, five on his art and the remainder on different aspects of his cooking, epicureanism, and general art of everyday living.
64. Masuda, "Botsu go 50 nen," 130–133.

Regional and International Variations

8

Savoring the Kyoto Brand

Greg de St. Maurice

Kyoto vegetables, Uji tea, Kyoto-style ramen . . . visitors to Kyoto encounter a veritable cornucopia of edible items proclaimed to be distinctly Kyoto-ish. Even outside the place itself, Kyoto whets appetites, with Kyoto-made ketchup on the shelves of an all-Kyoto store in Yokohama, a restaurant in Pittsburgh named Teppanyaki Kyoto, a section for Kyoto vegetables in an Okinawa grocery store, and an event in Nashville, Tennessee, featuring Kyoto kaiseki, the multicourse haute cuisine that is often used to represent the sophistication of Japanese cooking.

But which Kyoto do these things claim an affinity with? Multiple Kyotos exist, after all. There is Kyoto prefecture, the thirty-first largest of Japan's forty-seven prefectures at 2,866 square miles. There is also the prefectural capital, Kyoto City, which occupies 320 square miles of the prefecture and is home to 1.5 million of the prefecture's 2.6 million residents.[1] Much of the time, however, the Kyoto being channeled is the more diffuse, nebulous trope of the seemingly timeless ancient imperial capital. Kyoto City was founded as Heian-kyō in 794 by Emperor Kanmu. Its cityscape, full of temples and shrines that were spared the devastation that other Japanese cities experienced in World War II, draws tourists in increasing numbers. Within Japan, Kyoto stands for history and tradition, and is referred to as *nihon no kokoro no furusato*, the hometown of the Japanese heart/mind.[2] It is said that if Japan were a human, Tokyo would be the head, Osaka the stomach, and Kyoto the heart. This "Kyoto brand" extends to food culture and food products and is the focus of this chapter.

In Japan people frequently refer to places and their brands, Kyoto being one example of this. Consumer surveys conducted by Nikkei Research and Brand Management Institute indicate that Kyoto

City has become Japan's most appealing local brand and Kyoto prefecture the second strongest prefectural place brand in recent years. Seven of the top ten spots on Nikkei's list of edible products that evoke Japan's best qualities are occupied by items from Kyoto: Kyoto cuisine; Kyoto's *yatsuhashi*, a type of sweet; Kyoto sweets in general; Kyoto pickles; Kyoto vegetables; Kyoto miso; and Uji tea, from a town in Kyoto prefecture.[3] On top of this, more legally recognized geographical indications (such as Champagne or Yirgacheffe coffee) have been registered in Japan for Kyoto than any other prefecture, and the majority of these are edible products.[4]

Chef Ferran Adrià has commented, "It seems fitting that Kyoto should be the home of a cuisine, which, like the city itself, is born of an intimate communion between the work of man and the gifts of nature."[5] It is fitting, but should not be considered inevitable, that Kyoto developed such a tantalizing place brand. Obstacles have stood in Kyoto's way: Kyoto's traditional cuisines developed in the context of prohibitions against eating domesticated animals and in a place where fresh seafood was difficult to obtain; other cities have eclipsed Kyoto's economic and political influence (most obviously Edo/Tokyo, the subject of Brau's chapter in this volume, but also neighboring Osaka); and Kyoto prefecture has less arable land than other prefectures. That it was the longtime imperial capital is not sufficient to guarantee the power of its gastronomic brand centuries later, though many people assume as much.

Grant McCracken argues that a brand is a "bundle of meanings" that add value.[6] Historically the term "brand" referred to nonphysical signifiers such as names or visual representations that a seller used to distinguish its goods or services from similar ones.[7] Today people also treat physical entities themselves as brands. Not only are companies like McDonald's, Chanel, and Sony now considered brands, but people, places, and even professions are too.

The term "place brand" refers to two different phenomena. This chapter focuses on the Kyoto brand, a place brand in the sense that it consists of a commonly understood "aura" or patterned associations linked to a particular place. An example of this would be the 2006 handbook compiled by Kyoto City's Chamber of Commerce and Industry that explains the value and "Kyotoishness" (*Kyotorashisa*) of elements of the "Kyoto brand," including Japanese Buddhism, the summer Gion Festival, proper posture, and formal hospitality. This type of place brand is not limited to cities or prefectures, but exists at scales that are much more micro and macro. There is much talk within and outside Japan of Japan's brand—"Cool Japan," for example, is a notion adopted and promoted by the Ministry of Economy, Trade and Industry. The successful campaign to register washoku as UNESCO intangible heritage (see the Bestor chapter in this volume) was motivated in part by a desire to bolster Japan's brand in the wake of the earthquake, tsunami, and nuclear power plant destabilization of 2011, as well as the social and economic suffering that followed (an indication of the belief that strong place brands can transform a society—not just its economy—for the best). At the opposite end of the scalar spectrum, there are many municipalities and neighborhoods within Kyoto that have distinctive place brands, as does the Kamigamo neighborhood, which is famous for its Kamo eggplant and *suguki* pickles.

This first sense of the term "place brand" also captures Kyoto's appeal as a destination for millions of tourists from all over the world. Condé Nast Traveler has described the city as "where everything we think of as Japanese—its court culture, its art, its artisanry, and, oh yes, much of its spectacular cuisine—was born or perfected."[8] Coverage of Kyoto in foreign media often begins by deploying the trope of the "ancient imperial city" and then explaining its contemporaneity: a headline for an article about Kyoto on the Travel + Leisure website reads, "Japan's ancient capital has one foot in the 4th century and the other firmly rooted in the 21st," while *Monocle* magazine declares that "Kyoto is not just a museum piece, it is truly a 21st century city."[9]

"Place brand" can also be used in a narrower sense, however, to refer to entities whose names for selling products or services incorporate the place of origin or provenance. The marketing and selling of products using a Kyoto brand far precedes the current system for geographical indications, with examples including documented evidence of *Kyōyaki* ceramic ware and *Kyōgashi* sweets for the tea ceremony as far back as the seventeenth century.[10] Today the Japan Patent Office uses a "regional collective trademarks" system to legally recognize geographical indications.[11] Uji tea, Misaki wakame (a type of seaweed harvested off the Misaki coast of Iwate prefecture's Miyako City), and Shobara City's Hiba beef (from Hiroshima prefecture) are regional collective trademarks. In the summer of 2015 another approach for recognizing geographical indications emerged: the "Japan Geographical Indication protection system" run by the Ministry of Agriculture, Forestry and Fisheries.[12] Some place brands are not registered under either program, whether because an application is rejected or because those who manage a brand wish to restrict and retain control over its use. An example of this latter type, the Kyō Brand is used by Kyoto prefecture to certify, market, and sell prefectural agricultural and fisheries products ranging from "traditional" vegetables to pears and shellfish.

Recent developments in the globalization of food and agriculture have facilitated the spread of Kyoto's cherished traditions, crops, and gastronomic knowledge far beyond its borders. Today residents of major cities can experience kaiseki cuisine, seed catalogs on multiple continents allow home gardeners to grow traditional Kyoto vegetables like Kamo eggplant and Shishigatani squash, and places and products far afield take their names after Kyoto. In this context, how has Japan's culinary capital continued to exert its culinary capital?

If Kyoto's mouth-watering appeal was not inevitable, neither is it merely a happy coincidence for stakeholders in Kyoto's local food industry. Farmers, chefs, bureaucrats, retailers, food scholars, and others invested in local food culture constantly work to emphasize the distinctiveness of Kyoto's agricultural and food products in relation to heritage, craftsmanship, and Kyoto as a physical location conducive to agricultural and culinary excellence. Their efforts to promote a particular understanding of what Kyoto is, what it means, and what it should taste like make the brand meaningful.

This chapter focuses on these three points—heritage, craftsmanship, and geographical particularities—to illustrate their critical role in defining the Kyoto brand. It is based on fieldwork conducted in Kyoto in 2006–2008 and 2012–2013. It draws on newspaper articles, brochures, and documents about Kyoto's various place brands for agricultural products; semistructured and informal interviews I carried out with farmers, chefs, local government officials, local entrepreneurs, and consumers; as well as participant observation at events celebrating Kyoto's agricultural and culinary traditions, including farmers markets and agricultural fairs. Another source of valuable data was the Japanese Society for Innovative Cuisine (Nihon ryōri raboratorii), a monthly gathering of chefs and researchers stimulating culinary experimentation and discussion inspired by a predetermined theme. The chefs participating in the "Labo," as it is affectionately called, are professionals keen on better understanding what Kyoto cuisine is and keeping its traditions relevant to contemporary society.

The Taste of Tradition and History

Kyotoites and others have actively promoted conceptions of Kyoto as a historical city maintaining tradition for centuries and continue to do so today. At times local actors' efforts have been so successful that they became invisible and taken for granted. This is the case with "traditional Kyoto vegetables" (*kyō no dentō yasai*). Fifty years ago "traditional Kyoto vegetables" as such did not exist. Farmers grew the forty vegetable varieties that are now referred to as "traditional Kyoto vegetables" in limited quantities, as standardized hybrid vegetable varieties that were hardier, easier to transport, and could be prepared relatively easily, had become the norm. At the time no organizing concept grouping Kyoto's heirloom varieties together and celebrating them as local heritage existed. Concerned that these varieties might disappear, local farmers, chefs, researchers, and officials created an official definition for the term "traditional Kyoto vegetable" in 1988.[13] They decided to limit the list to varieties that had been locally cultivated before the Meiji period (1868–1912), when the capital of Japan was officially moved from Kyoto to Tokyo.

Creating a category, however, accomplishes little if the category does not gain traction in public consciousness. From the creation of a brand for prefectural produce (the Kyō Brand) to community and media outreach, networks of local stakeholders acted to promote these vegetables and strengthen the local agricultural economy. Pamphlets, posters, and information posted on the Internet deploy Kyoto's history and tradition as they describe and market local produce using phrases such as "passed down through generations," "heritage," and "thousand-year-old history." Thus a poster for the Kyō Brand (figure 8.1) features an enlarged photograph of Kyoto vegetables over which a list of "past customers" appears: historical figures of national importance such as Heian-era poet Ono no Komachi and nineteenth-century politician Sakamoto Ryōma. The text invitingly ends with an ellipsis, implying that those who eat Kyoto vegetables today may join this elite list.

In Kyoto one finds many physical testaments to history and tradition, including museums, plaques, and other forms of commemoration and documentation. The city of Mukō, southwest of Kyoto City, has erected a bamboo museum near a wide expanse of shady bamboo fields cultivated by farmers. The museum displays ornate baskets, delicate fans, whisks for making matcha green tea, and objects made from bamboo. Panels describe the varieties, biological characteristics, and local history of bamboo. The museum also contains a large display case dedicated to Thomas Edison, who lit his first light bulb using filaments made from Kyoto prefecture-grown bamboo.

Far from being simply relegated to the past, Kyotoites see themselves as incorporating heritage and history in their daily lives. Food culture is deemed important as a part of cultural life throughout the calendar year and the seasons, not as something set apart. In the fall and spring, temples and shrines in Kyoto prefecture hold ceremonies for the presentation of green tea to the gods, the imperial family, and in commemoration of individuals like the priest Myōei who were integral to the development of Uji tea. Temples and shrines like Yoshida Shrine, which houses the god of cooking and the god of sweets, host ceremonies meant to ensure the prosperity of local dining and drinking establishments. Vegetable farmers present their best specimens to local shrines and temples for important events like the Gion Festival. In doing so, they maintain ties between local agriculture and traditional culture. Every year the Kyō-ryōri (Kyoto cuisine) Association organizes an exhibition on Kyoto

FIGURE 8.1 A poster for Kyō Brand vegetables. Photograph by the author.

cuisine, offering the public an opportunity to learn about cooking from well-regarded chefs and also taste representative dishes from restaurants that might otherwise be beyond the average person's budget.

Terumi Aiba and fellow researchers found that most Japanese people associate the idea of *Kyō ryōri* (Kyoto cuisine) with kaiseki cuisine, *cha kaiseki* (the ritual meal of the tea ceremony), and Japanese cuisine.[14] Their respondents, like those I interviewed, stated that *Kyō ryōri* represents Kyoto's traditional culture. Identifying Kyoto and its foods with the "traditional" has become automatic for many people. The efforts of Kyotoites to brand the city as the gastronomic capital of Japan based on associations with history and heritage have played no small part in this.

FIGURE 8.2 Nishiyama area bamboo shoot sashimi. Photograph by the author.

Kyotoites intentionally invoke heritage and tradition when they think it will be effective. A woman whose family farms bamboo shoots just outside of Kyoto City, for instance, told me that when she attends events in Tokyo to try to secure customers, she makes a point of looking the part of the Kyoto native by dressing in a kimono. When she exchanges business cards with a chef or someone who could become a regular customer, she may send a gift of one of her high-quality, freshly harvested shoots when spring arrives. This practice, too, is a traditional means of trying to initiate a business relationship and reinforces popular understandings of the Kyoto brand.

Relishing Craftsmanship

Kyoto's farmers, chefs, retailers, local officials, and consumers also link Kyoto to craftsmanship. They laud the small-scale nature of the agricultural economy as a premium that adds value to their products, making them artisanal foods rather than mere commodities. This is true of Kyō Brand packages of the leafy green mizuna bearing the farmer's name and tea that is marketed with images of grandmothers hand-picking leaves in the hills. Farmers, consumers, retailers, and local officials say that local produce has "a face you can see"—the farmer's face, that is.

One reason Kyoto's Nishiyama area has developed such a reputation for its bamboo shoots has to do with craftsmanship. There is nothing haphazard about their occupation. Unlike farmers in other parts of Japan, who "merely" harvest bamboo shoots that grow in their groves, Nishiyama area farmers cultivate "bamboo fields" (*take batake*), even engaging in "soil-making" (*tsuchidzukuri*). Bamboo shoots are called *takenoko*, literally "bamboo children," and farmers save specific shoots to be "parents" for future harvests. When these plants have grown, farmers mark them with the number of the year they appeared. The hoes farmers use to harvest shoots are themselves the products of craftsmanship, specially made for each individual farmer. It takes ten years, they say, for a bamboo shoot farmer to develop his abilities to "see" underground with his arms to harvest shoots whose shape and position are not visible to the naked eye and "make" soil that will facilitate a good harvest of shoots the following year, no matter the weather. This meticulous work results in a craft food: fresh, quality shoots they insist should be boiled without the usual rice bran and can even be eaten as sashimi (figure 8.3), dipped in soy sauce and wasabi, because of an absence of the acridity found in ordinary shoots.

Heirloom variety cultivation is viewed as a craft, and shrines and temples host local agricultural fair competitions covered by the local media. Agricultural researchers explain that they believe these fairs serve both to recognize farmers' hard work maintaining agricultural traditions and to preserve knowledge about the particular traits that make specific heirloom varieties distinct. Growing a *manganji* pepper that looks like the ideal specimen, for instance, is not easy because pepper varieties crossbreed easily and are sensitive to environmental conditions. Local agricultural fairs serve as opportunities to recognize farmers' efforts with awards that make the local news.

Agricultural fairs for green tea allow farmers from different towns to compete. And at the national level, prefectures compete. A place that wins prizes consistently soon develops a reputation that can become a strong place brand. In Kyoto, Uji City and the town of Kyōtanabe have especially strong brands, the former for matcha (powdered green tea) and the latter for gyokuro (shade-grown, umami-rich, premium tea). Harvesting tea for a competition is a community effort that is a financial loss for the farmer unless he wins one of the top prizes, even when his town provides assistance with picking and processing. And it is far from easy. Farmers must coordinate with local grandmothers who are adept at harvesting leaves by hand, picking the tender shoots and newest

FIGURE 8.3 Picking green tea for a competition. Photograph by the author.

leaves, a time-consuming task. They must do so at the peak time and be wary of rain, which significantly diminishes the quality of the leaves. Processing the leaves in small batches is also a tricky endeavor. One local official commented to me that the steaming process alone determines half of the tea's taste. The farmers that I helped harvest tea for a national competition picked seventy-five kilograms of tea and ended up with about seven kilograms of dried tea leaves to send on to competitions. Farmers call tea *kitsunegusa*, literally fox grass; given the unpredictability of weather, the vulnerability of tea plants, the need to get timing right, and changing market dynamics, a good tea farmer must be as clever as a fox. Farmers confessed that they participate in the agricultural fairs out of a sense of pride; they find satisfaction in doing what they do well and would appreciate official recognition. If and only if they win, the price for the remainder of their submission increases dramatically. Teas that make it to the agricultural fair can already be worth ten times more than the ones sold at the central wholesale market.

Craftsmanship was essential to the development of Kyoto cuisine, especially considering the existence of prohibitions on meat consumption and Kyoto City's location far from the coast, which meant little availability of fresh seafood. To overcome these limitations, cooks resorted to several strategies. The first thing informants inevitably told me was that local cuisine relied on

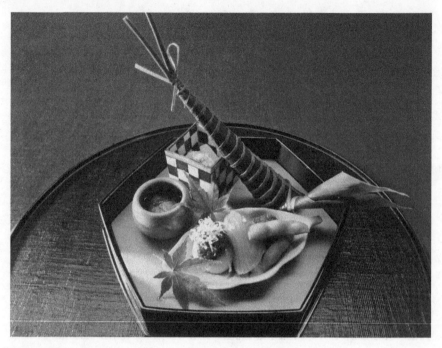

FIGURE 8.4 A Kyoto kaiseki course. Photograph by the author.

fresh, high-quality vegetables. Techniques were also developed to make the most of ingredients, particularly fish, that could be brought to the imperial capital and to make ingredients transported from great distances keep longer. For example, mackerel (*saba*) came from the Sea of Japan via the *saba kaidō*, or Mackerel Way, pickled in salt to better preserve it. Also much used in Kyoto cuisine is *hamo*, conger pike eel, with the Gion Festival even known as the *hamo* festival. Because it can live for up to twenty-four hours out of water, it could still be relatively fresh by the time it reached Kyoto and so did not require the use of preservation techniques. Rather than removing its many fine bones, Kyoto's chefs developed a way of cutting the bones into pieces (*hamo no hone giri*) that only sensitive eaters would notice. Then, of course, there is dashi or stock, said to be the backbone of Japanese cuisine. Traditionally, this is made with dried kelp (kombu) from Hokkaido and dried bonito (*katsuobushi*) from southern Japan.[15]

The craftsmanship aspect of the Kyoto brand is also evident in how food is used as a medium for materially expressing traditional culture. One chef explained that his restaurant serves a dish in which a grated daikon is dyed purple with peeled eggplant skins. This dish is meant to be appreciated at multiple levels: the grated daikon is a reference to the color of a Heian-era kimono that individuals especially well versed in Japanese history and culture are expected to identify. Customers may thus relish sensuous encounters with traditional culture in addition to delicious flavors and textures. For knowledgeable customers, restaurants will serve each course using special plates and bowls, each with its own history, perhaps made by a famous craftsman like Rosanjin (whose wares may be found in Kyoto restaurants like Kitchō and Hyōtei; see the Stalker chapter in this volume), some even with their own names. In this restaurant, I was served a classical kaiseki meal conceived of as an introduction to the cuisine, replete with basic cultural references like a bamboo-wrapped *chimaki* for Children's Day.

In today's Japan, the degree of craftsmanship that goes into a renowned restaurant's kaiseki cuisine will not be obvious to a first-time customer. Given that kaiseki can be exorbitantly expensive, it might seem that it is all about conspicuous consumption. Furthermore, Kyoto's gastronomic aesthetics dictate that a chef refrain from overly displaying his (and less frequently her) culinary prowess and ingenuity, instead using techniques that enhance the ingredients' best qualities. Kaiseki chefs, as I learned in the Japanese Society for Culinary Innovation (aka "Labo"), prize the elusive characteristic they call *hin'i*, a kind of restrained elegance that appears deceptively simple. Though these chefs

FIGURE 8.5 Agricultural fair judges smelling tea leaves in competition. Photograph by the author.

appreciate *B-kyū gurume* items like ramen, such foods have intense flavors rich in salt, fat, and sugar and possess little or no *hin'i*, unlike a strained dashi broth extracted from fine kombu kelp and bonito flakes. *Kyō ryōri* chefs may even pursue *hin'i* at the expense of deliciousness. At one Labo meeting, I was presented with two edamame (soy bean) pastes. The first consisted of beans that had been steamed, the second beans that had been boiled. The steamed paste had a creamier, fuller flavor, as though mayonnaise or butter had been folded in. I was told that though this first paste might be tastier, the second was better in terms of Kyoto cuisine because it possessed the subtle flavor of the beans, imbuing it with *hin'i*. This persistent pursuit of *hin'i* drives Kyoto chefs of all kinds to skim their dashi soup stocks, removing intensity of flavor, but refining it, making the taste subtler, more elusive. Chefs do not simply memorize what counts as refined, but rather consider their knowledge a practiced, embodied phenomenon. Takahashi Takuji of Kinobu restaurant explained to me that he refrains from eating a lot of red meat because even twenty-four hours after consuming it he finds his palate duller than usual, lacking the sensitivity critical to his occupation.

The link between a place and craftsmanship is weaker or less obvious than it once was, but it persists nonetheless. Specific places across the world are home to the perfume, fashion, and film industries, for instance, and certain cities have more culinary capital than others. The reasons for this likely include the efficiency that results from geographic proximity for collaborators and networks (even in the age of digital communication), the existence of definable communities of practice, regional cultural variation, and the existence of markets and local government policies that can support innovation and the preservation of heritage. Certainly, these factors have been important to Kyoto's edible brand. Even as globalization has diffused certain traditional resources across the globe and what has been called a "standard global diet" has emerged, tourism has helped Kyoto retain its culinary craftsmanship. This may seem ironic, as tourism is associated with the "inauthentic." Yet tourism can bolster a place's brand and create a market for items ascribed with various degrees of authenticity. Local nonprofit organizations and government institutions also maintain an internal focus, actively supporting culinary artisanship, a source of pride and identity for Kyotoites.

The current generation of Kyoto chefs realize that their craftsmanship cannot speak for itself it a globalized society; *Kyō ryōri* requires explanation. They consider themselves to be stores of expertise and information that are threatened with disappearance as Japanese consumption patterns change. Kyoto's chefs explain Kyoto's craftsmanship to customers, reporters, and even foreign anthropologists. They appear on international television, hold events for both local food experts and local residents, welcome media representatives to observe and film their activities, and regularly visit local schools to talk about their craft. Their professionalism and concern are apparent. Takahashi Eichi of Hyōtei restaurant explained that if television stations propose to send stars who elicit laughs to interview him, he declines. He accepts when they send reporters with a genuine interest in learning about Kyoto cuisine.

Kyoto is to Japan as savoring is to devouring. A leisurely meal in one of Kyoto's kaiseki restaurants, a dish with local bamboo shoots harvested that very morning, or a cup of Uji tea made by an expert blender: these present opportunities for slowly savoring Kyoto with all one's senses. The Kyoto brand for food and agricultural products is set in conceptual opposition to *B-kyū gurume* trends, though in fact the popular ramen chains Tenka Ippin and Kairikiya, which serve strongly flavored ramen, proudly proclaim their Kyoto roots, an example of the discrepancies that can exist between brand image or cultural ideal and actual reality.

The Taste of an Actual Place

Kyoto's geographical location and topography do not lend themselves to the natural emergence of a gastronomic power. Kyoto prefecture possesses less arable land than the average Japanese prefecture. Indeed, agriculture, fisheries, and food processing only contribute 0.4 percent to Kyoto's gross prefectural product.[16] As a case in point, contrary to what one might expect given the renown of Kyoto's Uji tea, Kyoto only produces about 4 percent of Japan's green tea.[17]

One would not look at this area and think it would become Japan's taste-making capital. Yet discursive expressions of Kyoto's location and geological particularities have contributed to its place brand. Farmers claim that the soil itself makes Kyoto's vegetables tasty. To what extent people believe this is difficult to gauge, but the power of this rationale is illustrated in a rumor I heard from multiple sources that someone stole soil from the fields of a farmer famous for his heirloom vegetables. When it comes to bamboo shoots, farmers and agricultural extension workers are more specific. The Nishiyama area's soil has a high clay content, which is said to give *takenoko* an ideal texture, coloring, and flavor. In the Nishiyama area, which has light-colored clay soil, farmers harvest bamboo shoots that sell at top prices due to their lemon yellow or yolk color.

Pamphlets and marketing materials also point to the quality of local water and a climate conducive to farming high-quality produce as reasons for the deliciousness of Kyoto vegetables, including bamboo shoots. Visitors to Kyoto cited these same attributes when I asked them what made Kyoto vegetables special. They frequently admitted that they could not explain the difference in taste, but stated that they nevertheless found Kyoto vegetables delicious.

Local tea industry experts attribute the quality of local tea to small fields in hilly areas that benefit from temperature variations. Alluvial soil is thought to be best suited for tea cultivation, which is why areas in the vicinity of the Uji River produce highly valued tea leaves.

The characteristics that differentiate teas from different places are harder to put into words than they are to discern. In tea tastings at agricultural fairs, I witnessed professionals putting their trained palates to work. Figure 8.6 shows judges for the Kyoto Prefectural Agricultural Fair for Tea smelling entries that have been steeped in boiling water. Here, the judges smell the leaves—not the liquid—and then rank them together, writing explanatory notes in chalk beside entries with less favorable rankings. I also participated in a training session for young men from a city near Uji who hoped to earn spots in the national tea-tasting competition. In the first round of the evening's competition they had to discriminate between the sensory qualities of four unidentified cups of tea passed around one by one and match them when passed around several times again in different order. The teas varied in quality and place of origin, but the tea deemed the most refined (and expensive) was a gyokuro from Kyoto prefecture that was selling for 25,000 yen a kilo. In other rounds, the young men had to tell teas apart based on the appearance and feel of dry leaves as well as the smell of steeped leaves. Even with the assistance of a novice participant's "cheat sheet," I failed at this competition, scoring far below the group's regular members, who had been training for some time. Their teacher, Morita Haruhide, a kind and dynamic tea blender who has taken first place three times in the national competition and has a virtually infallible palate, did not make any mistakes. That evening brought home to me the lesson that to discern the taste of a place requires not only an understanding of what it is, but also actual experiences tasting it. One individual's sensory experience consuming a Kyoto gyokuro—or a *junmai daiginjo* sake or a bowl of Edo soba (see the chapters by Stegewerns and Brau in the volume)—will never correspond exactly to another's. Yet it is clear that within the capacities and limitations of language a common vocabulary can be agreed upon to convey a nuanced understanding of sensory experiences that vary from one product to another. One can learn to taste the particular attributes that have led to the development of certain place brands.

Besides geological and climatic factors, chefs, researchers, and locals more generally stress the impact that geography has had on the taste of Kyoto. When

FIGURE 8.6 A poster for Kyoto meat. Photograph by the author.

asked why Kyoto's cuisine is characterized by a "light" taste, chefs often respond that Kyoto City is far from the ocean and traditional prohibitions on eating meat encouraged the development of a cuisine around high-quality, fresh vegetables. That Kyoto was the imperial capital, in a relatively central location, played a role as well. Its cultural, political, and economic influence meant that the city's residents had access to resources brought from great distances. To make the key ingredient, dashi requires bringing together *katsuobushi* from southwestern Japan and kombu from Hokkaido in Kyoto's soft water.

More recently, the social effects of geographic and political maps have played an important role in the discourse on food safety in relation to the meltdown and radiation leaks that occurred at the Fukushima Daiichi Nuclear

Power Plant in 2011. In the context of social anxiety about what is safe to eat (see the Kleeman chapter in this volume) and how individuals—particularly mothers—can be savvy consumers and caregivers, place of origin has become an index for food safety for Japanese consumers.[18] Many consumers I talked to throughout Japan indicated that they will only trust food that is grown in western and southern Japan, with Kyoto's brand ideally positioned because of Kyoto prefecture's distance from northeastern Japan. In one Kyoto restaurant that aims to serve food with as close to zero becquerels of radiation as possible, I heard that quite a few families had moved to Kyoto from northeastern Japan to make it easier for the parents to ensure that their children ate food they deem safe.

In my research, I discovered a less obvious reason why Kyoto's location matters to its brand: discriminating customers. Chefs told me that neighborhood customers—unbowed by the celebrity of these chefs—make it clear when they think something does not seem authentic and complain when they are disappointed. Kyotoites are capable of determining what is deemed authentic because they are socialized to do so. An informant explained that many people from outside confuse the approach of Kyoto's chefs, who try to bring out the best qualities of each ingredient, with a necessarily "light" or bland taste. Some restaurants even make this mistake. When we visited a well-established kaiseki restaurant that increased the saltiness of its food to adjust to a sultry summer in which guests—and their palates—would require more sodium than normal, this informant expressed her approval. Stereotypes about Kyotoites may not be entirely positive, but the reputation that people from Kyoto have developed for their pride in maintaining tradition has certainly contributed to Kyoto's brand power.

Conclusion

The popularity of Kyoto's edible products was never preordained. This success is the result of continuous efforts on the part of actors in the local food and agricultural industry to articulate what Kyoto is, means, and tastes like. History and tradition, craftsmanship, and the influence of Kyoto as an actual place are three elements that are emphasized repeatedly in the discourse on Kyoto's gastronomic distinctiveness.

As Nancy Stalker discusses in the introduction to this volume, however, branding and representation are one thing, historical facts and experienced realities another. Place brands and places as symbols always exist at some distance from the multifaceted, intricate places people inhabit and visit. Any place would leave ten different people with at least ten different impressions, refracted by such factors as class, ethnicity, and gender, as well as individual experiences. It can also be difficult to maintain brand power and messaging, as is clear when a celebrity, politician, or corporation experiences a sudden branding crisis.

What is striking about Kyoto's edible brand is that it has been articulated so consistently that it is taken for granted and yet is flexible, deployed even for products such as pork, candy, and coffee. National brand Suntory has promoted its high-end beer The Premium Malts with posters proclaiming—in the Kyoto dialect spoken by geisha—the deliciousness of its place of origin, its Kyoto brewery. Kyoto ramen, Kyoto waffles, Kyoto grilled-beef bento boxes—the adherence of these foods to tradition and the impact of Kyoto's location and geography on them may be minimal, but their use of the Kyoto name and iconography—geisha, temples, rock gardens, and the like—draws from historical efforts to market Kyoto and its products. As Takeshi Watanabe so aptly observes, contemporary Japanese eaters would likely find the food of the Heian period—that most associated with Kyoto in the popular imagination—strange and unsatisfying, in stark contrast with romanticized notions of the "ancient imperial capital." Yet predictably, even a poster for Kyoto meat (figure 8.6) co-opts these tropes, portraying not the product advertised but a geisha and the caption "The taste of tradition and culture: Kyoto meat."

Such flexibility may increase the distance between the brand and the experience. We can savor the Kyoto brand because people from Kyoto have developed a convincing understanding of what Kyoto is, means, and tastes like. This brand largely resonates with what visitors and consumers experience. But if the brand becomes diluted and confusing, the gap increases between what people anticipate and what they get, ultimately creating a brand crisis that makes it hard to savor Kyoto.

Thus far this threat has been mitigated because people in Kyoto—including those outside the local food industry—are committed to maintaining long-standing associations with history and tradition, craftsmanship, and idiosyncrasies rooted in actual places. Kyoto's consumers informally discriminate between the authentic and the inauthentic even as these categories change. Local residents of all kinds, in other words, determine to a great degree the continued existence of a meaningful—and mouth-watering—Kyoto brand.

NOTES

1. Kyoto Prefecture Department of Policy Planning, "Heisei 28 nen 7 gatsu 1 nichi genzai no shikuchōson betsu suikei jinkō," 2016.

2. See Christoph Brumann, "Outside the Glass Case," *American Ethnologist* 36.2 (2009): 276–299.

3. Nikkei Research, *Chiiki Burando Senryaku Sa-bei 2013: Chōsa Kekka no Gaiyō*, (Tokyo: Nikkei Research, 2013).

4. The system is for "regionally-based collective trademarks" and as of September 2013, Kyoto had 60 of Japan's 551 registered geographic indications.

5. Ferran Adrià, foreword to *Kaiseki: The Exquisite Cuisine of Kyoto's Kikunoi Restaurant*, by Yoshihiro Murata (New York: Kodansha, 2006), 6–7.

6. Grant McCracken, "The Value of the Brand," in *Brand Equity and Advertising: Advertising's Role in Building Strong Brands* (Hillsdale, NJ: Lawrence Erlbaum Associates, 1993).

7. Sonya Hanna and Jennifer Rowley, "An Analysis of Terminology Use in Place Branding," *Place Branding and Public Diplomacy* 4.1 (2008): 61–75.

8. Hanya Yanagihara, "Beauty and the Feast," *Condé Nast Traveler* 7.47 (2012): 109–112.

9. Jaime Gross, "T + L's Guide to Kyoto, Japan," 2009; Monocle, "Quality of Life Survey 2014," 2014.

10. Eric Rath, "New Meanings for Old Vegetables in Kyoto," *Food, Culture and Society* 17.2 (2014): 204.

11. Japan's system for regional collective trademarks (*chiiki dantai shōhyō*) was established by the 2005 amendment to Japan's Trademark Law. Over six hundred items have been designated as regional collective trademarks.

12. As of summer 2016 the new GI system had approved fourteen applications.

13. Rath, "New Meanings."

14. Terumi Aiba et al., "Modern Kyo-ryori (traditional Japanese dishes of Kyoto) through Image Analysis," *Journal of Cookery Science of Japan* 37.2 (2004): 189–197.

15. Alternatives to bonito include dried sardines, bluefin tuna, or, for vegetarian temple cooking, shiitake mushrooms.

16. Kyoto Prefecture Department of Policy Planning, Statistics Division, "Heisei 25 nendo fumin keizai keisan no suishin kekka ni tsuite," 2016.

17. Kyoto Prefecture Department of Agriculture, Forestry and Fisheries, Agricultural Products Division, "Heisei 27 nendo cha seisan jisseki no fuken betsu jun'i," 2015.

18. Nicolas Sternsdorff-Cisterna, "Food after Fukushima: Risk and Scientific Citizenship in Japan," *American Anthropologist* 117 (2015): 455–467.

9

Love! Spam

Food, Military, and Empire in Post–World War II Okinawa

Mire Koikari

In Okinawa, luncheon meat, or what locals call *pōku* (pork), has an extraordinarily visible presence. At a local restaurant, a bowl of Okinawan soba comes with at least one, and more often two, thick slices of pork. At grocery stores across the isles, various brands of luncheon meat—Hormel, Tulip, Midland, and so on—fill the shelves, competing with each other in taste and price (see figure 9.1). *Love! Spam*, a cookbook published by Okinawa Hormel, lists one hundred recipes featuring luncheon meat, including S curry, Spam taco rice, and Spam piccata.[1] A must-have ingredient in local storytelling, luncheon meat has also become an important narrative device with which Okinawans tell their stories of war, American occupation, and reversion to Japan, and express their longing for home cooking, which of course involves luncheon meat. Introduced as part of US military ration food at the end of World War II, luncheon meat has taken root in Okinawa, becoming a culinary-cultural icon of exceptional power and versatility.

This chapter explores how luncheon meat has created a vibrant narrative space in which Okinawans articulate their sense of self, culture, and history, past and present. Within the context of Japan, Okinawans' love for pork seems exceptional and even mind-boggling. In contrast to islanders' insatiable appetite for luncheon meat, those in the mainland express only mild curiosity and mostly indifference toward this gelatinous substance. Highlighting a difference between *uchinanchū* (Okinawans) and *yamatonchū* (mainland Japanese), luncheon meat could easily become a sign of Okinawa's regional

FIGURE 9.1 Display of canned luncheon meats at a supermarket. Photograph sby the author.

variation or, worse, a sign of its cultural-ethnic oddity, where a long-standing notion of racial-colonial hierarchy between Japanese and Okinawans, center and periphery, and the self and the other would be subtly invoked.[2]

Set within a larger transnational context, however, the material and symbolic prevalence of luncheon meat in Okinawa will instantly become recognizable as part of cross-border movements of meat, meal, and military in the twentieth century. The story of the canned pork meat carried by "militarized currents" across the Pacific is familiar.[3] In Hawaii, Guam, Korea, Okinawa, and the Philippines, the arrival of American soldiers was accompanied by an influx of military ration food, including luncheon meat whose taste and abundance symbolized the victor's power. Awestruck by American military prowess, local populations welcomed luncheon meat and other foreign items that poured into their communities, embracing the American way of life and altering their indigenous food and foodways forever.[4] As scholars of gender and empire point out, such dynamics could be set within an even larger analytic field of imperialism and domesticity. In the course of nineteenth- and twentieth-century imperial expansion, domesticity functioned as an "engine of empire," where the taming of the wild and unknown entailed establishing orderly homes in a frontier, inculcating proper domestic habits among the natives, and disseminating civilizing influences in gendered terms. Facilitating imperial expansion, domesticity—perceived as feminine, innocuous, and depoliticized—obscured the violence of empire, exerting even more power as a gendered tool of expansionism.[5]

Luncheon meat, which was invented shortly before World War II, is clearly part of such gendered dynamics of empire. Its proliferation followed the footsteps of American soldiers, and its homey brand obscured memories of war and violence.[6] Enjoying exceptional popularity in Okinawa, where more than 75 percent of the US military facilities within Japan are concentrated, luncheon meat reveals much about the militarization of everyday lives on the islands, exemplifying what Tomiyama Ichirō describes as the permeability of the boundary between *nichijō* (home front; everyday life) and *senjō* (war front; militarized state of affairs).[7] However, Okinawans have never simply been overwhelmed or overpowered by luncheon meat and the twentieth-century geopolitical dynamics it embodies. They have engaged in continuous negotiations with the canned pink meat, articulating their cultural and historical agency vis-à-vis the United States and Japan in various and often surprising manners. This chapter traces the colorful and multifaceted history of luncheon meat, which started as a symbol of American victory, became part of Okinawan home cooking, transformed itself into part of the Okinawan identity, and finally constituted a site of resistance against the erasure of Okinawan postwar experiences.

"No Wonder These Americans Won the War": Food and Survival in Postwar Okinawa

A story of luncheon meat in Okinawa starts with the Battle of Okinawa, one of the bloodiest encounters in the Pacific War. From early April to mid-June 1945, the so-called Typhoon of Steel launched by the US military caused enormous destruction across the islands, with Japanese violence vis-à-vis Okinawans adding further furies and tragedies to the killing field that was Okinawa. By the end of the battle, more than one-fourth of the islands' population had perished. Cut off from mainland Japan (Okinawa's former colonizer) and placed under the administration of US military (its new ruler), Okinawans, left with no place to live and little food to eat, were rounded up and taken to refugee camps to restart their lives.

It was within this context of transition—from Japanese rule to American rule, from the Pacific War to the Cold War—that Okinawans' everyday lives became inseparably intertwined with a militarized and militarizing product of luncheon meat. Okinawan narratives of the early postwar years are full of stories where everyday affairs at home were enmeshed with the material reality of military mobilization, demobilization, and remobilization. The wreckage of Japanese fighter planes was melted and reshaped into pots, pans, and kettles. The tops of Coke bottles discarded by American soldiers were cut off to create drinking glasses. To supplement their meager rations, Okinawans frequently resorted to appropriating (in reality stealing) various goods ranging from stationery to food to vehicles from US military bases, calling them *senkwa* (war booty) with a barely concealed sense of pride. Amid a series of sexual assaults of local women by American soldiers, American military parachutes were resewn into Western-style wedding dresses, and bullet casings were sliced to create wedding rings. As people's daily attire was improvised out of herringbone twill from US military uniforms, Okinawans called their new fashion *kuronbō* or "darky" because of the fabric's dark hue.[8] Luncheon meat was introduced into this militarized landscape of everyday life in Okinawa, where dynamics of race, gender, sexuality, and empire intersected to shape islanders' memories and experiences of war and postwar reconstruction.

Once in Okinawa, luncheon meat caused shock and awe. Amid acute food shortage and constant hunger, Okinawans found luncheon meat to be "unbelievably delicious" and even *nuchi gusui* (a source of life).[9] An initial impression of luncheon meat led to an understanding that "it was no wonder that Americans with access to such delicious food won the war," a sentiment repeatedly expressed in Okinawan memories of the early postwar days.[10] Linked with the victor's military prowess and material affluence, luncheon meat exuded exceptional power, becoming an object of adoration and admiration among Okinawans. From within this context one dish called *pōku tamago* (pork and eggs) emerged, becoming legendary fare whose popularity outlasted the occupation and continues to this day. Consisting of several slices of fried luncheon meat and eggs (either fried or scrambled), this simple dish was an unimaginably extravagant affair back then, something people often dreamed of but rarely had a chance to experience. As recalled by one Okinawan woman, her postwar encounter with the dish of pork and eggs was indeed unforgettable. Relocating from a rural community of Nakijin (known for its centenarians and traditional foodways) to a base town of Ginowan to attend Futemma High School (back then Nodake High School) in 1958, she ran into this dish for the first time at her friend's house. Ecstatic, she consumed not only her own portion but also that of her friend, surprising the latter's mother into serving the same dish every time she visited the family from then on.[11] *Pōku tamago* has gone on to become a popular item, regularly served at local homes and eateries and spawning a variation, *onipō* or *onigiri pōku tamago*, a Japanese-style rice ball with eggs and luncheon meat in the middle or on the top, as seen in figure 9.2.

FIGURE 9.2 *Pōku tamago onigiri*, or Spam and egg rice ball wrapped in seaweed. Courtesy of Wikimedia Commons.

Pork Culture of Okinawa: Indigenizing Luncheon Meat under the Shadow of American and Japanese Empires

As indicated by the proliferation of pork and eggs, luncheon meat did not remain a foreign product, nor did it retain its tragic memories of war and defeat for too long. Okinawans quickly adapted it, insisting on its affinity with local food and foodways. Food essays, cultural commentaries, and historical writings repeatedly explain islanders' enthusiastic acceptance of luncheon meat in terms of Okinawa's meat-eating culture and especially their traditional consumption of pork. On the islands where people love pork so much that they are said to consume each and every part of it except its sound (*nakigoe igaiwa subete tabetsukusu*), as the legend goes, it was natural and even inevitable that luncheon meat would become integrated into local culture. As one Okinawan writer explains, the fact that luncheon meat has taken root in Okinawa but not in mainland Japan is explained by the long-standing tradition of pork consumption in the former and the absence of such custom in the latter.[12]

Far from being a frivolous food talk or lighthearted cultural commentary, such accounts of luncheon meat and Okinawan tradition have been circulated as part of academic discourse, where scholars, especially home economists at the University of the Ryukyus (UR), authorize and authenticate the allegedly indigenous quality of luncheon meat. During the occupation, the UR was established under American auspices to promote science and technical education, which constituted a hallmark of Cold War US strategies abroad.[13] UR home economics was a gendered site of this postwar mobilization, where Okinawan women received training in American-style domestic science under the supervision of American home economists dispatched from Michigan State University (MSU).[14]

Hokama Yuki, a retired faculty member of the UR home economics department and a leading nutritionist on the islands, explains that luncheon meat became an integral part of everyday diet in Okinawa because islanders, having long consumed pork, found its taste to be familiar. As a source of protein, she goes on to state, luncheon meat played an important role in sustaining Okinawans in the early postwar years.[15] Kinjō Sumiko, also a former member of the program, makes a similar observation. Reflecting on the history of Okinawan food and foodways, she states that the preexisting habit of pork consumption explains why Okinawans readily adapted luncheon meat, bacon, and sausage during the US occupation and why more than 90 percent of imported luncheon meat in Japan is consumed in Okinawa. It is no surprise, Kinjō points out, that luncheon meat has become part of traditional Okinawan dishes such as *chanpurū* (Okinawan-style stir-fry), *ubushī* (Okinawan-style stew), and *jūcī* (Okinawan-style pilaf or gruel).[16] Naturalized and indigenized, luncheon meat becomes a depoliticized domestic object whose militarized origin gets lost in home economists' talks of centuries-old culinary custom and tradition.

It is not Okinawans alone who have spun tales of culture and tradition around canned pork meat, however. Luncheon meat has also provided a narrative device with which Americans articulate their own tradition of imperial expansionism. See, for example, "Hormel in Okinawa," a 1971 issue of the newsletter published by Hormel in Austin, Minnesota. As it tells the story of the company's advance into postwar Okinawa, it deploys the images and languages of manifest destiny, whereby American expansion in Asia and the Pacific is portrayed as inevitable. Accompanied by numerous photos, the newsletter showcases Okinawa as a new frontier where an abundant supply of orderly labor and cooperative business leadership will enable Hormel's international exploration and expansion. Emphasizing cooperation rather than conquest, it depicts Hormel's involvement in Okinawa as an instance of postwar multiculturalism and transnationalism enacted in the field of international business. Despite its benign facade, however, the tale of Hormel in Okinawa reflects and reinforces US imperial dynamics. To explain the value of Okinawa in the company's overseas venture, the newsletter turns to a map in which multiple lines radiate from Okinawa to Seoul, Taipei, Hong Kong, and Manila, a familiar representational practice of the US military that highlights Okinawa's strategic significance in the Cold War Asia-Pacific. That Hormel's business venture is inseparable from America's expansionist sentiment is even more explicitly noted in the remark that appears at the end of the newsletter: "With markets stretching from Canada to Australia, through Europe and the Far East, the sun quite literally never sets on Hormel!"[17]

While illuminating America's imperial tradition, luncheon meat also provides an occasion where a story of yet another expansionist tradition, that is, Japanese imperialism, was articulated. Indeed, in US-occupied Okinawa, luncheon meat repeatedly intersected with objects, discourses, and practices of Japanese imperial domesticity. Take, for instance, a record of meal planning at Okinawa Jitsumu Gakuen, a rehabilitation home of Okinawan youths where juvenile delinquents—in the case of boys, this often meant those who committed theft and other petty crimes, and in the case of girls, sexual transgression—were disciplined and rehabilitated. Its lunch menu on November 1, 1970, included *itamemono*, or stir-fry, which involved not only luncheon meat but also Ajinomoto, the Japanese brand name for MSG seasoning.[18] As Jordan Sand observes, the origin and history of Ajinomoto was inseparable from pre-1945 Japanese nation and empire building, as its genesis was traceable to the intersection of science and domesticity in the modernizing nation and its dissemination across Asia followed the route of its imperial expansion.[19] Okinawa is one of the sites where this iconic item of Japanese imperial domesticity had reached before World War II. During the occupation, Ajinomoto was a much-valued commodity, circulating through black markets but also distributed by American military wives whose food baskets often included an exceptionally large quantity of the item.[20] A stir-fry involving luncheon meat and Ajinomoto, fed to juvenile delinquents in a disciplinary space in US-occupied Okinawa, was undoubtedly a dish loaded with heavy flavors.

A link between luncheon meat and Japanese imperial tradition was embodied not only by objects such as Ajinomoto but also people such as Onaga Kimiyo, head of the UR home economics department and a leading promoter of American domesticity in occupied Okinawa. A well-known grassroots educator-reformer, Onaga offered countless workshops, lectures, and demonstrations on homes and homemaking during the 1950s and 1960s, instructing local mothers and wives on how to cook with luncheon meat and other foreign products that poured into the postwar islands. Admired as the "Mother of Okinawan women" due to her contributions to domestic modernization in Okinawa, Onaga was in fact a mainland woman whose pre-1945 career had deeply been embedded in the history of Japanese imperial expansionism. Originally from the northern hinterland of Yamagata, Onaga, a committed practitioner of the life improvement movement,[21] had taught home economics in colonial Korea, making a womanly contribution to the empire as she domesticated Japan's frontier. Arriving in Okinawa at the end of World War II, she reconfigured her career under the Cold War US reign to train—and discipline—Okinawan women in American- and Japanese-style domesticity.[22] Carried by Onaga's imperial trajectory that stretched from Tohoku through Korea and finally to Okinawa, luncheon meat developed a truly complex taste as it soaked up the legacy of not only American but also Japanese empire-building.[23]

Grandmother's Cooking: Luncheon Meat and the Taste of Home

In postwar Okinawa, Onaga was not the only female figure who facilitated local adaption of luncheon meat. There were other mothers and grandmothers whose stories are also deeply entwined with this war booty turned indigenous comestible. As the Okinawan motherly figures appear and reappear in various narratives involving luncheon meat, they not only promote Okinawan food and foodways as a source of health and longevity but also invoke a sense of nostalgia for Okinawan homes and home-cooked meals. The link between homes, mothers, and luncheon meat has been articulated in various manners. *Okinawa Ichiba* magazine describes luncheon meat as "a taste of Okinawan mothers" (*Okinawa no okāsan no aji*).[24] An advertisement by the Tulip, another distributor of luncheon meat and a competitor with Hormel, describes its product as "a source of Okinawan vitality" (*Okinawa no genki no moto*) and a source of the flowering of Okinawan domestic culture.[25] On the package of one of its products, Spam Curry, Okinawa Hormel declares that luncheon meat is an essential part of an "Okinawan dinner table" (*Okinawa no shokutaku*).[26]

No discussion of Okinawan mothers and grandmothers could take place without acknowledging the significance of Taira Tomi, a well-known actress whose seasoned performance as *obā* (grandmother) in *Nabī no koi*, *Chura-san*, and other films and television dramas propelled her to stardom and sparked an Okinawan boom across Japan in the late 1990s and the early 2000s. Her cookbook *Obā no sukina Okinawa chura ryōri* (Grandmother's favorite Okinawan recipes) introduces local cuisine accompanied by essays and commentaries, in which Taira praises the health and longevity of Okinawans and describes local food and foodways that have sustained such life style. Amid her talks on Okinawan culture and tradition, Taira pays special tribute to one "local" ingredient, that is, luncheon meat, an item indispensable in her recipes of *gōya champurū* (stir-fry with bitter melon, illustrated in figure 9.3), *māmina irichā* (stir-fry with bean sprouts), *pōku tamago*, and *pōku tamago onigiri*.[27]

FIGURE 9.3 *Goya champurū*, a stir-fry with bitter melon, luncheon meat, egg and tofu. Courtesy of Wikimedia Commons.

Reminiscing how luncheon meat used to be *kuwacchī* or *gochisō* (a treat), Taira explains that the canned pork meat was an ingredient of historic significance introduced by the occupiers. The US military brought luncheon meat to Okinawa, Taira explains, because Americans perhaps knew that pork was a favorite food among islanders.[28] As a sign of American goodwill, luncheon meat temporarily loses its militarized memory and stands as an object that embodies the occupiers' beneficence. Yet a taste of military and militarization associated with the canned meat will never completely go away. Included at the end of her cookbook is an advertisement for mail order delivery of Okinawan ingredients for mainland readers-consumers, which lists among others bitter melon, mango, luncheon meat, and, right next to it, a packet of the Old El Paso Taco Seasoning Mix.[29] The inclusion of the taco seasoning, an essential ingredient in "taco rice," another concoction popularized in postwar Okinawa, reminds one of changing configurations of the US military in which Hispanic Americans, in addition to African Americans, have been disproportionately represented. The presence of luncheon meat, together with the Old El Paso Taco Seasoning Mix, in Taira's cookbook complicates the tales and tastes of food, race, and empire in Okinawa and the larger Asia-Pacific region.

Okinawan mothers and their home-cooked meals are also conspicuously featured in *Okinawa tezukuri no aji: watashi ga gijutsu ichihansan* (Home-cooked meals in Okinawa: My number one cooking techniques), a two-part cookbook compiled by a group of Okinawan women who are members of local life improvement groups.[30] Included in the books are recipes for *mōi dōfu* (Okinawan-style tofu), *jagaimo no kakiage* (a deep-fried potato dish), and *āsa no kakiage* (a deep-fried sea-weed dish), all of which call for luncheon meat and, in the first two dishes, an additional ingredient of canned tuna, another item introduced to occupied Okinawa whose taste, as well as pronunciation, has become firmly ground into the tongues of Okinawans.[31] Here motherhood is tied not only to domestic space but also to technique, (re)articulating the basic tenet of the life improvement movement originating from Japan as well as that of Cold War domestic science education promoted by the United States.

The introduction to the first of the two books is written by Sho Hiroko, the first-ever female vice governor of the prefecture at the time and a leading nutritional scientist on the islands, who studied home economics at the UR and MSU during the occupation. A member of the Okinawan royal family, she is another indomitable motherly figure whose extraordinary career as a female scholar-politician has even exceeded that of Onaga. Not only does she provide an "academic stamp" to various recipes contributed by local mothers and wives, but she praises their dishes, including those that call for luncheon meat, as exemplars of cultural richness of Okinawa, where the climate is mild, the elderly are cared for, and neighborly ties remain strong. Casting her eyes beyond the islands, she even states that the spiritual wealth embodied in Okinawan culinary culture provides a model for Japanese people and indeed people around the world to emulate and embrace.[32]

The discourse of Okinawan wealth, health, and motherhood presented by Taira and Sho is complex. At one level, as they assert the value of Okinawan culture with mothers and grandmothers as its proud practitioners, they intervene in patriarchal dynamics on the islands, where women are frequently marginalized and overshadowed by men. Furthermore, as they praise the virtue of Okinawan domesticity and even suggest that Japanese mainlanders should learn from its cultural richness, they also challenge the long-standing colonial construction of Okinawa, whose racial inferiority vis-à-vis mainland Japan was allegedly evidenced by the islanders' "primitive" and "premodern" habits and practices at home.[33] At another level, however, their discourses also feed into and reinforce the dominant workings of power. Taira depoliticizes the history of luncheon meat, an item inseparable from postwar US military rule, while Sho (re)presents an exotic and essentialized image of "Okinawa," a discourse circulated during the Japanese colonial era. As scholars on Okinawa would readily point out, the understanding of Okinawa as an island community rich with indigenous culture and tradition and innocent of ill effects of modernity and progress is problematic, as it reinvokes the early twentieth-century construction of the atavistic and exotic (and romantic) Okinawa, an element salient in the Okinawan boom back then. Casting Okinawa as a preserver of values and traditions long lost in mainland Japan, the Okinawan booms in the past as well as present inscribe a dehistoricized and depoliticized image of "Okinawa," leaving power and hierarchy between colonizers and colonized obscured and even irrelevant.[34]

Complicit in the dominant dynamics of power, the Okinawan discourse involving mothers, grandmothers, and luncheon meat could also illuminate the distance and difference between Okinawa and Japan from critical perspectives. Such dynamics are often observed in the narratives of Okinawan migrants who lived in mainland Japan during or after the occupation. As they recount various difficulties and challenges they encountered, where prejudice and discrimination toward Okinawans were rampant, their stories frequently turn to one iconic object sent from home, that is, a care package containing luncheon meat. One Okinawan man recalls receiving such package while studying in mainland Japan. Struggling against poverty, isolation, and the cold weather, he found the package his mother sent from Okinawa, and especially the luncheon meat in it, to be a source of great comfort and solace. Not only did luncheon meat remind him of home because of its familiar taste, but it embodied his mother's care and affection, prompting him to say, "I can taste my mother's love in luncheon meat" (*Oya no nasake wa pōku no aji*).[35]

For another Okinawan man, luncheon meat sent from home was a source of cultural pride, in addition to being a reminder of home. Living in Tokyo, he frequently called up his mother, asking her to send luncheon meat, which he yearned for but could not easily obtain in the mainland. He recalls how he used to share the luncheon meat sent from home with a Japanese couple living next door, eventually turning them into "big fans of *pōku*." For him, luncheon meat was a sign of "richness of Okinawan culinary culture," which he was eager to display and even share with *yamatonchū* (Japanese mainlanders).[36] These narratives reveal the challenging circumstances Okinawan migrants experienced in mainland Japan, where connections to home, especially to luncheon meat, constituted an important element in their daily struggles for survival in an alien and often hostile environment.

In some narratives, luncheon meat does not simply invoke the figure of mother; it actually becomes one. This is seen in the narratives of Uechi Satoshi—a well-known Okinawan businessman, subversive cultural broker, and owner of an online store, Okinawaichi (Okinawan Market). Living in postreversion Tokyo as a university student, he, like many other Okinawan migrants, experienced a series of incidents triggered by Japanese prejudice and discrimination.[37] An encounter with luncheon meat within such a context was unforgettable. Wandering one day through a posh section of "imported food" at a department store in the Ginza district, he spotted luncheon meat (both Hormel and Tulip brand) among caviar, cheese, and other foreign luxury items on display. Surprised to see something so familiar and ordinary (for him) among fashionable goods imported from the West, he felt as though he had run into his own *kāchan* (mother) in the middle of the elegantly dressed ladies and gentlemen at a fancy dance party.[38]

Importantly, luncheon meat does not become essentialized or dehistoricized in his narrative. Uechi, who is originally from Yomitan, a community overrun by the Americans during the Battle of Okinawa and subsequently turned into a major base town during the postwar occupation, considers luncheon meat a political artifact that embodies the entangled histories of Okinawa, the United States, and Japan.[39] His critical sensibility is revealed in yet another episode he relates. In the 1990s, he was entrusted with management of Ginza Washita Shoppu in Tokyo, an Okinawan goods store established by the prefectural government to promote Okinawan tourism on the mainland. The store quickly became a site of contention, as a dispute broke out between Uechi and prefecture officials over whether or not it should carry luncheon meat. The government officials, learning about the presence of luncheon meat at the store, vehemently argued that luncheon meat was not an Okinawan product and demanded that Uechi immediately pull the item off the shelf. Uechi's response was equally adamant. He argued that luncheon meat was a symbol of the US occupation of Okinawa and that withdrawing it was tantamount to "denying the postwar history of Okinawa" (*sengo no Okinawa o hiteisuru*), where American military domination shaped people's everyday lives in countless ways. To Uechi, the government officials' demand to remove luncheon meat was nothing but an attempt to present pure and unsullied Okinawa, whose sanitized and comforting image would not only help sell tourism but also erase the history of American military rule on the islands and Japanese culpability in that very condition. Recounting how luncheon meat was a popular item among Filipino, Chinese, and Korean residents in Tokyo, moreover, Uechi not only extends his observation beyond Okinawa to the larger Asia-Pacific region, where the history of meat, military, and empire has been shared among more than one community. By shedding light on the existence of foreign migrants in Tokyo, he suggests that their experiences of marginalization and exclusion at the hands of Japanese were perhaps not too dissimilar to those of Uechi and other Okinawans.[40] In Uechi's narrative then, luncheon meat—his *kāchan*—becomes transgressive and even disruptive, subtly invoking the memories of war, military, and colonization shared across Asia and the Pacific and highlighting their embodied quality in the tiny can of scrap meat in a complex, subversive manner.

Conclusion

Okinawans' love for luncheon meat is a complex affair, then. The canned pork meat proliferating in Japan's southernmost island prefecture sheds light on cultural dynamics that we might otherwise overlook and facilitates critical thinking on historical ties that bind Okinawa, the United States, and Japan and proliferate still further into the larger terrain of Asia and the Pacific. A trans-Pacific mapping provided by luncheon meat offers an occasion to rethink and reinstate those marginalized—and often treated as "scraps"—in the mainstream historical narratives at the center of our analysis, where peripheral regions such as Okinawa, forgotten historical actors such as women and colonized minorities, and depoliticized space such as home reveal much about militarization and its attendant violence of twentieth- and twenty-first-century geopolitics.

NOTES

1. Naotsugu Yoshimura, *Love! Spam, the Cook Book, 100 reshipi* (Haebaru, Okinawa: 100 shirīzu shuppan purojekuto), 2009.

2. The book *Okinawa rūru* (Okinawa rules) lists forty-nine rules Japanese mainlanders might follow if they were to become real *uchinanchū*, i.e., Okinawans. One of the rules states that one should never run out of a supply of luncheon meat at home. Tokai seikatsu kenkyū purojekuto Okinawa chīmu, ed., *Okinawa rūru* (Tokyo: Chūkei shuppan), 38–41; Laura Hein and Mark Selden, eds., *Islands of Discontent: Okinawan Responses to Japanese and American Power* (Lanham, MD: Rowman and Littlefield, 2003); Chalmers Johnson, ed., *Okinawa: Cold War Islands* (Cardiff, CA: Japan Policy Research Institute, 1999).

3. For the term "militarized currents," see Setsu Shigematsu and Keith Camacho, eds., *Militarized Currents: Toward a Decolonized Future in Asia and the Pacific* (Minneapolis: University of Minnesota Press, 2010).

4. George H. Lewis, "From Minnesota Fat to Seoul Food: Spam in America and the Pacific," *Journal of Popular Culture* 33.2 (2000): 83–105; Ty Matejowsky, "Spam and Fast-Food 'Globalization' in the Philippines," *Food, Cultures, and Society* 10.1 (2007): 23–41; Miriam Kahn and Lorraine Sexton, "The Fresh and the Canned: Food Choices in the Pacific," *Food and Foodways* 3 (1988): 1–18.

5. Amy Kaplan, *The Anarchy of Empire in the Making of U.S. Culture* (Durham, NC: Duke University Press, 2002); Vicente Rafael, *White Love and Other Events in Filipino History* (Durham, NC: Duke University Press, 2000); Jane Hunter, *The Gospel of Gentility: American Women Missionaries in Turn-of-the-Century China* (New Haven: Yale University Press, 1984); Patricia Grimshaw, *Path of Duty: American Missionary Wives in Nineteenth-Century Hawaii* (Honolulu: University of Hawai'i Press, 1989); Nayan Shah, *Contagious Divides: Epidemics and Race in San Francisco's Chinatown* (Berkeley: University of California Press, 2001); Jane Simonsen, *Making*

Home Work: Domesticity and Native American Assimilation in the American West, 1860–1919 (Chapel Hill: University of North Caroline Press, 2006).

6. Carolyn Wyman, *Spam: A Biography* (San Diego: Harvest Original, 1999); Marguerite Patten, *Spam: The Cook Book* (London: Hamlyn, 2000); Dan Armstrong and Dustin Black, *The Book of Spam: A Most Glorious and Definitive Compendium of the World's Favorite Canned Meat* (New York: Atria Books, 2007).

For the notion of the US global military empire, see Mariah Hohn and Seungsook Moon, "Introduction: The Politics of Gender, Sexuality, Race, and Class in the U.S. Military Empire," in *Over There: Living with the U.S. Military Empire from World War Two to the Present*, ed. Hohn and Moon (Durham, NC: Duke University Press, 2010).

7. Ichirō Tomiyama, *Senjō no kioku* (Tokyo: Nihon keizai hyōronsha, 2006), 46–47.

8. The social history of US-occupied Okinawa constitutes an extraordinarily rich field of studies that illuminate the link among people's everyday lives, militarization of the islands, and Cold War geopolitical dynamics. See, for example, Toshiki Komazawa, *Amerika no pai o katte kaerō* (Tokyo: Nihon keizen shinbun shuppansha, 2009): Nahashi sōmubu joseishitsu, ed., *Naha onna no ashiato, Naha joseishi sengohen* (Naha: Ryukyu shinpōsha, 2001); Okinawa taimususha, ed., *Shomin ga tsuzuru Okinawa sengo seikatsushi* (Naha: Okinawa taimususha, 1998); Ryukyu shinpō shakaibu, ed., *Sengo Okinawa bukka fūzokushi* (Urazoe, Okinawa: Okinawa shuppan, 1987); Fumihiko Umino, *Okinawa natsukashi shashinkan, fukkimae e yōkoso* (Naha: Shinsei shuppan, 2012); Nahashi rekishi hakubutsukan, ed., *Sengo o tadoru, "Amerika yū" kara "Yamato no yū" e* (Naha: Ryukyu shinpōsha, 2007).

9. Munetaka Hirakawa, *Butaguni Okinawa: Anata no shiranai butano sekai* (Naha: Naha shuppansha, 2005), 177; Kiyoko Urasaki, "Senkwa no kanzume de nuchigusui," in Okinawa taimususha, *Shomin ga tsuzuru*, 201–202.

10. Nahashi sōmubu joseishitsu, *Naha onna*, 136.

11. Yumeko Misumi, "Pōku tamago sama!," in Okinawa taimususha, *Shomin ga tsuzuru*, 204–205.

12. Eiko Asato, "Amerika o chanpurū," *Taiyō*, April, No. 394 (April 1994): 78–79.

13. Katsunori Yamazato, *Ryudai monogatari, 1947–1972* (Naha: Ryukyu shinpōsha, 2010); Tadashi Ogawa, *Sengo Beikoku no Okinawa bunka senryaku: Ryukyu daigaku to Mishigan misshon* (Tokyo: Iwanami shoten, 2012).

14. Mire Koikari, "'The World Is Our Campus': Domestic Science and Cold War Transnationalism between Michigan and Okinawa," in *Cold War Encounters in US-Occupied Okinawa: Women, Militarized Domesticity, and Transnationalism in East Asia* (Cambridge: Cambridge University Press), 65–99.

15. Yuki Hokama, "Eiyōgen no yakuwari dai," in Ryukyu shinpō shakaibu, *Sengo Okinawa*, 64.

16. Sumiko Kinjō, "Okinawa no nikushoku bunka ni kansuru ichi kōsatsu, sono hensen to haikei," in *Nihon no shokubunka, dai 18 shū, ibunka tono sesshoku to juyō*, ed. Noboru Hōga and Hiroko Ishikawa (Tokyo: Yūzankaku shuppan, 1997), 227.

17. "Hormel in Okinawa: Okinawa de katsuyaku suru Hōmeru," *Hormal News* 45.11 (January 1, 1971): 10, Okinawa Prefecture Archives, Haebaru, Okinawa.

18. "Kondatehyō," in Kyūshoku jisshihyō, May 1, 1971–December 29, 1971, Jidō fukushi ni kansuru shorui, Okinawa Prefecture Archives, Haebaru, Okinawa.

19. Jordan Sand, "A Short History of MSG: Good Science, Bad Science, and Taste Cultures," *Gastronomica* 5.4 (April 2013): 38–49.

20. "Suggestions for Christmas Basket," Folder 134 (2), Box 134, Record Group 260—Public Affairs, and "Hinkonsha e purezento," December 12, 1963, Okinawa taimusu (a newspaper clip), Folder: Box 390 (2), Record Group 260–Public Affairs, Records of the U.S. Civil Administration of the Ryukyu Islands, 1945–1972, National Archives and Records Administration, College Park, Maryland.

21. For discussions of the significance of the life improvement movement in modernizing Japan, see Sheldon Garon, *Molding Japanese Minds: The State in Everyday Life* (Princeton, NJ: Princeton University Press, 1998).

22. Onaga Kimiyo jiden kankūkai, *Subarashikikana jinsei: Onaga Kimiyo jiden* (Naha: Wakanatsusha, 1985).

23. For Onaga's simultaneous involvement in Japanese and American imperial domesticity, see Koikari, "Mobilizing Homes, Empowering Women: Okinawan Home Economists and Cold War Domestic Education," in *Cold War Encounters*, chap. 5, 146–184.

24. "Okinawa no okazu," in *Okinawa ichiba* 10 (Summer 2005): 37.

25. "Okinawa no genki no moto," and "Irodori yutakana hanaga saku," posters, no date, courtesy of Tomimura shōji, Naha, Okinawa.

26. "Kantan! Okinawa no shokutaku shirīzu, Supamu Spam karē," accessed September 4, 2016. http://okinawahormel.co.jp/products.

27. Tomi Taira, *Obā no sukina "Okinawa chura ryōri"* (Tokyo: Sony magajinzu, 2002).

28. Taira, *Obā no sukina*, 91.

29. Taira, *Obā no sukina*, 95.

30. Okinawaken seikatsu kaizen jikkō gurūpu renraku kenkyūkai, ed., *Okinawa tezukuri no aji, watashi ga gijutsu ichibansan* (Urazoe, Okinawa: Okinawa shuppan, 1991); Okinawaken nōsangyoson seikatsu kenkyūkai, ed., *Okinawa tezukuri no aji, watashi ga gijutsu ichibansan II* (Urazoe, Okinawa: Okinawa shuppan, 1998).

31. Tuna is commonly pronounced as "tsuna" in mainland Japan. However, in Okinawa, the older generation of men and women often pronounce it as "tūna," retaining its original English sound, which they had acquired during the occupation.

32. Hiroko Sho, "Hakkan ni yosete," in *Okinawa tezukuri*, ed. Okinawaken seikatsu kaizen jikkō gurūpu renraku kenkyūkai, no page number.

33. Alan Christy, "The Making of Imperial Subjects in Okinawa," in *Formations of Colonial Modernity in East Asia*, ed. Tani Barloe (Durham, NC: Duke University Press, 1997), 146.

34. Osamu Tada, *Okinawa imēji o tabisuru: Yanagita Kunio kara ijū būmu made* (Tokyo: Chūōkōronsha, 2008); Yasuhiro Tanaka, *Fūkei no sakeme, Okinawa senryōno ima* (Tokyo: Serika shobō, 2010).

35. Sadamasa Kishimoto, "Oya no nasake wa pōku no aji," in Okinawa taimusushа, *Shomin ga tsuzuru*, 204.

36. Chōji Yamamoto, "Pōku o kirazuni maruyaki," in Okinawa taimususha, *Shomin ga tsuzuru*, 203.

37. Komazawa, *Amerika no pai*, 134–136.

38. Uechi's essay is quoted in Komazawa, *Amerika no pai*, 127–128. The original essay, entitled "Pōku kanzume no hanashi," was published on the online magazine *Okinawaichi*, July 11, 2001, http://uechi.exblog.jp/3260721.

39. For the significance of Yomitan in the post–World War II history of Okinawan resistance, see Norma Field, "Part I, Okinawa," in *In the Realm of a Dying Emperor: Japan at the Century's End* (New York: Vintage, 1993).

40. Komazawa, *Amerika no pai*, 128–130, 141–143.

10

Nikkei Cuisine

How Japanese Food Travels and Adapts Abroad

Ayumi Takenaka

"Nikkei cuisine," broadly defined as Japanese and Peruvian fusion food, shows how "Japanese food" is represented abroad, how the process of appropriation changes it, and ultimately, how "Japanese food" is defined and who defines it. Indeed, any "national cuisine" is created when there is a need to define it, and it is often defined in relation to, and in contrast with, others. This particular culinary encounter emerged more or less naturally from Japanese migration and from the emergence of Peruvian gastronomical fashions. But it also emerged through top-down government and elite initiative, including gastrodiplomacy, a form of cultural diplomacy that promotes and defines cuisine for nation branding and enhancing national status abroad.[1]

Today, Japanese food, or washoku, is rather ambiguously defined by the Japanese government as a dietary culture associated with "a social practice based on an essential spirit of the Japanese, 'respect for nature.'"[2] It is contentious to define washoku, which, in fact, entails multiple meanings defined by multiple actors. I illustrate this by showing how "Japanese food" evolved into a new genre of cuisine, "Nikkei food," in the Peruvian context.

My analysis is drawn from my long-term ethnographic research in Peru, on and off between 1996 and 2016, along with the content analysis of food blogs, food festivals, and cookbooks. In addition, to examine how the Japanese-Peruvian community reacts and relates to Nikkei food, I analyzed the contents of *Kaikan*, the official monthly magazine of the Japanese-Peruvian Association (APJ), the community's umbrella association, published between 2010 and 2013. My fieldwork in Lima, Peru, entailed visits to Nikkei restaurants,

Japanese-Peruvian homes, and community events as well as interviews with chefs, culinary specialists, and members and leaders of the community.

The Emergence of Nikkei Cuisine

For the past twenty years, "Japanese food" has gone through significant transformation in Peru. Once regarded as alien and unpalatable, this parochial food, consumed only by twenty-three thousand or so immigrants who arrived from Japan (mostly from Okinawa) between 1899 and 1930s, is now in vogue and forms a part of Peru's national cuisine as "Nikkei cuisine." This cuisine, generally defined as Japanese-Peruvian fusion, became popular at the end of the 1990s.[3] The number of Nikkei restaurants has increased rapidly in the past decades (the Peruvian Yellow Pages lists sixty in Lima alone), and gained visibility around the world with the advent of trendy Nikkei restaurants owned by renowned chefs, such as Ferran Ádria (Barcelona), Gastón Acurio (Lima), and Nobu Matsuhisa (New York).[4] Today Nikkei food is widely celebrated and promoted in the context of booming gastronomy in Peru.[5]

How Nikkei cuisine emerged has multiple stories, however, depending on how the cuisine is defined and who tells the story. The APJ, which actively promotes Nikkei food by organizing food fairs and offering cooking lessons, regards the food as rooted, first and foremost, in what was prepared and consumed by Japanese immigrants and their descendants, now estimated to number about ninety thousand. Accordingly, APJ traces the origin of Nikkei food to the "need of Japanese immigrants who arrived in Peru to nourish themselves."[6] What we know today as Nikkei food, thus, all began in the homes of Japanese immigrants, where they tried to replicate what they had eaten before, substituting what they lacked with local ingredients and improvising their food.[7] Thanks to Chinese immigrants who had arrived earlier as "coolie" laborers between 1849 and 1874, Japanese immigrants were able to utilize Chinese rice and vegetables, including key ingredients, such as ginger and soy sauce.[8] Since Japanese immigrants arrived in Peru's coastal areas to work on cotton and sugarcane plantations (like the Chinese predecessors), they had access to the vast sea. The Peruvian coastline, influenced by the cold and warm currents, offers one of the richest fisheries in the world, featuring over two thousand species of fish and sea products.[9] Japanese immigrants incorporated abundant seafood into their cooking, and seafood became emblematic of what is known today as Nikkei cuisine.

If Nikkei cuisine is defined as a type of cuisine consumed by the general Peruvian public, its origin must be traced to restaurants in Peru.[10] The formation of any cuisine must indeed depend on the willingness of some actors to transfer culinary traditions from the private sphere to the public.[11] According to Gastón Acurio, Peru's most renowned chef and a major promoter of Nikkei food, Nikkei cuisine emerged in Peruvian restaurants owned and run by Japanese descendants. One such restaurant was La Buena Muerte of Minoru Kunigami, a son of Japanese immigrants from Okinawa.[12] Like most other restaurants of Japanese-Peruvians, La Buena Muerte served Peruvian food, known as Creole food (la comida criolla), catering mostly to the general Peruvian public. In the small cevichería he started in the 1960s, Kunigami created fusion seafood, such as ceviche with ginger and wasabi, served as "sashimi," and tamal de kamaboko, fish cake made with Peruvian dried potatoes. Historically, many Japanese-Peruvians engaged in restaurant business in Lima after having completed (or escaped from) their contract work on plantations. In the late 1960s a quarter of Japanese-Peruvians owned or worked at restaurants.[13] Since they often worked and ate with Peruvian employees, restaurants served as a vehicle to exchange ideas and create distinct flavors by adding soy sauce and miso to typical Peruvian dishes.[14]

Nikkei cuisine as a brand offers yet another story. While the food we know today as "Nikkei" may have origins in Japanese-Peruvian homes and restaurants, it became labeled and popularized as such by non-Japanese Peruvians. First of all, the popularization of Nikkei food is owed to two renowned chefs from Japan, Nobu Matsuhisa and Toshiro Konishi, who arrived in Peru during the 1970s.[15] Nobu, a master sushi chef known for his adept skills in adapting Japanese food to local taste, invented tiradito, a signature dish of Nikkei cuisine, by mixing thinly sliced raw fish with lime juice and Peruvian peppers, seen in figure 10.1.[16] Toshiro followed in his footsteps by further popularizing fusion sushi through appearances on national television.[17] This fusion food was first labeled "Nikkei food" by Rodolfo Hinostroza, a Peruvian poet and a food writer, in his 1983 article in La Republica, a Peruvian daily. "Nikkei food," he wrote, "brings together the great rigor of the Japanese preparation of fish and seafood, and the spicy, aromatic sauces of Creole cuisine."[18] Following this, the status of "Nikkei food" as a new genre of cuisine was established firmly when Gastón Acurio promoted it as such in the context of the Peruvian gastronomic boom in the 1990s.

What Is Nikkei Cuisine?

Today, Nikkei cuisine is broadly defined as fusion food combining Japanese and Peruvian ingredients. Yet it does not refer to just any mixture. The creation of Nikkei cuisine, like any other cuisine, entails the process of selection and

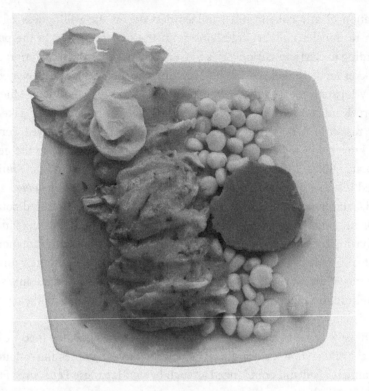

FIGURE 10.1 *Tiradito*, a Nikkei dish of raw fish in a spicy sauce, here accompanied by Peruvian corn and sweet potato. Via Wikimedia Commons.

legitimation of only certain ingredients. Japanese ingredients regarded as key in Nikkei cuisine are certain spices: *shōyu*, miso, Ajinomoto, *hondashi*, wasabi, and *kare* (curry), which all have entered the Peruvian culinary vocabulary today. The key Peruvian component, on the other hand, is aji, or Peruvian peppers. Also central are fish, shellfish, and other sea products.[19] Japanese food in Peru is strongly associated with seafood (thus, chefs who specialize in Japanese and Nikkei cuisines are all known as *itamae*, or sushi chefs). So Nikkei cuisine usually contains fish, in combination with Peruvian aji (as the theme of a recent gastronomic fair, Mistura, indicated, "There is no Peruvian cuisine without aji!").[20]

The most typical Nikkei dish is maki, and the most emblematic of all, according to Tsumura and Barrón, is *maki acevichado*, or ceviche roll, containing Peruvian-style marinated fish rolled up with rice, avocado, or seaweed. Similarly, Inka maki consists of avocado, Philadelphia cream cheese, and salmon, covered with sesame seeds; Samuray maki is with lobster, and Kamikaze maki with tuna or yellowtail (Más Que Sushi). Other typical Nikkei dishes include *tiradito*, sometimes referred to as "Nikkei ceviche," as well as steamed fish (known as *mushi*), curry-flavored fish (*chita con curry japonés*), and octopus with black olive sauce (*pulpo al olivo*).[21]

It is important to note that Inka maki is to be distinguished from the California roll. Even if they may look identical and the exact same ingredients may go into them, Inka maki, which in fact is marketed as "Machu Picchu Roll" in the United States, is Nikkei and Peruvian, according to culinary specialists in Peru, because it is fundamentally prepared *in Peru*.[22] What defines a cuisine, thus, depends not only on what it contains and how it is prepared, but also on where it is prepared and how it is marketed.

In addition, Nikkei cuisine is characterized, and celebrated, as a blend of opposites. "Japanese and Peruvian foods are so different . . . like oil and water," according to Tsumura and Barrón (2013), and it is this difference that creates dynamic and pleasant new flavors. In creating and defining Nikkei cuisine, therefore, differences associated with Japanese and Peruvian cuisines—and indeed cultures—are emphasized. The APJ characterizes Nikkei cuisine as Japanese simplicity blended with flavorful Peruvian spices.[23] According to *El Comercio*, a major national daily, Nikkei cuisine nicely balances out heavily seasoned Peruvian food by incorporating the Japanese tradition of using natural and neutral flavors.[24] Since Japanese cuisine is "diametrically opposed to ours in terms of portions," moderate serving portions are also identified as a characteristic of Nikkei cuisine.[25]

The difference emphasized sometimes goes beyond the realm of food. According to Tsumura and Barrón, Japan gave Peru the orderly, delicate, and meditative elements of cuisine, while Peru contributed daring spices and peppers both in form and in content. For some, Nikkei cuisine represents "values" associated with Japanese stereotypes prevalent in Peru. "Honesty" is deeply embedded in Nikkei cuisine, according to John Santa Cruz, and it offers a sense of "solemnity" and "calmness."[26] To Luis Arévalo Brilla, a non-Japanese Peruvian chef of a fancy Nikkei restaurant in Madrid, it is a cuisine of "discipline."[27] And Tsumura and Barrón describe Nikkei cuisine as "Peruvian food with a Zen spirit."

For some, Nikkei cuisine is a form of identity and a means to express one's identity. For Chef Hajime Kasuga, Nikkei cuisine is about "representing my culture on the plates": Nikkei cuisine is about me, he says, "because Nikkei, or fusion, is what we really are."[28] Chef Luis Arévalo Brilla does not know, or care, if what he cooks (in his "Nikkei" restaurant) is called Nikkei, Peruvian, or Japanese: "I only cook what comes out of my heart."[29] Even though the definitions and meanings of Nikkei cuisine have been debated, it does not matter if you use a Japanese ingredient or how you prepare it, states Santa

Cruz; Nikkei cuisine is about philosophy, concept, and identity. Nikkei cuisine, thus, has multiple meanings open to ideas and innovations.

Why Did Nikkei Cuisine Become Popular?

There are several factors behind the boom of Nikkei cuisine in Peru and beyond. The first dates back to a government policy of the 1960s and 1970s that aimed to boost seafood consumption in Peru. Despite the rich fishery off its coast, Peruvians previously had not had the custom of consuming much seafood.[30] It was attributed to lack of refrigeration and lack of knowledge of how to prepare seafood. The military government of Juan Velasco (1969–1975), in an attempt to amplify the Peruvian diet and avoid food shortages, ordered a fifteen-day monthly prohibition of beef consumption. This led to a massive consumption of seafood by the end of the 1970s and contributed to the boom in Nikkei food, which is closely associated with seafood.[31]

A second factor has to do with the global boom in sushi, and the transformation of Japanese food, across countries, particularly in the United States. Prior to the 1980s, raw fish was widely considered unpalatable, but partly because of the influence of celebrity and partly because of the local adaptation of sushi through the invention of the California roll, the number of sushi restaurants increased exponentially in the United States during the 1990s.[32] The popularization of Japanese food was boosted further by the rise of Japan as a global economic power and the increased visibility of the country and its culture. During the period of Japan's economic heyday, many Japanese chefs traveled to the United States, along with Japanese expatriate businessmen, making Japanese cuisine more available and accessible to the public. Gradually, sushi became a symbol of sophistication, health consciousness, and trendiness. And this sent ripples to Peru.

In addition, what boosted the Japanese culinary boom in Peru was the raised status of the Japanese-Peruvian community. The community's prestige is both a result and manifestation of the economic success of Japanese descendants as well as the emergence of prominent political figures, such as former president Alberto Fujimori. It is also attributed to financial resources poured into Peru from Japan and the cultural influence brought about by the migration of thousands of Peruvians to Japan beginning in the late 1980s.[33] The community has grown in status also as a result of the growing popularity of Japanese culture in Peru. The "massive presence of the Japanese *colonia*," as *La Republica* put it, influenced the proliferation of Japanese cuisine in Peru, referring not only to the symbolic power of the Japanese-Peruvian community, but also to its impressive community infrastructure, which has served as the country's main hub of Japanese cultural activities. This resulted in attracting more people, both Japanese and non-Japanese Peruvians, to the community's cultural center and elsewhere to eat and learn about Japanese food.

More importantly, perhaps, a key to the popularization of Japanese (and Nikkei) food lies in the broader gastronomic boom in Peru. Peru has gone through what former president Ollanta Humala called at the UN General Assembly in 2011 a "gastronomic revolution."[34] The "revolution" kicked in during the late 1990s when political violence abated and Peru began to experience economic growth by integrating into the global economy. In 2007, the Peruvian government recognized the country's gastronomy as "national heritage" and began to promote it nationally and internationally as an engine of economic development and national integration.[35] To advance these aims, the Peruvian Society of Gastronomy (APEGA), the trade association of Peru's elite chefs, was created in 2007. Their major activity is to organize Mistura, an international gastronomic festival, that has grown since its beginning in 2008 into a truly international extravaganza, attracting media attention, celebrity chefs, and over five hundred thousand visitors from around the world.[36] The food industry, which generated 11.2 percent of Peru's GDP in 2009, is now recognized as a key industry in Peru as a means to promote tourism, restructure the agricultural production systems, and export organic products.[37] The Peruvian government and the industry, thus, aim to consolidate the visibility of Peruvian cuisine abroad through the "gastronomic revolution." Gastón Acurio, a major protagonist of the gastronomic movement, elaborated on this: by consolidating "the place of Peruvian food in an economic vision . . . [we] will instill pride in local traditions and resources."[38] Mistura, he commented, is ultimately a "festival of Peruvian-ness."[39] Peruvian cuisine is promoted not simply as a motor of economic growth, but as a symbolic representation of the country's cultural diversity and rich traditions.

In promoting Peruvian cuisine, Nikkei cuisine has become identified as its key component. Even though "it may have roots in Japanese cuisine," assert Tsumura and Barrón, "there is no such thing as Nikkei cuisine in Japan."[40] As indicated in the title of their publication, *Nikkei Es Peru* (Nikkei is Peru), "Nikkei is Peruvian. It is in the DNA of our food."[41] In his cookbook on Nikkei cuisine (entitled *La Cocina Nikkei*), Gastón Acurio claims Nikkei cuisine as a "new Peruvian invention."[42] Figure 10.2 illustrates a dish from Acurio's acclaimed restaurant La Mar. The Peruvian media often feature rising Nikkei star chefs, such as Mitsuharu Tsumura, and treat them as representatives of Peruvian gastronomy.[43] Chef Tsumura responds affirmatively: "Nikkei cuisine represents our national identity. It demonstrates that we can live together happily."[44] The Peruvianness of Nikkei cuisine is reflected in the restaurant Chef Padro Luis Guimet opened, called Niquei with "q" to follow the spelling of Quechua, an indigenous and official language of Peru.[45] There he cooks and serves what he calls "Japanese food with Peruvian soul," a product of his three years of hard work conceiving the "Niquei concept."[46] According to the APJ, Nikkei cuisine undeniably has its own unique identity; neither completely Peruvian nor completely Japanese, it is now cooked and consumed not only by Japanese-Peruvians, but by all Peruvians.[47] It is an integral part of Peruvian national cuisine, representing, indeed, the country's cultural diversity, inclusion, and tolerance.[48]

In the context of booming Peruvian gastronomy, food has emerged as an important tool to consolidate unity in a society long marked by cultural divides and social inequalities. A critical component of this has been what Matta calls "ethnic revival." Precisely, national unity, or discourse thereof, has been constructed by incorporating formerly degraded "ethnic" cuisines, such as Andean and Amazonian foods, as part of Peru's national cuisine. In this process, certain select ingredients, such as quinoa and *kiwicha* (amaranth), were picked and valorized and marketed toward global audiences.[49] The

FIGURE 10.2 *Causa*, a Nikkei potato dish, here served with ceviche and shredded seaweed, at Gastón Acurio's La Mar restaurant. Via Wikimedia Commons.

nationalization of Nikkei cuisine was a part of this; once deemed alien and inferior, Nikkei cuisine has come to represent Peru's diverse culinary traditions as a national strategy to package "Peruvian cuisine" globally.

The process proceeded in a top-down manner. The Peruvian gastronomic revolution was led by Lima's elites of prestigious backgrounds, including politicians, journalists, food critics, and writers, as well as successful chefs and businessmen. Those people were able to reverse the historical perception of "backward" indigenous cuisines, precisely because of their economic success and power.[50] They did so by appropriating certain indigenous ingredients and accommodating them to the taste of the urban elite. In so doing, they also challenged indigenous populations to adjust their culinary traditions in such a way as to market to the international clientele. The national identity created through food, in this regard, is a symbol of hegemony, rather than a symbol of unity.[51]

The emergence of Nikkei cuisine entailed a similar process. Certain ingredients and culinary features were appropriated by Lima's elites of non-Japanese backgrounds and marketed as part of Peru's national heritage. In this process, the label changed—from "Okinawan" to "Japanese," then to "Nikkei," as did flavors, ingredients, and meanings, as well as cooks and consumers. This top-down approach, however, simultaneously made it possible for some of the culinary features immigrants originally brought from Okinawa to be widely known to the public and pave the way for their descendants to move onto the center of the national political stage.

The Evolution of Nikkei Cuisine

While Nikkei cuisine was appropriated by non-Japanese Peruvian elites, Japanese-Peruvians also appropriated its popularity to their own advantage. Today, the APJ, backed up by the Japanese government, actively promotes Nikkei cuisine as something unique to Peruvian culture. The first Nikkei Convention, held in 2016, and the annual Nikkei Festival (since 2014), feature Nikkei food, such as *maki acevichado*, as an emblematic aspect of Nikkei culture. The number of Nikkei culinary courses offered at APJ's Cultural Center has also grown rapidly. The official publication of the APJ, *Kaikan*, features one or two Nikkei restaurants every month, and food has grown into perhaps the single most important issue, judging from the coverage of the magazine's contents published between 2010 and 2013. Food brings in significant revenues to the community, according to Japanese-Peruvian community leaders I interviewed in 2012. Accordingly, leaders use Nikkei cuisine as a strategy to promote their community and culture as well as a way to affirm their privileged status in Peru.

As Nikkei cuisine gains popularity inside and outside Peru, Japanese-Peruvian chefs and other members of the community, indeed, feel proud of "their" food. Shinji Soeda, a Japanese-Peruvian chef, commented in an interview featured in *Kaikan* that because of the high recognition of Nikkei cuisine, "I now feel more proud of being Peruvian and having Japanese ancestry."[52] To many descendants of Japanese ancestry, it symbolizes their integration and social acceptance, over which they have long felt ambivalent. To the extent they feel accepted, Japanese-Peruvians also feel that they can appropriate back the "Japanese" element of Nikkei cuisine as their own contribution to Peru.

As Nikkei cuisine has crept into the mainstream culinary stage and more people of non-Japanese backgrounds have taken it over as chefs and promoters, Japanese-Peruvians have simultaneously begun to take Nikkei cuisine to the next level. They have created a new Association of Nikkei Cuisine and have plans to establish a Nikkei cooking school, not only to diffuse Nikkei food more widely, but also to control and authenticate it in the context of proliferation of a variety of "Nikkei" dishes. In trying to give it a new twist, some Japanese-Peruvian chefs have also chosen to go against the current trend of creating fusion by going back to "tradition." Namely, they try to be more "loyal" to traditional Japanese food and recreate "authentic" Japanese food, such as ramen.[53]

In the past couple of years, several ramen shops have popped up in Lima and gained growing popularity, mostly among the city's urban elites. Most of them, if not all, are run by Japanese-Peruvians who previously worked in Japan, either in factories or in ramen shops (*ramen-ya*) or both, as return migrants. Having been to Japan, they all aim to create "Ramen just like in Japan" and recreate a "real ambience of *ramen-ya* in Tokyo."[54] According to César and Fernando Hayashida, the owners of Doomo Saltado, one of the newly opened ramen shops in Lima, Japanese food is automatically associated with maki in Peru, but there is much more to it. Their ultimate objective, and dream, they say, is to recreate the flavors and smells of Japan that those Peruvians who were in Japan really miss now: "Along with safety, security, and orderliness, ramen is probably one of the things those Peruvians miss about Japan."[55]

The kind of Nikkei food those ramen chefs try to introduce to Peru, unlike most other Nikkei chefs, is not based on the fusion cultural heritage they typically claim; rather, it is based on what they newly acquired and experienced *in Japan*. The owner of popular Tokio Ramen, Juan Carlos Tanaka, explains that he incorporates into his ramen not only the ingredients he obtains from Japan, but also the "values" he learned in Japan—discipline, order, and punctuality. That is how he tries to be as "authentic" as he can get in recreating "real ramen of Japan."[56]

The return migration of Japanese-Peruvians, from Japan back to Peru (1989 onward) has provided ex-migrants with an opportunity to take a new turn in developing Nikkei cuisine in Peru. To the extent that they have gone "back" to tradition, the evolution of Nikkei cuisine may have come full circle. Yet the "Japanese" food those ex-migrants try to create is nowhere near what their immigrant ancestors ate or brought from Okinawa nor what they thought was Japanese. Neither is it the same as the food consumed in Japan when their ancestors emigrated around the turn of the twentieth century.

A culinary label carries multiple meanings. While most Japanese-Peruvians regarded "Japanese food" as what Japanese immigrants consumed in Peru, to Peruvians, it may have meant a dish with a touch of soy sauce or miso or anything diametrically opposed to Peruvian cuisine, as Tsumura and Barrón put it. To the young ramen chefs, such as César Hayashida and Juan Carlos Tanaka, "Japanese" food means food consumed in Japan today, such as ramen. And the Japanese government, in backing up the promotion of Japanese food in Peru, tends to define Japanese food in terms of ingredients brought from Japan.

In this way, Nikkei food is defined in multiple ways by multiple actors, sometimes in terms of who prepares it (by Japanese chefs) and who consumes it (Japanese immigrants), but sometimes in terms of what it represents (identity, spirit, culture), where ingredients originate (things indigenous to Japan or Peru), where it is prepared (in Peru), or what is popularly consumed in Japan (such as ramen).

The latest stage of the Nikkei cuisine evolution we observe with ramen is both a "new response to the culinary fusion" that has taken place in Peru over the past decades and a strategy of young emerging chefs to carve out a new niche in Lima's ever more competitive culinary market.[57] They may soon start adding Peruvian aji to their ramen. Whether aji ramen will be labeled Japanese, Peruvian, Nikkei, or something altogether different, depends on where Peruvian elites see marketable potentials, how consumers respond, and what resources the chefs bring and what tactics they use.

Conclusion

Japanese food in Peru has gone through significant transformation through the process of immigration, assimilation, and return-migration. When I first savored "Japanese food" in Lima in 1996, the food was of Okinawan style. The soba I ordered at a "Japanese" restaurant was Okinawa soba, different from the buckwheat noodle I was accustomed to while growing up in mainland Japan. When I went back to the same restaurant in 2011, the soba was no longer the same; it was more akin to the noodles of the mainland. Slurping the soba, I remembered a comment made by a Japanese-Peruvian in Okinawa, that local soba had lost a distinct flavor. Lamenting the extent to which Okinawa had assimilated to mainland Japan, he said: "Even soba tastes the same as in the mainland now."

Some descendants of Japanese immigrants in Peru do worry that their culture is being lost. Some also worry that the culture immigrants originally brought from Japan (or Okinawa) is being transformed into something completely different. A third-generation community leader I interviewed in Lima told me, however, that it should not really matter. What matters in the end is the "essence"—that is, the act of eating soba, regardless of its content. No matter what it is, he said, as long as we are eating soba—together—we can preserve our distinct identity. What matters, he points out, is the act of consuming what is *perceived* as Japanese (or Okinawan), regardless of who prepared the food, how it tastes, or where ingredients come from.

Food is a powerful tool to cultivate an identity as well as a tool to forge unity among a population. The transformation of Japanese food and the emergence of Nikkei cuisine both reflect the strategies of multiple actors. While the Peruvian government has promoted it to forge its nationhood, Japanese-Peruvians have used it to validate their own identity and the Japanese government, as a tool to enhance the Japanese brand abroad. We must not forget, however, that the ability to do so hinges on power and resources. While Japanese-Peruvians, with their resources and the support of the Japanese government, were able to exploit Peru's gastronomic boom to their advantage, poorer indigenous populations have been less able to reap similar benefits.[58] Although Nikkei food has recently gained enormous popularity in and out of Peru, this "most trendy food in Peru" is mostly consumed by, and known to, gastronomically conscious urban elites. The history of how "Japanese food" was presented, accepted, and transformed, therefore, is a story about how Japanese immigrants and their descendants adapted and "made it" in Peru, as well as how multiple actors, such as the Peruvian government, the Japanese government, and elite chefs, appropriated its symbolic meanings.

NOTES

1. Paul Rockower, "The State of Gastrodiplomacy," *Public Diplomacy*, Winter 2014, accessed December 15, 2014, http://publicdiplomacymagazine.com/the-state-of-gastrodiplomacy/.

2. Ministry of Agriculture, Forestry and Fisheries, "Washoku," 2014, accessed December 20, 2014, http://www.maff.go.jp/j/keikaku/syokubunka/ich/pdf/leaflet_e20k.pdf.

3. Amelia Morimoto, "Presencia nikkei en la cocina peruana I," *Discover Nikkei*, 2010, accessed April 26, 2010, http://www.discovernikkei.org/en/journal/article/3406/; Mariela Balbi, *La cocina según Sato* (Lima: Universidad San Martín de Porres, Facultad de Turismo y Hotelería, 1997); Mitsuharu Tsumura and Josefina Barrón, *Nikkei es Perú* (Lima: Telefonica, 2013); Toshio Yanagida, "Peru Nikkei shakai ni okeru 'washoku' to identity—'Nikkei shoku,' 'Nikkei ryori,' 'Nikkei fusion ryori'" (Washoku and identity of the Nikkei community in Peru), *JICA Yokohama Kaigai Iju Shiryokan Kiyo* (report published by JICA Yokohama Immigration Museum), 8.1 (2014): 1–28.

4. Morimoto, "Presencia nikkei" (2010); APJ (Asociación Peruano Japonés del Perú), "Cocina nikkei: La fusión hecha delicia," 2013, accessed December 29, 2013, http://www.apj.org.pe/temasemanal/26-01-07.

5. APEGA (Sociedad Peruana de Gastronomía), "El boom de la gastronomía peruana su impacto económico y social," 2010, accessed January 10, 2014, www.apega.pe; Mariano Valderrama León, "Gastronomia, desarrollo e identidad cultural el caso peruano," in Tsumura and Barrón, *Nikkei es Perú*.

6. APJ, "Cocina nikkei."

7. Morimoto, "Presencia nikkei" (2010).

8. Balbi, *La cocina según Sato*; Morimoto, "Presencia nikkei" (2010).

9. Balbi, *La cocina según Sato*,

10. Balbi, *La cocina según Sato*.

11. Raúl Matta, "Valuing Native Eating: The Modern Roots of Peruvian Food Heritage," *Anthropology of Food*, 2013, http://aof.revues.org/7361.

12. Gastón Acurio, *Las cocinas del Perú*, vol. 4: *La cocina nikkei* (Lima: Empresa Editora El Comercio, 2006); Morimoto, "Presencia nikkei" (2010); Balbi, *La cocina según Sato*.

13. Morimoto, "Presencia nikkei" (2010).

14. Tsumura and Barrón, *Nikkei es Perú*.

15. Tsumura and Barrón, *Nikkei es Perú*.

16. Shoko Imai, "Nobu and After: Westernized Japanese Food and Globalization," in *Food and Social Identities in the Asia Pacific Region*, ed. James Farrer (Tokyo: Sophia University Institute of Comparative Culture, 2010).

17. Tsumura and Barrón, *Nikkei es Perú*.

18. Balbi, *La cocina según Sato*; Tsumura and Barrón, *Nikkei es Perú*.

19. Amelia Morimoto, "Presencia nikkei en la cocina peruana," in *Cultura, identidad y cocina en e Perú*, ed. Rosario Olivas Weston (Lima: Universidad San Martín de Porres, 1996).

20. Tsumura and Barrón, *Nikkei es Perú*.

21. Tsumura and Barrón, *Nikkei es Perú*; APJ, "Cocina nikkei."

22. Tsumura and Barrón, *Nikkei es Perú*.

23. APJ, "Cocina nikkei."

24. El Comercio, "Comida 'nikkei,' lo japonés con gusto criollo," May 10, 2013, http://www.elcomercio.com/entretenimiento/Comida-asiatica-nikkei-gastronomia-Peru_0_916708381.html.
25. Tsumura and Barrón, *Nikkei es Perú*.
26. John Santa Cruz, "La cocina nikkey," *Revista digital de gastronomía y enología*, 2014, accessed January 15, 2014, http://www.gastronomiaalternativa.com/ga-23_32-la-cocina-nikkey.html.
27. *Kaikan*, October 2011, 13.
28. *Kaikan*, March–April 2011, 31; *Kaikan*, June 2012, 21.
29. *Kaikan*, October 2011, 13.
30. Balbi, *La cocina según Sato*.
31. Balbi, *La cocina según Sato*.
32. Matthew Allen and Rumi Sakamoto, "There's Something Fishy about That Sushi: How Japan Interprets the Global Sushi Boom", *Japan Forum* 23.1 (2011): 99–121.
33. Ayumi Takenaka, "The Rise and Fall of Diasporas: How Japanese-Peruvian 'Return' Migration Shapes Diasporic Relations," *International Migration*, first published online, February 20, 2014.
34. Mirko Lauer and Vera Lauer, *La revolución gastronómica peruana* (Lima: Universidad San Martín de Porres, 2006).
35. Matta, "Valuing Native Eating"; Valderrama, "Gastronomia."
36. El Comercio, "Mistura 2013: Estas son las cifras oficiales que dejó la feria," September 18, 2013, http://elcomercio.pe/gastronomia/peruana/mistura-2013-estas-son-cifras-oficiales-que-dejo-feria-noticia-1632897.
37. Valderrama, "Gastronomia"; Matta, "Valuing Native Eating"; APEGA, "El boom."
38. Elena Maria Garcia, "Super Guinea Pigs?," *Anthropology Now* 2.2 (2010): 22–32.
39. *Kaikan*, October 2011, 5.
40. Tsumura and Barrón, , *Nikkei es Perú*, 156.
41. Tsumura and Barrón, *Nikkei es Perú*, 156.
42. Acurio, *La cocina nikkei*.
43. Morimoto, "Presencia nikkei" (2010).
44. *Kaikan*, August 2011, 4.
45. *Kaikan*, October 2012.
46. *Kaikan*, October 2012, 18.
47. APJ, "Cocina nikkei."
48. *Kaikan*, October 2011.
49. Matta, "Valuing Native Eating."
50. Matta, "Valuing Native Eating."
51. Matta, "Valuing Native Eating."
52. *Kaikan*, March–April 2011, 31.
53. *Kaikan*, July 2013.
54. "Naruto Ramen," *Kaikan*, August 2011.
55. *Kaikan*, March 2013, 17.

56. *Kaikan*, January 2012, 26/

57. *Kaikan*, March 2013.

58. Matta, "Valuing Native Eating"; Elena Maria Garcia, "Culinary Fusion and Colonialism: A Critical Look at the Peruvian Food Boom," *ReVista: Harvard Review of Latin America*, Fall 2014 (online version), http://revista.drclas.harvard.edu/book/fusio%CC%81n-culinaria-y-colonialismo.

PART II

Japan's Food-Related Values

Food and Individual Identity

11

Miso Mama

How Meals Make the Mother in Contemporary Japan

Amanda C. Seaman

In her manga *Futari wa ninpu* (Both of us are pregnant), Kubota Miki depicts herself, pregnant, eating a bowl of ramen and drinking the fatty broth with gusto. Her neighbor, also pregnant, does not partake in these pleasures, leaving the broth aside. While the neighbor does not explicitly criticize the narrator's culinary choices, her successful labor and birth is pointedly contrasted with the narrator's own difficulties. At the end of the story, the narrator explicitly identifies her own weakness for tasty, fatty foods as the cause of her own complicated pregnancies, exclaiming, "I should have listened to my doctor!"[1] This story, one of many in the popular pregnancy manga series *Go-Shussan!*, suggests that what and how much a woman eats while she is pregnant are matters of great national concern. Indeed, expectant Japanese women today are inundated with advice from doctors and pregnancy manuals, advice that emphasizes strict management of weight gain through carefully controlling portion sizes and rigorously hewing to a particular, restrictive dietary regime.

Such concerns with diet's effects upon pregnancy are, of course, not new. From the early days of the Tokugawa period (1603–1868), instruction manuals advised pregnant women on what to eat and what to eschew. A cursory glance at the pregnancy advice manuals and magazines that line the shelves of Japanese bookstores today reveals that they still are dispensing advice to women on which foods to choose and which to avoid. While the substance of such advice has not changed that much over the centuries, it is framed and justified in very different ways. This chapter explores the history of Japanese attitudes toward food and the pregnant woman. Beginning with the early dietary regimes contained in Tokugawa advice literature, it traces how the prescriptions and proscriptions they offer persist despite the modernization of the medical system in the Meiji period and continue to be espoused today. It then addresses contemporary negative attitudes toward weight gain during pregnancy and the central role of food choice in weight-control efforts—in particular, the pointed association of a "traditional Japanese" diet with proper weight and the identification of "foreign" foods as inimical to prepartum health. Similar dietary ideologies inform food taboos surrounding breastfeeding—prohibitions that have changed little from Japan's premodern past, despite the fact that they are not supported by medical research. While the insistence that pregnant women need to eat a "Japanese diet" in order to ensure successful gestation is persistent, pervasive, and long-standing, its rationale has changed. Dietary control has shifted from being one element in a traditional canon of proper female behavior to a sign of self-sacrifice, self-control, and self-assertion by the mother herself.

Although there is a long history in Japan of food taboos related to pregnancy, evidence of them is far richer beginning in the Tokugawa era. This is due above all to the production and publication of manuals containing guidance for pregnant women, part of a broader genre of advice literature created in response to the growth and increasing prosperity of town-dwellers (*chōnin*). This literature was intended to instruct the merchant class in proper cultural and social behavior, formerly the province of aristocratic samurai families who had conveyed its precepts and expectations through traditional channels not open to other classes. A leading example of such literature directed at *chōnin* women was the *Onna chōhōki* (Record of women's treasures), written in 1692 by Namura Jōhaku.[2] In addition to sections on food and table etiquette (including the correct order in which to eat a formal meal, the proper use of chopsticks, and the polite way of drinking tea), penmanship, and weddings, the *Onna chōhōki* offered a substantial treatise on pregnancy and childbirth, in which diet played an important role. As William Lindsey has observed, Jōhaku and his readers "believed that food consumption during pregnancy also played a significant role in bringing forth a new life that was healthy, strong, free of disease and deformity."[3]

The *Onna chōhōki* classified the diet of pregnant women under four broad categories, two of which were advantageous (diets that would enrich the fetus and the mother, and that would increase breast milk production), and two of which were to be avoided (diets that could damage the fetus, and that could hurt the mother). Much of this theory of diet was based on ideas that came from Chinese medicine, the dominant medical practice in Japan during the

Tokugawa period. Some foods were to be avoided outright; crab and ginger, for example, were said to cause lateral births and crooked digits, respectively. More often, however, it was particular combinations of foods that posed a danger, either to the fetus's immediate, physical well-being—glutinous rice and chicken consumed together would cause the child to be born with a tapeworm or a parasite—or to its future prospects—eating sparrow together with rice wine, the text warned, made it more likely that the child would fall into lascivious ways.[4] These food prescriptions and taboos were aimed at alleviating maternal anxiety, since the mother's diet was thought to determine both the immediate and long-term outcomes of the fetus.[5] A proper diet was thus central to the maternal maxim: "Do everything properly and the baby will turn out fine."

The dietary guidelines codified in manuals such as the *Onna chōhōki* were still being observed at the beginning of the Meiji period, when midwives—responsible for delivering most babies in nineteenth-century Japan—came under intense scrutiny from medical modernizers. Deemed old-fashioned and nonhygienic, these lay midwives (*toriagerubaba*, literally "the old ladies who receive and lift up [the child]") were replaced in 1899 by younger women who had been trained in modern medical procedures.[6] Notably, while a number of pre- and perinatal practices were condemned as unhygienic and unsafe, many of the old dietary practices were maintained. When Kido Rin, head of the Fukuoka Hygiene Department, published a modern handbook for midwives, for example, its dietary advice for successful pregnancy and breastfeeding largely reflected traditions and beliefs from earlier centuries.[7]

Leaving the traditional pregnancy-related food prohibitions in place made sense when the crucial issue for pregnant women in Japan, particularly those in the countryside and the urban poor, was getting a balanced diet.[8] In the 1932 pregnancy and birth manual *Ansan to ikujiho* (Methods for safe birth and child-rearing), a chapter on "maternal environment and health maintenance" (*ninpu no kankyo to sessei*) distinguishes between the nutritional needs of city-dwellers, workers, and farm women, with the last group getting the most attention.[9] The manual emphasizes the need for proper prepartum nutrition, identifying rice, miso, vegetables, and fish as components of a balanced meal. After the baby is born, the lactating mother is instructed to eat a diet including tofu, Chinese cabbage, brown rice, fish, and other Japanese vegetables.[10] This emphasis on brown rice for lactating mothers reflected the frequency of *kakke* (beriberi) in the Japanese population, due in part to the preference for polished white rice.[11] The manual also lists foods to be avoided, including both sake and Western alcohol, sweets, and spices such as hot pepper and ginger. Enshrining this knowledge in a manual indicates the deep influence of traditional, premodern

Japanese dietary beliefs upon the newer field of "nutritional science" then being adopted in Japan.

The Japanese diet was severely challenged during the war years of 1931 to 1945. Even before Japan was blockaded by Allied forces in 1942, food shortages had become a problem, due both to diversion of much of the food supply to troops overseas and to a series of poor harvests in Taiwan and Korea.[12] The Red Cross's recommendations for pregnant women at the time reveal that the Japanese diet was calorie-poor: women in the latter half of their pregnancies (from five to nine months) were advised to consume 2,503 calories (compared to 2,262 calories during the first four months), with none of those calories coming from rice.[13] These guidelines were difficult to follow given shortages of meat, vegetables, and fruits, the latter crops largely abandoned in order to devote land to grain production.[14] As food shortages became more dire, even these recommendations were cut. After the war's end, it took several years for Japan to regain anything resembling food security.

The war also represented a profound dividing line in the practices of pregnancy and birth in modern Japan. Before the war, most babies were born at home, with midwives in attendance. After the war, however, American birthing practices were imported to Japan, leading to a dramatic increase in hospital births attended by doctors. Japan's rapidly rising standard of living, which allowed the first real experience of food security for a majority of Japanese, soon produced a previously unimaginable abundance and diversity of foodstuffs. As the Japanese diet shifted to include increasing amounts of processed ingredients (including snack food and fast food), nutrition and diet became matters of greater interest and concern.[15]

These changes and their presumed effects upon female (and fetal) health soon drew a response from the Japanese medical establishment that was reflected in the pages of birth manuals. In contrast to advice manuals published in the Meiji and Taisho periods, those from the 1960s and later paid much more attention to weight gain during pregnancy and its effective management. Most Japanese obstetricians now advise that women should only gain ten kilograms (twenty-two pounds) while they are pregnant, while midwives suggest an even more drastic limit of eight kilograms (eighteen pounds), likely due to their more limited access to medical facilities and interventions.[16] Some doctors follow the general guidelines of the Japanese Obstetrics Association, while other calculate the individual's ideal weight based on her prepregnancy BMI (body mass index).[17] During her pregnancy, the woman is constantly monitored, with her weight at each prenatal appointment recorded in her *boshi-techo*, or mother-baby health record. A weight gain considered to be excessive is marked in red. Between appointments, moreover, the patient is supposed to monitor her own weight and compare it to the medical practitioner's guidelines. The strict limits on weight gain are made even more trying by the fact that pregnant Japanese women are not supposed to exercise beyond simple stretching exercises and light walking, leaving them dependent upon self-control and "toughing it out" to manage their weight. As a result, if a woman finds herself slipping into the red zone, she is expected to simply "'hold back' and 'tame' her appetite."[18]

The concern over diet during pregnancy stems from a broader complex of beliefs and attitudes about the relationship between maternal and fetal well-being. Apart from worries that the baby will be born too large or that the mother will suffer from high blood pressure (a risk increased by high sodium levels in the Japanese diet), women and their doctors are prompted by more general anxiety that the baby will not be born healthy. As Tsipy Ivry notes in her recent comparative ethnography of Japanese and Israeli pregnancy and birthing practices, prenatal screening tests remain the exception rather than the rule in Japanese medicine. As a result, to maternal behavior and attitudes, rather than endogenous factors such as genetics or early gestational conditions, are ascribed a central role in ensuring successful pregnancies. It is little surprise, then, that in Japanese pregnancies nature is assumed to require the mother's helping hand; as Ivry states, "The process of gestation cannot be left to happen 'naturally' by itself if we aim for *anzan*, because not every *body* can give a good birth. The body that can give a good birth is the result of the continuous hard work of 'bodybuilding.'"[19] As the bodybuilding metaphor implies, becoming a mother is treated as serious work, requiring discipline, the control of one's desires and impulses, and thus self-sacrifice in order to create an appropriate and safe environment for the developing child. Food plays a crucial role in this process. Resisting the siren song of fatty, salty, and sweet foods, while difficult, is promoted as essential for ensuring fetal well-being.

Maintaining a strict diet that withholds most pleasurable items also trains the mother in the value of self-sacrifice, one of the fundamental tenets of traditional Japanese maternal ideology.[20] Indeed, from the moment of conception a woman's identity is redefined as that of *okaasan* (mother), and her primary interpersonal bond (and responsibility) is assumed to involve her gestating child rather than, for example, her husband.[21] Central to this concept of mother-baby bonding is the idea of *taikyō*, or "fetal education," in which the mother's behavior is believed to exercise a decisive influence over her unborn child.[22] Whereas in earlier centuries women were warned to avoid particular activities that might damage the fetus or lead to undesirable outcomes later in life, now they are encouraged to play Mozart or speak English during pregnancy in order to predispose their child to become a music lover or learn a second language. Here as well, diet plays a key role; eating a proper Japanese diet, mothers are told, not only aids the baby's physical development, but also conditions it from the outset to prefer healthy foods.

The desire to limit one's weight gain during pregnancy, on the other hand, reflects fears of disease and disorders in both mother and child that are thought to stem from "getting too fat." Many Japanese obstetricians and their patients remain convinced that weight gain poses serious risks for developing afflictions including gestational diabetes, pregnancy toxemia, and high blood pressure, despite research suggesting that maternal weight gains of up to fourteen kilograms (thirty pounds) have no statistical association with such ailments and in fact indicating that the real risk is with mothers whose body mass index (BMI) is too low.[23] The actress Mizuno Maki recalls being obsessed with her weight while she was pregnant, after being told that excessive weight gain would render her birth canal "too fat" for an easy labor and delivery—a notion that, while farfetched, reflects the new brand of "folk wisdom" surrounding pregnancy propagated by and among women via the Internet, manga, and pregnancy memoirs (including Mizuno's own).[24]

Equally disturbing is the potential for having a "too big" baby (also known as macrosomia), a fear dating back to at least the Tokugawa period, when women were told to bind themselves with a *hara obi* (belly band) in order to keep their fetuses from growing too large.[25] In her memoir *Zeitaku na osan* (A luxurious birth), Sakurazawa Erika recalls being told that her weight gain after eight months of pregnancy exceeded the eight-kilogram limit. According to her nurses, this was not simply bad for her health, but a harbinger of an oversized baby. It was better, they said, to "birth them small and then raise them big" (*chisaku unde [2000 gram gurai] ookiku sodateru*).[26]

This need to watch one's weight and to control one's appetite is reflected in manuals and magazines that are full of recipes and recommendations on what and how much to eat. Because Japanese women do not normally take prenatal vitamin supplements, a standard practice in the United States, it is critical for them to meet their dietary requirements through the foods they consume.[27] In one popular advice manual, *Ninshin daihyakka*, the section on nutrition emphasizes the importance of nutritional balance, controlling calories, and reducing sodium intake, offering a week's worth of recipes notable both for their low calorie counts and for their emphatic rejection of culinary indulgence. Carrot-milk gelatin pudding and plain yogurt with strawberries are apparently the only desserts deemed acceptable.[28] This approach is echoed by the manual *Hajimete no ninshin: shussan*, edited by the assistant head of the Obstetrical Department at Sanno Hospital in Tokyo (an institution long favored by the imperial household), which explains that "sweets are something extra, and you shouldn't eat too many of them."[29]

Just as notable, however, is the emphatic identification of "healthy eating" in this manual, and in others, with a traditional Japanese diet, presented as the best regime for ensuring proper maternal nutrition. A chart in *Ninshin daihyakka*, illustrating daily requirements of vitamins and minerals, makes this case directly and graphically: fish and mushrooms are recommended as key sources of vitamins B1, B2, and D; vegetables as a source of vitamin A, vitamin C, and folic acid; and seaweed, clams, and *yuba* (produced by skimming the skin from gently boiling soy milk) as sources of iron.[30] Western snacks and sweets are strictly taboo, a message conveyed in *Ninshin daihyakka* by a picture of a crossed-out cookie; if a woman absolutely *must* have sweets, then she "should choose a Japanese one like *manju* [bean paste cake], because they have fewer calories."[31] A few pages later, the reader is warned away from a seemingly healthy breakfast of toast and milk in favor of eggs and a green salad, since "even though [this] is harder to cook, you need to eat protein and vegetables."[32]

Even fruit appears to be frowned upon: the sample menus in *Ninshin daihyakka* contain almost no mention of it, while *Hajimete no ninshin: shussan*'s recommended servings are remarkably small (no more than eighty calories per day, equivalent to one small banana or thirteen strawberries).[33] This attitude likely stems from concerns about fruit's relatively high sugar content, as well as the fact that many fruits currently available in Japan are of foreign provenance.[34] Anthropologist Tsipi Ivry recounts a conversation with a Japanese obstetrician who advised his patients to avoid tropical fruits and instead to "eat fruit and vegetables that grew on the same land you grew up on"—an attitude rooted both in traditional Asian medicine's doctrine of balance of yin and yang and in a "grand environmental paradigm that sees people in general as being made of their environments."[35] In this respect, attitudes toward maternal diet in the manuals dovetail nicely with broader beliefs about the metonymic relationship between food and national identity, and with long-standing—if less openly stated—associations between the maternal and the national body.

The prenatal dietary picture that emerges from pregnancy magazines, while sharing many of the same nutritional and culinary concerns as the advice manuals, is nonetheless a more diverse and seemingly indulgent one. With more pages available to devote to recipes, the magazines offer a broader range of dietary options, with frequent lavish monthly features focused on seasonal foods. A recent fall issue of *Pre-mo* (a neologism meaning both "pregnant mother" and "premother") offered a glossy eight-page spread on foods for the season, including a number of vegetable stews, while the previous spring's issue detailed a week's worth of meals that the pregnant woman could make for her husband before she entered the hospital.[36] In a striking case of seeming to have one's cake and eat it too, the fashion-forward mook (a Japanese magazine-book hybrid) *Ninshin Seikatsu* even offered a flow chart for snack lovers, classifying their dessert preferences into three categories and suggesting snacks for each containing less than two hundred calories. Unlike the manuals, the mook allowed for chocolate as well as cake and ice cream—a concession, it would seem, to the dietary habits and preferences of young, urban, and cosmopolitan Japanese women. Even here, however, the dominant discourses of pregnancy and diet found in the manuals asserted themselves. While readers were allowed to taste the forbidden fruit, that taste was no more than a tantalizing nibble: one square of chocolate, the tip of the *gâteau chocolat*, or a sliver of the ice cream cone. Should this prove inadequate, there was always the option of twenty-five grams of nutritious, and virtuous, wakame seaweed.[37]

The concern for dietary discipline, moreover, does not end once a woman gives birth. Instead, the breastfeeding mother and her new child are considered to be just as susceptible to the effects—good and bad—of the food she ingests.[38] Here, as with pregnancy, the attitudes and advice given to modern Japanese women bear striking similarities to those offered in previous centuries. The beliefs on this score expressed in Kido's late nineteenth-century manual—for example, that women who ate overly rich or fatty foods were prone to breast infections, or that milk would rot in the breasts if not fully expressed—not only echo tenets of Chinese medicine disseminated and codified in the Tokugawa era, but also continue to be repeated in breastfeeding classes to this day.[39] Even the little bite of chocolate once allowed before birth now is taboo, since it is thought to make the breast milk cold.

As with other genres of advice literature, the manuals and magazines aimed at pregnant women mean not only to offer models of "proper" behavior, but also to respond to the problems and challenges faced by their readers, whether real or imagined. The end of this chapter therefore, focuses on how historic dietary prescriptions and proscriptions have shaped the childbearing experiences of Japanese women in the twenty-first century, focusing in particular on three Japanese actresses who wrote autobiographies describing their pregnancies in the early 2000s. In each of these accounts, the women recount terrible morning sickness, the negative effects this had on their appetites, and their subsequent relationships to food—relationships profoundly shaped by the advice given by their doctors, nurses, and midwives.

For the first of these women, Mizuno Maki, the doctor's orders not to gain too much weight while she was pregnant were made easier to follow at first by the constant nausea accompanying her morning sickness. As she describes in *Ninpu dokuhon* (The pregnant woman's reader) she found herself craving ramen and gyoza, but repelled by ice cream cones—reactions that made more sense to her when she discovered that she would be giving birth to a boy since boys traditionally are not supposed to like sweets and ice cream.[40] Despite these occasional cravings and the temptations posed by holiday meals, Mizuno reports little difficulty in maintaining her weight, a disciplined attitude toward diet reflecting both her own body-consciousness as a TV personality as well as her interest in healthy cooking (highlighted by the inclusion in the book of several recipes and photos of the meals she prepared while pregnant).[41]

A similar, if slightly less rosy, sense of dietary discipline can be found in Ishida Hikari's *Maarui seikatsu* (Round world), an account of the author's pregnancy. The picture that emerges from its pages is that of a privileged woman who, despite having a job, seems able to devote most of her time to being—and mulling over being—pregnant. Each day's entry records Ishida's activities, interspersed with thoughts about how happy she is to have a new life inside her ("Someone is in my belly," she remarks early on, "a person different from me").[42] While the early days of her pregnancy are marked by odd food obsessions (including a fascination with tomatoes), none are excessive or particularly indulgent; the records of her meals that accompany most days' entries are notable only for their restraint, their healthiness, and their stress on "balance."[43] Occasionally, the book hints at struggles to keep on the straight and narrow, with entries such as "Because my weight increased, I'll have to decrease the amount that I eat," or "No more snacks!"[44] On the whole, however, Ishida seems fully to have accepted the dogma of strict weight control, never complaining about having to restrict her diet.

Despite its whimsical appearance, Tomozawa Rie's *Mamma Tomosawa Ninpu-chan hen*—a scrapbook with pictures, cute illustrations, and cartoons arrayed across the pages—offers a far more serious, and ambivalent, account of how food anxieties shaped her own pregnancy. In diary entries, photomontages, and longer essays (called "columns") on medical procedures and encounters, Tomozawa graphically represents the stress she endured as a result of trying to control her weight. She obsesses about every weigh-in, carefully recording her weight when she wakes up and when she goes to bed, describes herself eating tiny portions, and suffers from anemia throughout her entire pregnancy. She even considers resorting to bulimic self-purging, recalling that "my friend, who was eight months pregnant, said, 'I threw up after dinner and my weight went down.'" The rest of the passage reflects her conflicting desires to remain small and to nourish the baby (nicknamed Fūsuke):

> Although I ate a lot at lunch, at night I need (!) to be careful. I have to relax and be carefree. That's probably what Fūsuke would say—to toss my worries aside and cherish the time I have left with Fūsuke, body and soul. I forget all about his darling body, thinking only,

"I want to give birth safely," and worrying that "I have to walk a lot" and "It's bad if I get fat." I forget the most important thing: Relax, and spend time with this other body.[45]

Two weeks later, her midwife tells her that she needs to gain more weight, which she is able to do. Eventually, despite a long and exhausting labor, her baby is born safely.

As these accounts make clear, Japanese women pay close attention to their own doctors and to the manuals and magazines that they read, all of which insist upon maintaining and controlling one's weight and eating modest portions of proper, "good" food. Despite the difficulties they encounter in following these often-rigorous dietary dictates, these women—like those in the *Go-shussan* manga—soldier on, driven by the conviction that doing so ultimately will ensure an easy birth. Unlike their ancestors in centuries past, however, who feared that forbidden foods would result in deformed children (i.e., ginger producing gnarled fingers and toes), these modern women see food itself as the potential enemy, with their pregnancies threatened by "too much of a not-so-good thing." Like women in the Tokugawa era, modern pregnant women are taught that proper prepartum behavior is necessary for a positive postpartum outcome. As Tsipy Ivry has noted, rather than attributing the outcome to genetics, many texts written by doctors continue to attribute a "good birth" (*anzan*) not to genes or other intrinsic factors, but to the disposition and commitment of the mother.[46] Now, however, proper diet demonstrates maternal self-sacrifice and self-control. Eating the "Japanese way" is not an intrinsic cause of fetal well-being and maternal safety, but a tool with which to shape the maternal body and render it the best possible vessel for the mother's own project of self-realization through self-abnegation.

NOTES

1. Kubota Miki, "Futari wa ninpu," in *Go-shussan*, ed. Horiuchi Mika, Takaha Mako, Matsui Natsuki, et al. (Tokyo: Asuka shinsho, 1998), 142.

2. William R. Lindsey, *Fertility and Pleasure: Ritual and Sexual Values in Tokugawa Japan* (Honolulu: University of Hawai'i Press, 2007), 12.

3. Lindsey, *Fertility and Pleasure*, 128. Such interests in culinary behavior can be found elsewhere in the *Onna chōhōki*, e.g., in its section on the proper way to deal with the symbolically important but inedible snacks given to newlyweds; see Eric Rath, *Food and Fantasy in Early Modern Japan* (Berkeley: University of California Press, 2010), 71.

4. Lindsey, *Fertility and Pleasure*, 129.

5. Lindsey, *Fertility and Pleasure*, 130.

6. Aya Homei, "Birth Attendants in Meiji Japan: The Rise of a Medical Birth Model and the New Division of Labour," *Social History of Medicine* 19.3 (2006): 410.

7. Homei, "Birth Attendants," 414.

8. Food security was not achieved at a national level until the postwar period, when general economic growth coupled with the introduction of government initiatives such as the school lunch program made it possible. Lizzie Collingham, *The Taste of War: World War II and the Battle for Food* (New York: Penguin, 2012), 289–290.

9. *Ansan to ikujiho* (Tokyo: Shufunotomo-sha, 1932), 24–27.

10. *Ansan to ikujiho*, supplement.

11. The Japanese long privileged polished rice, made by removing the nutrient-rich husk. Ironically, the consumption of this high-status food by middle- and upper-class families required them to inject themselves with B vitamins (scenes of which figure prominently in Tanizaki Junichiro's novel *The Makioka Sisters*), whereas the lower classes received better nutrition from the more humble brown rice in their pantries. The debate about the origin and cure for beriberi is nicely laid out in Alexander R. Bay's book *Beriberi in Modern Japan: The Making of a National Disease* (Rochester, NY: University of Rochester Press, 2012).

12. Collingham, *The Taste of War*, 278.

13. Nihon Sekijujisha, *Senji kokuminshoku* (Tokyo: Dainihon Shuppan, 1941), 136–137. My thanks to Eric Rath for sharing this reference with me.

14. Collingham, *The Taste of War*, 280.

15. A striking example of this transformation is the proliferation of high-fat instant ramen. Demand for Cup Noodle, first introduced in 1958, had reached four million servings by 1972; in less than twenty years, however, this number had grown more than five hundred-fold, with 2.2 billion units sold in 1989. See Frederick Errington, Tatsuro Fujikura, and Deborah Gewertz, *The Noodle Narratives: The Global Rise of an Industrial Food into the Twenty-First Century* (Berkeley: University of California Press, 2013), 43.

16. "Josanpu-san no hone" (The midwives' truth), in Horiuchi et al., *Go-shussan*, 190.

17. Tsipy Ivry, *Embodying Culture: Pregnancy in Israel and Japan* (New Brunswick, NJ: Rutgers University Press, 2010), 85.

18. Ivry, *Embodying Culture*, 86.

19. Ivry, *Embodying Culture*, 92–93.

20. This stands in contrast to the narratives of overconsumption that exist in Japan today and have been addressed by other chapters in this volume. The emphasis on restrictions in diet during pregnancy became more stringent from the late 1980s onward, suggesting a connection with the rise in postwar consumption of sweets and snacks. See, in particular, the chapters by Susan Napier and by Bruce Suttmeier. Keith Vincent's chapter demonstrates that these narratives existed before the war as well.

21. Ivry, *Embodying Culture*, 17.

22. Muriel Jolivet, *Japan: The Childless Society*, trans. Anne-Marie Glasheen (New York: Routledge, 1997), 77–79.

23. See H. Tsukamoto, H. Fukuoka, K. Inoue, M. Koyasu, Y. Nagai, and H. Takimoto, "Restricting Weight Gain during Pregnancy in Japan: A Controversial Factor in Reducing Perinatal Complications," *European Journal of Obstetrical Gynecology and*

Reproductive Biology 133.1 (July 2007): 53–59. On the connection between low maternal BMI and SGA (small for gestational age) births, see H. Watanabe, K. Inoue, M. Matsumoto, K. Ogasawara, H. Fukuoka, and Y. Nagao, "Risk Factors for Term Small for Gestational Age in Women with Low Pre-pregnancy BMI," *Journal of Obstetric Research* 36.3 (June 2010): 506–512; and Takimoto Hidemi, "Malnutrition during Pregnancy in Japan and Proposals for Improvement," *Acta Obstetrica et Gynaecologica Japonica* 58.9 (2006): 1514–1518. Low-birthweight babies also have a greater tendency to gain weight too quickly postpartum, a risk factor for childhood obesity: M. Oyama, K. Nakamura, Y. Tsuchiya, and M. Yamamoto, "Unhealthy Maternal Life-Style Leads to Rapid Infant Weight Gain and Prevalence of Future Chronic Diseases," *Tohoku Journal of Experimental Medicine* 217.1 (January 2009): 67–72.

24. Mizuta Maki, *Ninpu dokuhon* (A pregnant woman's reader) (Tokyo: Shueisha, 2005), 52.

25. For more on the *hara obi*, see Amanda Seaman, "The Ties That Bind: Pregnancy and the Persistence of Tradition," *Journal of Asian Medicine* 5 (2009): 39–56. In the earlier periods, giving birth to a smaller baby was medically sound given that all women did not have access to a midwife.

26. Sakurazawa Erika, *Zeitaku na osan* (A luxurious birth) (Tokyo: Shincho bunko, 2001), 102.

27. Interview with childbirth educator Brett Iimura, October 11, 2014.

28. *Ninshin daihyakka* (The pregnancy encyclopedia) (Tokyo: Benesse Mook, 2003), 170.

29. *Hajimete no ninshin • shussan*, ed. Oshiba Yuko (Tokyo: Lettuce Club Mook, 2006), 69.

30. *Ninshin daihyakka*, 171.

31. *Ninshin daihyakka*, 173.

32. *Ninshin daihyakka*, 173.

33. *Hajimete no ninshin • shussan*, 80. While both manuals allow the consumption of strawberries, it is worth noting that they, along with watermelons (*suika*) and melons (*meron*), are categorized as vegetables in Japan.

34. Apart from persimmons and Asian pears (*nashi*), most fruits currently consumed in Japan first appeared during the Meiji period or later, echoing the role played by increased fruit consumption in other dietary transitions around the world. See Vaclav Smil and Kazuhiro Kobayashi, *Food, Health and the Environment: Japan's Dietary Transition and Its Impacts* (Cambridge, MA: MIT Press, 2012), 32.

35. Tsipi Ivry, "Embodied Responsibilities: Pregnancy in the Eyes of Japanese Ob-Gyns," *Sociology of Health and Illness* 29.2 (2007): 265.

36. *Pre-Mo*, December 2007, 177–178; *Pre-Mo*, June 2006, 69–75. In the latter issue's recipes, calorie counts are provided in case the woman's labor proves to be false and she needs to eat the meals herself.

37. *Ninshin Seikatsu Goki* (Tokyo: Gakken, 2006), 77.

38. Bottle-feeding enjoyed a brief vogue in the postwar period, when a bottle-fed child's victory in the Ministry of Health's 1949 "healthiest baby" contest boosted the popularity of baby formula. This trend reversed in the following decades, however,

in the face of scandal (arsenic-tainted formula sold by the food conglomerate Morinaga was implicated in the death of 138 children), imperial example (the empress Michiko's decision to breastfeed her own children), and government policies like the 1974 breastfeeding campaign. See Errington, Fujikura, and Gewertz, *The Noodle Narratives*, 45.

39. Homei, "Birth Attendants in Meiji Japan," 414.
40. Mizuta, *Ninpu Dokuhon*, 43, 45.
41. Mizuta, *Ninpu Dokuhon*, 65–81.
42. Ishida Hikari, *Maarui seikatsu* (Tokyo: Gentosha, 2006), 7.
43. Ishida, *Maarui seikatsu*, 120.
44. Ishida, *Maarui seikatsu*, 120.
45. Tomozawa Rie, *Mama Tomozawa ninpu-chan hen* (Mama Tomozawa, pregnant lady) (Tokyo: Index Communications, 2006), 68.
46. Ivry, *Embodying Culture*, 92–93.

12

Better Than Sex?

Masaoka Shiki's Poems on Food

J. Keith Vincent

In this well-known 1897 haiku, the poet Masaoka Shiki (1867–1902), the primary theorist and practitioner of the haiku in its modern form, weaves together his three great themes of mortality, poetry, and eating.[1]

> **After I Am Dead**
> tell everyone
> he was a persimmon eater
> and a haiku lover
>
> **Waga shinishi ato wa**
> kakikui no
> haiku konomishi to
> tsutau beshi[2]

Despite its extreme brevity, the poem manages to encapsulate what is most important about Shiki. He loved to write and read, and he loved to eat. Over the course of his short life he composed almost 24,000 haiku.[3] He wrote prolifically in other genres as well. His collected works run to twenty-five thick volumes of poetry, criticism, novels, diaries, and essays, which he managed to produce despite dying prematurely at age thirty-four after a long and painful battle with tuberculosis of the spine that left him bedridden for the last seven years of his life. That Shiki lived even this long, many readers believe, was thanks to his quite literally death-defying appetite. Shiki ate, and wrote about eating, perhaps more than any other Japanese writer.[4] Many of his best poems describe the taste and texture of food and the sensual and convivial pleasures of eating. This chapter discusses what food meant to Shiki and what his writing about food says about him as a poet and a person. It argues that Shiki's fixation on food was not merely a biographical fact recorded in his writing, but that it had a profound impact on the kind of writer he became.

So what did food mean to Shiki? Shiki's interest in food did not have much to do with acquiring the kind of "culinary capital" discussed in the introduction to this volume. He did not see it as a means of expressing class distinction, nor was it tied to his national identity as a Japanese, as would be the case with many later writers. As a literary critic, Shiki famously argued that a good poet should not limit him- or herself to one genre, but should be well versed in the composition of haiku, *waka*, and *kanshi* (poetry in classical Chinese), as well Western forms of poetry.[5] This cosmopolitan attitude extended to food as well. He enjoyed all kinds of foods and did not dwell on their national origins. In this he was a typical Meiji cosmopolitan—just as happy with a beefsteak as he was sashimi, a lover of hot cocoa and green tea, of Asian pears, of ice cream, and, most famously, persimmons.

In the first instance Shiki saw food as fuel: it literally kept him alive by providing the energy and nutrients his body needed to defend itself against the disease that was slowly killing him. Food fueled his poetic imagination as well by inspiring him to stretch the descriptive powers of language to capture nuances of texture and taste. At the same time, by translating the sensuous pleasures of food into words, he was able to appreciate and savor what he ate more fully. His ability to intensify his pleasure in eating by writing about it became increasingly important as his health deteriorated, making chewing and eating more difficult. Writing about food also offered a way to relive past culinary pleasures in his imagination, a practice that may have had a curative effect on him.

Shiki never married or had any romantic relationships with women. In a typically half-humorous essay written in 1889 when he was twenty-two, he declared that all human beings have the same quantity of desire, but that it is apportioned differently depending on the person. Whereas some people experience powerful sexual desire (*shiki-yoku*), he himself was unburdened by it. In his case, he wrote, 70 percent of his desire was directed toward reading (*dokusho*) with 15 percent going toward eating (*shokuyoku*), and the remaining 15 percent toward "miscellaneous desires" (*zatsu-yoku*).[6] It's unclear what would be included in this mysterious third category. In any case, few readers have taken Shiki fully at his word on this matter. One famous argument claims that his "obsession with eating was a compensation for the loss of his libido or at least his inability to satisfy it as a result of his illness."[7] This seems a plausible enough explanation, although illness may not have solely prevented Shiki from satisfying his sexual libido. In fact the closest relationships he had were not with women but with men, with whom he formed powerful homosocial attachments. Given the increasingly heteronormative atmosphere of Meiji-era Japan, these relationships tended to be mediated by something other than sex.[8] The end of this chapter discusses how one such relationship was conducted through the exchange of food and writing about food. Food, for Shiki, I argue, was a powerful mediator of his connections to others: a lively nexus of material, cultural, and social values that offered him the incitement to write and to imagine and inhabit novel forms of sociality and intimacy.

Shiki's Appetite

Shiki always had a strong appetite. He was especially fond of fruits, a fact that is indelibly tied to the way he is remembered by Japanese readers. Years after his death in 1902, Shiki makes an appearance in novelist friend Natsume Soseki's 1908 novel *Sanshirō*. When Sanshirō first meets Professor Hirota on the train to Tokyo in the opening chapter, the professor impresses the young Sanshiro with having known Shiki and regales him with the following anecdote about Shiki and food.

> The man spoke of the poet Shiki's great liking for fruit. His appetite for it was enormous. On one occasion he ate sixteen large persimmons, but they had no effect on him. He himself could never match him, the man said.[9]

This is just one of many similar stories recounting Shiki's outsized appetite. Remarkably, his appetite never seems to have flagged even as his body succumbed to tuberculosis. Shiki was first diagnosed with the disease after coughing up blood in May 1889, when he was twenty-one. He remained relatively healthy for the next six years, but an ill-advised trip to China to work as a war correspondent in the Sino-Japanese War severely weakened him. He came close to death on the ship that brought him back to Japan and never really recovered. Beginning in the spring of 1896, the disease had begun to attack his spine, making it difficult for him to walk. His conditioned worsened progressively until, by the spring of 1902, he could no longer sit up or even turn over in bed. Most of what he wrote had to be dictated to others. And yet, even in these last months of his life, with his back and buttocks covered in painful sores, and his gums oozing puss and blood, Shiki ate with gusto. He kept eating fruits even after the tuberculosis bacteria had ravaged his digestive tract to such an extent that they could pass through almost wholly undigested.

Most people who are this sick find it hard to imagine wanting to eat at all. But Shiki continued to eat and also to write about what he was eating. His private, handwritten journal *Stray Notes While Lying on My Back* contains meticulous records of everything he ate on a daily basis over the last year of his life. September 10, 1901, almost exactly a year before his death, has this typical entry:

> Shit my pants Bandages changed

And then, without missing a beat, in the very next line:

> Lunch: Three bowls of rice gruel with potatoes, bonito sashimi, miso soup with onions and eggplant, tsukudani, two Asian pears, one apple.[10]

This is an enormous amount of food for the lunch of an invalid, but it was not unusual for Shiki. A typical day's menu comprised approximately 3,800 calories. Of his total household income of about fifty yen per month in his final years, 65 percent went to pay for food, the vast majority of which was consumed by Shiki alone, while his mother and sister got by on much less. As one scholar has pointed out, this ratio of total income to food expenditure is equivalent to that of an average household amid the devastation of immediate postwar Japan.[11] In the case of Shiki's household in the early twentieth century, the skewed ratio indicates not grinding poverty but prodigious consumption. Another scholar has calculated that Shiki spent as much on sashimi every month as he did on rent.[12] Shiki's appetite for food was legendary among his circle of family, friends, and disciples, who recognized in it his fierce desire to survive and keep writing. As his contemporary Ioki Hyōtei recalled, it was Shiki's appetite that enabled him, "even after being confined to a six-foot bed for seven or eight long years, to keep fighting, never yielding in his battle with a cruel, atrocious, almost unmanageable monster of an illness."[13]

It is no doubt true that Shiki's appetite helped him keep living. Food provided Shiki with crucial nutritional and psychological nourishment. In the April 20, 1901, entry in his diary, *A Brushful of Ink*, which he published on a daily basis in the newspaper *Nippon*, Shiki begins by thanking his many readers for suggesting various remedies for his illness. While he is grateful for their well-meaning advice, however, he informs them that his disease "is not only incurable, but has also reached the final stage such that not even the most miraculous treatment or magical medicine would do any good. It is even beyond the reach of God at this point." He continues:

> The only treatment that I do have available to me is "eating tasty things." As to what is "tasty," I determine this based on many years of experience and on my mood at the moment. I don't allow anyone else to tell me what is good and what is not. Things that one only eats

> rarely are good, but I can eat sashimi every day and never tire of it. Fruits, pastries, and tea are delicious even if you can't digest them. Skipping breakfast makes lunch taste better and dinner is better if one's fever is low. But I usually eat even if it is running high.[14]

Although difficult to render in translation, Shiki's sense of humor comes through here in the way the slightly overblown formality of the epistolary *sōrōbun* style contrasts with the colloquial phrase "eating tasty things" (*umai mono wo kū*). The latter phrase is set off by scare quotes as if it were a rare and little-known treatment in need of explication. It is true that at this time there was no treatment available for tuberculosis, so getting enough to eat was crucial. But something else is going on in this passage as well. Just as was the case with his taste in literature, Shiki had very strongly held opinions about food.[15] Expressing himself so firmly on matters of taste was a way of constituting and fortifying his sense of self even as his body rotted away. At the same time, telling his readers that "tasty things" were the only cure was his sly way of getting his readers to send him care packages of food, and many of them gladly took the hint. Friends, disciples, and readers across the country responded by sending Shiki food to cheer him up and to help in his recovery. His diaries and correspondence in his last years overflow with haiku and thirty-one-syllable tanka written to express his gratitude for these gifts of food, as in this poem from 1901:

> For the sick one
> a gift of sea bream
> on a rainy day in May
>
> Byōnin ni
> tai no mimai ya
> satsuki-ame

As Miyasaka Shizuo, one of Shiki's most sensitive readers, has observed, the sea bream is an auspicious fish, meant for celebratory occasions, so there is something incongruous and poignant about a gift of sea bream for someone as sick as Shiki was at this time. And yet the easy rhyme between "tai" (sea bream) and "mimai" ("paying a visit on a sick person") makes it seem appropriate despite this incongruity, while expressing the cheering effect the gift clearly had on Shiki. The use of the Sino-Japanese term *byōnin* (translated here as "the sick one") to refer to Shiki himself is typical of his characteristic tendency to see his own situation from a third-person point of view and with a self-deprecating sense of humor that helped him to cope with an increasingly miserable situation.[16]

But food offered Shiki more than just nourishment for his ailing body and good cheer from his friends and readers. He often claimed that it enabled his writing more directly. In an essay titled "Fruits," written in 1896, the first year he spent mostly confined to his bed, he begins with elaborately crafted descriptions of the taste of pears, peaches, strawberries, persimmons, and other fruits, and then discusses how fruits fuel his writing. "Beginning this summer," he writes,

> I have started to crave fruits, and I eat them whenever I sit down to write something. Once I start writing, if I feel like giving up, I eat more, and I feel cool and encouraged; the thoughts come easily and my brush flies. My writing owes a great deal to fruits.

This is followed by five poems featuring the act of reading or writing haiku in conjunction with eating. The following two, each of which associates writing implements with food, are typical:

> this little knife
> for sharpening pencils
> And peeling pears
>
> Kogatana-ya
> enpitsu wo kezuri
> nashi wo hagu
>
> On my red ink stone
> skins of grapes
> scattered about
>
> Shusuzuri ni
> budō no kara no
> sanran su[17]

Another of many examples of poems where fruits seem quite literally to fuel Shiki's writing is this well-known 1897 haiku, which is preceded by the headnote "Upon reaching the bottom of my haiku box late one night":

> After reading and
> ranking three thousand haiku
> two persimmons
>
> Sanzen no
> haiku wo kemishi
> kaki futatsu[18]

The "three thousand haiku" mentioned here could refer to poems Shiki was reading in his capacity as the editor of the haiku column for the newspaper *Nippon*, which ran large-scale haiku contests for its readers starting in 1893 that attracted thousands of entries.[19] The poem could also refer to an evening spent on his life's work of collecting and categorizing seventeen-syllable poems by earlier poets. By the time he died in 1902, Shiki had collected more than 120,000 poems into a massive index known as the *Haiku bunrui* (Haiku categorized), an invaluable resource for poets in the genre that still remains in print today.[20] He had also eaten many thousands of persimmons.

But perhaps the most important way in which food mattered to Shiki as a poet was in the specifically writerly challenge of describing the taste of food in words. This challenge might be described as a variant of what I shall term the "cooking show paradox." Viewers watching *Top Chef* or *Lydia's Kitchen* or *The Barefoot Contessa* are cut off completely from the tastes and smells on the television set, and yet those very tastes and smells are precisely what these shows are supposed to be about. Unable to convey them directly, the best the cooking show can do is help viewers imagine them through a set of proxies that can be conveyed audiovisually. That people do watch cooking shows and enjoy them as much as they do is testament to the fact that the producers have come up with many clever ways of conveying the taste and aromas of food without ever having access to viewers' taste buds and noses: the sounds of simmering sauces, the crunch of fried foods, the fresh colors of a salad, and the look on the judges' faces as they chew and swallow. Poetry about food presents an even greater challenge, since poets have only words on the page at their disposal. But Shiki took on this challenge enthusiastically, especially in his later years. As his teeth fell out and his digestive tract was destroyed by disease, he was increasingly unable to enjoy the foods he loved, so he wrote about food as a way to supplement his enjoyment of it, as in this poem from *Stray Notes While Lying on My Back*:

> I sink my teeth in
> and overripe persimmon goo
> drips all down my beard
>
> Kaburitsuku
> jukushi ya hige wo
> yogoshikeri[21]

The persimmon here is a gooey mess, with sweet, gelatinous insides. The five syllable in the verb *kaburitsuku* ("to sink one's teeth into something") takes up the whole first line, suggesting that the poet is taking his time with this messy fruit. The initial sharp "k" sound yields to a softer "b" as he bites into the persimmon. The beard makes the mess seem even stickier and renders it more visible. At the time he wrote this poem, Shiki was so sick that he did not have the energy to raise his head or clean the persimmon off his beard. And yet he lists not one but "three persimmons" among the items he ate for lunch that day.[22] The action of biting into the persimmon would not have felt the same as it once did when his mouth was healthy. But in writing the poem, he intensifies his pleasure in eating it, while also conveying that pleasure to his readers. The poem is a good example of Elaine Scarry's discussion of how authors use "instructions" to readers on how to imagine "the actual structure of production that gives rise to the perception" to achieve a "vivacity" in verbal description.[23] It is hard to read this poem without imitating the action of biting into the persimmon, and imagining how it would feel and taste.

If this poem focuses on the sensuous texture of the persimmon, in others Shiki focuses on the visual appeal of fruits, as in this poem

> deepest purple
> unto black
> this bunch of grapes[24]

> Kuroki made ni
> murasaki fukaki
> budō kana[25]

Published in the newspaper *Nippon* on September 9, 1902, this haiku also appears in *Stray Notes While Lying on My Back*, where Shiki often jotted down early drafts of his poems alongside the lists of what he was eating. In the last months of his life, Shiki would take a shot of morphine and use the pain-free moments to paint and write poems about the fruits and flowers in his sickroom, so *Stray Notes* includes many watercolor paintings and sketches alongside haiku. In this poem he seems to be thinking about how to mix just the right color to paint the grapes. The poem uses the more angular katakana phonetic characters instead of rounded hiragana, creating a kind of visual staccato that accentuates the five "k" sounds in the first two lines.[26] The angular lines of the katakana and plosive "k" sounds contrast with the lusciousness of the voiced consonants and rounded vowels in the word for "grapes" (*budō*) in the last line. The combined effect of this passage from sharp to soft is like biting into a cool grape bursting with juice. (In the English translation, I have tried to approximate this with the "t" and "k" in "unto black" leading into the softness of a "bunch of grapes.") If the reader can almost taste the grapes thanks to these techniques, it is because the poem captures both their appearance—their "deepest purple" color—and what it would feel like to bite into them, in a way that is similar to the poem quoted earlier on the gooey persimmon.

The focus in these poems on the act of eating in all of its sensual immediacy was something new in Japanese poetry at the time. As Takeshi Watanabe points out in his chapter for this volume, works of classical Japanese literature such as *The Tale of Genji* and *The Pillow Book* rarely mention food, and when they do, they display little interest in how it tasted.[27] One critic Watanabe cites suggests that this was because "Heian cuisine tasted awful, and food was not something to be enjoyed."[28] In his book on the culture of the seasons in Japan, Haruo Shirane offers another plausible explanation. "In the classical poetic tradition," he writes, "sight, sound, and smell were considered to be elegant sensations while taste was regarded as vulgar."[29] For these reasons texts in the high classical tradition rarely mention food. It was only in the Edo period, when political stability and burgeoning national trade routes brought about the growth of a richly diverse gastronomic culture, that food items fully enter the lexicon of Japanese poetry. Shirane notes that by the nineteenth century one popular poetic reference manual for seasonal terms (called a *saijiki* in Japanese) contained "as many as 480 food words out of around 3400 seasonal words—that is, some 14 percent of the total."[30] But if food had at last become a legitimate topic for poetry in this period, it tended to feature in poems not in its immediate materiality, but as a social symbol of one kind or another. Thus food items tended to appear in occasional poems written in thanks for gifts of food, as indices of wealth or poverty, or as indicators of the season. The following well-known poem by Yamaguchi Sodō (1642–1714), on the sights, sounds, and tastes representative of early summer, is a good example:

> Green leaves for the eyes
> in the mountains the cuckoo's cry
> the first bonito

> Me ni wa aoba
> yama hototogisu
> hatsugatsuo[31]

A classical poet would have been more than content with the first two of this poem's three seasonal words: the visual reference to green leaves and the sound of the cuckoo, both of which were well-established indicators of early summer in the classical tradition. But Yamaguchi's inclusion of a third seasonal word, the "first bonito," locates this poem squarely in the context of the Edo period's commercial gastronomic culture. The phrase refers to the bonito (also known as "skipjack") fish caught just as it comes into season in early summer, typically brought by runners direct from the Kamakura to market in Edo. For an Edo-ite the "first bonito" was the quintessential indicator of this season. Its presence here marks the poem as a good example of the vernacular *haikai* tradition; the contrast between the first two lines and the third would have given contemporary readers a little thrill as the poem comes down to earth and shows its rootedness in local Edo culture.[32] The poem also has a hint of class snobbery typical of the Edo sophisticate: only the relatively well-off connoisseur could afford to purchase the first bonito of the season. While such poems in which food items served as markers of season or class were common in the Edo period, it was less common to see poems describing the appearance, taste, or texture of food itself, as in Shiki's gooey persimmon poem.[33]

Shiki's innovative focus on the taste and texture of food in his poetry can be explained partly by his protracted illness. He was especially aware of the sensual pleasures of eating both because he had always been an enthusiastic eater, and because in his later years he began to lose the ability to chew his food. In an essay on Shiki's relation to food, Kurosawa Tsutomu, a literary critic and dentist, notes the crucial importance to one's mental and physical health of the ability to chew food properly. Kurosawa quotes the following passage published in another of Shiki's public diaries on May 9, 1901, in which he reflects on what it has meant to him to have a strong bite. "I have realized something lately," Shiki writes.

> Even though I have been confined to my bed for so long now, the fact that I have still been able to digest most kinds of food must have to do with my strong jaw muscles. It is surely no coincidence that I have long had the habit of continuing to chew my food when it has already been chewed, of further softening what is already soft, even the rice in a bowl of congee. It is perhaps because I tend to chew and chew like this (*kaku kami-kami taru tame ni ya*) that my top and bottom molars, which are most important for manducation, have finally been damaged such that now they cause me great pain, making it impossible for me to bring my top and bottom teeth into complete alignment. Now that it has come this far I have no choice but to swallow without chewing even the softest of foods. Swallowing without chewing not only makes it hard to taste what you are eating, it also causes one's stomach to ache and cramp. I have thus been robbed in one fell blow of both the nutrition necessary for my health and of one of my greatest pleasures in life. As my body thus weakens and I continue to suffer in anguish night and day, the question suddenly occurs to me: "For what reason do human beings hold on to life?"[34]

The question is of course rhetorical, and as long as Shiki is asking it and writing about his suffering, the reader feels that he will indeed "hang on to life." But the passage makes clear how crucial the pleasures attached to eating were to him. Shiki ends the essay with a long poem (*chōka*) in the archaic lyrical style of the eighth-century *Man'yōshū*, the very earliest collection of Japanese poetry. The poem reads:

> my back teeth
> that once twittered like birds
> and crushed like mortars
> seem to have rotted away
> I cannot eat
> the grains of the fields
> or the fish of the sea
> biting into a fruit
> causes me pain
> and the sweet and bitter greens
> of Musashino
> I must boil
> into a slurry of rice gruel
> so the days pass by
> as each breath I draw
> grows thinner
>
> saezuru ya
> kara-usu nasu
> oku no ha wa
> mushibami-kerashi
> hatatsu mono
> io wo mo kuezu
> ko no mi wo ba
> kamite mo itamu
> Musashino no
> amana karana wo
> kayujiru ni
> mazete mo
> nineba
> iya hi ke ni
> ware tsuku iki no
> hosori yuku ka mo[35]

Kurosawa argues that Shiki responded to his loss of the ability to chew food by writing poems in which he imagines or remembers himself eating. This so-called memory therapy (*kaisō ryōhō*), which is currently used in Japan as a way to prevent dementia in elderly patients, was a way of reliving the pleasure of eating foods that he could no longer enjoy.[36] In her book on food in Japanese literature, Tomoko Aoyama notes (modifying a quote about literature from critic Terry Eagleton) that food, like literature, "looks like an object but is actually a relationship."[37] In Shiki's case, he would often write about important memories in his life connecting food with people he was close to, as a way of dealing with the isolation caused by his illness. His many haiku on fruits and other foods are often inspired by his relationships with other people. In yet another essay titled "Fruits," serialized in the journal *Hototogisu* in March and April 1901, he relates beautifully written anecdotes having to do with memories of eating fruits. In each one, a barrier of some kind is overcome and Shiki manages to gorge himself on some delicious fruit. The focus is not on the taste of the fruits themselves, but on the whole experience of acquiring and eating them. And yet, by the time he does eat them, he has built up so much anticipation in readers' minds that they can almost taste the fruits. The following passage recalls a memory from the summer when he was hospitalized after coughing up blood while on the ship that took him back from a short stint as a war reporter in the Sino-Japanese War (1894–1895) and his two favorite disciples, Takahama Kyoshi and Kawahigashi Hekigotō vie to bring him strawberries.

> I went into the hospital in Kobe in late May 1895. Kyoshi came and then Hekigodō came too, so I was well taken care of. But I was extremely weak and could hardly drink a cup of milk or soup. The doctor gave permission for me to eat just a few strawberries, so I had some every morning without fail. The strawberries in the stores were not fresh, so Kyoshi and Hekigodō took turns picking some for me directly from the fields. Lying in my hospital bed, I pictured the two of them gathering those strawberries in a strawberry field sloping gently upward. Before long a basket of strawberries was set upon my bed. I never forgot those strawberries, so when I came back to my house in Tokyo I took great pleasure in planting a Western strawberry bush on the fence of my garden.[38]

Shiki had already written of this memory once in his 1896 essay on fruits cited earlier, in which he described how fruits fueled his writing.[39] In writing this passage five years later, he would seem to be eating these strawberries over and over. He anticipates their arrival as he imagines Kyoshi and Hekigodō picking them, savors them when they arrive, and then remembers them for years after. The taste of the fruits is clearly enhanced by his affection for the two young men who went to such trouble to bring them to him. But just as the past cannot ever be fully recaptured, the object of one's desire can never be full attained. In the following poem written in 1900, Shiki describes food in a situation where it is inaccessible, thus invoking desire—and recapitulating what I called the "cooking show paradox," whereby food is seen but not tasted.

> The cakes on the altar
> look beautiful
> winter solstice
>
> Butsudan no
> kashi utuskushiki
> tōji kana[40]

The "altar" in this poem is sometimes translated as "household altar," or "buddha shelf," where it is customary to place food as an offering to one's deceased relatives. The word I have translated as "cakes" (*kashi*) is a broad category that can encompass both sweet and savory, so has no exact equivalent in English. I chose "cakes" because of the poem's emphasis on the appearance of these treats, rather than their taste. Clearly Shiki chose the word "beautiful" (*utsukushiki*) because these are cakes you can see but not eat. The image encapsulates what it is like to have lost someone, to have memories and feelings associated with the person but to be unable to touch him or her physically. The poet can't have his cakes and eat them too and the seasonal reference to the winter solstice, the shortest day of the year, further intensifies this awareness. This day, the poem seems to say, is painfully short, and the shortness makes the cakes more beautiful and the feeling of loss more acute.

In Shiki's second essay on fruits, he addresses the fact that not everyone likes the same fruits. Most people like fruits in general, he writes, but when it comes to which ones are best, no one can agree.

> Some people like persimmons best, but others dislike them because they are not tart enough and don't taste like fruits. Other people like Asian pears, while still others will eat any fruit except Asian pears. Some like strawberries, others praise grapes. Some like peaches for their elegance, while others say there is no fruit as delicious as the apple. To each his own.[41]

This passage, in the middle of a long and rambling essay, seems relatively mundane on first reading. That not everyone likes the same fruits is true enough. On multiple readings, however, the passage speaks to something more profound: the impossibility of ever experiencing the world as someone else does. Differences in taste, and the concomitant failure of language to convey just how a particular fruit tastes to a particular person, is both a reminder of our final separation from each other and a spur to try harder to bridge the gap. Shiki was perhaps even more acutely aware of this because he lived with pain and illness for so long. Physical pain, like the taste of food, is an intensely subjective experience. Only the sufferer can understand it directly. Writing cannot in itself communicate taste or convey exactly what it feels like to be in pain. But it can come close, and in doing so, it can lessen our sense of separation from others.[42]

Two years before his death in 1900, Shiki met the poet and future novelist Nagatsuka Takashi. Nagatsuka had been deeply impressed by Shiki's call for a new and more realistic style of poetry in his *Letters to the Waka Poets* (*Utayomi ni atauru sho*), which was then being serialized in the newspaper *Nippon*. He traveled to Tokyo from his hometown in Tochigi prefecture and showed up at Shiki's home in Negishi on March 27 intending to ask Shiki for his guidance in writing tanka, a form of classical poetry in thirty-one syllables that Shiki is credited with updating for the modern age.[43] Seeing a rickshaw parked outside Shiki's home on that day, Nagatsuka lost his courage to knock. But he came back the next day when no other guests were visiting, and Shiki received him warmly.[44] Nagatsuka, who was just shy of his twenty-first birthday, was quite beautiful, and according to an account by their mutual friend and fellow tanka poet Itō Sachio, Shiki fell hard for him. Donald Keene draws on Itō's account in his recent biography of Shiki, noting: "It was clearly not a physical relationship—by the time that Shiki and . . . Nagatsuka . . . became intimate friends, Shiki was a hopeless cripple confined to his sickbed. But, Itō wrote, it gave Shiki great pleasure to impart to Nagatsuka not only his knowledge of tanka composition but also his philosophy, and he showed Nagatsuka a warmth that went beyond that of teacher and student."[45] While Keene refers to Shiki's "love" for Nagatsuka, Itō has a harder time coming up with the right word to describe their relationship. It was "too idealistic to be that between father and son" and "too emotional to be that between a teacher and his disciple."[46] Like the taste of a delicious food that evades verbal description, the nature of their relationship was known only to the two who tasted it.

One can, however, get some sense of their relationship from the eighteen extant letters Shiki sent to the Nagatsuka in the last two years of his life that have been included in Shiki's collected works.[47] Sixteen of these are thank-you notes for an item of food that Nagatsuka sent to Shiki; one is an offer to Nagatsuka to come and take some scrap writing paper that Shiki has collected. The last is a letter in which Shiki encourages Nagatsuka to open a school and educate the farmers in his hometown, which is said to have inspired Nagatsuka to write *The Soil*, a novel about farm life in his village that would make him famous years later.[48] Thus all eighteen letters have to do in some way with food or writing. The list of food items that Nagatsuka sent to Shiki shows great thoughtfulness and inventiveness. Most are local specialties from around Nagatsuka's hometown in Tochigi prefecture, including angelica tree shoots (*tara no me*), thorny olives (*nawashirogumi*), chestnuts, mulberries, hachiya persimmons, a hare, two pheasants, three snipes, plum *yōkan* jelly from Mito, and a "mountain" of freshwater minnows (*yamabe*). Shiki's letters express his appreciation for the gifts and his affection for Nagatsuka. "Thanks for the sparrows," he writes in early February 1901, "I ate them the day before yesterday, yesterday, and today."[49] Often he includes poems as well. On September 27, 1900, in thanks for a gift of chestnuts he writes:

> when I think that these
> chestnuts are a gift from you
> they taste great!
>
> Kimi ga kureta
> kuri da to omou to
> umai yo[50]

A year later, having received the three snipes, he writes:

> my loneliness
> just decreased three whole birds' worth
> snipes in autumn
>
> Sabishisa no
> san'wa herikeri
> shigi no aki[51]

Remarkably, several of Shiki's letters mention that the food item that Nagatsuka has sent him has been damaged or spoiled on its way to him. The fact that he feels comfortable telling Nagatsuka this suggests how close the two men felt to each other. The chestnuts received on September 20 are full of bugs, the mulberries are crushed, and the *yamabe* minnows are crawling with maggots. Shiki takes the damage in stride. He gives Nagatsuka some advice on better techniques of packing and preservation, and he writes in each case that he has eaten some of the food anyway (even the maggot-filled minnows). Shiki was used to living with decay. He knew how to take what he could of the unspoiled parts of life and get the most out of them. In the following haiku, he suggests that the bugs in the chestnuts make Nagatsuka even more dear to him:

> a heartfelt gift
> of bug-eaten chestnuts
> arrived today
>
> Magokoro no
> mushiguikuri wo
> moraikeri[52]

It is highly likely that Nagatsuka sent even more than sixteen packages of food to Shiki over these years and that Shiki was either not well enough to write thank-you notes or the notes do not survive. The long poem I discussed earlier in which Shiki laments the loss of his ability to chew food concludes with two envoys, one of which mentions another gift that most likely came from Nagatsuka. The poem uses the ancient name for the region in Tochigi prefecture where the town of Yūki is located, where Nagatsuka grew up.

> spring quails
> sent from the town of Yūki
> in Shimōsa
> How desperately I wish
> I had teeth to eat them with
>
> Shimōsa no
> Yūki no sato yu
> okurikoshi
> haru no uzura wo
> kuwan ha mogamo[53]

This envoy takes the form of a thirty-one-syllable tanka, the poetic form in which Nagatsuka had apprenticed himself to Shiki. Tanka are traditionally associated with romance between men and women, but this one is clearly expressing Shiki's love for Nagatsuka and perhaps also his painful awareness that he will never be able to express it physically. The poem's four "k" sounds suggest the strong bite that Shiki has lost to illness, fading into the mush of the word "mogamo" at the end, an archaic particle indicating desire characteristic of the poetry of the *Man'yōshū*. While this word lends the poem an antique tone, the use of the colloquial word "kū," for "eat," makes it modern, and very much in line with Shiki's efforts to update the genre. Whereas other words in Japanese for "eating" (such as *taberu* or *itadaku*) derive etymologically from words for "receiving" food from a social superior, *kū* refers directly to the physical act of eating. It was a favorite of Shiki's, no doubt because of its crisp "k" sound and its more primal connection to the act of eating. It features in many of his best poems, including this one, far and away the most famous of all modern Japanese haiku, and the one for which Shiki is best known:

> I bite into a persimmon
> and the temple bell tolls
> at Hōryūji
>
> kaki kueba
> kane ga naru nari
> Hōryūji

The poem has Shiki doing what he liked best: biting into a persimmon, back when his bite was still healthy in the fall of 1895. Most scholars agree it was written on October 26 of that year, when he stopped in the ancient capital of Nara on his way back to Tokyo after having spent that summer and fall recovering in Kobe, Suma, and finally in Matsuyama from his ill-fated his trip to China. The implied cause-effect relationship between the act of biting into a persimmon and the booming of the temple bell adds a humorous note to the poem, as if the persimmon contained a switch inside it that caused the bell to go off, startling the poet. The persimmon here is not an overripe persimmon as in the previous poem, but rather a small round "palace persimmon" (*goshogaki*). These are known for their crisp flesh, more like an apple, and are produced around Nara, where the great seventh-century Hōryūji temple complex is located. The four "k" sounds in the first two lines evoke the crunch of the persimmon and perhaps the crackling of fall leaves underfoot, while the long vowels in "Hōryūji" mimic the sound of the temple bell. Once again, there is a combination of hard "k" sounds with softer sounds, suggesting what it feels like to bite into the fruit. That persimmons were Shiki's favorite fruit may well have had something to do with the satisfying "mouth feel" of these two "k"s—and perhaps also with the fact that the word "kaki" is a homonym for "writing" in Japanese.

All poetry functions in the space between words and things, but there is something about forms like haiku and tanka that awakens the reader in a particularly intense fashion to the vibrant materiality of language and the world-making power of words.[54] This may have to do with the their extreme brevity, which makes every syllable of every word count, or with the way they articulate the world into aesthetically satisfying, "bite-size" fragments of seventeen or thirty-one syllables.[55] These aspects of haiku and tanka seem to have provided

Shiki with a sense of secure connection to the world, even as his physical body rotted away.[56]

As I noted at the beginning of this chapter, some critics have claimed that food took the place of sex for Shiki. As Donald Keene writes, Shiki's "lack of interest in women . . . puzzled his disciples."[57] Robert Tuck notes that Shiki's love life is "one of the minor unsolved mysteries of Meiji literary history."[58] But rather than trying solve this "mystery" as his disciples and many critics since have done—by scouring his archive for signs of a woman with whom he might have been involved[59]—it may be more productive to think of the ways in which Shiki's "sexuality" is not such a "mystery" at all, but something right there on the page, in the words he uses, in the evident delight he takes in them and the relationships that they mediate. This is especially clear in his many poems about food, as they express the pleasures both of eating and of connection with others. Food, after all, is a lot like sex, and a lot like poetry too: never just word or thing, but something in between.

Acknowledgments

I am grateful to the two anonymous reviewers for their extremely helpful and candid critiques of this chapter in its earlier form. Thanks also to Nancy Stalker and to Susan Ferber for their careful editing and for their patience.

NOTES

1. This chapter is dedicated to Professor Donald Keene.
2. This and all other translations are my own. "After I am dead" (*Waga shinishi ato wa*) is a headnote, not part of the poem proper. Masaoka Shiki, *Haiku: 3*, vol. 3 of *Shiki zenshū*, 25 vols. (Tokyo: Kōdansha, 1975), 88–89.
3. The Kodansha *Shiki zenshū* (*Collected Works of Shiki*) lists 23,647 haiku written by Shiki, including 18,191 included in his notebooks and/or published, 3,372 that he crossed out, and 2,085 "gleanings" (poems that were either first drafts, were published but then left out of his diaries, etc.). See *Shiki zenshū*, 3:729. All of Shiki's haiku have been conveniently compiled in a searchable database by the Shiki Museum in his hometown of Matsuyama. It can be found here: http://sikihaku.lesp.co.jp/community/search/index.php.
4. Shiki is discussed prominently in a number of books on food and Japanese literature, including Tomoko Aoyama, *Reading Food in Modern Japanese Literature* (Honolulu: University of Hawai'i Press, 2008); and Kōzaburō Arashiyama, *Bunjin Akujiki* (Tōkyō: Shinchōsha, 2000).
5. See, for example, Shiki's *Letters to the Waka Poets* (*Utayomi ni atauru sho*), where he chastises *waka* poets for their ignorance of other forms of poetry other than

waka. Masaoka Shiki, "San Tabi Utayomi Ni Atauru Sho," in *Karon; Senka*, vol. 7 of *Shiki zenshū*, 26–28.

6. Masaoka Shiki, "Dokusho-Ben," n.d., http://www.aozora.gr.jp/cards/000305/files/3608_17700.html.

7. The critic is the poet Saito Mokichi, as quoted in Aoyama, *Reading Food*, 21–22. See also Tsutomu Kurosawa, "Byōja No Bungaku: Masaoka Shiki Ni Okeru Yamai No Bungaku III: Gyōga Manroku Kō," *Ijigaku Kenkyū* 9 (December 10, 1994): 1–70, p. 45.

8. For a discussion of literary fiction that narrates the onset of heteronormativity in Japan, see Keith Vincent, *Two-Timing Modernity: Homosocial Narrative in Modern Japanese Fiction*, Harvard East Asian Monographs 352 (Cambridge, MA: Harvard University Asia Center, distributed by Harvard University Press, 2012).

9. Sōseki Natsume, *Sanshirō: A Novel*, trans. Jay Rubin (London: Penguin, 2009), 13.

10. Masaoka Shiki, "Gyōga Manroku," in *Shiki zenshū*, 11:406.

11. See Natsuo Sekigawa, "Shiki Saigo No Hachinen: Shokuryoku to Hyōgenryoku," *Tanka Kenkyū* 66.10 (2009): 106–112.

12. Toshinori Tsubouchi, *Masaoka Shiki no "Tanoshimu chikara"* (Tokyo: Nihon Hōsō Shuppan Kyōkai, 2009), 160.

13. Quoted and translated in Donald Keene, *The Winter Sun Shines In: A Life of Masaoka Shiki*, Asia Perspectives: History, Society, and Culture (New York: Columbia University Press, 2013), 20.

14. Masaoka Shiki, "Bokuju Itteki," in *Zuihitsu 1*, vol. 11 of *Shiki zenshū*, 91–227, p. 168.

15. Robert Tuck captures this characteristic of Shiki in his forthcoming book on Shiki and Meiji print culture: "Shiki's career was also distinguished by his pugnacious and polemical critical writings, the source of many of the pronouncements for which he is best known. Early in his critical career, for instance, he would famously declare that around nine-tenths of the work of Matsuo Bashō (1644–1694), haikai's greatest poet of all time and worshipped as a literal god during Meiji, was made up of 'bad, awful poems (*akku daku*).' In another well-known moment of literary iconoclasm, he would state in his 1898 discussion of *waka* that the legendary Ki no Tsurayuki (872–945) 'was a terrible poet (*heta na utayomi*), and [his anthology] the *Kōkinshū* is a collection of garbage.'" Robert Tuck, *Idly Scribbling Rhymers: Poetry, Print, and Community in 19th Century Japan* (New York: Columbia University Press).

16. Shizuo Miyasaka and Masaoka Shiki, *Shiki Shūku Kō: Kanshō to Hihyō* (Tōkyō: Meiji Shoin, 8), 429–430.

17. The entry ends on this somber note, "Now I am assailed by new ailments. What's worse, winter has arrived and there is no prospect of nuts or fruits any time soon. My brush has come to a stop." Masaoka Shiki, "Kudamono," in *Shōragyokueki*, vol. 11 of *Shiki zenshū* (Tokyo: Kōdansha, 1975), 84–85.

18. Masaoka, *Haiku; 3*, 88.

19. On haiku competitions in Meiji newspapers, see Tuck, *Idly Scribbling Rhymers*.

20. For the Shiki "database" of more than 120,000 seventeen-syllable poems, see Masaoka Shiki, ed., *Bunrui Haiku Taikan*, 13 vols., Bunrui Haiku Taikan (Tōkyō: Nihon Tosho Sentā, 1992).

21. The poem appears in *Stray Notes While Lying on My Back* on October 25, 1901, in which he writes that he has begun to sell his books in order to buy food, "realizing that I have not much longer when I will still be able to eat, which makes me want to eat as many delicious things as possible while I still can." Masaoka, "Gyōga Manroku," 11:479.

22. Also listed are "tuna sashimi, two bowls of rice, *narazuke* pickles, milk, biscuits, and salt crackers."

23. Elaine Scarry, *Dreaming by the Book* (New York: Farrar, Straus and Giroux, 1999).

24. I owe the word "unto" in this translation to Janine Beichmann's fantastically minimalist translation of the same poem: "Purple / unto blackness: / grapes!" See Janine Beichman, *Masaoka Shiki: His Life and Works* (Boston: Cheng & Tsui, 2002), 98.

25. Masaoka Shiki, *Shokan 2*, vol. 19 of *Shiki zenshū*, 473.

26. One Shiki scholar suggested to me that Shiki used katakana in his late diaries when he was feeling especially ill because the straight lines and angles of katakana required less energy to produce than the rounded ones of hiragana.

27. Shiki himself made note of this relative lack of references to food in classical literature in a characteristically systematic way. In an 1897 notebook he listed thirty-six food items and copied out passages in which they appear in classical literature, including what may be all of the rare references to food in the *Tale of Genji*. The editors of his collected works speculate that a "hidden motif" of this work may be that it was a way to continue to enjoy food even after he had become bedridden. See Masaoka Shiki, "Shokubutsu-Kō," in *Kenkyū Hencho*, vol. 20 of *Shiki zenshū*, 579–591.

28. Kiyoyuki Higuchi, *Taberu Nihon Shi*, Asahi Bunko (Tōkyō: Asahi Shuppansha, 1996). The passage is translated by Watanabe.

29. Haruo Shirane, *Japan and the Culture of the Four Seasons: Nature, Literature, and the Arts* (New York: Columbia University Press, 2012), Kindle ed., locations 4276–4277.

30. Shirane, *Japan and the Culture*, Kindle locations 4282–4283.

31. I have modified the translation of this haiku based on the version that appears in Faubion Bowers, ed., *The Classic Tradition of Haiku: An Anthology* (Mineola, NY: Dover Publications, 1996), 12.

32. For a useful discussion of the popular and sometimes irreverent *haikai* aesthetic from which the modern haiku is derived, see Haruo Shirane, "Haikai Language, Haikai Spirit," in *Traces of Dreams: Landscape, Cultural Memory, and the Poetry of Bashō* (Stanford, CA: Stanford University Press, 1998), 52–81.

33. Shiki had a particular aversion to the seasonal word *hatsugatsuo*, which he considered so overused as to have become cliché. See his entry on May 8, 1902, in his diary, *A Drop of Ink*. Masaoka, "Bokuju Itteki," 182.

34. Masaoka, "Bokuju Itteki," 183–184.

35. Masaoka, "Bokuju Itteki," 184.

36. On this, see Kurosawa, "Byōja No Bungaku."

37. Aoyama, *Reading Food*, 2.

38. Masaoka Shiki, "Kudamono," in *Zuihitsu 2*, vol. 12 of *Shiki zenshū*, 491–501.
39. Masaoka, "Kudamono."
40. Masaoka, *Haiku: 3*, 366.
41. Masaoka, "Kudamono," 494–495.
42. It was Kurosawa Tsutomu's essay on Shiki, cited earlier, that crystalized this insight for me. The literary critic Christina Crosby makes a similar point in her moving memoir of life after becoming paralyzed in a bicycle accident. "Only through writing," she writes, "have I arrived at the life I now lead, the body I now am. I've done this work in language, because my profession is the study of literature. It's what I have and what I know. I have found solace in tropes, since figurative language helps us approach what's otherwise unapproachable or incommunicable." Christina Crosby, *A Body, Undone: Living on after Great Pain*, Sexual Cultures (New York: New York University Press, 2016), 12.
43. On Shiki's efforts to modernize and "reform" tanka poetry (also known as *waka*) see Robert H Brower, "Masaoka Shiki and Tanka Reform," in *Tradition and Modernization in Japanese Culture*, ed. Donald Shiveley (Princeton, NJ: Princeton University Press, 1971), 379–418.
44. For a remarkable record of what Shiki did and who came to visit on almost every day of his adult life, culled from dozens of sources, see Wada Katsushi, ed., *Shiki no isshō*, vol. 14 of *Shiki senshū* (Nagaizumi-chō Japan: Zoshinkai shuppansha, 2003), 534–535.
45. Keene, *Winter Sun Shines In*, 191.
46. Sachio Itō, "Masaoka Shiki-Kun," in *Kaisō No Shiki*, in *Bekkan 2*, vol. 23 *Shiki zenshū*, 98–101.
47. Between April 13, 1900 and August 19, 1902.
48. Takashi Nagatsuka, *The Soil*, trans. Ann Waswo (London: Routledge, 1989).
49. Masaoka, *Shokan 2*, , 610.
50. Masaoka, *Shokan 2*, 558.
51. Masaoka, *Shokan 2*, 623.
52. Masaoka, *Shokan 2*, 623.
53. Masaoka, "Bokuju Itteki." 184.
54. On the "vibrancy" of matter, and food in particular, see chapter 3, "Edible Matter" in Jane Bennett, *Vibrant Matter: A Political Ecology of Things* (Durham, NC: Duke University Press, 2010).
55. In one of many discussions of haiku in his series of lectures *The Preparation of the Novel*, Roland Barthes writes, "The act of syllabification has been linked to manducation: movement of the lower jawbone; we chew our words: bites)." Roland Barthes, Kate Briggs, and Nathalie Léger, *The Preparation of the Novel: Lecture Courses and Seminars at the Collège de France (1978–1979 and 1979–1980)* (New York: Columbia University Press, 2011), 24.
56. This argument has been made by Suenobu Yoshiharu in a recent book. He writes, "If haiku works by taking the phenomena of the external world that appear to the eye and articulating them into 5-7-5 syllables, by thus 'haiku-izing' the flow of the world and time, Shiki was able to regain the connection to that world that he had lost

when he coughed up blood and to boldly recover a sense of wholeness in his life." Yoshiharu Suenobu, *Masaoka Shiki, Jūgunsu*, Shohan (Tōkyō: Heibonsha, 2011), 97.

57. Keene, *Winter Sun Shines In*, 190.

58. Robert Tuck, "The Poetry of Dialogue: Kanshi, Haiku and Media in Meiji Japan, 1870–1900" (ProQuest Dissertations Publishing, 2012), http://search.proquest.com/docview/1034267673/, 120.

59. See, for example, Horiuchi Tsuneyoshi, *Koi suru Masaoka Shiki* (Matsuyama, Japan: Sōfūsha shuppan, 2013).

13

The Devouring Empire

Food and Memory in Hayashi Fumiko's Wartime Narratives and Naruse Mikio's Films

Noriko J. Horiguchi

As this book's introduction discusses, foodways have become an important source of identity and "soft power" in contemporary Japan, with the active involvement of the Ministry of Agriculture, Forestry, and Fisheries and the Ministry of Foreign Affairs. Although today the government's focus is on accumulating culinary capital as part of Japan's soft power, its investment in foodways as a national project began in the Meiji period (1868–1912) as a strategy to elevate Japan's economic and military strength in the power contest among the imperial nations. To boost Japan materially, physically, and metaphorically and build a "rich nation, strong army" (*fukoku kyōhei*), food played important roles in discourses that ranged from laws, nutrition science, and school textbooks to newspapers, magazines, novels, and films, all of which interacted in recreating the bodies and identities of Japanese empire.

On the one hand, food is a source of material and corporeal sustenance that feeds and builds the bodies of the people in modern Japan; lack of food endangers the survival of the nation and its subjects. This is most evident in the ways the Japanese empire (1868–1945) collapsed. Starvation and malnutrition contributed to 60 percent of the casualties of soldiers and civilians, and to 80 percent of the deaths of Japanese soldiers in the Philippines.[1] On the other hand, food is a rich source of metaphor and allegory. As an allegory, the bodies of people, as parts of the national body (*kokutai*), starve, search for, consume, and remember food as a source of distinction and power—or lack thereof—in the contest with other nations.[2] Furthermore, food and the act of eating create a symbolic relationship between the colonizer and the colonized. The colonizer as the subject devours, thus building up its own body and, by extension, the body of the empire; the colonized serve food, or themselves as food, for the Japanese empire.

During the period of Japan's expansion and collapse as an empire, Hayashi Fumiko (1903–1951) moved through the space of both *naichi* (homeland or inner territories) and *gaichi* (outland or overseas territories), wrote often about food and hunger, and produced some of the most critically acclaimed and popular texts of modern Japanese literature. Hayashi depicts women's physical movements at the intersection of personal, culinary desire and political, expansionist aspiration, thus elucidating the power dynamics of the Japanese empire, its subjects, and the Western imperial nations. Hayashi's narratives and memories expose the relationship between the colonizer and the colonized through the lens of food; in her writing, the eating subjects of the empire desire and devour food, while the subjected bodies of the empire are devoured as food. Thus Hayashi's writing is a prime example of modern literary narratives on food and hunger, which can be read as an allegory of national/imperial history. It is also a medium for remembering and critiquing the national and imperial identity of Japan in the prewar, wartime, and immediate postwar periods. Hayashi's novels, and Naruse Mikio's (1905–1969) postwar film adaptations of them, thus function as a medium that recreates in the present the memory of the Japanese imperial past.[3]

Memories of hunger and food consumption are central to Hayashi's writing. In her autobiographical novel *Hōrōki* (*Diary of a Vagabond*, 1928–1929), which instantly won critical acclaim and made her the most popular writer in 1930s Japan, the heroine's single-minded pursuit of food is clear in her disposition that "to eat and to write are the only two reasons for living."[4] Hayashi's descriptions of travel, hunger, and food stand out in the literary history of modern Japan because she was the first modern writer to depict hunger and food from women's perspectives.[5] Her heroines pursue, work with, and represent food as they physically move from prewar naichi in the 1920s to wartime gaichi in the 1930s and early 1940s, and then to postwar Japan in the late 1940s.[6] Thus Hayashi's representation of working-class women's travel and food consumption contrasts with Kaiko Takeshi's depiction of a middle-class, masculine project of travel, food, and consumerism in the 1970s and 1980s (as examined in Bruce Suttmeier's chapter in this volume).

In Hayashi's *Hōrōki*, the narrator-heroine is from the heart of the Japanese homeland (naichi) but sympathizes with the oppressed residents of the outer territories and colonies, such as Hokkaido, Japan's northernmost island, and Karafuto, territory won in the Russo-Japanese War. And it is the narrator's specific perceptions, principles, and practices of food that expose the plight of subjects of the empire who are marginalized because of their class, gender, and ethnicity. As I show in detail below, the narrator critiques the Japanese empire that devours/exploits its subjects by using principles that challenge the Cartesian dualism of the subject as mind/soul and the object as body/food.[7] By erasing the distinction between the subject who eats and the object that is eaten, the narrator involves the bodies of subjects of the empire both as agents of power and as subordinated subjects who move or are mobilized within the spaces of the empire in a direct, intimate, and invasive manner.

For example, in *Hōrōki* the narrator-heroine's food practices are drastically different from and defy the state's standards of normative food practices for the middle class. These standards contributed to the economic and political capital and power of the subject and, by extension, of Japan as a nation and empire. The heroine states:

> The living room in the next-door neighbor's house is lit ... and a
> tasty smell and sound are emanating from the kitchen downstairs.
> I have not eaten for two days. My stomach is immersed in empty
> thoughts, antipathy ... and nostalgia for travels. How on earth can
> I survive?[8]

In this remark, the narrator's outlook subverts the division of mind/soul and body/food as separate entities, because her stomach thinks and feels. With her senses of sight, smell, and sound, the narrator perceives a nurturing and brightly lit middle-class household. In contrast to the ideal of healthy Japanese bodies that constitute a materially and militarily strong modern nation, the narrator is deprived of food, thus endangering her existence. Her distance from the stable middle-class household is also evoked by her yearning for travel.

A family nation-state (*kazoku kokka*) that nurtures its subject was an idea created and promoted by the Japanese government beginning in the 1890s. The notion of modern family as a community, nation, and empire was in many ways built upon the new practices of production, distribution, and consumption of food. Since individual families represented microcosms of the family nation-state, communal eating by families symbolized the communality of the nation. As scholars such as Katarzyna Cwiertka in anthropology-history and Fukuda Ikuhiro in literature point out, instead of the individual tray used in different spaces and times by each member of the family in the Edo period (1600–1868), a low dining table (*chabudai*), for use while seated on the floor, began to be used in the late 1880s. This led to the popularization in the 1960s of a high dining table used with chairs and contributed to creating the modern family whose members share food and conversation in the same space and time.⁹

However, *Hōrōki*'s narrator-heroine in prewar naichi challenges the modern ideal of a nurturing family as the microcosm of the united family nation-state of Japan:

> Human beings fight alone;
> There is no need for the force of the crowd.
> Eating meals does not depend on the culture of family or nation.¹⁰

The narrator's sole concern is her own survival, without dependence on family or nation. As she physically moves through the spaces of prewar naichi in search of food and in her aspiration to become a writer, she lives outside the institutionalized womanhood of the "good wife, wise mother." For example, she declines the marriage proposal of a man called Matsuda-san by noting that "to be fed by a man is harder than to chew mud."¹¹ Rather than forming the stable community of a family headed by a male breadwinner, she is committed to her writing: "I will go to the back side of Japan (*ura nihon*) with my yellow manuscript of poems, my only wife and husband."¹²

The narrator-heroine in *Hōrōki* moves through various spaces and social strata as she craves, consumes, and works with food. In small rented apartments, cafés, bars, and a confectionary factory, she associates with others who are holding blue-, pink-, and white-collar jobs, such as a café waitress, factory worker, prostitute, clerk at a stock-trading company, and professional fiction writer. As she does so, she decries the plight of working-class women in prewar naichi by subverting the dualism of the subject that eats and the object that is eaten. For example, she not only identifies specific foods such as eggs, rice, and tonkatsu (pork cutlets) as the objects of her desire, purchase, and consumption, but also identifies with the foods that are desired, purchased, or consumed. In one line she writes, "I woke up feeling sad, like fish at a fish store."¹³ Thus erasing the distinction between the subject/self and the object/food, she compares herself with food items that are sold for daily consumption at low prices. The narrator's devalued self and body in the marketplace are also evident in her depiction of and association with her coworkers in the factory. At a boarding house of a factory, she notes, "The woman called Ohatsu-chan . . . was taken by a man when she was twelve and was kidnapped to Manchuria. . . . She was soon sold to a geisha house."¹⁴ The narrator's reference to the abduction of a girl working at a factory in naichi to the Japanese empire's gaichi exposes the plight of gender- and class-specific bodies that are sexualized for trade.

In addition, Hayashi's depiction of the narrator-heroine and her coworkers as items of food asserts their equality based on their subjugation due to gender and class, even though she also recognizes different regional (ethnic/racial) origins, whether in naichi or gaichi. At a boarding house, for example, the narrator writes, "I lay down with three pillows next to each other with a woman from Karafuto and another woman from Kanazawa. Somehow, I was feeling sad, like an eggplant that was exposed at a small store."[15] Here we can see that the narrator associates herself with the marginalized and/or colonized population. She also identifies with the colonized race as a commodity for trade: "When night falls, I sing a useless song with the sorrow of an aborigine (*dojin*) who has been bought by the white men's nation."[16]

Rather than conveying a "rich and strong" family empire that nurtures its subjects, depictions of food in *Hōrōki* indicate economic and physical abuse of the narrator-heroine's body and its association with the marginalized populations of the empire. In the following poem, she rebels against the social and sexual victimization of working women by comparing Japan with food:

> I saw Mount Fuji . . .
> The sharp heart of the mountains
> Threatens my broken life
> And looks down coldly into my eyes.
> Mount Fuji is an image of Japan.
> . . .
> Mount Fuji is now an old and rotten bean-jam bun (*manjū*) made of mud.
> . . .
> Attention, Mount Fuji!
> Here is a woman who stands alone and does not bow to you.
> Here is a woman who mocks and laughs at you.[17]

The narrator reduces Japan, with its cold heart and gaze from on high, to a piece of rotten food. Her choice of a *manjū* (a white bun with dark bean-paste inside) may refer to Mount Fuji's white, snow-covered exterior and dark interior of brown soil. But to describe Japan as a sweet bun that is now "old and rotten" emphasizes the stark difference between the expectation of Japan as a source of delicious, nourishing food and the reality of a nation that offers only inedible mud.

Although her depictions of food rebel against the empire of Japan, the narrator-heroine in *Hōrōki* nevertheless aspires to recreate the periphery of that empire as a utopia for the socially marginalized and exploited: "The old newspaper that wrapped the daikon pickles (*takuan*) states that there are still tens of thousands of meters of wasteland in Hokkaido. I think it would be fun if our utopia could be created in such an uncultivated land."[18] She longs for the demise of the society that deprives her of food and devours/expropriates her body. Yet she continues to imagine uncultivated land, somewhere nonspecific but on the periphery of Japan, as an unexplored place of salvation: "I thought Tokyo would be filled with many good things, but there is nothing."[19] "Somehow, I came to want to go to a foreign country. . . . I want to go somewhere far away."[20]

Acting on wishes to travel abroad, both Hayashi the author and her characters traveled to the colonies and outposts of the Japanese empire and wrote about food and hunger. One such text is *Hokugan butai* (*Northern Bank Platoon*, 1938), written in the context of the Japanese nation-state's imperial ambition and expansion. By the time she wrote *Hokugan butai*, Hayashi had become a wealthy, critically acclaimed writer. In 1938, she voluntarily joined the Pen Squadron formed by the Agency of Information (*jōhōkyoku*) and became a war reporter. Hence, in accordance with the Japanese government's aim, Hayashi traveled to gaichi China with a group of writers and reported on the circumstances and sacrifices of Japanese soldiers to readers in the naichi. Although technically *Hokugan butai* is a war report and *Hōrōki* a novel, my comparative analysis below places them on the same plane, examining them both as amalgams of power and knowledge.[21] *Hokugan butai* resembles *Hōrōki* in combining poetry with prose in what read like journal entries depicting a single woman's physical mobility in a state of hunger. More importantly, *Hokugan butai* recreates its narrator's national identity as she marches with Japanese soldiers in the wartime gaichi of China.

Food and hunger are a recurring theme in *Hokugan butai*, as they are in *Hōrōki*. The narrator of *Hokugan butai* writes, for example, "Since I came to this battleground, I have gradually become a human being who is like a piece of glass, which eats nothing."[22] "Even if meals of only miso soup and rice continued for eternity from this point forward, I don't think my appetite would ever complain again."[23] In *Hōrōki*, hunger threatens the survival of the narrator-heroine, who rejects nation and empire in favor of the individual. In contrast, in *Hougan butai*, hunger sharpens the narrator's sense of Japanese national identity. Her desire for miso soup and rice reflects the dominant state discourse that defined a proper "Japanese meal" (*kokumin shoku*) as miso soup, rice, and vegetables. As scarcity of rice became severe and distribution of rice to the battleground became difficult, frugal consumption of food became a symbol of nationalism in naichi and gaichi alike. Food shortages and the government's encouragement of meager consumption of food discursively leveled the differences between regions, classes, and occupations.[24] Thus the descriptions of hunger in *Hokugan butai* are infused with the norms of the food practices and state-driven nationalism of imperial Japan in the late 1930s. In this sense, the narrator's hunger and participation in the homogenized diet of the soldiers enable her to become part of Japan.

In addition, the narrator-heroine of *Hokugan butai* emphasizes communal eating of the rationed food distributed by the Japanese military: "We share food with everyone. We also share tobacco. Water from the water bottle, too."[25] This sharing of food with members of the family empire in wartime gaichi contrasts sharply with the actions of the narrator in *Hōrōki* in prewar naichi, who strives to earn money so that she can buy a bowl of white rice on her own, independent of a family or empire. In *Hokugan butai*, marching, starving, and then sharing rationed food with Japanese troops in the battle zones of China lead the narrator to identify with the soldiers: "I accompanied Yōsukō Northern Troop . . . I am no different from the soldiers."[26] Thus the heroine's body in *Hokugan butai* is "mobilized by the system and conforms to the external impetus of the government, its politics and economy," just as Suttmeier observes in his analysis of Kaiko Takeshi's novel *Atarashii tentai* (*The New Celestial Bodies*, 1972) elsewhere in this volume.[27] Although the time periods are different, these are examples of literary texts that demonstrate the interaction of literature and its political and economic contexts.

The narrator-heroine of *Hokugan butai* shares not only food with the Japanese soldiers on the battlefield, but national values of "self-discipline," Japanese uniqueness, and prescribed gender roles as well. Whereas the descriptions of the narrator-heroine's relationship with food in *Hōrōki* help her create the multiple identities of economically, ethnically, and racially marginalized and colonized peoples of the Japanese empire in prewar naichi, the narrator-heroine in *Hokugan butai* reconstructs a single identity as a "pure Japanese," based on a dualism of Japan as the subject/spirit and China as the object/body, with both as clearly separate entities. On the one hand, the narrator in *Hokugan butai* notes the degradation of the Japanese soldiers and war reporters to the status of beggars for food: "We make breakfast by pouring water from the water bottle into the leftover rice in a mess kit from last night. It's as if we are beggars."[28] On the other hand, she describes Chinese soldiers with "begging facial expressions" on a dirty and stagnant battlefield that she compares to "rotten fruit."[29] In other words, she compares the Chinese soldiers with "beggars" who tread on a field that is as impure as rotten food. In contrast, the she glorifies the Japanese soldiers who continue to advance on soil that she compares to a "red carpet," despite their being gnawed by hunger: but the Japanese soldiers have "gotten rid of excess," so that their "spirit becomes extremely pure."[30] She further writes that her "memory of this battleground will become a pile of salt" that will purify her self.³¹ Whereas the Japanese are associated with pure "spirit," she writes that the corpse of a Chinese soldier

> looked like nothing but an object to me. While having heart-rending sentiments and admiration for our soldiers who were carried away on stretchers a while ago, I feel like a cold stranger to the dead body of this Chinese soldier. My feeling toward the dead body of that Chinese soldier is completely empty. . . . Moreover, in my consciousness of peoples (*minzoku*), this is the conflict between enemies that cannot come together.³²

As she marches with the soldiers in China, the narrator's discourse on food comes to conform not only to the nation-state but also to the prescribed gender role of woman as a nurturing mother:

> At a farm on the side of the Daisai Lake, I held an infant who was about two years old. I don't recall anything that made me so pleasant and glad. The smell of mother's milk was attached to the dusty clothes, and for a moment I thought of my hometown where I was born.³³

It is an infant who exudes the smell of mother's milk that brings the narrator closer to her "hometown." Home as *kuni* (nation) in *Hōrōki* signifies the narrator's hometown, and so does this statement in *Hokugan butai*. However, home in *Hokugan butai* also signifies "homeland" (*sokoku nihon*) and the family nation-state, with which she can connect by marching, starving, and sharing rations with the soldiers.³⁴ For example, the narrator writes of soldiers of the empire: "Until they achieve heroic and incomparable deaths magnificently, they always think of their homeland. They are good husbands, fathers, and older and younger brothers."³⁵ Unlike the physically abusive and financially exploitative men in *Hōrōki*, soldiers as the children of the emperor in *Hokugan butai* are courageous and righteous family members whom she wishes to take care of as a nurse: "Soldiers are all kind and gentle" and "pure."³⁶ "I want to . . . look after the injured and sick soldiers.³⁷

Although she must return to Tokyo, the narrator-heroine of *Hokugan butai* wishes to stay in the war zone in China, where she can connect with Japan and become a member of the family nation-state. "I will never forget, for the rest of my life, the feeling of love for the country . . . I don't care about my house in Tokyo."³⁸ She concludes: "I want to stay behind."³⁹

As discourses on hunger and food practices, *Hōrōki* critiques and *Hokugan butai* exalts Japanese national identity as Hayashi's narrator-heroines move through the spaces of naichi and gaichi in the 1920s and 1930s. In Hayashi's novel *Ukigumo* (*Floating Clouds*, 1949; figure 13.1), adapted as a film by Naruse Mikio in 1955, food narratives and the medium of memory negotiate the hegemonic relationship between the colonizer and the colonized during the Pacific War and the Allied occupation of Japan in the postwar period.[40] The heroine Yukiko's sharply contrasting food practices/privileges, first in Japan's wartime imperial outpost in Indochina and then in the defeated Japanese nation, stripped of empire and militarily occupied, vividly show the rise and demise of—and citizens' nostalgia for—the Japanese empire.

The heroine in *Ukigumo* lives in the immediate postwar period, when destruction has leveled the land and food shortages have homogenized the diet of the Japanese populace. In this environment, she recreates prewar naichi and wartime gaichi in her memory. Yukiko is an unmarried working woman, with no stable home or family, and her mobility in naichi and gaichi counters the ideal of domestic stability associated with the "good wife, wise mother," whose place is defined as home in the Civil Code (1898). After leaving her native home in Shizuoka in prewar naichi, Yukiko moves to Tokyo to attend typing school and stays at her brother-in-law's house. This mobility outside her native home in prewar naichi seems to signal her loss of respectability as a candidate for

FIGURE 13.1 A dining scene in wartime French Indochina in Naruse Mikio's *Ukigumo* (Floating clouds, 1955).

the role of a sacred wife and mother, and leads to her sexual exploitation by her brother-in-law. Yukiko is repeatedly raped by him while staying at his house in prewar naichi.

Yukiko's social, economic, and physical conditions change when she obtains a position as a typist for the Ministry of Agriculture and Forestry and moves to Dalat, French Indochina, which had fallen under Japanese control in 1942. The only time Yukiko enjoys a sense of freedom, power, and security is when she is in wartime gaichi Indochina as an occupier. Her new position becomes clear when the bureaucrats Tomioka and Kano toast her arrival and participation in Japan's imperial project: "Let's have a toast. To Koda Yukiko, who has come all the way to Dalat on occupation duty!"[41] There, at the periphery of the Japanese empire, Yukiko stays in a French-style mansion that the Japanese bureaucrats are using as their official residence and dines with them. In this colonial setting, her newfound elite identity is particularly apparent through her food-related practices.

In Naruse's 1955 film of the story, the space of the French-style mansion, its dining room, and the act of eating in it visually narrate Japan's identification with the Western imperial powers that subjugated nations such as Indochina. The white tablecloth, white wine, and Yukiko's white dress signify not only the novelty of her experience but the Japanese empire's initial identification with Western imperialism, its subsequent displacement of the "white" Western imperial power, and its assertion of control over the darker-skinned Annamese, symbolized by the maid Niu, who serves the food to Yukiko and the Japanese bureaucrats.[42]

Yukiko's luxurious formal dinners in French Indochina may give the impression that she is on vacation or outside the social norms of Japan.[43] This is true in the sense that it required substantial economic and cultural capital to experience and appreciate the culinary exoticism of French food during wartime. However, the food practices/privilege of the Japanese occupiers in Indochina also enforced the dominant state discourse on Japan's status as an empire at the time. Historian John Dower uses dining practices as a metaphor to explain Japanese imperialism: "While most of the rest of the world fell under the control of the Western powers, Japan emulated them and joined their banquet."[44] Instead of contrasting itself with the Western Other, the Japanese empire in *Ukigumo* achieves culinary identity, distinction, and prestige by identifying with the West and then displacing it.

The depiction of the dining scene in the early 1940s in *Ukigumo* attains another layer of meaning in Japan's modern cultural history when we consider the changes and continuity in the culinary discourse since the Meiji period. As M. William Steele's study shows, in the 1870s, when negotiating with the Western imperial powers, the Japanese imperial court adapted the foodways of the West.[45] The changes in food choices and table manners at the imperial court when receiving foreign dignitaries were part of the Japanese government's attempt to be treated as an equal by the Western powers. As the people in Japan began to "eat Western," and as Japan planned, built, and expanded itself as an empire from the late nineteenth century to mid-twentieth century, the connections between food, politics, and empire were reasserted in the texts written by Hayashi Fumiko, who lived from the Meiji through the Showa era.

Against the backdrop of Japan's all-out war with the Allied Forces in the early 1940s, *Ukigumo* depicts low-ranking Japanese bureaucrats and their female assistants ousting the French imperial power from its former colony of Indochina, yet simultaneously adapting French foodways. To use feminist bell hooks's term, subjects of the Japanese empire participate in "eating the Other"—in this case the French—"adapting and hybridizing foreign foods and settings to suit domestic tastes."[46] "Domestic tastes" and the dominant imperial agenda in *Ukigumo* include expropriation of food and natural resources in gaichi and adaptation of the West's food practices to symbolically and materially enrich and strengthen the empire of Japan. The representation of Yukiko's— and, by extension, Japan's—culinary capital in *Ukigumo* also exposes the power dynamic within the Greater East Asia Co-Prosperity Sphere, in which the lifestyles, including dining practices, of the Japanese colonizers as the superior leaders involve the subordination of the colonized Annamese people as inferior servants. Thus "Japan" in Hayashi's *Ukigumo* is embodied in Indochina, at the economic and gastronomic margins of the empire, in support of the state's agenda of expansionism.

In 1945, Yukiko returns to the postwar ruins of Japan and reassumes her prewar social standing as an impoverished and mobile working woman. As a war repatriate, she no longer works for the Ministry of Agriculture and Forestry and struggles to survive physically and financially. In Tokyo, she rents a dark storage room as her residence (figure 13.2), where she meets and dines with her lover Tomioka, who is reunited with his wife in postwar Japan. In the film adaptation of the story, Yukiko appears to be assuming the role of a servant by preparing and serving food to Tomioka, who sits at a small table on the tatami floor, in stark contrast to the Western-style dining table at which Yukiko had sat as Tomioka's equal and enjoyed wine served by the Annamese woman Niu in wartime Indochina. Under the Allied occupation, Yukiko's physical and economic restrictions are all poignantly clear as she uses a tin kettle to pour tea into a cup for Tomioka in a storage room.

FIGURE 13.2 Yukiko and Tomioka dining together in her rented storage room in postwar Japan under the Allied occupation in Naruse's *Ukigumo*.

Yukiko's lowly social position in postwar Japan is also evident in her relationship with the American soldier Joe. She sells her body to him and compares herself to Niu, the Annamese woman who was under Japanese control in wartime Indochina.[47] The market (material and corporeal) value of Yukiko's body seems to be determined by the food and other materials Joe brings to her rented room. There is no depiction of monetary exchange between Yukiko and Joe. Instead, Yukiko receives chocolate, Coca-Cola, and a radio for her sexual services. Yukiko's sex work and the abortion she undergoes after being impregnated by Tomioka signify the invasion of her body in postwar Japan.

Under these physical and economic postwar conditions, Yukiko feels nostalgia for wartime Indochina. However, Yukiko's postwar nostalgia for the lost empire is also accompanied by her reflections on the egotistical and destructive policies and actions of the Japanese occupiers who expropriated the labor, food, and natural resources in Indochina.[48] Although the film omits this, in the novel the narrator explains: "The long history of these tea fields that had been carefully managed for so many years made her [Yukiko] feel ashamed of the highhanded tactics that the Japanese had used to take over everything—even these fields—in a short amount of time."[49] The narrator further wonders: "Were not the Japanese—who were suddenly rummaging about among the treasures of other people that had taken them centuries to develop—nothing but robbers?"[50] Although Yukiko is nostalgic for the status and privilege she enjoyed in the empire, her own postwar degradation and privation give her empathy for subjugated peoples.

Hayashi's literary texts, and Naruse's film adaptation of *Ukigumo*, include prominent examples of food narratives and memories that both challenge and recreate Japan's national and imperial identities in relation to its subjects, geopolitical territories, and the Western imperial powers. In *Hōrōki*, the heroine eats in ways that violate the norms for food practices in Japan's middle class, among Japanese females, and by those of Japanese ethnic/racial identity. In *Hokugan butai*, the narrator-heroine experiences a new sense of national identity by sharing rations with Japanese soldiers in China. In *Ukigumo*, Yukiko's nostalgia for colonial privilege in Indochina, symbolized by the Japanese occupiers' French food practices, evokes the days of Japan's empire in postwar Japan, when those days have been irretrievably lost. As we have seen in these texts, women's social, gender, and political positions change as their bodies move through the Japanese empire and as their food conditions change. Hayashi the author and her characters' personal cravings intersect with the state's imperial ambitions and downfall. Their food narratives and memories illuminate the juncture between physical hunger and political aspiration, and between culinary consumption and the economic and political accumulation of capital, which reinvent the national and imperial identities of Japan. In this sense, Hayashi was not only the first female modern writer in Japan to depict hunger from the personal perspectives of women, but also the first female writer to describe culinary and political desires that celebrate and critique the imperial history of modern Japan.

NOTES

1. On starvation, malnutrition, and war casualties, see Fujiwara Akira, *Uejini shita eiyū tachi* (The spirits of the soldiers who starved to death) (Tokyo: Aoki shoten, 2001). Saito Minako's *Senka no reshipi: Taiheiyō sensōka no shoku o shiru* (Recipe for war: Food in the Pacific War) (Tokyo: Iwanami shoten, 2002), also discusses starvation and malnutrition as the major cause of casualties in both gaichi and naichi.

2. See *kokutai* as nature and metaphor in chapter 2 of Noriko J. Horiguchi, *Women Adrift: The Literature of Japan's Imperial Body* (Minneapolis: University of Minnesota Press, 2011).

3. Naruse Mikio (1905–1969) was known for his mastery of literary adaptation, and came to adapt Hayashi Fumiko's novels because his own subject matter was especially close to hers. Naruse's films, like Hayashi's novels, often depict single

women who are understood to be engaged in personal struggles at the periphery of society for their daily economic survival. Naruse produced six film adaptations of Hayashi's novels: *Meshi* (Repast, 1951), *Inazuma* (Lightning, 1952), *Tsuma* (Wife, 1953), *Bangiku* (Late chrysanthemum, 1954), *Ukigumo* (Floating clouds, 1955), and *Hōrōki* (A vagabond's song, 1962). His career as a director culminated in the early to mid-1950s, when he directed film adaptations of Hayashi's novels. See Catherine Russell, *The Cinema of Naruse Mikio* (Durham, NC: Duke University Press, 2008) and conclusion of Horiguchi's *Women Adrift*.

4. See Yukiko Tanaka, *To Live and to Write: Selections by Japanese Women Writers, 1913–1938*, Women in Translation (Seattle: Seal Press, 1987), 99.

5. Tomoko Aoyama, *Reading Food in Modern Japanese Literature* (Honolulu: University of Hawai'i Press, 2008), 26.

6. Among Hayashi's contemporaries, there are a few female authors who present women who work with or offer their perspectives on food. For example, Sata Ineko's (1904–1998) "Café Kyoto" ("Resutoran Rakuyō," 1929), published at the same time that Hayashi's *Hōrōki* (1928–1929) was serialized, depicts conditions of women's labor and café waitresses' personal and professional relationships with their coworkers and customers. This story presents café waitresses as somewhat tragic but glamorous. A recent translation of "Café Kyoto" is available in Samuel Perry's *Five Faces of Japanese Feminism: Crimson and Other Works* (University of Hawai'i Press, 2016). On the topic of travel, food, and empire, Yosano Akiko, in her 1928 travelogue *Manmōô yūki* (Travels in Manchuria and Mongolia, translated into English by Joshua Fogel), rejoices at the multiethnic culture of the Japanese empire in Manchuria, where she had a taste of Russian, Chinese, and German food. But Yosano pays only passing attention to food. The ideals and ideologies of hybridity, coexistence, and harmony in her writing broke down as tension between the Japanese and Western imperial powers, and Chinese resistance to Japan, quickly led to the creation of a strict dichotomy between superior Japan and inferior China. Okamoto Kanako's (1889–1939) *Shokuma* (The Gourmand, ca. 1939) is one of the few Japanese works of fiction of this period that presents female characters' viewpoints on food. Composed at the same time as Hayashi's *Hokugan butai*, *Shokuma* is notable in depicting a woman who critiques food prepared by a master male chef. See Aoyama, *Reading Food*, 146–150.

7. On food and philosophy, see Deane W. Curtin, "Food/Body/Person," in *Cooking, Eating, Thinking: Transformative Philosophy of Food*, ed. Deane W. Curtin and Lisa M. Heldke (Bloomington: Indiana University Press, 1992).

8. Hayashi, *Hōrōki* (Diary of a vagabond) (Tokyo: Shinchōsha, 1979, 2000), 266. All translations from *Hōrōki* are mine unless otherwise indicated. Joan Ericson's translation is available in *Be a Woman: Hayashi Fumiko and Modern Japanese Women's Literature* (Honolulu: University of Hawai'i Press, 1997).

9. On communal eating, see Katarzyna Cwiertka, *Modern Japanese Cuisine: Food, Power and National Identity* (London: Reaktion Books, 2006), 88–96; and Fukuda Ikuhiro, *Inshoku to iu ressun: Furansu to nihon no shokutaku kara* (Lessons from eating and drinking at dining tables in France and Japan) (Tokyo: Sanshūsha, 2007), 90–101.

10. Hayashi, *Hōrōki*, 446.

11. Hayashi, *Hōrōki*, 51.
12. Hayashi, *Hōrōki*, 137.
13. Hayashi, *Hōrōki*, 127.
14. Hayashi, *Hōrōki*, 99.
15. Hayashi, *Hōrōki*, 88.
16. Hayashi, *Hōrōki*, 87.
17. Hayashi, *Hōrōki*, 142–144.
18. Hayashi, *Hōrōki*, 43.
19. Hayashi, *Hōrōki*, 322.
20. Hayashi, *Hōrōki*, 353.
21. The boundaries of genre are not fixed, but malleable and subject to challenges and negotiations by authors and readers.
22. Hayashi, *Hokugan butai* (Northern bank platoon), in vol. 12 of *Hayashi Fumiko zenshū* (Complete works of Hayashi Fumiko) (Tokyo: Bunsendō, 1977), 297. All translations from *Hokugan butai* are mine.
23. Hayashi, *Hokugan butai*, 297.
24. Cwiertka, *Modern Japanese Cuisine*, 115.
25. Hayashi, *Hokugan butai*, 257–258.
26. Hayashi, *Hokugan butai*, 300.
27. See Bruce Suttmeier's chapter in the present volume.
28. Hayashi, *Hokugan butai*, 311.
29. Hayashi, *Hokugan butai*, 306, 212.
30. Hayashi, *Hokugan butai* 295, 281.
31. Hayashi, *Hokugan butai*, 332.
32. Hayashi, *Hokugan butai*, 283.
33. Hayashi, *Hokugan butai*, 333.
34. Hayashi, *Hokugan butai*, 330.
35. Hayashi, *Hokugan butai*, 308.
36. Hayashi, *Hokugan butai*, 256.
37. Hayashi, *Hokugan butai*, 214.
38. Hayashi, *Hokugan butai*, 241.
39. Hayashi, *Hokugan butai*, 214.
40. *Ukigumo* (Drifting clouds) is Hayashi's last complete novel and arguably one of the most important works of postwar Japanese literature. Naruse Mikio's film adaptation of her novel with the same title won the designation "best film" in *Kinema junpō* in 1955, the year it was first released.
41. Hayashi, *Floating Clouds*, trans. Lane Dunlop (New York: Columbia University Press, 2012), 30.
42. Naruse's *Ukigumo* is a black-and-white film, but the script specifically indicates the color of Yukiko's dress as white. See Mizuki Yōko, screenplay of *Ukigumo*, vol. 106 of *Kinema junpō bessatsu* (Kinema Junpō, supplementary volume) (Tokyo: Kinema junpō sha, 1954), 80.
43. Russell, *Cinema of Naruse Mikio*, 280. Russell writes that "Tomioka served as an official in the Imperial Forestry Ministry, and Yukiko was posted there as a typist, but the imagery is more that of a country retreat than a workplace."

44. John Dower, *Embracing Defeat: Japan in the Wake of World War II* (New York: Norton, 2000), 21.

45. M. William Steele, "The Emperor's New Food," in *Alternative Narratives in Modern Japanese History* (New York: Routledge, 2003), 110–132.

46. bell hooks, "Eating the Other: Desire and Resistance," in *Black Looks: Race and Representation* (Boston: South End Press, 1993), 21–40.

47. Hayashi, *Floating Clouds*, 94.

48. The narrator's reflection of wartime behavior may have been colored by the fact that the novel was published during the US occupation, when strict censorship rules were still in place.

49. Hayashi, *Floating Clouds*, 98.

50. Hayashi, *Floating Clouds*, 38.

Food Anxieties

14

Eating amid Affluence

Kaikō Takeshi's Adventures in Food

Bruce Suttmeier

The discovery of a new dish does more for human happiness than the discovery of a star.
—Brillat-Savarin, *Physiologie du Goût*[1]

On the morning of December 2, 1978, the writer Kaikō Takeshi gathered a group of like-minded friends at a posh culinary academy. "For quite some time now," he explained, "I have dreamed of a feast where I could eat without end," a "true feast," not like the stomach-straining banquets of some Roman emperor, but a meal "where I could eat without the upsetting aftereffects of consumption, without the drowsiness accompanying such feasting."[2] He sought a meal, as he wrote, that he could savor and digest for hours on end, a meal that would, "like a great literary work," leave him both "exhilaratingly emptied" and "wholly enriched."[3] What he sought, one might say, was distress-free consumption, extravagance without much consequence, indulgence without its usual costs. In practice, the meal that December day was an exercise in assorted indulgences. Lasting nearly twelve hours, it featured a multipage menu, filled with painstakingly produced French delicacies. Its second course alone had eighteen separate dishes, its third course twenty-one. The wine list featured a 1945 Chateau Lafite Rothschild and a 1929 Chateau Cailou. The dishes were gold-rimmed Limoges, the glasses Saint Louis crystal, the dinnerware Christofle silver. Yet, despite Kaikō's desire to be free from the price of indulgence, he acknowledges, in part, the absurdity of his ambitions. The middle-aged men come prepared with pockets full of heartburn medicine. Their wives come dressed in loose-fitting, beltless outfits "resembling muumuus or maternity dresses."[4]

I begin with this meal to highlight the complex intersections of "consumption" and "desire" in the late 1960s and 1970s, a period of rising affluence and growing consumer demand, a period when middle-class inclusion—achieved in large part through the acquisition of household commodities—grew to encompass much of society.[5] High-growth policies were doubling incomes and spurring consumption, standardizing mass trends in domestic space and cultural practice. Food culture by and large saw similar trends of standardization, with industrially prepared food occupying an ever-larger place on the Japanese plate. Frozen food production, a mere 5,000 tons in 1960, jumped to 141,000 tons by 1970 (and to over half a million tons by 1980).[6] Restaurant dining—an often-unattainable luxury before the 1970s—became increasingly routine, especially in the flourishing of fast-food franchises.[7] Tastes, one might say, were becoming homogenized in the service of convenience, accessibility, and industrial efficiency. In his novels and essays of the period, Kaikō focuses little on mass tastes, writing instead about food at the economic and gastronomic margins, both rarified delicacies and grubby street food. And yet, in his celebrations of consumption, like the feast at the culinary academy, we see the discomforts consumption can bring, discomforts that often center on the consuming body. This chapter traces Kaikō's efforts, through a 1972 satirical novel, to wrestle with the conflicting sides of consumption: both its pleasures and its unsettling origins in economic, not bodily, forces. His tale ends in a flight from consumption, an escape from consumer society, and yet the ambivalence of the narrative solution speaks to the era's conflicted sentiments toward consumption: both its aversion to its excesses and its attraction to its pleasures.

The Demands of Consumption

Kaikō (figure 14.1) was best known for his writings on the Vietnam War, from his Saigon dispatches for *Shūkan Asahi* magazine in the mid-1960s, to his well-regarded novels of the war and its aftermath, *Into a Black Sun* (1968) and *Darkness in Summer* (1972). But the early 1970s saw his writing focus increasingly on travel and food, including his best-selling fishing adventures such as "Fish On" (1969) and the work I focus on here, his "food novel" *A New Star* (*Atarashii tentai*), first serialized in 1972. The story follows an unnamed middle-aged, middle-class, mid-level bureaucrat in the Ministry of Finance who one day is summoned to his superior's office and given a new assignment. He is "to become a special officer for economic research," ostensibly tasked with

FIGURE 14.1 A woodcut of Kaikō by his daughter, Kaikō Michiko, from her book *A Museum with Paintings* (*E no aru hakubutsukan*), 1986. Courtesy of Hoikusha Press.

assessing how eating establishments around the country are responding to economic circumstances. But this position is simply a sham, a cover for the actual job he needs to accomplish, which, his supervisor tells him, "is to steadily, increasingly eat up (*shōka*) our budget surplus . . . since, if the money goes unused, our next quarter's budget will be decreased by that unused amount."[8] As the narrator recalls later to a friend, "From here on out, every day, I am on orders to eat lavishly. Day after day, week after week of extravagant eating. That is my job, eating up ministry funds."[9]

Beginning work as the new "Special Officer for Research on Relative Economic Conditions" (*sōtaiteki keiki chōsakan*), he visits scores of small local shops selling chicken skewers and other quick fare, each time dutifully reporting back to his supervisor and each time getting upbraided for insufficient spending. "You should spend more freely. . . . Start taking more planes, more taxis. You should be going to places that use up more of your expense account."[10] This triggers increasingly extravagant travel: Hokkaido for mackerel and Shimane for eel, Morioka for soba noodles, Kōchi for its seared bonito fillets. When this too fails to consume enough funds, he is ordered to frequent high-priced restaurants—Maruume in Tokyo's Yotsuya district, Wadakin in Matsusaka city—and then, finally, he is instructed to combine far-flung visits to fancy restaurants to create "extended meals." "Take, for example, a Chinese meal," his supervisor explains. "You could start in Tokyo with cold-dish appetizers, go to Yokohama for shark fin or bird's nest soup, travel to Kobe for beef or fish, and finish in Nagasaki for dessert. . . . You've got to choose only the most superdeluxe restaurants (*chō ichiryū*), since it's a problem if the food is of the highest rank, but the price is not. Let's avoid those places with top-of-the-line food at bargain prices."[11] Demanding ever more consumption, the supervisor offers the celebrated appetite of the writer Balzac as a model to emulate: a man who, in one legendary meal, ate a hundred oysters as an appetizer, followed it with meats of all kinds—including a whole duck—and finished with twelve pears. In comparison, he tells the main character, "You're just lazy . . . what you're accomplishing is just embarrassing."[12]

Finally, one night at an expensive Akasaka restaurant, as snifters of expensive cognac are passed around, the narrator feels a shudder pass through his body and, suddenly, he senses his entire project collapse. It took but the lightest of touches, he notes, "like a fingertip grazing him, but that was enough. . . . In an instant, everything was upended. It all fell apart, was smashed, flattened, pulverized. All pleasure, excitement, intoxication, gone. 'It's over,' he thought. 'I quit.'"[13]

The narrator's body, to this point an obedient servant of his superior's wishes, rejects any further consumption. The shudder, the slight touch that he feels—whether a twinge of conscience or an acknowledgment of some limit reached—triggers a withdrawal of all somatic incentives for consumption: pleasure, excitement, intoxication. And yet, what is striking about this scene, the penultimate scene in the book, is how little pleasure, excitement, and intoxication have driven his eating to this point. In even the early scenes, before expectations for consumption escalated so absurdly, the narrator expresses no desire for food, no longing for a specific restaurant or dish. The demand to consume is strictly an externally imposed mandate, an imperative that ignores (even scorns) his internal signs of hunger or appetite. Within the structure imposed by his superior, the only value of the food lies in its material cost, its ability to eat up the ministry's budget. Any incentive to consume is displaced from the physical onto the economic. Granted, the narrator is shown at nearly every meal taking pleasure in the food he consumes. At the renowned beef restaurant Wadakin, he takes his first bite and describes how "the flavors of milk and butter filled his mouth, followed by a developing aroma that was warm and savory. The meat was voluptuously soft, tender enough to be cut with chopsticks, its texture exquisite, abundant, straightforward. He swallowed the small piece, engrossed in its flavors, saliva filling his mouth. 'It's wonderful,' he exclaimed again and again."[14] But this pleasure never structures his actions, never moves his body later to reclaim this experience. That is to say, what makes this such an odd staging for a story of gourmet dining and travel is that the impetus for eating never originates in the body.

But perhaps detaching such appetites from a bodily source is a more revealing dramatization of the nature of desire in the current economic age. Capitalism, in addressing individuals, interpellates them as consumers, soliciting in them always-new desires and offering products to satisfy them. And yet, at the bottom of all desire, as the critic Slavoj Žižek and others remind us, is a push to reproduce itself as further/other desires (thereby never finding full satisfaction).[15] Food in Kaikō's novel is never sought as the natural consequence of hunger or appetite, social connection or social distinction. It is never dramatized as an object of desire. Rather, the pursuit of food follows the logic of capital, articulated here by the supervisor. Consumption, by his reasoning, has its end not in any physical fulfillment, but in its own ceaseless self-perpetuation.[16]

In nearly all stories of extravagant eating, the body unsurprisingly serves as the generator of desire, maybe no more hyperbolically and hysterically than in Tanizaki Jun'ichirō's 1919 short story "Gourmet Club" ("Bishoku Kurabu"). Kaikō knew this work well in the 1970s, when the story, as he described it in a 1979 essay, was "neither a very famous work nor a widely known short story."[17] Tanizaki's story describes a dining club, comprised of five moneyed dilettantes, whose lives revolve around stimulating their jaded palates. Whenever one would mention an enticingly new dish, "immediately fierce gluttony would run like electricity through the little group . . . their eyes and faces took on a curious shine . . . a wild, degraded look, like that of the hungry ghosts of Buddhist lore."[18] The desire for food is a bodily compulsion, sensual, erotic, and constantly suggestive of the sexual act. Indeed, by the story's end, as the group members stand in a darkened room awaiting their meal, one man, A., senses a woman in front of him. "Her soft hair brushed against his forehead. Her warm breath caressed his neck . . . the woman's cool but soft palms stroked A.'s cheeks."[19] Anyone who knows the story knows the strange, sensual turns of this episode, with the woman's fingers, stuck into his mouth, becoming inexplicably indistinguishable from the "wondrous flavor" of Chinese cabbage he tastes as he bites down.[20] Here, appetite equals a bodily, carnal desire, and that desire—for novelty, for gratification—is what impels their eating.

Consumption, ruled by a logic of bodily desire, drives them around the country to find enticing food. When this "collection of idlers" thinks of the turtle soup at Maruya in Kyoto, "Their redoubled appetites were felt rumbling up from the pits of their stomachs. So, impelled by their desire for turtle, they endured being shaken about on the night train for Kyoto." They are then "off to Osaka to have sea bream and hot tea over rice, or to Shimonoseki for blowfish. Longing for the taste of Akita sandfish, they made expeditions to the snow-blown towns of the north country."[21] Like Kaikō's protagonist, they are compelled to the ends of Japan for gastronomic delicacies, but in Tanizaki's universe, the body is always the staging ground for this desire. In Kaikō's novel, by contrast, such trips are compelled not by corporeal (or even gastronomic) demands but by travel's capacity for capital consumption. Indeed, throughout Kaikō's text, activities commonly inscribed onto circuits of pleasure are unceremoniously defined as conduits of capital expenditure.

Food and Place in 1970s Japan

Kaikō's own penchant for traveling in the 1970s and 1980s, a globe-trotting, masculinist project described in several of his essay collections, finds form in the novel in the many scenes of small-town eateries. Farmers and fishermen, bar maidens and laborers of all kinds populate his pages with a salty, dialect-heavy speech, describing local specialties, telling dirty jokes, and initiating the narrator into a particular social (and gastronomic) community. His travel to Shiretoko peninsula on the easternmost edge of Hokkaido, for example, is a thirty-page narrative idyll, including everything from didactic discussions of the Ainu etymology of *shiretoko* to local history via his cab driver, from long descriptions of local mackerel to an extended discussion of the preparation of a house specialty, salted sea cucumber ovaries.[22] Most of his travels follow this framework, making visible the particularities of a place, articulating the local through both elegant exposition and distinctive dialogue. These convey the text's anthropological ambitions, its proclivity for didactic instruction, and its earnest evocation of a small-town community and its distinctive food.[23]

With travel such an essential element of Kaikō's figuration of food, it seems useful to examine his novel alongside the period's most ubiquitous framing of traveling, "Discover Japan," the famous and "wildly successful" corporate effort to get urban residents to travel in the 1970s. This long-running commercial campaign, called "the most successful advertising campaign in Japanese history," was created in the wake of Osaka's grand international exhibition, Expo 70, to "boost domestic travel in the anticipated post-Expo slump."[24] The ubiquitous posters for this campaign showed young female travelers in a remote rural setting—a small mountain temple, an old, weathered farmhouse—encountering a local resident, an elderly monk, a seaweed gatherer, some personification of "tradition" that enabled contact with a more "authentic" sense of Japanese culture and, by extension, a "temporary recuperation of a lost self."[25] The campaign scripted travel as an encounter with an authentic, localized scene, an occasion for the quotidian self to momentarily escape its deracinated modern state. In the anthropologist Marilyn Ivy's interpretation, the campaign "summed up the cultural nostalgia for an entire decade," urging Japanese to "discover what remains of tradition in the midst of its loss."[26]

In the ad campaign, as in Kaikō's text, travel has its origins in economic anxiety, in a drive for increased consumption. These origins are obscured in "Discover Japan" by the drama of encounter the ads offered, their affective appeal in their promise of contact with tradition. But Kaikō's narrative, too, "forgets" these economic origins for long stretches of the novel as the protagonist travels and eats around the country. His time in Shiretoko and idylls in Shimonoseki are all untroubled by the demands of consumption. Consumption is, in these stretches, framed as a wholly pleasurable encounter, edifying, satisfying, filled with nostalgic discovery. Throughout the book, the body may not be driving his movements, but it is certainly authenticating what he tastes, identifying local flavors as nostalgia-filled remnants of a bygone Japan. Even in the urban center, tasting a Tokyo restaurant's laboriously prepared rice—each small batch cooked in an iron pot over wood flames—the protagonist notes how "the rice shined brilliantly in the bowl, each and every grain striking a perfect balance of separation and cohesion with its neighbors." A fellow diner effusively exclaims that he hadn't "had rice like this in ages," that he was "experiencing Japanese rice again after all these years."[27] Indeed, the site of consumption seems less significant here than the geographical origin of the food itself (rural/remote) and the temporal positioning of the cooking methods employed (the rice is prepared, in the words of the proprietress, "in the old style" [*mukashi fū ni*]).[28]

Strangely, the food itself seems immune to the text's satirical critique of consumption. In scene after scene, food is lovingly described, from its production (through long discussions with farmers, ranchers, and others), to its distribution (seen in the long exegesis on shipping Okayama peaches), to the moment of elated consumption. The work may sporadically lampoon the supervisor and other high-ranking bureaucrats for their philistine opinions and crass manners at the table, but the food itself, regardless of its price or provenance, is accorded a kind of reverence. The obsessive devotion of those who prepare it demands the dedication of a master (*kyoshō*) to a craft (a formulation he uses often in the text). When this lovingly prepared food invariably brings its pleasures, it is as if the body were asserting the food's liberation from the reductive circuits of capitalism. And yet every time the narrator pushes away from the table and returns to his "work," the economic logic of his project reasserts itself.

Attempting to Flee the Demands of Desire

Any examination of the novel must recognize its broad satirical ambitions, its efforts to mock, through its central narrative premise, the duplicity, avarice, and absurdity of governmental (and other) appetites. This can be seen, perhaps most clearly, in the work's final few pages, as the protagonist, his body now rejecting any further consumption, flees the high-priced restaurant. He escapes to the remote mountains, seeking only water. He wanders for days and drinks from the pure mountain streams, "never tiring of it . . . [the experience] inducing an unexpected wistfulness (*natsukashisa o oboesaserareru*) such as one feels when passing the same illuminated storefront window decade after decade."[29]

One night, though, at the small cabin where he is staying, he suddenly begins to feel an enormous rumbling from deep within his body. He rushes to the bathroom, his stomach spasming. He lowers his pants and before he knows it, all the food he has consumed, throughout the entire book, begins to flush from him. As the text puts it, "Everything from Kagoshima to the Shiretoko peninsula began to flow out of him (*Kagoshima kara shiretoko hantō made ga ryūshutsu shihajimeta*)."[30] What follows is a list of every item consumed in the book— "Takoyaki from Yurakuchō. Takoyaki from Kobe. Doteyaki from Dotombori. Stewed whale tongue. Rolled burdock root"—a list that continues for nearly a page and a half, noun phrase after noun phrase, totaling 150 items in all, ending with "Water. Water. Water." The list concludes and "a rapturous elation" takes hold of his body. "In this way," he notes, "the entire budget was gone."[31]

It's hard not to read this final scene—the fleeing to the mountains, the excretion of all he has consumed—as a broad lampooning of the individual rejecting the demands of modern consumerism and, by extension, rejecting contemporary life itself. "Everyone and everything could just eat shit (*issaigassai, kusokurae*)," he tells himself after bolting from the restaurant. "He wasn't going to work anymore. He wasn't going to run about anymore. . . . No matter what anyone asked of him, he would refuse. . . . The alcohol, the meat, the flavors, the aromas: it could all just eat shit. Everything swallowed would be thrown up, everything eaten flushed out, he would serve nobody, dedicate himself to nothing." As he notes at the end of this mini-diatribe, "Satiation was but a prelude to wretchedness (*hōman no shungo ni kōryō ga atta*)."[32] The extraordinary, even comic levels of consumption throughout the story are matched by an equally comic renunciation.[33] In Kaikō's parodic parable, the escalation of consumerist demands ends in absolute asceticism, a rejection of all food, all work, all human connection. Indeed, the nation too is flushed from his system, all of it, from far-north Shiretoko to Kagoshima in the distant south. The character's final state is a nod to the sheer impossibility of escaping modern consumer culture. The madness of his original project is matched by the madness of his eventual solution.

And yet, while the protagonist's body may be ejecting and rejecting all the food he has consumed throughout the story, Kaikō's text cannot quite bring itself to do the same. It cannot lump all this food into an indistinguishable mass. It cannot relegate these delicacies to the trash heap of narrative history. Instead, on the work's final pages, it offers up the food to readers yet again, meticulously recalling and enumerating each one, cataloging each item with the name of the town or restaurant name associated with it. What is this long list of food but a kind of menu, a reminder, even in this context, of the pleasures each item brought? And how does the larger text function, in addition to its status as satire, but as a kind of culinary travelogue and advertisement for dining around Japan, an inventory and celebration of the national cuisine?[34] The nostalgic pleasures of small-batch, wood-fired rice or Wadakin beef do not dissipate at the novel's end, but rather, re-emerge in the text's curious impulse to recount each and every item consumed. With desire dramatized in this story as the economic and governmental dictates of consumer capital and not the physical cravings of the body, as a structural force and not a natural urge, the narrative concludes by fashioning an escape from all the institutional structures that govern everyday life. In such a staging, the body, unable to obey the command to consume at ever-greater levels, flees these structures to escape desire itself. But the narrative, it appears, cannot dispose of its desires, since the list itself signifies an effort to revive, recall, and retain those objects that brought such pleasure. It is a retrospective desire, a mode of longing structured as nostalgia. But perhaps that is the point: efforts at escaping consumerist society can only find respite by looking backward, to the past, to tradition, to a necessarily imaginary image of earlier times. Perhaps it is a nostalgia for a time when "real desire" could arise "naturally," without the mediating presence of consumer society dictating our desires to us. The moral angst around rampant consumerism, articulated here through satire, ends not in meaningful resistance but in ambivalent nostalgia, not just in the final pages but in the many nostalgia-tinged scenes throughout the book. The 1970s may have seen increasingly critical responses to consumer society, and yet those critiques, like Kaikō's, cannot shake a nostalgia for the pleasures consumption brings.[35] Here the madman in the mountains may reject all forms of consumption, but his story can't help but long for the pleasures of the plate.

NOTES

1. Jean Anthelme Brillat-Savarin, *The Physiology of Taste, or, Meditations on Transcendental Gastronomy*, trans. M. F. K. Fisher (New York: Vintage Books, 2011), 15. This quote from Brillat-Savarin's 1826 work appears as the epigraph to Kaikō's 1972 novel *A New Star* (*Atarashii tentai*), with its title borrowing from Sekine Hideo and Tobe Matsumi's 1967 Japanese translation (*Atarashii gochisō no hakken wa jinrui no kōfuku ni totte tentai no hakken ijō no mono de aru*). I borrow Brillat-Savarin's (and Fisher's) terminology of "star" (*étoile*) to translate Kaikō's title. The quote was also featured on the cover of the first edition.

2. Kaikō Takeshi, "Ōsama no shokuji" (The king's feast), in *Saigo no Bansan* (Tokyo: Bungei Shunjū, 1979), 170.

3. Kaikō, "Ōsama no shokuji," 169.

4. Kaikō, "Ōsama no shokuji," 172.

5. For a succinct overview of commodity acquisition in the 1950s and 1960s, see Yoshimi Shunya, "Consuming America, Producing Japan" in *The Ambivalent Consumer: Questioning Consumption in East Asia and the West*, ed. Sheldon Garon and Patricia L. Maclachlan (Ithaca, NY: Cornell University Press, 2006), 75–82. For a brief discussion of the survey where 90 percent of Japanese respondents said their standard of living was in the "middle," see Marilyn Ivy, "Formations of Mass Culture," in *Postwar Japan as History*, ed. Andrew Gordon (Berkeley: University of California Press, 1993), 241–242.

6. Katarzyna J. Cwiertka, *Modern Japanese Cuisine: Food, Power and National Identity* (London: Reaktion Books, 2006), 160.

7. Harada Nobuo, *Japanese Food and the Culture of Japan: A Social History of Japanese Cuisine* (*Washoku to nihon bunka: Nihon ryōri no shakai shi*) (Tokyo: Shōgakkan, 2005), 209–210.

8. Kaikō Takeshi, *Atarashii tentai* (A new star) (Tokyo: Ushio Shuppansha, 1974), 18–20.

9. Kaikō, *Atarashii tentai*, 14.

10. Kaikō, *Atarashii tentai*, 106.

11. Kaikō, *Atarashii tentai*, 228–229.

12. Kaikō, *Atarashii tentai*, 280.

13. Kaikō, *Atarashii tentai*, 288–289.

14. Kaikō, *Atarashii tentai*, 195.

15. Slavoj Žižek, *The Parallax View* (Cambridge, MA: MIT Press, 2006), 61.

16. See Eiko Siniawer's chapter in this volume for a discussion of how consumption produces a logic of waste.

17. Kaikō Takeshi, "Appetites of Japanese Writers" ("Nihon no sakkatachi no shokuyoku"), in *Saigo no Bansan*, 141. Not until the "gourmet boom" of the 1980s was this early story "discovered," reprinted, and, in 2001, translated into English.

The rediscovery, it seems, was occasioned by Tanemura Suehiro's 1989 publication of several of Tanizaki's early works. See Tanemura Suehiro, *Bishoku kurabu: Tanizaki Junichirō Taishō sakuhinshū* (Gourmet club: A collection of Taisho-era works by Tanizaki Junichirō) (Tokyo: Chikuma Bunko, 1989). As Nancy Stalker points out in chapter 7 in the present volume, Rosanjin opened his eating club, named Bishoku kurabu (The Gourmet Club), in 1920, the year after Tanizaki's story was published.

18. Tanizaki Junichirō, "The Gourmet Club," in *The Gourmet Club: A Sextet*, trans. Paul McCarthy (New York: Kodansha, 2001), 101. All subsequent quotes are from McCarthy's translation.

19. Tanizaki, "The Gourmet Club," 133.

20. Tanizaki, "The Gourmet Club," 136.

21. Tanizaki, "The Gourmet Club," 102.

22. Kaikō, *Atarashii tentai*, 121–125.

23. Kaikō can be considered an early example of the elevation of local, artisanal foods, insofar as he heralds an area for accruing "culinary capital," to borrow Nancy Stalker's term from her introduction to this volume, through a distinctive regional cuisine.

24. Marilyn Ivy, *Discourses of the Vanishing: Modernity, Phantasm, Japan* (Chicago: University of Chicago Press, 1995), 34–36.

25. Marilyn Ivy, "Tradition and Difference in the Japanese Mass Media," *Public Culture* 1:1 (Fall 1988): 21.

26. Ivy, "Tradition and Difference," 22.

27. Kaikō, *Atarashii tentai*, 165–166.

28. Kaikō, *Atarashii tentai*, 167.

29. Kaikō, *Atarashii tentai*, 294.

30. Kaikō, *Atarashii tentai*, 294.

31. Kaikō, *Atarashii tentai*, 298.

32. Kaikō, *Atarashii tentai*, 289.

33. The text's efforts to critique consumerism are further demonstrated in an important anecdote that comes at the novel's end, just after the protagonist has fled the restaurant. The narrator leaves the character's mountain wanderings to recount the story of a famous French gourmand who can effortlessly identify the grape variety, region, name, and vintage of each wine he drinks, all while blindfolded. He astounds all those around him. He is then presented with a glass and he takes a sip. His face contorts, and he anxiously takes a second sip and a third, his face filled with confusion as he yells, "What a strange wine. I've never tasted anything like it." The crowd around him snickers and he yells, "What *is* this? What *is* this?" "It's water," they answer. "It's water. Just water" (Kaikō, *Atarashii tentai*, 291–292). The gourmand, the consummate consumer, has so lost himself in the esoteric that he has forgotten the most elemental ingredient of life. He is a connoisseur without common sense. The crowd surrounding the sommelier serves as a kind of Greek chorus, informing the character of his folly. In the novel's final words, we find the narrator ecstatically muttering the same words, "It's water. It's water. It's just water" (298), as if trying to warn readers of their own folly, a folly, perhaps, in that their own narrow consumption habits leave

them blind to life's essentials. But here too we see the text's ambivalence: the character who purports to speak the truth, who wants to expose the folly of our out-of-control, misbegotten consumption, appears to be insane. What are we to make of the message if the messenger is mad?

34. We see this in the publisher's efforts as well. The *obi* on the 1974 edition reads like a railway company's iteration of local delicacies: "Izumo eel, Hokkaido mackerel, Akita kiritanpo, Towada red salmon . . . Matsuzaka beef sashimi, Kagoshima sakezushi . . ." all in all, twenty-four pairings of place and food. See Kikuya Kyosuke, *Kaikō Takeshi no iru fūkei* (The scenes in Kaikō Takeshi) (Tokyo: Shūeisha, 2002), 147.

35. I borrow this idea of nostalgic responses to consumerism from Jordan Sand, who traces its path through the 1980s and 1990s. See Jordan Sand, "The Ambivalence of the New Breed: Nostalgic Consumerism in 1980s and 1990s Japan," in *The Ambivalent Consumer: Questioning Consumption in East Asia and the West*, ed. Sheldon Garon and Patricia L. Maclachlan (Ithaca, NY: Cornell University Press, 2006), 85–111.

15

An Anorexic in Miyazaki's Land of Cockaigne

Excess and Abnegation in Spirited Away

Susan Napier

At first glance, the films of Miyazaki Hayao show a rich and positive relationship with food. In fact so intense and generally enticing have been Miyazaki's filmic presentations of food that one of his American fans actually created a sequence entitled "25 GIFS that prove that Miyazaki is a Total Foodie." The GIFS range from Miyazaki's first feature film, *The Castle of Cagliostro*, in which the hero, Lupin, is seen arguing with his comrade Daisuke over an immense bowl of spaghetti, to several scenes from what was at the time his most recent film, *Ponyo*, in which the eponymous heroine, a former fish turned human, is introduced to such earthly delights as ham sandwiches and ramen.

In every film by Miyazaki, food plays a role and usually a strongly positive one, but there is one major film of Miyazaki's where food plays a much more multivalent and ambiguous role. This is in his masterpiece *Spirited Away (Sen to Chihiro no kamikakushi)*. *Spirited Away* is an immensely satisfying, family-oriented film, highly suitable for children who, in the West at least, make up the main audience for animated films. At the same time, *Spirited Away* also possesses disturbing and even transgressive elements, carnivalesque action, and subversive outrageousness. The story of an initially whiny ten-year-old girl forced to find work in a bathhouse of the gods in order to rescue her magically transformed parents, *Spirited Away* is both an affecting coming-of-age story enacted within a stunningly realized magical setting and also a satiric and sometimes dark commentary on contemporary postindustrial society.

Food plays a major role in this fantasy world and in a variety of intricate and seemingly antithetical ways—sometimes as bitter medicine, sometimes as nurturing comfort cuisine, at other times pathologized as a dangerous and addictive substance, and at still other times performing an openly transgressive role linked to vomitus and excrement. But the fundamental antithesis in the film is between excess and abnegation. In *Spirited Away* food becomes both a form of empowerment and an element of abuse, a means of control and discipline and a celebration of extravagance and decadence. It also becomes a way not only of commenting on the excesses of contemporary society but at the same time of suggesting a path toward a more meaningful existence. Based around the conceit of a bathhouse retreat for tired Japanese gods, the film brings up not only traditional cultural issues such as purity and defilement, but also harks back to early Shinto mythology where food, vomitus, and waste inform the earliest appearance of the major gods of the Shinto canon.[1]

Food, naturally, is linked to the body, and another striking aspect of *Spirited Away* is its fascination with the changing body—both in terms of positive transformation and monstrous transmogrification. The fact that the film is animated, rather than live action, is extremely important. *Spirited Away* uses sophisticated animation techniques to portray a dazzling variety of bodies in various states of metamorphosis. These fantastical metamorphoses are not simply visually exciting but also enable the film to comment memorably on the realities of modern society through the defamiliarizing medium of animation and the equally estranging genre of fantasy, a genre often linked to animation.

Fantasy and animation combine in *Spirited Away* to create a world that is grotesque and carnivalesque. The trope of the constantly changing carnivalesque is particularly suited to the fluid, ever-changing nature of contemporary culture. In *Spirited Away* the body is never fixed, immobile, or autonomous; instead it "continues to evolve and transform in ways that reflect both an internal transformative dynamics . . . and the effect of external processes," as David Harvey describes the body in the contemporary world.[2]

As it does with food, the film depicts the body in antithetical ways. On the one hand, in its portrayal of the film's heroine, Chihiro, it shows her body as a literal manifestation of anorexia. We see her reject food and watch as her body begins to extinguish itself. On the other hand, the film shows another major character—the ghostly/monstrous No Face, going from a virtually bodiless spectral presence to a gigantic monster of consumption, characterized by his enormous gaping mouth, and then to an emblem of bulimia as the character vomits forth what it had previously ingested.

Bulimia and anorexia are linked to the very real ills of contemporary society, but in *Spirited Away* they manifest in a fantastic world inhabited by gods and dominated by the looming presence of a gigantic bathhouse.[3] One of Miyazaki's most inspired creations, the bathhouse, at least for the gods who are its clients, is a place of rest and relaxation, equipped with soothing and healing waters, dancing, singing (and perhaps other less salubrious forms of entertainment), and, of course, feasting. The bathhouse offers every kind of comfort, a kind of cozy utopia of the senses. Even its workers seem relatively satisfied, coming across as vivid personalities taking part in a busy collectivity.

In many ways the bathhouse represents traditional Japan, a world in which the gods are still very much alive and where meaning is derived from hard work and shared goals. But the bathhouse also resembles the fantasy paradise of Cockaigne, a staple of medieval European folklore, illustrated in figure 15.1. Cockaigne is a magical dreamland characterized in particular by the omnipresence of delicious and available food, where roasted pigs wander around with forks and knives plunged into their sides "spontaneously offering themselves" to be eaten. Cockaigne also offers other pleasures: healing springs, beautiful gardens, and promiscuous sex.[4]

FIGURE 15.1 Peter Brueghel the Elder, *The Land of Cockaigne*, late sixteenth century. Courtesy of Metropolitan Museum of Art via Wikimedia.

Interestingly, I could find no folkloric or high-culture equivalent of Cockaigne in Japanese texts. The closest equivalent I could discover was the *Shuhanron emaki*, a picture scroll made during the sixteenth century, centering around a debate between the virtues of rice versus sake that finally settles on a "middle way" of moderation.[5]

The bathhouse in *Spirited Away* embodies all of the major elements of Cockaigne—sumptuous food, beautiful gardens, relaxation, healing waters, and even implied sexual pleasures. There is a significant difference between Cockaigne and the bathhouse, however. Although the gods certainly fit the paradigm of the lucky visitors who manage to enter the European dreamland, the workers in the bathhouse are far from idle gluttons. Tomoko Shimizu describes the gods as *himajin* (people of leisure) who are forced into idle existences through spread of modernity that has deprived them of meaningful work.[6] In contrast, Chihiro, the young human heroine of *Spirited Away* who takes on herself the task of rescuing her magically transformed parents, must rely on hard work rather than magic spells in order to effect the rescue. She enters into a labor contract with Yubaba, the elderly witch who runs the bathhouse with an eagle eye for profit.

Ayumi Suzuki has interpreted Yubaba and her bathhouse as a sharp satire on capitalist Japan, seeing Yubaba as the bourgeois capitalist boss who thrives off of the labor of her underlings.[7] Certainly Yubaba is the least appealing character in the movie, dwelling in a luxurious Western-style penthouse and caring more for gold than for her own child. Her greed and manipulativeness are set off even further by the existence of her kinder twin sister, Zeniba, who lives in a simple cottage in the country.

However, Yubaba's workers do not seem particularly unhappy, and the atmosphere of the bathhouse is one of positive energy.[8] Furthermore, it is abundantly clear that Chihiro is redeemed from whining brathood by hard work and the taking on of more and more challenging tasks. In this regard, rather than a critique of capitalism, the bathhouse suggests a return to traditional Japanese values, encapsulated in its work ethic, its traditional architecture, and of course its time-honored function of providing baths, a culturally specific rite in Japan for at least a millennium.

What the film is really critiquing is the frenetic consumption that late twentieth-and early twenty-first-century capitalist culture have ingrained into society. Herman Pleij in his book *Dreaming of Cockaigne* suggests nonjudgmentally that "by medieval standards, modern day Europe represents in many aspects the realization of Cockaigne, fast food is available at all hours, as are climactic control, free sex, unemployment benefits and plastic surgery that seemingly prolongs youth."[9] *Spirited Away*'s vision of a similar world is far more judgmental. As the film continues, the world of *Spirited Away*, while initially traditional, increasingly begins to suggest a modern Japanese version of Cockaigne, as both its guests and its workers get caught up in a frenzy of pleasure-seeking consumption.

The film begins with an extraordinary scene in which excess and abstinence are revealingly intertwined: On their way to a new home, Chihiro and her parents discover an abandoned theme park. Within the theme park a seemingly empty restaurant beckons the parents with an array of delicious-smelling foods. Undaunted by Chihiro's stubborn refusal to eat, the parents dig in, her father explaining to her that she need not worry because they have "cash and credit cards." Chihiro wanders unhappily away to find a riverbank and a bridge that links her side of the river to the opposite bank, where the enormous bathhouse sits. Upon crossing the bridge she encounters a strange boy who tells her to get away. She returns to the mysterious restaurant only to find her parents transforming into gigantic pigs. Lurching and grunting, they fall to the floor amid a clatter of broken plates and spilled food, spewing viscous liquid out of their mouths. Terrified, Chihiro runs back to the riverside only to find that her limbs are turning transparent. Just as she seems about to entirely disappear, the strange boy, whom we later discover is named Haku, comes and offers her a small berry. Telling her not to be worried about turning into a pig, he forces the berry on a reluctant Chihiro. She gulps it down with clear distaste, but her body immediately returns to normal.

This intense and disturbing introduction embodies the fundamental dynamic associated with food in much of the rest of the film, a tense back and forth between excess and denial. Food is clearly pathologized in this scene. The parents' gluttonous orgy comes across as genuinely revolting; they are literally wallowing in food to the point of almost vomiting it out again. The parents' greed and unthinking consumption turns them into pigs—or is this perhaps their real form? Certainly we are primed to see them as materialistic and shallow—they drive a shiny Audi and the father, bragging about cash and credit cards, is obviously proud of his financial status. The parents' greed and grotesque punishment thus becomes Miyazaki's pointed comment on our abjectly material and consumerist world and also probably on the "foodie' culture that has overwhelmed contemporary Japan, satirized in manga, films, and novels from the 1980s on.[10]

In contrast to her parents' piggish behavior, Chihiro unconditionally resists temptation with a strongly disapproving expression while her parents obliviously snarfle huge helpings of mystery edibles. Making her rejection even clearer, she runs away from the unpleasant scene. It is perhaps no coincidence that Chihiro's body begins to vanish after witnessing her parents' gluttony. While the ostensible reason may be that an enchantment is being worked upon her, what really seems to be happening is that Chihiro is enacting a very swift version of anorexia. Disgusted by and alienated from her own parents, lost in an alienating world over which she has no control, Chihiro at the riverside begs for the world around her to "be a dream" and "to disappear." In fact, she cannot make this nightmare vision disappear, and it is she instead who begins to vanish.

The question of control is important. Susan Bordo has linked anorexia in contemporary society to "our modern fear of loss of control over our future," pointing out that the body is "perhaps one of the few areas of control we have left in the twentieth century."[11] Chihiro's move to a new house is one that she has no control over. In our first glimpse of her, her body language quivers with defiance—she is lying on her back in the car, her sneakered feet pointed up at the ceiling. In all, her body language enacts both a kind of passive aggression (lying down) and defiance (shoes pointed at her parents), a potent mixture that suggests the basic style of the anorexic—suppressed anger and the need for control. Chihiro's rejection of food begins as a kind of rejection of parental authority and ends up, when she tries to reject the food that Haku gives her, as an attempted denial of the frightening outside world. Eating, or rather not eating, becomes an "emotional instrument" to the anorexic, as Joan Brumberg describes it, and perhaps one reason for the power of this opening episode is the deeply suppressed emotions at its base.[12]

Of course Chihiro 's "anorexia" is symbolic, suggesting her vulnerability and loss of control. In Japan anorexia had been in the news since the 1980s, and it is now considered a genuine health problem for young Japanese women, although the number of actual anorexics is still small.[13]

In contrast to her rather chunky father, Chihiro is slight and almost boyish. She is a *shojo*, a young girl on the cusp of puberty. In this regard, Haku's reassurance to Chihiro that eating the magic berry will not turn her into a pig is revealing. While the obvious interpretation is that she is afraid of magical transformation, there also may be an underlying assurance that she will not turn into a gluttonous, overweight adult. By accepting the bitter medicine that Haku provides, Chihiro is accepting not only the "correct" kind of food (nourishing and nurturing) but also stands in contrasts to her gorging parents.

As her parents turn into pigs, there is the very real fear that they may be eaten. Chihiro must rescue her parents not merely from their transformation but also from being devoured. Although the witch Yubaba is figured as a nonhuman, her human appearance suggests an implicit theme of cannibalism, or more, symbolically a cannibalistic world where humans feed on each other. This theme will reappear later when the spirit No Face devours the bathhouse attendants in a frenzied rampage.

The theme of humans being eaten by magical beings is well known cross-culturally. In the West, perhaps the most famous example of this is the story of Hansel and Gretel, which resonates with *Spirited Away* in its use of tropes, such as food that is magical and delicious and an old witch who threatens to consume humans.

A culturally closer example is an early twentieth-century tale by one of Japan's most beloved writers, Miyazawa Kenji. Entitled "The Restaurant of Many Orders" ("Chumon no ooii ryoriten"), the story is cited by Miyazaki as one of his favorite children's works. In this dark fantasy two human hunters lost in the mountains find a "restaurant" where they are nearly eaten by the very prey they were hunting. A devout Buddhist and passionate vegetarian, Miyazawa imbues his story with the traditional Buddhist horror of killing and eating animals.

Miyazaki's vision in *Spirited Away* is less a religious than an explicitly social and perhaps moral critique. The piggish parents clearly represent the materialism and superficiality of Japan's contemporary consumer society, where the privations of wartime and the aesthetics of nonconsumption are forgotten or ignored. Furthermore, unlike Miyazawa's hunters who arrogantly consider eating delicious food to be their right, there is a frantic, even desperate quality to the parents' consumption in *Spirited Away*, implying a basic and overwhelming spiritual and emotional void to their lives. Miyazaki's and Miyazawa's visions unite in their ironic and frightening notion of the consumer potentially becoming the consumed.

In contrast to her unthinkingly all-consuming parents and to her former recumbent self, Chihiro must aggressively seek work at the bathhouse in order to rescue her parents. The work she performs is supremely basic and physically demanding—washing both the bathhouse and the customers. Far from being the typical *shojo*, who is characterized by irresponsibility, play, and consumption of consumer goods, Chihiro and her *shojo* body are now marked by hard manual labor. Continuing with the idea of *Spirited Away* as a critique of capitalist society, we can also see Chihiro's initial virtual "melting" as related to Bauman's vision of modern society, where "persons" and "things" have lost their solidity.[14] This is underscored when Yubaba takes away one of the characters that make up Chihiro's name so that she becomes "Sen" rather than Chihiro.

With even her name slimmed down, Chihiro seems grateful to toil alongside the magical bathhouse workers and take care of the gods who are the bathhouse's magical guests. She is helped in this new attitude by her consumption of three rice balls secretly given to her by Haku, who explains that he has put "magic" in them. The real magic is the nostalgic purity of the rice balls, inducing tears in Chihiro and also, reportedly, in the Japanese audience, who would associate rice balls with home and childhood. While much of the food in *Spirited Away* links with banqueting, excess, and gluttony, the rice balls in their simplicity evoke an earlier, purer Japan. As with the bitter-tasting berry that Haku gave her at the beginning, the rice balls suggest proper, nourishing Japanese food. In her acceptance of Haku's gift Chihiro edges away from anorexic denial while at the same time remaining distant from her parents' pathologized consumption of exotic alien cuisine.

The rice balls appear to give Chihiro the necessary spiritual fortitude to cope with new challenges, as is clear in the extraordinary Stink God episode that follows. In this episode a so-called Stink God, a creature whose smell and appearance is revolting, insists on making his way into the bathhouse. As a newbie and a despised human, Chihiro is given the task of bathing the creature. This scene, in which Chihiro washes the spirit to discover that it is actually a grievously polluted river god, is important for a number or reasons. The most obvious is the fact that this is the first scene in which we see Chihiro developing agency. Chihiro takes over the bathing of the spirit and discovers his real identity, through her unearthing of a rusted bicycle that is shackling the Stink God to the polluted river.

Chihiro's role in this scene is crucial, as we see her leading the other attendants in freeing the river spirit of his stinking shackles, but the river god / Stink God himself is fascinating in terms of his initially transgressive role within the narrative. The Stink God resembles "a turd with a face" in the eyes of some viewers, and this description is strengthened by the abominable smell that emanates from him. The entrance of this gigantic monster of filth into a structure identified with cleanness and purity is transgressive on many levels. If we take it as an excremental image, the Stink God suggests the literal underbelly of society, the logical final result of a world of massive oblivious consumption.[15] The Stink God's invasion of the bathhouse suggests that the bathhouse is more vulnerable than it first appears. The nature of the material that comprises the turdlike mass is clearly linked to real-world modern culture—bicycles, cans, bedsprings, and other assorted detritus of contemporary society.

Excrement's transgressive role is manifest in one of the most famous myths of Japan, in which feces play a starring role. This is the tale of the sun goddess, Amaterasu, and her problematic brother, Susannoo, as recorded in one of Japan's earliest collections of myths, the *Kojiki*. In this account Susanoo becomes exultant after winning a contest with his sister and proceeds to get drunk and violent. Breaking down the ridges between rice paddies, he proceeds to "defecate and strew feces about" in the hall where the harvest festival was celebrated.[16]

We have already seen how the Stink God brings feces or at least feces-like material into the bathhouse. Fortunately, when he transforms into a river god, he becomes associated with a more wholesome sort of food in the form of a magical dumpling that he gives Chihiro in gratitude for her help. Like Haku's berry, which saves Chihiro from disappearing, the dumpling is apparently bad tasting but possesses strong magical powers, which become obvious in a subsequent Susanoo-esque episode involving the problematic spirit No Face. This episode is in some ways the most disturbing and exciting part of *Spirited Away*, revolving around food- and body-related elements.

No Face at first appears harmless. Chihiro initially encounters him, a black-robed and hooded creature with a white, masklike face, as she walks across the bridge to the bathhouse. At that time, and in her other early encounters with him, he comes across as attenuated and ghostly, possessing neither voice nor feet, seemingly hovering just outside the narrative's action.[17] Once inside the bathhouse, his first act appears to be a generous one, arranging for Chihiro to receive a pile of special bath tokens that help her cleanse the Stink God. But his subsequent behavior becomes increasingly problematic.

Not only had the Stink God / river spirit left the dumpling for Chihiro, he also scattered gold pieces for the bathhouses attendants, who go after them with greedy alacrity. No Face has understood the seductive power of gold, and that night he uses gold pieces to lure one of the bath attendants close enough to be swallowed. The swallowing of the bath attendant not only provides No Face with a voice (albeit a borrowed one), but also sets off an orgy of consumption on the part of both the spirit and the bath attendants.

Swelling to gigantic size, No Face becomes a grotesque vision of the ultimate customer/consumer, demanding increasingly gargantuan amounts of food that he tosses down an ever-widening, teeth-rimmed throat, located in his upper stomach region. In a beautifully rendered scene we see No Face from a low angle, towering Pantagruel-like above a litter of food that would ordinarily be seen as auspicious banquet cuisine. Now pathologized, the food seems to take on a life of its own, imbuing the scene with a sense of desperation and excess.

The bath attendants too become part of this consuming frenzy as they run over each other to collect the gold pieces that No Face doles out. They also literally dance to his whims, singing and twirling in an attempt to keep him entertained. No longer caring for any other customers, the bathhouse and its attendants have become a land of Cockaigne for a single visitor.

But the void in No Face is not simply physical hunger. When the desperate Yubaba brings Chihiro in to try to quell his actions, No Face reveals that he wants more than food. "I want Sen [Chihiro]," he moans, "I'm lonely."

The increasingly empowered Chihiro is unfazed by the creature's desperate yearning, however. Calmly refusing a proffered pile of gold pieces, she forces part of the river god's magic dumpling down No Face's gaping mouth. This action leads to perhaps the most extreme scene of excess ever to appear in a Miyazaki film. With the dumpling functioning as a purgative, No Face's already grotesque body distends, deforms, and erupts, vomiting forth the swallowed bath attendants and regurgitated food. Energetically spewing masses of dark liquid, No Face chases after Chihiro on a wild race through the bathhouse.

This grotesque scene of excess, with its Rabelasian and carnivalesque overtones, deserves closer examination. Not only does it evoke Susanoo's drunken frenzy in his sister's banquet hall, and also a vomiting scene in the *Shuhanron* scroll, but it also suggests a more current form of excess. The greedy, grotesque, and all-devouring No Face can be seen as the distorted face (or lack thereof) of consumer capitalism. Empty inside, No Face attempts to fill an emotional void by paying absurd amounts of money (money that, as we discover later, reverts to filth) for food, entertainment, and companionship and finally ends up shoveling live creatures down his maw. In this excessive but exhilarating scene, No Face transgresses all limits of civilized behavior, becoming a rampaging embodiment of desire. It is not by chance that his prime characteristics are an anonymous mask and a gaping mouth. The blank masks suggest an attempt at controlling outward manifestations of the self, hiding one's identity and real desires through a cover of anonymity. But the gaping mouth, of course, subverts this pose, indicating the raging need within.

Bakhtin in his study of Rabelais's *Pantagruel* states that the most important of all human features in the grotesque is the mouth, a "wide-open bodily abyss."[18] Bakhtin also points out that the gaping mouth in medieval Europe was linked to the diableries, mystery plays performed at carnival related to the demonic. No Face's mask and cloak is reminiscent of Death. Thus, while the scene is genuinely thrilling, it also calls up images of death and destruction, as the attendants are in a sense cannibalized by their own customer, who parallels their own downward spiral into empty consumption.

In contrast, Chihiro stands aloof from the rampage. Where her initial posture of rejection was related to a negative form of anorexic control, Chihiro's current stance suggests maturity and a positive form of self-abnegation. Rather than rejecting food, Chihiro now becomes the giver of food, offering part of the magic dumpling to No Face in order to calm him down. Chihiro, in her refusal to give into No Face's blandishments and in her ultimate rescue of the bathhouse attendants by sacrificing the last part of the dumpling she had been saving for her parents, becomes a kind of still point in a carnivalesque vortex.

The episode with No Face can also be read as a vivid comment on the contemporary phenomenon of bulimia. Unlike anorexics, as Bordo comments, the bulimic pursues not rejection or abnegation but giving in to urges and then punishing oneself for one's excess. As Bordo explains, "Bulimia emerges as a characteristic modern personality construction. For bulimia precisely and explicitly expresses the extreme development of the hunger for unrestrained consumption (exhibited in the bulimic's uncontrollable food binges), existing in unstable tension alongside the requirement that we sober up." This binge-and-purge dynamic "embodies the unstable bind of consumer capitalism."[19]

Thanks to the bitter medicine of Chihiro's dumpling, No Face purges himself of his own grotesque appetites and begins to vomit back the attendants he had only recently consumed. But this is not enough. Just as Chihiro's parents are punished for their gluttony, No Face is also "punished" by exile from the bathhouse. Again, we have an echo of Susanoo's story as Susanoo, after his rampage, is exiled by the gods and forced to live on earth.

No Face distinctly improves once he is banished. He is accompanied on his exile by Chihiro, who explains that "he's bad only in the bathhouse." This suggests that some potent combination of No Face's emptiness and need for fulfillment in relation to the attendants' suppressed greed has created a uniquely combustible situation. Once he has been given the bitter medicine and been removed from the bathhouse, both he and the bathhouse return to a more tranquil state.

This has been accomplished by a considerable sacrifice from Chihiro. We see Chihiro's empowerment in her ability to offer precious food and in her decision to leave the bathhouse, not only to get rid of No Face but also to rescue Haku, her savior at the beginning of the film. Once again, food is involved: Haku in dragon form returns from a mission for Yubaba in a damaged state, body out of control and blood flowing from his mouth. We learn later that something is "eating him from the inside." Chihiro is able to save him, partly through feeding him another section of the dumpling that she had hoped to keep for her parents' rescue, and partly through her ability to fill Haku's own emotional emptiness through the power of her love. Although never as despairingly empty as No Face, Haku too initially appears to have a hollowness about him. Chihiro's love and care for him replaces whatever evil was eating him and helps in solving the mystery of his identity in the final third of the film.

This final part of the film takes Chihiro, No Face, and two other bathhouse denizens into a different but still recognizably fantasy world, the cottage of Zeniba, Yubaba's kindlier twin sister. The cottage is reached by an old-fashioned train, linked by some critics with death, especially since the other passengers are all shadows.[20] However, these shadows, while implying death, can also be considered anorexic manifestations of a vanishing culture, that of old Japan.

Although the way to Zeniba's cottage is shadow haunted, the cottage itself in all of its traditional solidity provides a reassuring form of refreshment and renewal to the exiles from the bathhouse. Zeniba's form of refreshment also includes food, but in comparison to the extravagant Japanese banquet food of the bathhouse, she offers comfort food of the most basic Western kind—cake and colorful cookies, accompanied by a pot of tea. More Beatrix Potter than Pantagruel, this delightfully homey vision includes the memorable vision of No Face sitting at dining table daintily eating cake. The fact that this food is instantly recognizable, unlike the mysterious substances that Chihiro's parents gorged on at the beginning of the film, supports the sense that order has been re-established.

The scene at Zeniba's house is the most tranquil and reassuring in the entire film. Although Zeniba is clearly the hostess, there seems no other form of hierarchy, and everyone seems comfortable eating, drinking, and working. Food appears finally to be in its proper place, as a pleasant element in a tranquil social world.

But Miyazaki does not leave us there. Instead he brings in one last element to suggest another way of relating to the world, through sexuality and love, rather than through food. In contrast to the shadows, Chihiro is now a robust and vital young girl, open to love and adventure. Just as tea is finished, Haku, once again in dragon form, appears at Zeniba's door, restored to virile good health. He takes Chihiro on his back to return to the bathhouse in a magnificent flying scene of the kind that Miyazaki is justly famous for. This flying scene is also a scene of revelation, for Chihiro now remembers that she has met Haku before and that he too is a river god, although his river has been dammed up due to development. Chihiro's revelation of his true identity frees Haku from the last of the spells with which Yubaba had held him and he returns to human form while still flying. In these final scenes the film moves away from food with all its demands, appeals, and power, into the realm of the transcendent, as Chihiro's flying body has finally transcended the shackling world around her.

When Chihiro and her parents depart from the fantasy world, it appears that Chihiro no longer remembers her adventures. However, the fact that her adventure has vanished from surface memory does not mean that it has vanished from her unconscious. Chihiro's identity has now been bolstered and matured through her struggles and eventual triumphs in the Cockaignian world of the bathhouse. The land of excess has paradoxically become a place where honest work uplifts and ennobles the young. The returning Chihiro exemplifies the possibilities of transcending consumer culture to create an identity based on more solid foundations.

NOTES

1. Miyazaki was highly conscious of *Spirited Away*'s links with indigenous Japanese culture and folklore, announcing that one of the movie's aims was to help viewers be aware that its world "was a descendant in a long line of Japanese folklore [and] to once again arouse in them the consciousness that they are the inhabitants in this island nation," emphasizing the importance of finding out the nation's past and history. In *Miyazaki Hayao zenshou* (Tokyo: Film Art, 2007), 227.

2. David Harvey, *Spaces of Hope* (Berkeley: University of California Press, 2000), 98.

3. Gitte Marianne Hansen mentions *Spirited Away* in her article "Eating Disorders and Self-Harm in Japanese Culture and Cultural Expressions," *Contemporary Japan: Journal of the German Institute for Japanese Studies* 23.1 (2011): 49–69.

4. Herman Pleij, *Dreaming of Cockaigne: Medieval Fantasies of the Prefect Life* (New York: Columbia University Press, 1997), 141.

5. Takeshi Watanabe describes it as depicting "an alternative, yet contemporary Utopia where food is bountiful and strife is limited to friendly debate." Takeshi Watanabe, "Wine, Rice or Both: Overwriting Sectarian Strife in the Tendai Shuhanron Debate," *Journal of Japanese Religious Studies* 36.2 (2009): 259–278, p. 273. Otherwise, I could find nothing close to the debauched revels depicted in the Cockaigne manuscripts. Even later works such as the satirical stories of Saikaku tend to involve sexual excess more than the gustatory kind.

6. Tomoko Shimizu, "Ghiburi monstazu to kankaku no toporoji," *Miyazaki no sekai* (Tokyo: Chikushobo, 2005), 109. In contrast to the *himajin* spirits, the frog workers at the bathhouse are apparently caricatures of "hard working money worshipping salarimen," according to Miyazaki (*Miyazaki Hayao zenshou*, 232).

7. Ayumi Suzuki, "A Nightmare of Capitalist Japan: *Spirited Away*," *Jump Cut: A Review of Contemporary Media*, No. 51 (Spring 2009), https://www.ejumpcut.org/archive/jc51.2009/SpiritedAway/.

8. If we wanted to be orthodox Marxists, we could argue that the bathhouse workers are victims of a false consciousness, but if that is so, it is one shared by the director. Throughout his oeuvre, Miyazaki shows characters who are happy in performing hands-on manual labor that is productive and, in the case of the former sex workers of Tataraba in *Princess Mononoke*, genuinely redemptive.

9. Pleij, *Dreaming of Cockaigne*, 5.

10. Movies such as the 1985 film *Tampopo* also satirized foodie culture in a carnivalesque fashion.

11. Susan Bordo, *Unbearable Weight: Feminism, Western Culture, and the Body* (Berkeley: University of California Press, 2003), 139, 141.

12. Joan Jacobs Brumber, *Fasting Girls: The History of Anorexia Nervosa* (Cambridge, MA: Harvard University Press, 1988), 14.

13. The female critic, Nakajima Azuas, commented on anorexia as early as the 1980s in works such as *Communikeshon fuzen shokogun*. More recently, Japan's medical world has started to wake up to the dangers of anorexia and bulimia, as

shown in an article in the June 2006 issue of *Marie Claire*: "Anorexia: The Epidemic Japan Refuses to Face Up To." Food rejection is not confined to females or to modern Japanese culture. According to Eric Rath in *Food and Fantasy in Early Modern Japan* (Berkeley: University of California Press, 2010), an important feature of traditional food was decorative food made *not* to be eaten. If food is traditionally appreciated in Japan in ways that also involve *not* eating it, then Chihiro's parents' gluttony becomes even more unappealing and her judgmentalism even more understandable.

14. Zygmunt Bauman, *Liquid Modernity* (Malden, MA: Polity Press, 2000), 85.

15. See Bakhtin's discussion of excrement in *Rabelais and His World*, , trans Hélène Iswolsky (Bloomington: Indiana University Press, 1984), 224–226. Also see Susan Morrison, *Excrement in the Late Middle Ages* (New York: Palgrave Macmillan, 2008), 6–8, for an interesting discussion of the symbolic role of excrement in medieval Europe.

16. *The Kojiki*, translated by Donald L. Philippi (Tokyo: Princeton University Press and University of Tokyo Press, 1969), 79.

17. Famously, No Face's rampage was actually a late addition to the movie. Realizing that the original conception of the film would mean a movie that lasted over three hours and go way over budget, Miyazaki and his crew decided quite late in shooting to place the wispy creature that Chihiro encounters on the bridge into a costarring role in order to bring the narrative to an earlier close. See *Miyazaki Hayao zenshou*, 228. In my opinion the creativity inspired by this late decision (paradoxically the result of budget and time constraints) opens up the film in a far freer and more exciting way than the earlier version would have allowed. Miyazaki himself said of *Spirited Away* that he "opened the top of his brain" to let out the riot of action and images that characterize the last third of the movie.

18. Bakhtin, *Rabelais and His World*, 317.

19. Bordo, *Unbearable Weight*, 201.

20. The old-fashioned train is reminiscent of the train in Miyazawa Kenji's most famous story, *Ginga tetsudo no yoru* (*Night train to the stars*), which is deeply associated with death as it carries the spirits of dead children and others, such as the drowned victims of the *Titanic* disaster.

16

Discarding Cultures

Social Critiques of Food Waste in an Affluent Japan

Eiko Maruko Siniawer

In the 1980s, cartoonist High Moon created in a single cell the scene of a lavish wedding banquet with tables crammed full of food and drink, and a multitiered wedding cake waiting to be eaten. All eyes were on the chef in toque and apron, who thrust his arm into the air to present another plate of food: "Eh," he said, "This is a sample of the next dish. Those who still want to eat it, raise your hand!" This food was rendered by High Moon as a commodity put on display, with the language of "sample" (*mihon*) evoking a parallel to any other product that a customer might decide to consume. The chef's request for the guests' preferences was described in the sardonic caption as "modest saving at a wedding reception," commenting on the relative restraint of not automatically serving every person another course of food whether or not they could actually eat it. But the emptiness of the gesture in the context of such an extravagant event was underscored by High Moon's wordplay: in the caption, he replaced two of the characters in "wedding reception" (*kekkon hirōen*) with homophones that, when read in reverse order, meant "waste" (*rōhi*).[1]

Food, in this cartoon and others by High Moon, was depicted as an object no longer valued as a product of nature that nourished the body and soul or as a necessary resource that sustained life. It had become instead a commodity like any other in a society accustomed to luxury, and this commodification was exemplified by the rampant and thoughtless wasting of food. Food waste, for High Moon, was an issue through which he engaged critically with broader societal concerns that he addressed, not just in his stylistically simple and characteristically straightforward cartoons, but also in other realms of his professional life. High Moon was the pen name of Takatsuki Hiroshi, a professor with a doctorate in engineering, a specialist in the field of waste management, and the director of the Miyako Ecology Center (Miyako Ekorojī Sentā), an educational facility opened in Kyoto in 2002 to promote environmental conservation. Originally published in the monthly magazine *Haikibutsu* (*Waste*), his cartoons numbered over six hundred and were compiled in a seven-volume series. They were also displayed at the Kyoto International Manga Museum (Kyoto Kokusai Manga Myūjiamu) in 2010 and have been used as an educational tool by various environmental organizations.[2]

High Moon's cartoons were part of a rising chorus of voices in government reports, newspaper articles, books, magazines, and children's literature that decried the waste of food in a time of plenty. From around the mid-1970s, food waste was criticized for reasons other than the squandering of desperately needed nutritional value. Especially by the 1980s, the malnourishment, hunger, and food shortages of the wartime and immediate postwar years had long been consigned to memory, and practices from four decades earlier—like guests bringing their own rice balls to wedding receptions rather than being served food—had faded into the distant past.[3] It was against a backdrop of affluence, particularly from the 1980s onward, that food waste garnered substantial attention as a problem, be it as discarded scraps from the production process, unused food gone bad in household refrigerators, leftovers on people's plates at home or in restaurants, or uneaten food thrown out by stores.

Much quantitative data was marshaled to illustrate the problem. In the 1990s, the electronics conglomerate Tōshiba concluded that 70 percent of food stored in the home would eventually go to waste.[4] Quantified in terms of energy, or caloric supply minus caloric intake, each Japanese person wasted a little over seven hundred calories a day in the early 2000s, according to the Central Environmental Council of the Ministry of the Environment (Chūō Kankyō Shingikai).[5] Quantified in terms of weight, the Ministry of Agriculture, Forestry and Fisheries (Nōrin Suisanshō) calculated that eleven million tons of food waste were created in 2005, up to seventeen million tons in 2010.[6] One concern was the food wasted annually by ubiquitous convenience stores and supermarkets, reported to be around six hundred thousand tons.[7] There were also alleged indications that waste consciousness was weaker in the younger generation. In a survey conducted by the Japan Consumer Information Center (Kokumin Seikatsu Sentā), 83 percent of respondents in their twenties, compared to 59 percent in their sixties, said that they had disposed of food that was untouched.[8] What was striking about the creation of this data was the concern with understanding what were considered wasteful behaviors as well as the ways in which food waste was defined as a pressing societal issue.

The discourses about food waste that framed this quantitative material bemoaned the treatment of food as a commodity in a mass-consumerist, materialist, and affluent Japan. For various social commentators, consumer advocates and educators, environmentalists, and agriculturalists, food and food waste thus became topics that lent themselves to broader commentary on the excesses of rampant consumption, the alienation of commodities from their production, the environmental implications of a culture of disposability, and the endangerment of the country's self-sufficiency.

To counter the food waste problem as well as the social and cultural phenomena with which it was entwined, these didactic discourses imbued both food and the act of wasting with meanings resurrected from an era before mass consumption, mass production, and mass disposal. Food was to be reconnected with nature, agriculture, and the farmer, and appreciated as a resource by a skilled housewife; and the act of wasting was endowed with resuscitated moral and spiritual virtues. In redefining food and food waste in these ways, the past was nostalgically remade to combat the perceived societal ills of the present and thus avoid the perils of the future.

The Waste of Overconsumption

In what was called "the age of satiation" or "gluttonous saturation" (*hōshoku no jidai*), admonishment of wasting food stemmed less from a fear of food shortage than from the sheer obscenity of overabundance and excessive consumption. High Moon's cartoon of the plush wedding reception was a visual illustration of the conspicuous consumption of food also criticized by *rakugo* artist and politician Tatekawa Danshi. Food, Tatekawa observed, was "on parade."[9] This was also a theme in a children's book series written by Shinju Mariko in the 2000s about No Waste Grandma, or Mottainai Bāsan, who strictly policed her young grandson's daily life for wasteful habits. In one episode at a buffet with his mother, the grandson reached up to the beautifully displayed feast to fill his plate, only to become stuffed before finishing what he had so eagerly taken. At the end of the meal, the grandson and his mother sat with their hands on their stomachs, plates of uneaten food spread out before them. An angry No Waste Grandma scolded them both with a didactic comment on the bottom of the page: "Leftovers are thrown away. Just take what you can eat, and don't leave anything on your plate. How wasteful!"[10] The overabundance of food, the mindset of eating all one possibly can, the encouragement to take more than can be consumed, and the uneaten leftovers that result were all criticized by No Waste Grandma as wasteful.

For freelance journalist Sunada Toshiko, the "era of excess" starting in the 1980s was characterized by the proliferation of food choices and opportunities to consume food. People did not just want ice cream, but a specific flavor; they not only wanted rice, but a specific variety. Bento beckoned consumers, as a younger generation came to think of them not as something that was made in the home to be eaten outside of it, but something that could be purchased outside of the home to be eaten inside. Food could be had at vending machines, fast-food joints, convenience stores, and a plethora of restaurants. One could also eat in front of a vending machine, in a classroom, at a baseball stadium, and in the theater. All of this excess, Sunada suggested, went hand in hand with waning attention to wastefulness.[11] Similar to the premise of the No Waste Grandma books, Sunada implied that the lack of waste consciousness perpetuated societal and cultural practices that were intrinsically wasteful.

Writing from the perspective of someone who was part of an earlier generation that was taught not to leave food uneaten, Takekuma Yoshitaka similarly observed that there had never been a time with such overabundance of food and explicitly criticized how, by the early 1990s, food had become a commodity not unlike an object. In Takekuma's view, consumers chose what food to consume as they would choose any other commodity to buy—based on attributes such as price, attractiveness, and convenience. This was not a new idea at the time of Takekuma's writing; in the mid-1970s, the Better Home Association (Betā Hōmu Kyōkai) had published a book that explained the overconsumption of food as a particular variation on the habit of purchasing a lot of things, and doing so blindly and without a plan.[12] For Takekuma, a health professional, this consumerist mindset led to the consumption of food that was not good for the body, especially processed and prepared foods. Neglected were those foods that had life (*inochi*), like rice, meat, fish, and vegetables.[13] Like Takekuma, cartoonist High Moon denigrated meals made outside of the home as embodying the commodification of food and concomitant fetishization of convenience. In one particular cartoon (figure 16.1), he drew a wall of machines, reminiscent of those that sold train tickets, with the options for transportation replaced by pictures of food. Consumers sat down in front of the machine, put money into the slot, pushed the button under their desired selection, and the food would come shooting out of faucets straight into their mouths.[14] A queue of consumers formed in front of the machines, with one particular man eyeing his watch as he waited impatiently for the completion of the transaction before him. In another piece (figure 16.2), High Moon commented on the allure of both convenience and price, depicting a long line of customers in front of a stall selling bento as a store clerk handed out fliers advertising how economical it would be to purchase three meals a day here. With the line consisting mainly

FIGURE 16.1 Hai Mūn, *Gomikku "haikibutsu"* (1999). Courtesy of Nippo Corporation.

FIGURE 16.2 Hai Mūn, *Gomikku "haikibutsu"* (1986). Courtesy of Nippo Corporation.

of middle-aged women, one of whom had a child with her, it was implied that the home-cooked meal was being replaced by prepared meals being marketed as warm and comforting. Next door to the bustling bento shop were a greengrocer and a fish market with nary a customer in their vicinity. The woman working at the greengrocer sunk her head into her hands, looking forlornly at the busy bento place, and the fishmonger let out a yawn. As a point of information, High Moon noted under the cartoon that there were some sixteen thousand such bento places in the country.[15] While Takekuma pointed out how the emphasis on convenience and price had sacrificed the health benefits of fresh produce, High Moon's juxtaposition of stores offered a broader critique of a culture of convenience.

In other cartoons, High Moon placed more emphasis on the virtues of fresh produce and suggested that the commodification of food was responsible for severing in people's mind the connection between its cultivation and its consumption. Or put another way, there was something unnatural about food presented for consumption, such that people no longer thought of food as a product of nature but as an object manufactured for purchase. In one particular cartoon (figure 16.3), two mothers were walking with their children, supermarket bags in their hands, the large store itself prominent in the backdrop. One of the children, a young girl, smiled and pointed as they passed by a bed of cucumbers: "Mommy," she declared, "those cucumbers are bent!

FIGURE 16.3 Hai Mūn, *Gomikku "haikibutsu"* (1986). Courtesy of Nippo Corporation.

They're probably sick." Contrasted with those crooked cucumbers growing on the vine were perfectly straight ones peeking out of the disposable supermarket bags, packaged on a styrofoam tray and wrapped in clear plastic. High Moon's caption, indicating that fruits like grapes with seeds and tangerines untreated with wax were becoming unusual, proposed that even fresh produce was becoming unnatural when manipulated to meet the aesthetic expectations of consumers. The cucumbers, in this case, had been turned into attractive objects divorced from nature and the natural.[16]

Also in this cartoon, High Moon hinted at the waste of food packaging (the styrofoam tray, clear plastic wrap, and plastic bags) that would become garbage. In other instances, he was more pointed in his criticism of the garbage generated by the consumption of instant and prepared foods packaged for convenience. In one cartoon, a mother proudly showed off the canned and instant foods on display in her kitchen where the counter and cupboards used to be. Two sad-looking children sat at the kitchen table, flanked on either side by garbage cans overflowing with trash.[17] The widespread concern with the garbage created by a disposable food culture was echoed by journalist and writer Sano Shin'ichi, who criticized the containers used for cup ramen and microwavable meals. He also listed the contents of the 230 tons of garbage thrown out by the 4,500 bars and cabarets in the Ginza district of Tokyo on any given day, including the bottles once filled with brandy and cognac, chopsticks, pork and chicken bones, and yakitori skewers.[18] Consumption of food created waste, through preparation and packaging, which was inherent in a culture of disposability that encouraged the belief that, to quote Sano, "affluence could only be experienced in proportion to what was thrown away."[19]

In this context, food itself was a disposable commodity that instantaneously turned into garbage at the moment it was discarded. Food waste was thus framed not just as a problem of consumerism, but of environmental harm as well. The Japan Consumer Information Center, for one, examined food waste in conjunction with its concerns about the environmental implications of the "garbage problem." Homing in on kitchen garbage (nama gomi), the center conducted a survey of 937 people in the early 1990s and asked what specific strategies they were using to reduce their creation of that particular kind of trash. That 61 percent of respondents were not making too much food, 60 percent did not have leftovers, and 60 percent were not buying too many groceries was presented as a heartening sign that food was being valued, but the finding that about 30 percent of survey takers had thrown out food without eating much of it cast doubt over the reliability of these statistics in particular and of self-reporting in general.[20] Of particular concern to Yanagibashi Tetsuo, of the Japan Consumer Information Center's Product Testing Division, was food being thrown out untouched. But the phrasing of this question seemed to invite an alarming response, since it asked if one had ever exhibited this wasteful behavior, without concern for frequency.[21] The answers to this question, broken down by age, were published prominently on the front page of a special feature about wasteful eating in a magazine about food, above three images: a photograph of several sanitation workers loading up a garbage truck, another of a man sweeping up around a mound of garbage bags at a dumping area, and a hand-drawn cartoon of the earth with an anxious face and a bead of sweat running down its face as it emitted a cloud of dark smoke.[22] The attention dedicated to investigating the phenomenon of wasting food coupled with the way in which the data were gathered and presented reinforced the link between food waste and the environmental degradation caused by the garbage problem.

Drawing a connection between the overabundance of food and the environmental impacts of the accumulation of garbage was common, especially from the late 1980s onward. The citizens of Gifu prefecture involved in its No Waste Movement (Mottainai, Gifu Kenmin Undō), for example, called for the reduction of garbage and carbon dioxide emissions. To this end, they conducted a survey about waste consciousness in which they asked people when they felt a sense of wastefulness. Of the 2,637 respondents, many reported that they thought of wastefulness when they left food uneaten. Supporting a recommendation made by the prefectural Office for the Promotion of a Circulatory Society (Junkan Shakai Suishinshitsu), one article in a major daily newspaper recommended that the prefecture adopt a policy of encouraging "half menus," or dishes of smaller portions, as part of its environmental countermeasures to reduce garbage.[23] At a time when most people were not taking home leftovers from restaurants or composting their spoiled food, uneaten food was synonymous with garbage.

That food was being treated like a disposable commodity was also lamented because it was viewed as a reflection of people's lack of appreciation for food as a valuable resource. This was not a new sentiment in the 1980s and beyond, but one that had been expressed in the context of resource anxieties in the 1970s. A book published in 1976 by the Better Home Association opened by painting a dire picture of the trend toward poor harvests due to unusual weather conditions, constraints on fishing imposed by the establishment of economic zones in the sea, and dependence on the importation of food.[24] This last concern—that Japan would have difficulty subsisting on its domestic food supply alone—was an oft-repeated refrain in the 1970s and subsequent decades.[25] In the 1976 version of its book, the Better Home Association claimed that there was no other nation that had as much difficulty obtaining food as Japan; over thirty years later, the association published an updated book about how not to waste precious food that began, on its first page, with an illustrated graphic of an anthropomorphized map of Japan, importing 60 percent of its food with its right hand while throwing out 30 percent of its food with its left.[26] The book went on to give Japan's food self-sufficiency rate in 2004 as 40 percent, placing this number on a graph alongside the higher rates of England (74 percent), Germany (91 percent), the United States (119 percent), and France (130 percent).[27] These statistics appeared in a number and variety of publications about food waste. In a 2008 book in the No Waste Grandma series, for example, author Shinju Mariko contrasted the hardships of poverty, war, and starvation experienced by children in other countries with an emblematic Japanese girl named Hanako-chan who was picky about what she ate and left food on her plate. Presented here to underscore the folly of wasting food were the three iconic numbers: Japan's food self-sufficiency rate, the percentage of food imported, and the percentage of food wasted.[28]

At first blush, it may seem as though there was a tension between the ways in which food waste was criticized—as reflecting the excessive availability of food and as exacerbating food insecurity. But the concerns about Japan's food insecurity were typically oriented toward the future, one in which the country would be in a perilous position because excess and wastefulness in the present would continue. The Better Home Association book from 1976 worried about what would happen as the world population increased and food resources became more limited in the future; its 2007 version explained, alongside the graph of comparative food self-sufficiency rates, that over the previous forty years, food waste as measured in caloric terms had doubled.[29] It was the continuation of trends into the coming decades that was the source of alarm—the sense of food insecurity was not rooted in food shortages in contemporary Japan, but reflected anxieties about both the supply of food and national security in the future. Feared were the impending consequences of the kind of consumerist society that had given birth to the rampant wasting of food.

The Meanings of Food

To counter the wasteful discarding of food, the treatment of food as a disposable commodity in an affluent society of consumerist excess was juxtaposed against an ideal association of food with nature—food should be valued as having life and as having been cared for and nurtured by farmers. This conception of food and food production was sometimes promoted for pragmatic reasons and in pragmatic ways. The Ministry of Agriculture, Forestry and Fisheries, for example, sought to market farming as an attractive occupation as part of its effort to recruit farmers, increase food self-sufficiency, and mitigate a potential food shortage crisis.[30] For others, the celebration of nature, farming, and farmers was not so practical, infused instead with moral and spiritual meaning. In author Shinju Mariko's rendering, No Waste Grandma chastised the fussy Hanako-chan for not appreciating the blessings of nature, and the Better Home Association criticized the wasting of food as an inexcusable offense to those who produced it.[31] Juxtaposing food waste with food production in a cartoon titled "Today's Food Situation," High Moon drew on one side a typical middle-class couple tossing out uneaten food (a bowl of rice, a fish, and a whole green vegetable) into an already full garbage can. On the other side was a farming couple, mouths turned downward and sweat dripping from their brows as the woman carried a tank on her back to water crops and the man pulled fish up with a net. High Moon quantified this wastefulness in monetary terms, explaining that leftover food cost the nation 11.1 trillion yen, while 12.4 trillion yen was the production value of the agricultural and fishing industries. Along with these numbers, the cartoon strikingly illustrated the ease with which one couple threw out food while the other produced it with such difficulty, painting food waste not just as financially costly but also as an affront to the hard work and effort of farmers.[32]

Developing a more personal relationship among farmers, distributors, and consumers that revolved around an appreciation of quality produce was one of the primary aims of the Association for Thinking About the Throwaway Age (Tsukaisute Jidai o Kangaeru Kai). Established in 1973, the group was based in Kyoto and, among other activities, encouraged the spread of organic farming in surrounding areas.[33] In a book entitled *Vegetables Are Your Friend* (*Yasai wa tomodachi*) that was published in the late 1990s, the association recommended that consumers have face-to-face interactions with farmers so as to know and care about who grew their produce, in what kinds of fields, and why any pesticides were used.[34] To model the connection between the cultivation of food and how it was eaten, every section of the recipe book, organized by kind of vegetable, opened with an explanation of when and how it was grown. Similarly, in a book published by a group (Light of the Family Association, or Ie no Hikari Kyōkai) that had long been oriented to a rural and agricultural constituency, health professional Takekuma Yoshitaka extolled the virtues of the agricultural and fishing industries and their provision of life-supporting rice, meat, fish, and vegetables.[35]

Tasked with treating this produce properly was the skilled housewife, for whom numerous books were written about how to use food fully. The lessons fell into several relatively fixed categories: how to purchase the right amount of food so that excess food did not have to be thrown out; how to store foods to maximize their longevity and minimize the chances that they would be forgotten; how to distinguish between the "best by" and "consume by" dates so as to not discard food still safe to eat; and how to prepare foods so that all edible parts were used.³⁶ Specific, iconically wasteful mistakes included cramming the refrigerator full of food such that produce would go bad in its dark recesses, throwing out perfectly good food just because the "best by" date had passed, and tossing out the edible green leaves of the daikon radish. Such instructions were presented in didactic books reminiscent of those that had extolled the virtues of household frugality and thrift in the tighter times of the prewar and immediate postwar periods, and their orientation toward women reflected the endurance of the idea, crafted into its postwar incarnation through the New Life Movement (Shin Seikatsu Undō) starting in the late 1940s, that women were the chief managers of household consumption.³⁷ In a time of abundance, the archetype of the skilled housewife was remade such that frugality and rational management were not means for modernization or economic growth, but were markers of social and environmental consciousness.

Indeed, using food fully was not just a pragmatic skill to be learned and mastered, but also a moral virtue. In a public service announcement produced by the advertising firm Dentsū Osaka in 1982, four young children in the animated spot were invited to dinner at a Buddhist temple by its priest. Not unlike Hanako-chan, the children made the mistake of being finicky and refusing to eat foods that they did not like. Almost gleeful in their disregard for the food, they laughed while proclaiming their dislike for specific foods, with one boy tossing aside a carrot that bounced off a resting cat's head and onto the ground. That night, they were haunted in their nightmares by food—a carrot, daikon radish, eggplant, cucumber, bean, and stalk of rice—that encircled them and repeatedly chanted, "wasteful, wasteful" (*mottainai, mottainai*). The next morning at breakfast, the priest explained that they had been visited by the "no-waste ghost" (*mottainai obake*). The four children ate everything on their plates, to the approval of the priest, having demonstrated that they learned the lesson that was explicitly and succinctly presented on screen at the end of the announcement: "Cherish food."³⁸ What haunted the children was unadulterated produce, not a styrofoam cup of instant ramen, and the act of not wasting such products from nature was imbued with moral and spiritual meaning by the setting of the Buddhist temple, the didacticism of the priest, and the supernatural haunting by the no-waste ghost.³⁹ The educational spot borrowed from a popular animated television series, *Tales of Old Japan (Nihon mukashibanashi)*, both its subject and its style of animation that was intentionally evocative of a time well before the early 1980s when it aired.⁴⁰ The nostalgic feel of the animation as well as the elderly priest who interpreted the message of the no-waste ghost for the children cast the cherishing of food as a moral virtue from times past that should not be discarded in the present.

Reflections on Affluence

In a time of abundance, food was a site of social commentary not just about the discrete problem of food waste, but also about the characteristics and manifestations of affluence in postwar Japan. Through the topics of food and food waste, various authors, reformers, bureaucrats, critics, citizens, and activists engaged in broader discourses about commodification, materialism, excessive consumption, environmental degradation, and resource insecurity. And they attempted to infuse understandings and mindful uses of food with moral virtues that were nostalgically remade from a time before mass production, mass consumption, and mass waste.

Such criticism of the wastefulness inherent in the excessive consumption of commodified food, and indeed of the logics of mass consumerism, was a straightforward and explicit expression of what was illustrated through the plight of the narrator in writer Kaikō Takeshi's 1972 novel, *A New Star* (*Atarashii tentai*). As Bruce Suttmeier discusses in his chapter in this volume, food for Kaikō's narrator was reduced to a quantifiable expenditure that he was compelled to consume in excess. The wastefulness of the enterprise took physical form toward the end of the novel, when the narrator excreted all that he had eaten—the food itself having been transformed into waste. Like the various people discussed in this chapter who spoke about reconnecting food to nature and virtues of times gone by, Kaikō too offered nostalgia for earlier times and a return to nature as respites from consumer culture. But in Suttmeier's reading, Kaikō was ultimately pessimistic about the possibility, and ambivalent about the desirability, of an enduring escape from mass consumerism. The social critics of food waste in the 1980s and beyond were not so pessimistic, perhaps because of the prescriptive and didactic nature of many of their concerns and much of their writing.

It may initially seem as though discourses about food waste took a critical stance on food and foodways quite different from the laudatory approach of foodies and others, who were more focused on the pleasures and culinary capital of washoku in particular or Japanese food in general. Yet many of those who criticized food waste at least implicitly acknowledged the multidimensional nature of food and foodways in the 1980s through the 2000s. Food and foodways were often about excess, convenience, and indulgent luxury, but could also be about healthy appetites and spiritual and bodily sustenance. This optimism was inherent in the didacticism of the discourse—the choice of local, handmade, or artisanal foods over convenience store bento or instant ramen was a way to navigate and negotiate the ills and potential perils of a mass consumerist and affluent Japan.

NOTES

1. Hai Mūn, *Gomikku "haikibutsu": Manga*, vol. 1 (Tokyo: Nippō Shuppan, 1986), 30. On wedding receptions as an occasion for particularly egregious food waste, see Ōsawa Masaaki, "Gomi kinenbi: Obutsu to gomi to haikibutsu no naritachi to watashitachi no seikatsu," *Seikatsu to kankyō* 52.6 (June 2007): 38.

2. The magazine *Haikibutsu* was founded in 1975 and was published by the Nippō Company, which specialized in disseminating information about waste. On the Miyako Ecology Center, see Miyako Ekorojī Sentā, "Kankyō (eko) o manabu nara," http://www.miyako-eco.jp; Nihon Kankyō Hogo Kokusai Kōryūkai, "'Eigoban, Kyoto-shi no gomi no dashikata, gomikku besuto korekushon, CD' no shuppan," http://www.jeeeco.org/project/gomicbest.html; Kyoto Kokusai Manga Myūjiamu, "Manga gomikku 'haikibutsu' sakuhinten," http://www.kyotomm.jp/event/exh/gomic2010.php.

3. John W. Dower, *Embracing Defeat: Japan in the Wake of World War II* (New York: Norton, 1999), 96.

4. *Mainichi shinbun*, May 18, 1999.

5. Chūō Kankyō Shingikai, "Shokuhin risaikuru seido no minaoshi ni tsuite (iken gushin)," February 2, 2007, 4.

6. Chūō Kankyō Shingikai, "Shokuhin risaikuru seido," 4; Nōrin Suisanshō, Shokuryō Sangyōkyoku, Bio Masu Junkan Shiryōka, Shokuhin Sangyō Kankyō Taisakushitsu, "Shokuhin rosu sakugen ni mukete: 'Mottainai' o torimodosō!," September 2013, 2.

7. On convenience store food waste and efforts to mitigate it, see Gavin Hamilton Whitelaw, "Shelf Lives and the Labors of Loss: Food Livelihoods, and Japan's Convenience Stores," in *Capturing Contemporary Japan: Differentiation and Uncertainty*, ed. Satsuki Kawano, Glenda S. Roberts, and Susan Orpett (Honolulu: University of Hawai'i Press, 2014), 135–160.

8. "Tokushū: Muda na tabekata shite imasen ka," *Tabemono tsūshin* 276 (March 1994): 5.

9. Tatekawa Danshi, *Kuimono o somatsu ni suru na: "Nami no Nihonjin" no shoku bunka ron* (Tokyo: Kōdansha, 2000), 3.

10. Shinju Mariko, *Mottainai koto shite nai kai?* (Tokyo: Kōdansha, 2007), 23.

11. Sunada Toshiko, "Tabemono ga kawatta, tabekata ga kawatta: 'Mottainai' wa takoku no kotoba?," *Tabemono bunka* 149 (September 1990): 34–37.

12. *Tabemono o taisetsu ni suru dokuhon* (Tokyo: Betā Hōmu Kyōkai, 1976), 2.

13. Takekuma Yoshitaka, *Kome to kaihan: Somatsu ni suru to bachi kaburu* (Tokyo: Ie no Hikari Kyōkai, 1991), 12, 14, 26, 76, 78.

14. Hai Mūn, *Gomikku "haikibutsu": Manga*, vol. 4 (Tokyo: Nippō Shuppan, 1999), 115.

15. Hai Mūn, *Gomikku "haikibutsu"*, vol. 1, 41.

16. Hai Mūn, *Gomikku "haikibutsu"*, vol. 1, 22.

17. Hai Mūn, *Gomikku "haikibutsu"*, vol. 1, 4.

18. Sano Shin'ichi, "Sutereru bōdai na tabemono: Daitoshi Tokyo kara no repōto," *Tabemono tsūshin* 276 (March 1994): 7–8. Part of the special feature "Tokushū: Muda na tabekata shite imasen ka."

19. Sano, "Sutereru bōdai na tabemono," 8.

20. Yanagibashi Tetsuo, "Katei no daidokoro kara deru nama gomi," *Tabemono tsūshin* 276 (March 1994): 10. Part of the special feature "Tokushū: Muda na tabekata shite imasen ka."

21. Yanagibashi, "Katei no daidokoro kara deru nama gomi," 10.

22. "Tokushū: Muda na tabekata shite imasen ka," 3.

23. *Asahi shinbun*, October 7, 2003.

24. *Tabemono o taisetsu ni*, 1–2.

25. On the idea of a "resource poor" Japan, see Eric Gordon Dinmore, "A Small Island Nation Poor in Resources: Natural and Human Resource Anxieties in Trans-World War II Japan" (PhD diss., Princeton University, 2006).

26. *Tabemono o taisetsu ni*, 1–2; Betā Hōmu Kyōkai, *Taisetsu na tabemono o muda ni shinai hon* (Tokyo: Betā Hōmu Shuppankyoku, 2007), 1.

27. Betā Hōmu Kyōkai, *Taisetsu na tabemono*, 4.

28. Shinju Mariko, *Mottainai bāsan to kangaeyō sekai no koto* (Tokyo: Kōdansha, 2008), 44–47.

29. *Tabemono o taisetsu ni*, 1; Betā Hōmu Kyōkai, *Taisetsu na tabemono*, 4.

30. Julia Adeney Thomas, "Using Japan to Think Globally: The Natural Subject of History and Its Hopes," in *Japan at Nature's Edge: The Environmental Context of a Global Power*, ed. Ian Jared Miller, Julia Adeney Thomas, and Brett L. Walker (Honolulu: University of Hawai'i Press, 2013), 304.

31. Shinju, *Mottainai bāsan to kangaeyō*, 47; Betā Hōmu Kyōkai, *Taisetsu na tabemono*, 1.

32. Hai Mūn, *Gomikku "haikibutsu": Manga*, vol. 6 (Tokyo: Nippō Shuppan, 2007), 50.

33. On the organic farming and consumer cooperative movements in Japan, see Katarzyna J. Cwiertka, *Modern Japanese Cuisine: Food, Power and National Identity* (London: Reaktion Books, 2006), 169.

34. Tsukaisute Jidai o Kangaeru Kai and Anzen Nōsan Kyōkyū Sentā, eds., *Yasai wa tomodachi: Sanchoku yasai no jōzu na tabekata* (Tokyo: Nōsan Gyoson Bunka Kyōkai, 1998), 3.

35. Takekuma, *Kome to kāchan*, 26.

36. See *Tabemono o taisetsu ni*; Tsukaisute Jidai o Kangaeru Kai and Anzen Nōsan Kyōkyū Sentā, *Yasai wa tomodachi*; Betā Hōmu Kyōkai, *Taisetsu na tabemono*; and Shinju Mariko, *Mottainai koto shite nai kai?* See also Akiyama Hiroko, *Kaiteki ni sugosu kufū*, vol. 2 of *Edo no kurashi kara manabu "mottainai"* (Tokyo: Chōbunsha, 2009).

37. See Sheldon Garon, "Fashioning a Culture of Diligence and Thrift: Savings and Frugality Campaigns in Japan, 1900–1931," in *Japan's Competing Modernities: Issues in Culture and Democracy, 1900–1930*, ed. Sharon A. Minichiello (Honolulu: University of Hawai'i Press, 1998). On the New Life Movement, see Sheldon Garon, *Molding Japanese Minds: The State in Everyday Life* (Princeton, NJ: Princeton University Press, 1997); Andrew Gordon, "Managing the Japanese Household: The New Life Movement in Postwar Japan," *Social Politics* 4.2 (Summer 1997): 245–283.

38. Kōkyō Hōkoku Kikō, "Mottainai obake" (1982). The announcement can be viewed at http://www.youtube.com/watch?v=6be2IvKKdo4.

39. It was not unusual for the idea of not wasting (*mottainai*) to be associated with Buddhist origins or meanings. As one example, Shinju Mariko explained that she had modeled No Waste Grandma after the Buddha. See "Koramu tokushū: Mottainai!," *Gendai* 40.2 (February 2006): 234.

40. AC Japan, "1982 nendo sakuhin," accessed January 21, 2014, http://www.ad-c.or.jp/campaign/work/1982/index.html.

17

The Unbearable, Endless Anxiety of Eating

Food Consumption in Japan after 3/11

Faye Yuan Kleeman

On March 11, 2011, the Great Eastern Japan Earthquake (Higashi Nihon daishinsai) shook the archipelago nation and caused the demise of about twenty thousand people. As of 2014, there were still more than a quarter of million people in temporary refugee housing.[1] It has become the biggest natural disaster of the postwar era, and the harrowing effects will surely last for a long time to come. The earthquake and tsunami, the subsequent catastrophic damage, the continuing inability to control the radiation leak at the Fukushima nuclear power plants, the displaced populace, and the contamination of the food production all became symptoms of a protracted postbubble gloom. They symbolize a Japan that has lost its way in economic advantage and its ability to solve problems in a critical moment. The triple disaster exacts a somber toll on the collective psyche of the Japanese people.

The situation was further complicated by series of reports in the summer of 2013 when the government revealed that the stricken nuclear power plant at Fukushima had probably been leaking high volumes of radioactive-contaminated water into the Pacific Ocean for more than two years, ever since March 2011. As of now, how, when, and whether the leak can be contained is anyone's guess.[2] This revelation of one of the continuing impacts of the disaster on the environment, in particular on the safety of the food supply in Japan and its neighboring countries, has produced endless anxiety. The anxiety is further exacerbated by distrust generated by the lack of transparency on the part of the government in dealing with the Tokyo Electric Company (TEPCO) and the public. This precarious thin line of confidence in the authorities deteriorated even more as the result of the Special Secrecy Law (*tokutei himitsu hogo hō*) passed by both houses in the Diet and encoded into law on December 6, 2013, a law allowing the government to designate a wide range of information (that has to do with defense and national security) as "special secrets."[3] Activists and scholars who are concerned with transparency regarding the condition of the Fukushima nuclear power plant are particularly troubled.[4]

This is not the first time the collective Japanese psyche has been in a deep funk. The tumultuous year 1995 epitomized the bleak postbubble era, which was aptly labeled the "lost decades." It was a year demarcated by two major natural and manmade disasters: the sarin attack by the religious terrorist group Aum Shinrikyō and the Hanshin earthquake that made the Japanese public question the trajectory of its adrift generation of youth and the competence of the government to deal with the aftermath of the quake.[5] Nonetheless, even in those darkest moments, while the populace worried about the aftereffects of the quake and domestic terror attacks, they at least never had to worry about the safety of their food. This gnawing sense of anxiety toward an odorless, shapeless, invisible element that may be plaguing the food supply has cast a long shadow on the public consciousness.

The social critic Miyadai Shinji's frequently cited work on post-1995 Japan, *To Outlive the Endless Everyday Life*, comes with a useful subtitle: *A Complete Manual for Overcoming Ōmu*.[6] Miyadai juxtaposes the "endless mundane everyday" with the "communality of the postnuclear war" as the two systematic polarities of Japanese society in the 1980s. Speaking mostly to a younger generation, which he characterizes as the bloomer-sailor generation, Miyadai suggests that, in this era of the endless mundane, one no longer should expect the "scintillating extraordinary" or "a beautiful future," but should instead find the wisdom of surviving endless boredom.[7] This passivity as a strategy for living echoes Asada Akira's earlier prescription of "escapism" (*tōsō*).[8]

This escapism is, of course, a play on the homonym *tōsō*, which can mean "escape" or "struggle" (a key term that defined his parent's generation and the student/political movement of the 1960s and 1970s). Deftly applying Deleuzian schizoanalysis, Asada proposed escape rather than maturation as a means to elude and transcend the systematic control of normative society. Asada, often touted as the poster child of the 1980s New Academism, and Miyadai, a prominent public intellectual of the 1990s, and their brand of inaction as resistance seem to have settled into the psyche of the public. For example, a survey titled "Consciousness on Food after the Earthquake," conducted between June and July

2011, reveals much concerning how Japanese attitudes toward food have changed after the quake. To the question "What is your biggest concern regarding food?" almost 70 percent of the respondents indicated "food safety" as their primary concern (followed by rising prices [21 percent] and self-sufficiency [5.4 percent]). However, to the question "Has your consciousness of food safety heightened since the quake?" 63.7 percent indicated that there was no change (with 13.8 percent indicating heightened awareness and 22.3 percent slightly heightened).[9] This seemingly contradictory attitude attests to the fissure between the abstract epistemology of the issue (though continual reports on TV, newspaper, magazines) and the cognizance of the concern that might actually bring forth change.

This cognizance gap may also explain different responses to an ad campaign for domestic audiences and its overseas responses. In October 2012, the popular male vocal group Tokio made a commercial for the organization called Food Action Japan (FAJ). The campaign was called "Let's Support Eastern Japan by Eating" (Higashi Nihon o tabete ōen kyanpēn 2012). FAJ is a subsidiary organization affiliated with the Ministry of Agriculture, Forestry and Marine Products, with its sole mission being to "expand the consumption of domestically grown agricultural products and to increase Japan's food self-sufficiency."[10] On its website it touts its not too catchy slogan: "Let's increase food self-sufficiency" (*Minna de shokuryō jikyūritsu o appu!*) This relatively noncontroversial ad, once uploaded to YouTube, generated many negative comments from Japanese and particularly overseas viewers. Though a few did express their support for the campaign, most responses were highly negative, some jeering at its naiveté and its cheerful manipulation of a serious issue using celebrities; some viewers criticized the commercial's hidden agenda to gloss over the food safety worries the public has had since the March 11 eastern Japan earthquake.

Food Consumption and (National) Ideology

On the surface, this ad campaign may be just a public relations campaign by governmental bureaucrats gone amok, but it also exposes the fracture between the government's desire to regain the public's trust concerning domestic food consumption and a deeply skeptical public that is still reluctant to buy into this optimism. One cannot help but compare this national mobilization through food consumption with the wartime campaign against conspicuous consumption as represented by slogans such as "No need [for material goods] until victory"), which prioritized the national interest over personal desire.

The backlash experienced by the ad campaign further highlights the cynicism of the Japanese media, leading many to comment that overseas sources are more reliable on this matter. In light of the fact that the primary goal of the organization that made the ad is to achieve food self-sufficiency in Japan, the divergence between the national interest (i.e., promoting domestic food self-sufficiency and increasing consumption) and the food safety concerns of the public cannot be overlooked. Again, as mentioned before, consumption of food is not a mere physiological process but can be a highly ideological activity. Examples of crises, natural or manmade, that changed the course of collective food consumption habits are abundant. For example, the Meiji era (1868–1912) "civilization and enlightenment" movement ushered in a meat consumption food culture that fundamentally altered the Japanese diet. The Russo-Japanese War (1904–1905) popularized canned food for its portability. The aluminum utensils used by the soldiers later evolved into the bento box.[11] Not only did what one eats or how one eats change due to external forces, but the behavior surrounding food consumption also transformed. Japanese men started to cook, employing standardized handbooks and recipes, again during the Russo-Japanese War, on the submarines battling Russian navy.[12] During World War II, the scarcity of food forced the government to impose a rationing system and spurred all sorts of innovations in stretching available food (e.g., new methods of cooking that reduced the amount of food used by 10 percent) and incorporating unusual resources such as grass, mulberry leaves, and stems of potato plants into the everyday diet.[13]

In the postwar era, and particular into the high-growth period, the Japanese relationship with food underwent a drastic change. Shimada Akio divides this relationship into four stages of "plentiful food" (*hōshoku*): "abundance" up to the 1960s; "gluttony" up to the 1980s; "opulence" up to the 2000s, and the "disintegration of food culture" since then.[14] Abundant and readily available food transformed Japanese traditional attitudes toward food from "a gift of grace from heaven" (*ten kara no tamamono*) to a mere consumptive commodity.

Hatanaka Mioko's 2013 book, *Fashion Food, Yes!* (*Fasshon fūdo, arimasu*) traces the numerous food fads that swept through the nation from the 1970s to the 2010s. Various food fads (which Hatanaka refers to as "fashion food") typify this commodification, as does the obsessive pursuit of the newest, rarest, and most expensive cuisines to enhance the consumers' social status and culinary capital. This gave birth to a fetishism of food in popular programs such as *Iron Chef* (where top chefs of Japanese, French, and Chinese cooking competed with each other weekly to claim the title) or the cultish manga *Oishinbō*, in which the meaning of life seems to be centered on the protagonist's quest for the "ultimate gourmet." Driven by the media catering to young women (women's magazines such as *Hanako, An-an, Non-no*, etc.) and armed with disposable incomes, young, professional women chase after the latest food fad (e.g., Italian food [*itameshi*] replacing French, the traditional gourmet cuisine;

the tiramisu boom; the sweets boom) like chasing the latest fashion. Thus, the consumption of food has become akin to the consumption of popular culture. *Fashion Food, Yes!* unpacks the Japanese relationship to food, explaining how the consumption of food went from an act intended to satisfy hunger or delight the taste buds to an embodied cultural experience in the bubble era.

If fashion food symbolized the excesses of the bubble era, Yūki Masami's series of dialogues with four writers on the interface of food and culture, *To the Other's Fire: The Interface of Food and Culture (Tabi no hō e: Shoku to bunka no intāfēsu*, 2012) served as the counternarrative to this mindless consumption.[15]

In a sense, these two recent popular books on food consumption serve as frames to bracket the shifting attitudes toward food and changes in consumption patterns during the period of rapid economic growth period and the postbubble and post-3/11 eras. Whereas Hatanaka's *Fashion Food, Yes!* focuses on the cultural commodification and social meaning of food fads, Yūki Masami's exploration of the interface between food and culture occupies another pole of the relationship with food. A literary and ecological critic, Yūki examines the ecological impact of eating as represented in literary works in order to convey the dynamic relationships between food, nature, and human endeavor in the post-3/11 world. The book consists of four in-depth conversations (accompanied by critical essays) with authors Ishimure Michiko (Minamata and eating locally); Taguchi Randi (contamination and border space); Morisaki Kazue (communal eating and diaspora); and Nashiki Kahō (food and sexuality/sensuality). For the purpose of the current discussion, I focus on Ishimure and Taguchi.

Ishimure Michiko (b. 1927) is perhaps the most renowned ecological writer in Japan. Her fictional works have highlighted the plight of those impacted by Minamata disease. Her narrative *The Sea of Suffering and the Pure Land: My Minamata Disease* (1969) depicted the rustic life of fishing villages like Uchiumi and Shiranuikai on post-Minamata Kyūshū.[16]

Ishimure writes with a detached compassion of villagers and fishermen knowingly eating food harvested from the polluted ocean because they have no other way to sustain their livelihood. A haiku is quoted several times through the text:

Minamatabyō
wakame to iedo
haru no mikaku

Though it is called Minamata disease
seaweed, it is
the taste of spring

This points to the dilemma facing the victims of this environmental disaster. This (somewhat perverse) practice goes beyond the Grow Local and Eat Local campaign (*chisan chishō*), the slow-food movement, and LOHAS (Lifestyle of Heath and Sustainability) that have gained popularity since the turn of the millennium as alternative lifestyle choices. Rather, it is grounded in an earlier national campaign called *shokuyō*, or "healthy food" movement, that promoted local, vegetarian food and a brown rice diet. Proposed by the military physician and pharmacist Ishizuka Sagen (1851–1909) and tacitly supported by the Meiji government, the Healthy Food Association (Shokuyōkai) advocated many practices and concepts that were based on traditional Chinese medicinal/food theory, such as the idea that the food you eat directly impacts human health and that you should consume specific foods to maintain a harmony of yin and yang elements (*yinyō chōwa*), as well as a grain-based food theory and a whole-food theory (thus *genmai* brown rice was favored over processed white rice). But Ishizuka's most influential and long-lasting legacy may be the idea of *shindō funi*, which literally means the body and the earth are one. Originally a Buddhist term, *shindō funi* emphasizes the symbiotic and mutually nurturing relationship between the body/self and the land/nature in consuming food.[17]

Born more than a quarter-century later than Ishimure, the contemporary writer Taguchi Randi (b. 1959) similarly emphasizes deference to the land where one lives and eats. She goes beyond a mere observer to literally partake in the local food scene. In her series of travel writings, Taguchi presents a worldview that is divided into strangers (*yosomono*) and natives (*tochinomono*), and the connection between the two is often through food, or to be more precise, the act of sharing food. For Taguchi, eating the food presented by natives is the most fundamental way of knowing a place and its people, even if the food is radioactively contaminated. The author visited Budische village in the Republic of Belarus (old Ukraine), a village ravaged by the Chernobyl nuclear disaster from which six hundred villagers had been relocated, leaving behind only fifty-five old folks who refused to leave. Taguchi noted the deeply rooted affinity the remaining residents have for their village, even if it is still highly radioactive. Volunteers and visitors from abroad who visit do not eat local food. Taguchi, however, stayed with one family and shared dinner with them.

> I ate home cooking made by Anna. Well, even though it is homemade, there is not much food culture in Belarus to speak of. It may sound ungrateful, but Anna is not a good cook. Most of the time she just lays out all the food on the table and most of it is unheated. However, cheese, yogurt, bread, jam—everything is homemade.

> The radiation accumulated in the grass. Cows eat the grass, so they are, of course, contaminated. The milk produced by the cows, fruits made into jam, wheat that bread is made from, everything is highly contaminated, I thought to myself. These are all natural and organic foods loaded with Cesium 16. However, human beings are simple animals. One gets hungry, and all these delicious foods are freshly made without any additives, so I ate. They did not taste radioactive. Truly, it was the taste of natural food.[18]

For Taguchi, it is this physical (and ritualistic) act of participation that makes her merge with the locality. But even for a firm believer in participant observing, Taguchi has her limits:

> I am very reluctant to go into places where people are still living in protective gear. Perhaps it is because I am a traveler who travels on my own volition. It is an iron rule that a traveler partakes of whatever food is presented to her. When in Rome, do as the Romans do. However, I was not able to bring home the strawberry jam the villagers gave me as gift. In short, I am just a half-baked, halfhearted human being.[19]

Both Ishimure and Taguchi emphasize the physiological, (animalistic) instinctive aspect of eating (to relieve hunger) by the destitute villagers as a genuine, natural act of eating to critique the industrialized and commoditized "fashion food" culture that they see prevailing in Japan. In other words, they are using the ideal of eating naturally, an embodied experience that manifests in the *shindō funi* belief system, as a counternarrative to the cultural eating.

Taguchi herself is one of many people who felt disillusioned about the materialistic, consumption-oriented postcapitalist Japanese society after the burst of the economic bubble. Like many, she left her city job and moved into the mountains of Nagano and started farming as part of the self-sustaining eating natural movement often referred to as "rural-mountain capitalism" (*satoyama shihonshugi*). In her essay collection *Hopes in a Nuclear Era*, she interweaves her visit to the Budische village, Japan's bubble economy, and the 3/11-related nuclear incident at the Tōkaimura power plant into a mosaic of personal contemplation of greed, nuclear power, and villagers who live radioactive lives. The author concludes, "Even without money, if one can grow one's own food, one will not perish."[20] The nostalgic turn to the rural mountains can be seen as a strategy to culturally distance oneself from the urban area and, economically, to survive the lack of opportunity in big cities after the burst of the bubble.

Certainly, we need to read with caution this overtly romanticized fetishism of "one's own land." Henmi Yō, another journalist-essayist who also visited the same village, noted in his essay collection *People Who Eat* (*Mono o kū hitobito*) that "the price for food where the villagers were relocated is so expensive. The villagers believe that compared to young people, the radioactive impact is much less severe in old people. To reduce the number of mouths that one has to feed, many old villagers returned to the forbidden zone and wait for their death slowly."[21]

Conclusion

Japanese modes of eating continue to undergo changes due to various sociocultural factors and not simply because of the 3/11 disasters. For example, the concept of family restaurant sprouted up in the suburbs in the late 1970s and early 1980s to accommodate the suburbanization of postwar middle-class nuclear families, but recent reports suggest that the clientele is no longer families but rather mostly senior citizens who use the restaurants for socialization or young singles who use it like a Starbucks. In the era of "eating alone" (*koshoku*) some restaurants provide lone diners with a specially designed space so they don't have to interact with other customers or serving staff. The evolution of gender relationships in Japan is framed in terms of food consumption, with young men who show no interest in pursuing girls known as herbivore men (*sōshoku danshi*) and eager, assertive young women pursuing what they want known as carnivore women (*nikushoku joshi*).

But apart from this sociocultural change in the way one consumes, the more critical issue at hand is a lack of food safety that impacts some but not all of the populace. The 3/11 disaster in Fukushima is still relatively new, and its long-term health impact is unclear, which prompts the Japanese to look to Chernobyl to try to prognosticate. What we know is that the myth of absolutely safe nuclear power has been discredited, but the final impact remains unknown.[22] Even among scientists, there are differences of opinion in the case of Chernobyl, with scientists' estimates of the damage to human life ranging from a million (Helen Caldicott) to six thousand cases of thyroid cancer projected among children and adolescents.[23] Most experts think it is still too early to tell in the case of Fukushima, as thyroid cancer usually takes four to five years to surface in children who have been exposed. While scientists still debate the degree of danger to health, the nagging fear among the general public is real. And the fear sometimes is as crippling as the health hazard; the Japanese Ministry of Education reports that children in Fukushima prefecture have now become the most obese in Japan, since the nuclear accident prompted schools to curtail outside exercise, even in areas where the risk from radiation was relatively insignificant. This endless anxiety and uncertainty, I believe, will gradually nudge the public to rethink its relationship with food, nature, and the land. Food nationalism is deeply rooted in Japanese popular discourse, which echoes sentiments of distrust of unknown food sources from outside of the country. Yet, unlike the outright rejection of imported rice (mostly from California, Thailand, and Vietnam) hyped by the media in the 1990s, food production by domestic and imported sources, food that grows in nondisaster areas, and food from disaster areas should be evaluated in accordance with a transparent, standardized, and easy-to-understand system for all consumers.

NOTES

1. Information from the Fukushima prefecture government website updated on August 31, 2016. http://www.pref.fukushima.lg.jp/site/portal/ps-kengai-hinansyasu.html
2. *New York Times*, July 10, 2013.
3. The law snuck through the parliament, supported mostly by the Liberal Democratic Party and Kōmeitō, on October 25, 2013, and was signed into law on December 6, 2013, without much public awareness or extensive debates. Polls showed that even of those who support the law, about 60 percent think that it has not been sufficiently discussed, while almost 90 percent of those who oppose the law think it was not sufficiently debated. See the following link for details: http://www.asahi.com/articles/TKY201312070534.html.
4. For example, see the various articles on the issue by Kimura Shinzō, who is a radiation health specialist who has been conducting fieldwork in Fukushima and the vicinity since 2011. http://www.yomiuri.co.jp/feature/eq2011/information/20111111-OYT8T00478.htm; http://www.asahi.com/area/niigata/articles/TKY201309150136.html; http://www.asahi.com/news/intro/OSK201209300089.html; etc.
5. See Hayamizu Kenrō's recent book titled *1995* (Tokyo: Chikuma shobō, 2013) for reflections on many other events and trends that happened the same year.
6. Miyadai Shinji, *Owarinaki nichijō o ikiro: Ōmu kanzen kokufuku manyuaru* (Tokyo: Chikuma shobō, 1998).
7. *Burusera* is a slang term coined by combining *burumā* (bloomers), the bottom of Japanese schoolgirls' gym suits with *sērāfuku*, the typical uniform for high school girls. The term became popular in the 1990s when the fascination with *shojo* (girls) prompted some shops to specialize in selling young girls' used underwear, often accompanied by photos of young girls wearing the item. Miyadai researches the phenomena in detail in his book *Sefuku shōjotachi no sentaku* (Tokyo: Kōdansha, 1994) and views it as a reflection of youth culture.
8. Asada Akira, *Tōsōron sukizo kizzu no bōken* (Tokyo: Chikuma shobō, 1986)

9. The survey was conducted through the Internet and geared toward housewives. It generated 970 responses. See *Shokuseikatsu dēta sōgō tōkei nenpō 2012*, 173.

10. The mission statement in Japanese includes the statement: "Kokusan nōsanbutsu no shōhi kakudai wa shokuryō jikyūritsu kyōjō o jitsugensu" ("An expansion of the consumption of national products would result in an increase in food self-sufficiency"), using the term *kokusan*, which literally means "national/domestic products." Accessed on November 4, 2013, http://syokuryo.jp/fan/logo.html.

11. For a detailed discussion on the transformation of kitchen utensils and the working environment, see Murase Shirō, "'Shoku' o 'dōraku' ni suru hōhō: Meiji sanjūnendai shūhiseikatsu no tebiki," in *Disukūru no teikoku: Meiji sanjū nendai no bunka kenkyū*, ed. Kaneko Akio et al. (Tokyo: Shinyōsha, 2000), 165–172.

12. Murai Gensai, *Zōho chushaku Shokudōraku* (Tokyo: Shibata shoten, 1976).

13. Ehara Ayako, *Nihon shokumotsushi* (Tokyo: Yoshikawa kōbunkan, 2009), 279.

14. Shimada Akio, "Shindo funi no shisō," *Wa*, special issue, "What Is Shoku?," 16 (2004): 74–83. The Japanese food self-sufficiency rate hit its apex in 1960 with 79 percent of the food consumed in Japan produced domestically. It has since decreased every year. The latest number available is 68 percent, though the calorie-based self-sufficiency rate is only 39 percent (2012). See http://www.maff.go.jp/j/zyukyu/zikyu_ritu/012.html, http://www.maff.go.jp/j/zyukyu/zikyu_ritu/012.html.

15. *Tabi* literally means "other's fire" is said to be the etymology of journey *tabi*, as going on a journey means eating, warming, and lighting with a stranger's fire.

16. Ishimure Michiko, *Kukai jōdo waga minamatabyō* (Tokyo: Kōdansha, 1969).

17. In the Buddhist context, *shin* (the body) refers to *shōhō* (the proper consequences of past deeds) while *do* (the land) refers to *ehō* (the environment that accommodates that consequence), and the two are undivided. This idea of *shindo funi* was also taken up by Korean society in 1989 and has now become the official slogan of the Korea Agricultural Association.

18. Taguchi Randi, *Yorube naki jidai no kibō* (Tokyo: Shunjusha, 2006), 194–195.

19. Taguchi Randi, "Zōn nite II," *Ōru yomimono* 67.1 (2012): 150.

20. Taguchi Randi, *Yorube naki jidai no kibō*, 160.

21. Henmi Yō, *Mono kū hitobito* (Tokyo: Kadokawa shoten, 1997), 275.

22. The Health and Labor Department's website provides detailed information on food and radiation, though it is very technical and less than user friendly. See http://www.mhlw.go.jp/shinsai_jouhou/shokuhin.html#syokuhin.

23. United Nations Scientific Committee on the Effects of Atomic Radiation report, 2008.

Afterword

Foods of Japan, Not Japanese Food

Eric C. Rath

In 1946 an English-language guidebook to Japanese food began with the following warning:

> Initiation of foreigners into Japanese dishes must be a gradual one proceeding from the familiar to the unfamiliar. Raw fish in slices ("sashimi") and pickled vegetables ("konomono"), so dear and delicious to the Japanese palate, should be reserved for the initiated—these are dangerous things to offer to the beginner; dangerous because they may repel and disgust those who will come to appreciate Japanese delicacies when introduced to them from other easier approaches where they have to tackle with the line of least resistance.[1]

Today, sashimi and Japanese pickles, represented frequently by slices of yellow *takuan* (daikon pickled in rice bran) and round, red *umeboshi* (pickled apricot), have become familiar in the food scenes in North America and Europe to the point that no one would begin an introduction to Japanese food on a cautionary note. It is a different world than the age when the Japanese Tourist Bureau published *Notes on Japanese Cuisine*, the first postwar introduction for foreigners to the foods of Japan. Sushi can be purchased in train stations in Europe and sports stadiums in the United States; and in New York, California, Texas, and other locales, trendy ramen restaurants now compete with Japanese steakhouses of an older generation.

The fact that Japanese food has become globally recognizable and appreciated was brought home to me when I discovered sushi in a remote Tibetan region of China in 2010. Thanks to a university

FIGURE A.1 Longen with Thubten Chokorling Monastery in the foreground. Photograph by the author.

service project and funding from the US State Department, I traveled to the Tibetan Autonomous Prefecture of Golok (Tib. Mgo log; Ch. Guoluo) in rural Qinghai province to live in the community of Longen, which is about eight hours by car from the provincial capital of Qinghai. Longen, seen in figure A.1, is home to about one thousand households in a valley thirteen thousand feet above sea level. It is a town where yaks have the right of way on the dirt streets and their dried dung fuels home-cooking fires (see figure A.2). Longen has two rows of shops including a short stretch of restaurants across from Thubten Chokorling Monastery, known in Chinese as Longensi, which is the main reason for the settlement and gives the community its name.[2]

Like restaurants elsewhere in Asia, the eateries of Longen attract trade with photos of food outside. Gazing up at the offerings of one of these establishments I was stunned to see a photo of sushi and Japanese udon between images of dumplings and hearty soups that are traditional Tibetan fare (see figures A.3 and A.4). When I entered the restaurant and asked the staff whether they sold Japanese food, I was disappointed to learn that their specialty was Tibetan soup, cooked in metal bowls heated so hot they need to be carried to the table with tongs. The Japanese food photos were purely decorative in an area where some Tibetans call crab and lobster "sea bugs."[3]

FIGURE A.2 Longen with yaks. Photograph by the author.

Marveling at the fact that images of Japanese food were attractive even to locals more accustomed to yak and mutton than Japanese wheat noodles and sushi, I concluded that finding sushi in Tibet was about as likely as meeting a yeti. But when a friend took to me a more upscale Tibetan restaurant two hours away in the town of Dawu, I had a second surprise. The Black Tent Restaurant was quintessentially Tibetan with a name evoking the traditional dwellings in which many nomads in the region still live. On the menu were Tibetan dumplings (*momo*), bread with meat stuffing (*sha palep*), and other representative Tibetan dishes, but so too was "Korean Sushi"—a sushi roll consisting of nori wrapping a stuffing of rice, slices of cucumber, egg, vegetables, and Spam, all presented beautifully on a white and blue plate, seen in figure A.5. It was a revelation for me to see that not only that canned meat had spread to rural China, but also that sushi had become a way of consuming it in an area where rice is as foreign as potted meat. Tibetans in Golok traditionally consume barley and rely on meat and dairy products in their diet, not rice or even many vegetables.

As Korean sushi at a Tibetan restaurant in China illustrates, Japanese food is now so global that trademark dishes are on the verge of losing their identification with Japan. Other examples of this phenomenon are the many Chinese buffets in America's heartland that allow customers to serve themselves sushi alongside macaroni and cheese, pork ribs, and General Tso's Chicken (aka

FIGURE A.3 Exterior of a Tibetan restaurant in Longen across from Thubten Chokorling Monastery. Photograph by the author.

General Chicken), which is an American culinary invention.[4] Customers at these establishments blur the conceptual categories of Western and Asian cuisine as they pile foods onto their plates.

Purists might object to these messy plates of food for many different reasons, and the fact that Japanese food is on the verge of losing its "Japaneseness" has made the Japanese government anxious for the last several decades. Worried that eateries selling "Japanese food" were serving substandard fare, in November 2006, the Japanese government attempted to launch a licensing program for Japanese restaurants outside of the country to ensure customers of their authenticity. The scheme famously backfired with cries in the media that Japan was launching the "sushi police!"[5] A more successful initiative to promote Japanese food abroad was the 2012 effort to list "Japanese traditional dietary cultures" (washoku) with UNESCO, which Ted Bestor has analyzed in this volume. Japan's application to UNESCO indicates specifically the desire to seek a heritage listing for washoku as a symbol of the country's recovery from the 2011 earthquake and tsunami, which prompted many of Japan's trading partners to ban the import of Japanese agricultural and seafood products and damaged the country's food service industry.[6] The successful UNESCO listing, awarded in 2013, endorses Japanese food as healthy and desirable to eat.

FIGURE A.4 Signboard advertising the "Clay Pot Non-vegetarian Restaurant" (*Rdza khog ldum log za khang*) in Longen. Photograph by the author.

The vitality of Japan's food service industry, which closely correlates to the health of its general economy, had experienced sluggish growth preceding these disasters, and has only recently recovered from them.[7]

Japan's promotion of washoku internationally is also meant to shape eating habits at home. In 2013 the noted food expert and cultural historian Kumakura Isao, listed on the Japanese government's 2012 UNESCO application as heading the "Investigative Commission to nominate WASHOKU on the Representative List of the Intangible Cultural Heritage," wrote candidly that the traditional dishes and modes of eating promoted as washoku were actually "facing extinction" in Japan. The government sought UNESCO recognition, Kumakura explained, less to promote Japanese food globally than to reinvigorate home cooking domestically. Kumakura listed the root causes of the decline of washoku as resulting from the prevalence of eating out, purchases of ready-made meals, and mothers allowing their children to dictate the types of foods prepared at home.[8] According to Kumakura, professional cooking has displaced the homemade meal, whether that means dining out or bringing carryout meals and prepared dishes home. Kumakura's conclusions highlight the success of Japan's restaurants, which

FIGURE A.5 Tibetan dumplings (*momo*) and "Korean" sushi from the Black Tent Restaurant in Dawu, prefectural country seat of Golog. Photograph by the author.

have garnered awards domestically and fame abroad, as Nancy Stalker discusses in this volume. But rather than blame the restaurant industry, Kumakura faults mothers for the decline of home cooking due to their poor food choices and failure to prepare more "traditional" dishes for their families or simply to cook at all.

Despite such alarmist and sexist language, most meals in Japan are still made and consumed at home. In 2013 dining out comprised just around 20 percent of monthly food expenses per capita and purchases of precooked meals amounted to 12.7 percent of total food expenses monthly, meaning that the bulk of food and beverage costs for households were for ingredients for cooking at home.[9] According to 2014 statistics, dining out has also been on the decline in Japan, measured by a 12.7 percent reduction in spending for dining out per capita from 1995 to 2011.[10] With less dining out separately, more families are eating dinner at home together, according to countrywide surveys from the Cabinet Office Center for the Advancement of Food Education (Naikaku shokuiku suishin shitsu), which has measured an uptick in the rate that respondents eat their evening meal together every day from a rate of 56.8 percent in 2009 to 65 percent in 2014.[11]

Kumakura alleges that people, specifically housewives, are not cooking Japanese food with enough frequency, but that does not appear to be the case either. In the same year that Kumakura published his essay, a 2013 Internet survey by the beverage maker Takara Shuzō asked three thousand people ages twenty to sixty about what they consumed at home. It discovered that 46.2 percent ate predominantly Japanese (washoku) meals, 43.7 percent replied that about half of their meals were washoku, and only 5.2 percent responded that they never ate washoku.[12]

Despite the fact that in 2013 almost 90 percent of the respondents in the aforementioned survey claimed to consume washoku for at least half the meals they ate at home, the Japanese government, like their spokesman Kumakura, depicts washoku as being in decline. The Ministry of Agriculture, Forestry and Fisheries and the Agency for Cultural Affairs, joint authors of Japan's 2012 UNESCO application, describe the "practitioners of washoku" as "all of the Japanese people." But their application essay contends that "due to the increase of single-family households, dismemberment of local communities and standardization of dietary lifestyles, WASHOKU's presence and viability have recently gradually decreased."[13] Washoku then is less about what the Japanese report to eat—and who they actually eat with—than about using food to designate societal norms. "Washoku is a social practice . . . passed down in the home at shared mealtimes," according to the official definition on the UNESCO website.[14] By this reasoning, washoku depends on a family structure with several generations living under one roof, not "single-family households." If the government cannot make intergenerational families live together, it can at least try to shame them into eating together, or at the very least raise popular awareness of the importance of elders in a country where in 2016 nearly one out of four people is over age sixty-five, a population expected to exceed one in three people by 2035.[15]

Along with critiquing perceived failings in modern family and social life, the UNESCO washoku campaign is meant to encourage the consumption of ingredients produced in Japan. The reference to the "dismemberment of local communities" in the UNESCO application is shorthand for agricultural and coastal areas that have seen a decline in population and economic opportunities, which greater farm and fishery incomes might stem if only demand for the products of these areas increased. Additionally, the fact that no other developed country is so dependent on food imports as Japan fuels worries among politicians and the media about the nation's food self-sufficiency.[16] Consequently, a major reason for promoting what the government identifies as washoku is to spur demand for foods produced domestically and to expand the exports of these foodstuffs abroad to shore up the agricultural sector and the fishing industry.

That traditional Japanese dietary cultures have become a matter for government policy should not disguise the fact that the notion of a national cuisine is still young in Japan, only little more than a century old. The earliest references to the words signifying Japanese cuisine—*honpō ryōri, Nihon ryōri, Nihon shoku*, and *washoku*—appeared in the last decades of the 1800s, and were coined to designate native practices in contrast to the Western and Chinese cuisines arriving on Japan's shores.[17] Washoku, defined as "traditional dietary cultures," evokes connections with the past without referencing historical specifics.

Nevertheless, many Japanese food scholars have endeavored to prove that the essence of Japanese cuisine is not modern at all. Some researchers have focused on prominent foodstuffs in Japan to trace a linkage between cooking and ethnic identity. The noted ethnologist Tsuboi Hirofumi (1929–1988) wrote his famous study *Potatoes and the Japanese* (*Imo to Nihonjin*) to explore the idea that dry-field farming, and the culture surrounding it, was as important historically as rice paddy agriculture in some locales in Japan.[18] Following Tsuboi's lead, later authors examined the centrality of other foodstuffs and ways of cooking to the Japanese in works such as *Konbu and the Japanese* (*Konbu to Nihonjin*), *Buddhist Vegetarian Cuisine and the Japanese* (*Shōjin ryōri to Nihonjin*), and *Grilled Chicken and the Japanese* (*Yakitori to Nihonjin*).[19] Such texts are keen to point out the unique qualities of both Japanese food culture and the Japanese people that their authors claim have coexisted for centuries if not millennia. Perhaps the most famous example of the genre is *Foodstuffs and the Japanese* (*Shokumotsu to Nihonjin*) by the historian Higuchi Kiyoyuki, a survey text once popular in university courses. Higuchi argues (erroneously) that the wide variety of plant and animal life once consumed in Japan contributed to the Japanese having intestines eighty centimeters longer than Europeans, which according to Higuchi was needed for the Japanese to digest all of the things found in their homeland.[20] For Higuchi, there is a special and ancient connection between the Japanese people and their diet that can measured if not in centuries than in the length of their bowels.

Other specialists backdate the crystallization of Japanese cuisine by trying to determine when different components of the diet, chiefly rice, and the custom of eating that grain with soup, pickles, and side dishes, first came together. Watanabe Minoru's *History of Japanese Foodways* (*Nihon no shokuseikatsushi*), published in 1964, an influential text formerly used in high schools and women's colleges, where most food studies classes are taught, dates the formation of washoku to the late sixteenth century and the development of a gourmet Japanese cuisine to the early modern period (1600–1868).[21] A more recent definitive work written by a team of respected scholars, *A History of*

Japanese Foodstuffs (*Nihon shokumotsushi*), published in 2009, likewise upholds the notion that Japanese cuisine is a product of the sixteenth through nineteenth centuries.[22]

Japanese cuisine, when defined according to these studies as certain foods combined with a type of menu format—that is, a meal of rice, miso soup, pickles, and a few side dishes—might be dated to the eating habits of the ruling and economic elite in the early modern period or an earlier time, but that is not the same as saying that such a mode of eating was the dominant one in that age or any other. The leading historian of Japanese food, Harada Nobuo, contends that rice did not become the universal staple grain in Japan until the early 1960s.[23] More to the point, the notion that the people in the islands of Japan for millennia before 1600 or centuries after who ate meals other than rice, miso soup, pickles, and side dishes were somehow consuming something nonnormative, primitive, or substandard—that is to say, non-Japanese—needs to be challenged more rigorously in scholarship. Why a typical farmer's meal before World War II consisting of a pot of boiled grains (rice, barley, millets, and even corn) flavored with miso and mixed with vegetables and tubers is any less "Japanese" than a meal in which the rice, soup, and vegetables are served separately reveals the bias of scholarship that has tended to identify the meals of the urban elite as constituting authentic "Japanese" cuisine. When modern notions of culinary identity and cuisine are projected backward into the past, one might uncover precedents for some perceived modern norms, but at the expense of ignoring more complex historical realities.

To borrow the terms of the French culinary historian Jean-François Revel, historians of Japanese food have focused too much on the "cuisine that talks too much," which is the diet of the elite chronicled in gastronomic writings, when they need instead to reclaim the "silent cuisine" of the peasantry and bourgeoisie that evolved slowly and did not have an inventor, but has produced a legacy of fine eating.[24] Food scholars cannot be blamed for the fact that they have tended to focus on the diet of the elite due to the paucity of sources for documenting the diet for ordinary people in premodern Japan. As historian Susan Hanley has noted, "With few exceptions, food usually doesn't figure prominently, if at all, in the various diaries extant from the Tokugawa period."[25] The lack of documentation for understanding the diet of the peasantry, some 80 percent of the Japanese population in the Tokugawa (early modern) period, prompted cultural geographer Arizono Shōichirō to go so far as to say that there are no records for what commoners ate on a daily basis in that era.[26]

A subtler and more problematic reason for the emphasis on elite as opposed to ordinary foodways is the choice that scholars have made to peg the history of Japanese food to the chronology of political history. Authoritative studies in Japanese and English are organized by chapter according to governmental periods. Both Sasagawa Rinpū and Adachi Isamu's 1973 study *A History of Food in Early Modern Japan* (*Kinsei Nihon shokumotsushi*) and Morisue Yoshiaki and Kikuchi Yūjirō's classic text, first published in 1952, then in a revised edition in 1965, as *A Revised History of Food: The Development of the Foodways of the Japanese People* (*Kaikō shokumotsushi: Nihonjin no shokuseikatsu no hatten*), divide their late medieval and early modern chapters according to the Azuchi Momoyama (1573–1600) and Edo periods (1600–1868).[27] In a history of food, references to the political context are unavoidable and necessary, which is why Naomichi Ishige's *The History and Culture of Japanese Food* begins each chapter with a description of the historical setting, a narrative largely confined to developments in rule and society.[28] A more recent Japanese work, mentioned previously, *A History of Japanese Foodstuffs*, published in 2009, is also organized according to conventional historical categories of prehistoric, ancient, medieval, early modern, and modern.[29]

Such an approach to any history seems familiar and logical, but at times the emphasis on the political situation means an unnecessary spotlight on the dietary habits of those at the top of society. The anecdote of how a court chef pleased warlord Oda Nobunaga (1534–1582) by making food more provincial in taste than the manner of the capital's elite is often retold in food histories, and the cultural historian Murai Yasuhiko includes the vignette in his history of kaiseki cuisine.[30] Such tidbits may be interesting, but it is questionable why the taste preferences of a sixteenth-century warlord, who would be tried for crimes against humanity were he alive today, should be of lasting interest in a work that purports to survey the food history of a country.

The essays in the present volume as well as the scholarship of Barak Kushner and George Solt on the history of ramen offer useful corrections to the prior focus on elite foodways, but to counter the hegemony of models of Japanese cuisine as elitist, researchers may also need to revise the chronology of Japanese culinary culture according to parameters that do not align with political history but do express changes in the diet that affected most of the population.[31] Such a history would be important for prioritizing food, and it might also spur a debate about the chronological boundaries all historians of Japan currently use to demarcate the past.

Rather than peg food history to changes in political regimes, a revised chronology of Japanese food history should be attentive to factors such as innovations in technology, introductions of new ingredients from abroad, the popularization of important staple foods, and the debut of noted recipes. Consideration of such factors suggests that there was a greater contrast in the food culture of the eighteenth century compared to the seventeenth century than there was between the period immediately before and after 1600, which is the date usually used to divide the medieval and early modern periods.

In the eighteenth century, more farmers owned stone mortars, allowing them to more readily mill grains like buckwheat and wheat, which require processing, into flour for foodstuffs like gruel and noodles, thereby diversifying their diets. Farmers also switched to using a hammer-shaped pestle rather than a straight pestle, an advance that made it easier to hull grains, mash soybeans for miso, and pound rice cakes.[32] Important staple foods introduced in the 1500s and 1600s became more widely consumed by the eighteenth century, providing essential sources of food energy in places where other crops could not be grown. Corn became a major staple in Shikoku after its arrival in the seventeenth century.[33] Sweet potatoes arrived in the Kantō area in the first decades of eighteenth century and became an essential food in the southern Kyushu domain of Satsuma by the end of that century.[34] Double cropping became more widespread after 1700 as farmers planted barley or vegetables after their rice crops. In the Hokuriku, Kinai, and San'yō regions, and in northern Kyushu, rates of double cropping reached 60 to 70 percent and even 90 percent in some areas in the eighteenth century.[35]

In the major cities, use of stoves (kamado) became more common in the homes of wealthy townspeople in the eighteenth century, allowing for a more varied diet than cooking over an open hearth.[36] When waterwheels came to be used for grinding and polishing rice in cities, urbanites gained greater, more affordable access to polished rice and refined wheat and buckwheat flours for noodles.[37] Printed culinary books (ryōribon) debuted with Tales of Cookery (Ryōri monogatari) in 1643, but the golden age of such writings and of Edo cuisine occurred in the latter half of the eighteenth century.[38] The first specialized text on confectionery was published in Kyoto in 1718, and sweet makers in Edo (Tokyo) established a guild in 1721, and their counterparts in Kyoto created a similar organization in 1775.[39] The confectioners' success was thanks on the one hand to ample sugar imports from the Dutch, who were turning a handsome profit on the sweetener by the latter half of the eighteenth century, and on the other hand to the rise of the domestic sugar industry. Satsuma domain began selling sugar from Ryukyu from the first decades of the eighteenth century, and sugar cultivation and processing spread on Japan's main islands in the same century.[40] Sugary sweets even showed up in rural households by the end of the eighteenth century.[41] Japan's restaurant trade has a long history, but it was firmly established after 1700 and enjoyed tremendous growth in the latter half of the eighteenth century.[42] The 1700s are also the age of the invention of many traditional Japanese dishes, including tempura and sushi rolls wrapped in nori.[43] Soba became the preferred noodle dish in Edo in the eighteenth century.⁴⁴ And roasted sweet potato (*yaki imo*) shops became a common sight in the warrior capital, with grilled eel (*kabayaki*) becoming a dish synonymous with the same city in that century.⁴⁵

In the same way that a focus on food might prompt a reconsideration of the important transitions in the early modern period, food scholars have already suggested extending the endpoint of the early modern era to the 1920s or early 1930s, noting the continuities in the diet for most of the population from the nineteenth century to the first decades of the twentieth century. The story of how urban elites began enjoying exotic Western dishes like beef curry, croquettes (*korokke*), and pastries in the Meiji era (1868–1912) is often told, but the diet for most of the population that lived in rural villages in the 1920s and 1930s was little different than it was a century earlier. Outside of the cities, people ate what they produced locally during this time.⁴⁶ Vaclav Smil and Kazuhiko Kobayashi's recent study of Japanese dietary transitions finds only slight changes in food energy supply for the first four decades of the twentieth century, indicating that, while the diet of people in the cities may have become more Westernized, cooking and eating remained largely unchanged for the bulk of society.⁴⁷

As important as looking for new transitions is, so too is the search for continuities. For example, the arrival of rice agriculture in the Yayoi period (c. 400 BCE–300 CE) should not overshadow the enduring role of gathered foods in the diet such as chestnuts, acorns, and horse chestnuts. Scholars examining the Toro excavations in Shizuoka, which date to the Yayoi period, have concluded that the amount of rice grown would have been insufficient to support the population, especially if some of the rice was destined to become sake. The archaeological site suggests that gathered foods such as chestnuts, acorns, and horse chestnuts remained important sources of food energy for the Yayoi age.⁴⁸ Indeed, nuts continued to be key staples up through the first half of the twentieth century in the Japan Alps, in mountainous areas of Shikoku, and in other regions of Japan.

Acorns and chestnuts as well as foxtail millet (*awa*) and barnyard millet (*hie*), seen in figure A.6, that were once staples have disappeared from the current Japanese diet, but their absence has largely been ignored by scholars and government officials who fret over the disappearance of "traditional Japanese dietary cultures." One could argue that since people stopped eating nuts and millets after World War II, these foodstuffs no longer have a place in traditional food culture, especially if they reportedly do not taste good. Yet it is also essential to recognize the gaps in the recent definitions of Japanese cuisine that deny these once common foodstuffs a place. It is the role of scholars to acknowledge the full diversity of Japanese food culture today and historically and

FIGURE A.6 Barnyard millet (*hie*) (*left*) and foxtail millet (*awa*) (*right*). Photograph by the author.

then seek to document it in the widest sense and experience rather than limit attention to rarified versions of dietary culture such as national cuisine, which are modern constructs. In other words, we need to focus on the foods of Japan, not on Japanese food.

NOTES

1. Katsumata Senkichiro, *Notes on Japanese Cuisine* (Tokyo: Japan Travel Bureau, 1946), 2.
2. I describe the monastic diet at Longensi in Eric C. Rath, "Mealtime at a Tibetan Monastery," *Gastronomica* 10.2 (2010): 17–21.
3. Dorje Trangpo, leader of the training program for yogis at Longen, personal communication, 2010.
4. On the invention of General Tso's chicken, see Barak Kushner, *Slurp! A Social and Cultural History of Ramen—Japan's Favorite Noodle Soup* (Leiden: Koninklijke Brill NV, 2012), 20.
5. Rumi Sakamoto and Matthew Allen, "There's Something Fishy about That Sushi: How Japan Interprets the Global Sushi Boom," *Japan Forum* 23.1 (2011): 99–121.

6. Eric C. Rath, "How Intangible Is Japan's Traditional Dietary Culture?," *Gastronomica* 12.4 (2012): 2–3.

7. Masayuki (Alex) Otsuka, "Japan Food Service—Hotel Restaurant Institutional: Japan HRI Food Service Sector Report 2014," Gain Report JA 3526, USDA, 2013, 4. Accessed from gain.fas.usda.gov, September 17, 2014.

8. Kumakura Isao, "Nihon no dentōteki shoku bunka to shite no washoku no inkikata," in *Nihon no shoku no kinmirai*, ed. Kumakura Isao (Kyoto: Shibunkaku, 2013), 3–5. I develop this discussion and several of the themes in this chapter further in Eric C. Rath, *Japan's Cuisines: Food, Place and Identity* (London: Reaktion Books, 2016).

9. The results were based on a survey of 10,000 households, of which 8,478 responded. Statistics Bureau, "Yearly Average of Monthly Receipts and Disbursements per Household (Total Households), 2013." Accessed from www.stat.go.jp/english/data, September 17, 2014.

10. Ministry of Agriculture, Forestry and Fisheries, "Heisei nijūyonnenban shokuryō, nōgyō, nōson hakusho sankō tōkeihyō," 16. Accessed from www.maff.go.jp, September 18, 2014.

11. There were 2,732 respondents in the 2009 survey of men and women above the age of twenty and 1,658 respondents in the same age range in 2014. Of the 5.5 percent respondents in 2014 who reported never dining with their families, more than half of them (58.1 percent) reported wanting to be able to eat with them more often. Santōsha, *Shokuseikatsu dēta sōgō tōkei nenpyō 2014* (Tokyo: Santōsha, 2014), 193; Santōsha, *Shokuseikatsu dēta sōgō tōkei nenpyō 2016* (Tokyo: Santōsha, 2016), 330.

12. Santōsha, *Shokuseikatsu dēta sōgō tōkei nenpyō 2014*, 254–255.

13. "Nomination File No. 00869 for Inscription in 2013 on the Representative List of the Intangible Cultural Heritage of Humanity," PDF document, 4, 7. Accessed from www.unesco.org/, August 26, 2014.

14. "Washoku, Traditional Dietary Cultures of the Japanese, Notably for the Celebration of New Year," www.unesco.org, accessed August 26, 2014.

15. Anne Allison, *Precarious Japan* (Durham, NC: Duke University Press, 2013), 35.

16. Vaclav Smil and Kazuhiko Kobayashi, *Japan's Dietary Transition and Its Impacts*, (Cambridge, MA: MIT Press, 2012), 196.

17. In the *Asahi shinbun* newspaper the word *honpō ryōri* debuted in 1879, *Nihon ryōri* in 1880, *Nihon shoku* in 1884, and *washoku* in 1892. Kikuzō Database, database. asahi.com, accessed May 21, 2013. I am grateful to Michiko Ito for alerting me to this.

18. Tsuboi Hirofumi, *Imo to Nihonjin: Minzoku bunkaron no kadai* (Tokyo: Miraisha, 1979).

19. Okui Takashi, *Konbu to Nihonjin* (Tokyo: Nihon Keizai Shimbun Shuppansha, 2012); Toriimoto Yukiyo, *Shōjin ryōri to Nihonjin* (Tokyo: Shunjusha, 2006); Tsuchida Mitose, *Yakitori to Nihonjin: Yatai kara hoshitsuki made* (Tokyo: Kōbunsha, 2014).

20. Higuchi Kiyoyuki, *Shokumotsu to Nihonjin* (Tokyo: Kōdansha, 1979), 13. Higuchi first won wide acclaim for his books *Umeboshi and the Japanese* (*Umeboshi to Nihonjin*) published in 1974 and *Sequel to Umeboshi and the Japanese* (*Zoku, Umeboshi*

to Nihonjin), which appeared the following year. See Saitō Tokio. *Nihon shokubunka jinbutsu jiten: Jinbutsu de yomu Nihon shokubunkashi* (Tokyo: Tsukuba Shobō, 2005), 265.

21. Watanabe Minoru, *Nihon shokuseikatsushi* (Tokyo: Yoshikawa Kōbunkan, 1964); Nishiyama Matsunosuke, ed., *Tabemono Nihonshi sōkan* (Tokyo: Shinjinbutsu Ōraisha, 1994), 385.

22. Ehara Ayako, Ishikawa Naoko, and Higashiyotsuyanagi Shōko, *Nihon shokumotsushi* (Tokyo: Yoshikawa Kōbunkan, 2009).

23. Harada Nobuo, *Rekishi no naka no kome to niku: Shokumotsu to tennō, sabetsu* (Tokyo: Heibonsha, 1993), 282.

24. Jean-François Revel, "Retrieving Tastes: Two Sources of Cuisine," in *The Taste Culture Reader: Experiencing Food and Drink*, ed. Carolyn Korsmeyer (New York: Berg, 2005), 52.

25. Susan B. Hanley, *Everyday Things in Premodern Japan: The Hidden Legacy of Material Culture* (Berkeley: University of California Press, 1997), 88.

26. Arizono Shōichirō, *Kinsei shomin no nichijō shoku: Hyakushō wa kome o taberarenakatta ka?* (Ōtsu: Kaiseisha, 2007), 2.

27. Sasagawa Rinpū and Adachi Isamu, *Kinsei Nihon shokumotsushi* (Tokyo: Yūzankaku Shuppan, 1973); Morisue Yoshiaki and Kikuchi Yūjirō, *Kaikō shokumotsushi: Nihonjin no shokuseikatsu no hatten* (Tokyo: Daŕichi Shuppan, 1965).

28. Naomichi Ishige, *The History and Culture of Japanese Food* (London: Kegan Paul, 2001).

29. Ehara, Ishikawa, and Higashiyotsuyanagi, *Nihon shokumotsushi*.

30. Murai Yasuhiko, "Kaiseki ryōri no rekishi," in *Kaiseki to kashi*, ed. Tsutsui Hiroichi (Kyoto: Tankōsha, 1999), 17.

31. Kushner, *Slurp!*; George Solt, *The Untold History of Ramen: How Political Crises in Japan Spawned a Global Food Craze* (Berkeley: University of California Press, 2014).

32. Ishige Naomichi, *Men no bunkashi* (Tokyo: Kōdansha, 2006), 105–106.

33. Kondō Hideo, *Shikoku: Tabemono minzokugaku* (Matsuyama, Ehime: Atorasu Shuppan, 1999), 30.

34. Segawa Kiyoko, *Shokuseikatsu no rekishi* (Tokyo: Kōdansha, 2001), 45; Arizono, *Kinsei shomin no nichijō shoku*, 34.

35. Kimura Shigemitsu, *Nihon nōgyōshi* (Tokyo: Yoshikawa Kōbunkan, 2010), 166.

36. Penelope Francks, *The Japanese Consumer: An Alternative Economic History of Modern Japan* (New York: Cambridge University Press, 2009), 36.

37. Harada Nobuo, "Kinsei ni okeru funshoku," in *Zakkoku II: Funshoku bunkaron no kanōsei*, ed. Kimura Shigemitsu (Tokyo: Aoki Shoten, 2006), 106–107.

38. Harada Nobuo, *Edo no ryōrishi: Ryōribon to ryōri bunka* (Tokyo: Chūō Kōronsha, 1989), 11.

39. Akai Tatsurō, *Kashi no bunkashi* (Kyoto: Kawara Shoten, 2005), 214.

40. Yao Keisuke, "Jūhasseiki ni okeru Dejima Oranda shōkan no satō yunyū ni tsuite," *Shigaku zasshi* 105.3 (1996): 62; Gregory Smits, *Visions of Ryūkyū: Identity and Ideology in Early Modern Thought and Politics* (Honolulu: University of Hawai'i Press, 1999), 141.

41. Francks, *The Japanese Consumer*, 57.
42. Kumakura Isao, "Nihon ryōriyashi josetsu," in *Ryōriya no kosumorojī*, ed. Takada Masatoshi (Tokyo: Domesu Shuppan, 2004), 30.
43. Hirano Masa'aki, *Shōyu, tenpura monogatari*, vol. 11 of *Hirano Masa'aki cho, Nihon ryōri tankyū zensho* (Tokyo: Tōkyō Shobōsha, 1979), 205–206; Ishikawa Hiroko, ed., *Shokuseikatsu to bunka: Shoku no ayumi* (Tokyo: Kōgaku Shuppan, 1988), 17.
44. Ishige, *Men no bunkashi*, 158.
45. Nagayama Hisao, "Edo no shokubunka," in *Edo jidai "seikatsu bunka" sōkan*, ed. Nishiyama Matsunosuke (Tokyo: Shinjinbutsu Ōraisha, 1992), 38–39.
46. Arizono, *Kinsei shomin no nichijōshoku*, 1.
47. Smil and Kobayashi, *Japan's Dietary Transition*, 83.
48. Ehara, Ishikawa, and Higashiyotsuyanagi, *Nihon shokumotsushi*, 26.

Glossary

Ajinomoto: Japanese brand of monosodium glutamate (MSG) seasoning, associated with adding umami (see Chapter 6) to dishes. Also the name of the multinational company that makes the product and promotes the concept of umami worldwide.
āsa: type of Okinawan seaweed
atsukan: warmed sake
awa: foxtail millet
ayu: sweetfish, a relative of smelt, native to East Asia
bento: a prepared, packed meal typically consisting of rice, pickles, and entrées, typically served in a box
B-kyū gurume: "second-class gourmet" or "B-grade gourmet," a food movement that celebrates Japanese comfort foods like fried noodles (yakisoba) and *okonomiyaki* savory pancakes
chabudai: a short-legged table used by diners seated on the floor on tatami mats
chanko nabe: a one-pot Japanese stew (*nabe*) commonly eaten by sumo wrestlers in training; contains large quantities of protein such as chicken, fish and tofu, and vegetables such as daikon or bok choy, although there is no fixed recipe
chanpurū: Okinawan-style stir-fry
chisan chishō: "Grow local and eat local," slogan of local food campaigns
chōka: long poems consisting of multiple lines or phrases in 5-7 meter; often associated with the eighth-century Man'yōshū, the oldest existing collection of Japanese poetry
choko or ochoko: ceramic sake cups

chōnin: city-dwellers, usually associated with the merchant and artisan classes during the Edo period (1603–1868)

daiginjōshu: relatively small-batch slow- and cold-brew sake, for which at least 50 percent of the rice grain has been polished off

daikon: long white radish frequently used in Japanese cooking

dashi: the foundation soup stock for Japanese cuisine, usually made from KATSUOBUSHI, KOMBU, or both. Also known as *hondashi*, this stock is used as the basis for a wide variety of dishes.

donburi: "rice bowl dish" consisting of fish, meat, vegetables or other ingredients simmered together, often flavored with dashi, soy sauce, and mirin, and served over rice served in an oversized rice bowl. Popular varieties include *oyakodon* (literally "parent and child bowl," steamed chicken and egg), *katsudon* (pork or chicken cutlet and egg), and *gyūdon* (simmered beef and onion).

Edo: earlier name for the city of Tokyo, also used as an era name for the years 1600–1868.

Edokko: "children of Edo," Edo natives of the merchant and artisan classes who took pride in their identity and played a central role in the flourishing of Edo's urban culture

fugu: pufferfish, typically served as sashimi or sometimes in a NABE; can be lethally poisonous and must be carefully prepared to remove toxic parts. Chefs must undergo years of training to earn qualifications to serve fugu in restaurants. The liver, often considered the tastiest part, is also the most poisonous.

furusato: one's hometown or native place

futsūshu: alcohol-added plain sake that does not qualify for one of the four designated categories within the group of alcohol-added sake because of the large addition of alcohol and/or the low degree of polishing

gaichi: overseas territories, a term used for Japan's colonies and areas of influence during Japan's imperial era (1895–1959)

gaijin: foreigners, non-Japanese. The term usually indicates Euro-American Caucasian foreigners; it is sometimes used for foreigners from South Asia, the Middle East, or Africa, but not generally used for individuals from East Asia.

gaki: hungry ghosts in Buddhist reincarnation philosophy. While above being reborn in hell or as an animal, hungry ghosts were condemned by their previous sins, such as greed, to wander on earth, invisible, famished, and never satiated.

genshu: undiluted sake

ginjōshu: relatively small-batch slow- and cold-brew sake, for which in between 40 and 49 percent of the rice grain has been polished off

gochisō sama: phrase associated with dining etiquette meaning "Thank you for treating me," said after meals to host or chef

gōya: bitter melon, typically used in the Okinawan dish *gōya champuru*, a stir-fry of pork, eggs, tofu, and bitter melon

gyōza: pan-fried dumplings typically filled with pork, scallions, and ginger and served with a dipping sauce of soy sauce and vinegar

gyūdon: sweet, simmered beef and onions over rice, sometimes topped with a raw egg and typically served with pickled ginger and shichimi, a red-chili spice mixture of seven ingredients

haiku: a form of short poetry, traditionally consisting of seventeen syllables in three phrases of 5-7-5 and containing a seasonal reference. The essence of the haiku form is the juxtaposition of two images or ideas.

hara obi: belly-band made of cotton or stretchy materials to restrict the size of a fetus or, more generally, to keep the abdomen area warm

hie: barnyard millet

Higashi Nihon daishinsai: the Great Eastern Japan Earthquake that occurred on March 11, 2011, off the Pacific coast of Tōhoku with a magnitude 9.0–9.1

hin/hin'i: an aesthetic term that indicates restrained, simple elegance

hiragana: one of the two Japanese syllabaries that, together with Chinese characters (kanji), form the Japanese writing system. Hiragana contains forty-six characters with rounded shapes and is a phonetic lettering system, in contrast with logographic kanji. It is used to inflect verbs and adjectives, for particles and other grammatical function words, and to spell out native words for which there are no kanji or whose kanji are obscure. Also see KATAKANA.

hōshoku: gluttony, abundance, opulence; sometimes used to indicate the disintegration of traditional food culture

ichijū sansai: "One soup, three side dishes." With white rice, this is the formula for "standard" Japanese-style meals.

iki: Edo chic, an aesthetic originally associated with geisha and their patrons.

itadakimasu: phrase associated with dining etiquette meaning "I will receive" said before meals to indicate gratitude

itamae: sushi chef

itamemono: stir-fried foods

izakaya: informal Japanese pub offering many types of food along with beer, sake, cocktails, and other drinks. Food is normally ordered slowly over several courses rather than all at once and shared by the entire table.

jagaimo: potato

jizake: sake made with local ingredients

junmaishu: pure rice wine; sake made without the addition of alcohol, sugar, or taste-, aroma- or color-enhancing elements (although, in sharp contrast to the case of natural wine, added yeast is not treated as an impure element)

kabayaki: eel grilled over charcoal

kāchan: fond name for mother, more formally *Okāsan*

kaiseki: a formal multicourse dinner that usually employs fresh, seasonal ingredients and strives to balance the taste, texture, appearance, and colors of food. Dishes are arranged, garnished, and presented on plates in a manner designed to enhance both the food's appearance and the meal's seasonal theme. Courses generally include an appetizer (*sakizuke*), sashimi (*mukōzuke*), a simmered dish (*takiawase*), a grilled dish (*yakimono*), and a hearty course, such as a hotpot (*shiizakana*), along with soups, palate cleansers, pickles, and desserts at the chef's discretion.

kaiten-zushi: "rotation" sushi, where the plates with sushi are served via a rotating conveyor belt that moves past every table or counter seat, from which diners choose their selections. The final bill is calculated based on the number and type of plates each diner accumulates. Some restaurants use miniature boats traveling on water or miniature train cars to deliver sushi.

kakiage: a type of tempura made with mixed vegetable strips, such as onion, carrot, and burdock, and sometimes shrimp or squid, deep fried into small round fritters; often served as a topping for udon

kakke: beriberi

kamado: traditionally, a Japanese wood- or charcoal-fueled cook stove, although in contemporary use usually indicates any stove or cooking range.

katakana: one of the two Japanese syllabaries that, together with Chinese characters (kanji), form the Japanese writing system. Katakana contains forty-eight short, angular characters and is a phonetic lettering systems, in contrast with logographic kanji. It is used for transcription of foreign language words into Japanese, for emphasis, for onomatopoeia, and for technical and scientific terms. Also see HIRAGANA.

katsuo: type of fish, ideally skipjack tuna, but sometimes substituted with less-expensive bonito

katsuobushi: dried, fermented, and smoked skipjack tuna or bonito, used in paper-thin shavings. It is a staple of Japanese cuisine that provides an umami quality to food and is a main ingredient, along with kelp (kombu) in making dashi stock.

kimoto: Edo-period slow-brew method of making the yeast-starter for sake, where no lacto-acid is added to the starter. It differs from YAMAHAI in the sense that the painstaking labor of crushing the steamed rice with wooden poles is conducted.

kōji: a mold that is sprinkled on steamed rice during sake production and turns the starch in the nucleus of the rice grain into glucose

kokumin shoku: "Food of the people/citizens," a term used to indicate nationally approved meals used especially during wartimes

kokushu: national alcoholic drink; recent term that is central to the mainly government-led campaign to promote the idea that sake is Japan's national alcoholic drink

kombu: kelp (*Saccharina japonica*) or certain other dried seaweeds of the Laminariaceae family; staple of Japanese cuisine that is a main ingredient, along with katsuobushi in making dashi stock

konbini: convenience stores in Japan, such as 7-11 and Lawson's

korokke: deep-fried croquettes that can be filled with a variety of ingredients. The most common version uses mashed potato and ground beef. Other popular versions include crab in cream sauce, pumpkin, and curry.

koshoku: eating alone, an increasing trend

kyōdo ryōri: regional cuisine, with connotation of ancient historicity

kyoshō: master, virtuoso, artist

kyūshoku: school lunch programs at public elementary and secondary schools that educate students about nutrition, etiquette, and national food history while requiring hands-on participation in serving food and cleanup

MAFF: acronym for Japan's Ministry of Agriculture, Forestry, and Fisheries

māmina irichā: Okinawan-style stir-fry with bean sprouts

manjū: a category of traditional Japanese confection, typically with an exterior made from flour, rice powder, and buckwheat and a filling of sweet bean paste, made from boiled azuki beans and sugar. Many areas of Japan have their own regional *manjū* specialties.

mazui: adjective meaning bad tasting

meibutsu: famous product of a city or region, for example, tea from Uji, apples from Aomori, and udon from the Sanuki region

mirin: a type of rice wine with very high sugar content that is a staple in Japanese cooking

miso: fermented soybean paste, a staple ingredient in Japanese cooking used for sauces and spreads, pickling vegetables or meats, and mixing with dashi stock to serve as miso soup. Typically it occurs in red or white varieties. It can also be made with barley, rice, or other ingredients in place of soybeans

mōi dōfu: Okinawan-style tofu

momo: Tibetan dumpling

mono no aware: "the pathos of things," term coined by Motoori Norinaga to describe the emotional tenor of classical literature, especially *The Tale of Genji*.

mottainai: often-used term meaning wasteful, implying it is a shame to waste something such as food

munōyaku: without chemical fertilizers

muroka: unfiltered sake made via filtration with carbon, rather than straining or pressing

nabe/nabemono: one-pot stew dishes often cooked at the table on portable stoves, typically served in winter. Diners choose the ingredients they want from the pot, and further ingredients can be added. They are either eaten with the broth from the pot or with a dip. Characteristic dishes include ODEN, SHABU-SHABU, SUKIYAKI, YOSENABE, and YŪDOFU.

naichi: homelands, a term used for Japan's four main islands, as opposed to its colonies (GAICHI) during Japan's imperial era (1895–1959)

namazake: unpasteurized sake

nichijō: home front; everyday life

nigiri: hand-molded rice, also used to indicate nonroll sushi consisting of hand-molded rice topped by raw fish or other ingredients. Also see ONIGIRI.

Nihonjin no mikaku: Japanese sense of taste

Nihonjinron: the theory of Japaneseness

Nihonshoku: Japanese food

nihonshu: rice wine; written with the same Chinese character as sake, but preceded by characters for "Japan" to make a distinction with Western alcoholic drinks from the late nineteenth century onward

nikushoku joshi: "carnivorous women," a term coined to indicate the trend of aggressive young women who remain single. See the male complement, SŌSHOKU DANSHI.

nimono: dish consisting of a vegetable, seafood, or tofu simmered in a dashi stock typically flavored with soy sauce, sake, and sugar until the liquid is absorbed by the main ingredient(s). Characteristic types of *nimono* include *nikujaga*, a beef and potato stew, and *kakuni*, stewed pork belly.

ningen kokuho: living national treasure

nuchi gusui: Okinawan term meaning source of life

oden: type of NABE using several ingredients such as boiled eggs, daikon, *konjac* (jellied devil's tongue), and processed fishcakes stewed in a light dashi broth. Hot Japanese mustard (*karashi*) is often used as a condiment.

Oishinbo: a long-running gourmet food manga (comic) written by Tetsu Kariya and drawn by Akira Hanasaki. The title combines the Japanese word for delicious, *oishii*, and the word for someone who loves to eat, *kuishinbo*.

okaasan: mother

okonomiyaki: meaning "grilled as you like," a pancake-like dish that can contain a variety of ingredients including vegetables, seafood, meats, cheese, and rice cake (mocha). It is typically topped with a savory sauce, mayonnaise, and finely ground seaweed.

omakase: a meal consisting of dishes selected by the chef

omotenashi: the traditional spirit of Japanese hospitality, entertaining guests whole-heartedly

omuraisu: a Japanized Western dish of ketchup-flavored fried rice wrapped in an omelet; often topped with a demi-glace sauce.

onigiri: hand-molded rice ball, a quintessential Japanese convenience and comfort food. It can contain a variety of ingredients in the center, such as UMEBOSHI (pickled plum) or salted salmon, or consist of rice mixed with seasonings, such as sesame salt (*gomashio*), then molded. Often covered with seaweed (nori).

onigiri pōku tamago: rice ball with eggs and luncheon meat such as Spam popular in Okinawa and often abbreviated as *onipō*

Osechi ryōri: traditional New Year's meal, typically served in a multilayered lacquered box (*jūbako*) shared by the whole family and containing dishes considered symbolic of happiness and wealth for the coming year, such as sweet rolled omelet (*datemaki*), fishcake (*kamaboko*), sweet black soybeans (*kuromame*), and candied chestnuts with sweet potatoes (*kuri kinton*)

ōte meekaa: big producers. In terms of the sake industry these are producers who have turned their breweries into factories, where sake is made throughout the year under computer and temperature control. Almost all are located in the premodern and early-modern brewing centers of Nada and Fushimi.

pakku sake: cheap industrial sake, made in big factories, and sold in paper 1.8-liter and 3-liter cartons.

ponzu: tart, watery citrus-based sauce used frequently in Japanese cuisine; often combined with soy sauce, the mixed product is also referred to as ponzu.

rakugo: traditional comic form of storytelling performed in small venues called *yose*

ryōribon: culinary books

ryōtei: luxurious, traditional Japanese restaurant, usually serving kaiseki cuisine

sake: rice wine

sashimi: dish of very fresh raw fish or meat sliced into thin pieces

seishu: clear sake. One of the legal definitions of sake is that it has been strained. However, passing sake through a cloth with relatively big holes is nowadays also defined as straining, so clear sake includes white cloudy sake.

senbei: rice crackers that come in various shapes, sizes, and flavors, usually savory but occasionally sweet
sensai-sa: sensitivity, subtlety
setsuwa: a loose genre of premodern Japanese literature specifying didactic, anecdotal literature
shabu-shabu: a NABE dish consisting of thinly sliced meat and vegetables dipped in water boiling in a pot at the dining table and eaten with a sesame or ponzu dipping sauce
sha palep: Tibetan bread with meat stuffing
shindō funi: "body and earth are one"; East Asian aphorism encouraging people to eat foods from their local areas
shizenshu: natural sake, made with rice for the cultivation of which no chemical fertilizers were used
Shōjin ryōri: Buddhist vegetarian cuisine, typically consisting of seasonal vegetables, foraged wild plants, and tofu
shokuchūshu: food sake; versus the Western concept of pairing, where drink contributes to the food appreciation, "food sake" tends to be neutral and does not contribute to the taste and aroma of foods
shokuiku: food education, especially associated with elementary and secondary school curricula, which highlights food, body, nutrition, and communal consumption and connections among agriculture/fisheries, environment, and society.
shokunin: professional cook or chef
shokuyō: healthy food movement, dietetics; often championed by Shokuyōkai, or Healthy Food Associations
shōyu: soy sauce
shuppinshu: extremely small-batch sake made especially for the annual sake competition in Hiroshima
soba: buckwheat or thin noodles made from buckwheat flour, served either chilled with a dipping sauce, or in hot broth as a noodle soup.
sobaya: restaurant specializing in buckwheat noodles
sōshoku danshi: "herbivore men," a term coined to indicate the trend of passive young men who remain unmarried. See the female complement, NIKUSHOKU JOSHI.
sukiyaki: a type of NABE dish consisting of thinly sliced beef, tofu, vegetables, and starch noodles stewed in sweetened soy-based sauce and often eaten with a raw egg dip
tai: sea bream, a large flat-bodied fish considered the best tasting of the white meat fish. Although the species varies in color according to environment, red sea bream are most typical in Japanese cuisine and considered a symbol of good fortune
takuan: type of pickle made with daikon radishes, typically yellow in color and pickled using rice bran
tanka: form of classical Japanese poetry considered one of the major genres of Japanese literature; characterized by five lines with the syllable patter 5-7-5-7-7
tempura: vegetables, seafood, and occasionally meats dipped in batter and deep-fried. Tempura is usually served with a dipping sauce based on soy sauce.

teppanyaki: Japanese style of food preparation, with meat, seafood, and/or vegetables grilled or fried on a hot steel plate at the table

tezukuri: handmade

tōji: head sake brewer, in charge of the team brewing the sake; in former times usually a seasonal laborer from another region, nowadays still distinct from the brewery owner, in many cases

tokuri: ceramic sake carafes, usually holding 180 or 360 ml of sake

tonkatsu: pork cutlet breaded with panko (Japanese breadcrumbs), deep fried, and usually served with shredded cabbage and a savory sauce

tonkotsu: style of ramen that originated in the Fukuoka region of Kyushu characterized by its thick, cloudy white broth, made from boiling pork bones on high heat for up to twenty hours

toriagerubaba: traditional midwives

Toshikoshi soba: noodles eaten on the evening of December 31 for good luck in the new year.

tsū: term meaning connoisseur in current use; first used in the Edo period to indicate a "man about town" known for his savoir-faire

Tsukiji: biggest wholesale fish and seafood market in the world and also one of the largest wholesale food markets of any kind, located in central Tokyo, but relocation has long been planned and is anticipated in 2018

tsukudani: an intensely flavored side dish made of small pieces of seafood, meat, or seaweed simmered in soy sauce and mirin, typically eaten with white rice

ubushī: Okinawan-style stew

uchinanchū: term for Okinawans

udon: thick wheat noodles usually served hot in a mild broth of dashi and soy sauce; can be topped with a variety of ingredients including chopped scallions, sliced fish cake, tempura crumbs, or seasoned, deep-fried tofu (*aburaage*)

unagi: freshwater eel, typically served grilled over charcoal with a sweet, savory sauce (*tare*). Saltwater eel is known as *anago*.

umai: masculine variant adjective of *oishii*, meaning good tasting or tasty

umeboshi: pickled plum or apricot, typically flavored with *shiso* (perilla or beefsteak leaves)

wabi/wabi-sabi: an aesthetic term that indicates rough, natural, and asymmetrical characteristics, often associated with the tea ceremony and with the term *sabi*, which connotes solitude and austerity

wafū pasuta: Japanese-style pasta with ingredients like cod roe, soy sauce, and seaweed

waka: poems composed in Japanese, in contrast with poetry composed in classical Chinese by Japanese poets, known as *kanshi*.

wasabi: Japanese horseradish, a condiment served with sushi and sashimi, among other dishes

washoku: Japanese dietary culture or cuisine

yaki imo: roasted sweet potatoes, traditionally sold by street vendors

yakisoba: fried noodle dish, typically containing small pieces of meat and vegetables and seasoned with a savory sauce

yakitori: charcoal-grilled chicken parts served on skewers and seasoned with a sweet soy-based sauce or salt. Includes many varieties such as *momo* (thigh), *nankotsu* (cartilage), *tebasaki* (wing), and *negima* (chicken and green onion).
yamahai: Meiji-period slow-brew method of making the yeast-starter for sake, where no lacto-acid is added to the starter. Omits painstaking labor of crushing the steamed rice with wooden poles (see KIMOTO).
yamatonchū: term used by Okinawans to refer to Japanese mainlanders
yatai: a street stall for food
yinyō chōwa: "harmony of yin and yang elements"; in food parlance, eating a balanced diet of foods identified with yin or yang
yōkan: thick, jellied dessert typically made of red bean paste, agar, and sugar and served in slices. It can also be made with white bean paste, chestnuts, persimmons, figs, sweet potatoes, and other ingredients.
yosenabe: a type of NABE dish consisting of meat, seafood, egg, tofu, and vegetables, in a miso- or soy sauce-flavored broth.
yōshoku: term invented in the Meiji period to describe "Western foods" as a category
yuba: tofu skin; the thin layer that forms on the surface of soy milk when boiled, collected, and dried into yellowish-colored sheets. Considered a delicacy in Japanese cuisine.
yūgen: an aesthetic term that indicates a beauty that is mysterious, profound, and beyond words

Index

acorns, 323
Acurio, Gastón, 189, 193
Adachi, Isamu, 321
Adams, William, 39
Adrià, Ferran, 133, 154
aesthetics: "aesthetic disposition" and, 56–57; associated with Edo, 67, 70–71, 75; consumerism and, 293; of court cuisine, 49–50; craft aesthetic, 38–39; cultural heritage and, 113; Japanese, 35–36, 46, 75, 128–129, 144; of Kyoto, 163; simplicity of, 46, 133; visual appeal of washoku and, 147
Agency for Cultural Affairs (Bunkachō), 105, 318
agriculture: consumerism and, 292–293; cultural heritage and, 100; double-cropping, 322; Eastern philosophies and, 61; at Expo 2015, 111; food waste and, 295–296; in Kyoto, 155, 157–161, 165; in Peru, 193; place brands and, 155–156; subsidization of, 108; UNESCO designation and, 107–108. *See also* bamboo; fruit; tea; vegetables
Aikawa-Faure, Noriko, 104

Ajinomoto (MSG seasoning), 120, 177, 190. *See also* umami
alcoholic beverages. *See* beer; sake
Alexander, Jeffrey, 19
Allison, Anne, 19
amaranth (*kiwicha*), 194–195
Anderson, Lara, 135
Anholt, Simon, 5
Anime News Network, 110
anorexia, 274–275, 278, 282–283, 285n13
"antenna" stores, 10
Aoki Tamotsu, 112–113
Aoyama, Tomoko, 19
APJ (Japanese-Peruvian Association), 187, 191, 194–195
Appadurai, Arjun, 100, 135
Arizono Shōichirō, 320
Arte de Cozhina (Rodrigues), 38
artisanship, 74, 159–165
Asada Akira, 303
Asahi (newspaper), 122
Ashkenazi, Michael, 19
Assman, Stephanie, 19
Austin (TX), 4
authenticity, 12–13, 100–101, 109–114, 164, 169, 196

ayu (sweetfish), 140
Ayumi Suzuki, 276
Azuchi-Momoyama period, xvii, 321

B-kyū gurume (second class gourmet foods), 5–9, 164–165
bamboo, 157, 159–160, 165
Baumann, Shyon, 10, 16
beef: Kobe beef, 8; in Peru, 192; sukiyaki, 8; wagyū (Japanese beef), 102
beer, 10, 137, 145, 169
Belasco, Warren, 50
bento boxes, 124, 140, 169, 291–292, 298
Bestor, Theodore, 19
Better Home Association, 290
Bird, Isabella, 7
Bocuse, Paul, 2, 36
bodies: in Hayashi's writing, 245–246, 253, 254; in *Spirited Away*, 274
bonito, 50, 70, 120, 128, 162–164, 228–229
Bordo, Susan, 26
Bourdain, Anthony, 1
Bourdieu, Pierre, 20–21, 56
brands/branding: brand consciousness, 112–114; Japan as, 62; of Japanese cuisine, 35, 100; Kyoto as, 74, 153–156; Nikkei cuisine as, 189; sake and, 82–86, 91; soba and, 74; umami and, 119, 126, 130. See also place brands
breastfeeding, 214, 218n38
A Brushful of Ink (Shiki), 223
Buddhism: and attitudes toward food during Heian period, 51–53, 58; food waste and, 297–298, 301n39; Kyoto and, 154; and morality tales (setsuwa) about food, 53–55; theme of humans being eaten and, 279
bulimia, 274–275, 278, 282–283, 285n13

California Roll, 1, 10
Cang, Voltaire, 106
cannibalism, 278–279, 281–282
capitalism, 265, 265–267, 274, 276–277, 279, 281–282

Careme, Marie-Antoine, 133
Carletti, Francesco, 40
Caron, François, 41
The Castle of Cagliostro (Miyazaki), 273
ceramic tableware: Bizen, 141; Oribe, 141; Raku, 38; Shigaraki, 141; Shino, 137; *wabi* (aesthetic), 141
Chang, David, 1–2
chanko nabe (sumo wrestler stew), 145
Chapel, Alain, 36
Chernobyl nuclear disaster, 307–308, 309
chestnuts, 234, 323
Cheung, Sidney, 8
China: cuisine of, 8, 314; Hayashi and, 247–249; immigration to Peru and, 188; influence of on Japanese cuisine, 51, 60, 102–103, 140; medicine and, 208–209, 214; Shiki and, 222, 236
chōnin (urban townspeople during Edo period), 208
chopsticks, 38, 50, 54–55, 57, 72, 75, 208
Clavell, James, 39
cleanliness, 36, 38, 41, 75. See also hygiene
clothing, 159
Cockaigne, fantasy land of, 275–277
Cold War, 7, 146, 173, 176–178, 180
Cole, Tyson, 4
colonialism: food and in Hayashi's writing, 243, 246; in French Indochina, 251; Japanese, 25, 180–181, 243, 246, 251; Okinawa and, 180–181; in Taiwan, 90
confectionery, 322. See also sweets
Conklin, Dave, 76
connoisseurship, 15, 73–75, 138
consumerism, critique of, 26; food anxiety and, 305; food waste and, 289–293, 298–299; Kaikō Takeshi and, 262–269; *Spirited Away* as, 277, 279, 284
consumption: desire and, 262, 265; "Discover Japan" ad campaign, 267; *A New Star* and, 268–270; *Spirited Away* and, 281
convenience foods, 26. See also fast food

INDEX   341

convenience stores, 290
cookbooks, 171, 178–181, 193
Cooking Papa, 16
Cool Japan, 5, 85, 107, 112, 154
corn, 321
court culture, 49–50, 53, 155
craftsmanship, 159–165
croquettes, 102, 134
culinary capital, 56, 67, 73–74, 76–77, 156, 164, 221, 242
culinary nationalism: etiquette and, 57, 72, 108, 208; food-based media and, 18; in Heian period, 49–53, 61; promotion of Japanese cuisine and, 22, 114; Rosanjin and, 135–137, 143–146; umami and, 125–127, 130–131
curry, 10, 134, 190, 323
Cushman, Tim, 4
customers, 168
Cwiertka, Katarzyna, 19, 102, 134, 244

daikon, 142
Darkness in Summer (Kaikō Takeshi), 261
dashi, 50, 119, 121–124, 128, 162, 164, 167, 190. *See also* hondashi
Deshima, 41
desire, 262, 265–266
deterritorialization, 4
diet: contemporary Japanese, 108; early European impressions of Japanese, 40; in Heian culture, 49; influence of Buddhism on, 52–54; luncheon meat and, 176; macrobiotic, 144; in Meiji period, 102; Peruvian, 192; in pregnancy, 207–216; sake and, 87; soba as diet food, 76; standard global, 164; Westernization of Japanese, 127, 130, 208, 213, *See also* Japanese cuisine
"Discover Japan" ad campaign, 266–267
domestic education: food waste and, 297; shokuiku (food education), 108–109; US in Okinawa, 176
domesticity, 172, 177, 180, 262
double-cropping, 322
Dreaming of Cockaigne (Pleij), 276

Ducasse, Alain, 2
Dutch, 41, 322
Dutch East India Company, 41

earthquakes: Great Kantō earthquake of 1923, 139; and tsunami of 3/11, 3, 18, 27, 61, 107, 168, 302, 315
eating disorders, 274–275, 278, 282–284, 285n13
Edo (period), xvii, 21, 228–229, 321–322, *See also* Tokugawa period
Edo Sobalier Society, 73–75
Edokko, 66, 68–76; hari, 70; iki, 70–71, 75–76
eel, grilled (*kabayaki*), 68, 323
empire. *See* imperialism; Japanese empire
environment, food waste and, 293–294
escapism, 303
Escoffier, Georges Auguste, 133
etiquette, dining, 57, 208
excrement, 280–281
exoticism, culinary, 12–13
Expo 70, Osaka, 137
Expo 2015, Milan, 111, 135

family nation-state (*kazoku kokka*), 244
Farrer, James, 4, 20
Fashion, Food, Yes! (Hatanaka Mioko), 305
fast food, 66–68, 70, 76, 130, 262, 276, 290
Ferguson, Priscilla Parkhurst, 135
fermentation, 44, 92n1
festivals, 43–44; Edo, 67; Gion, 105, 154, 157, 162; Nikkei Festival, 195
fish: *ayu* (sweetfish), 140; bonito, 228–229; food safety and, 306–307; *hamo* (conger pike eel), 162; Kyoto cuisine and, 162; mackerel (*saba*), 162; Nikkei cuisine and, 190–191; as part of traditional Japanese diet, 39–40
Fisher, M. F. K., 135
fisheries: of Kyoto, 155; subsidization of, 108; UNESCO designation and, 107–108

food anxiety, 302–303, 309–310
food fads, 290–291, 305–306
food packaging, 12, 293–294, 297
food safety, 167–168, 302–310
food self-sufficiency, 26, 294–295, 304, 318
food technologies, 9, 322
food trucks, 10
food waste: consumerism and, 289–293, 298–299; environmental harm and, 26, 293–294, 297; financial costs of, 296; food insecurity and, 26, 294–295; food use as moral virtue and, 297–298; High Moon's cartoons and, 287–288; No Waste Movement, 294; quantitative data on, 288–289
foodies: North American vs. Japanese, 10–16; *Spirited Away* and, 277
Freeman, Paul, 134
French cuisine: effect of Japanese cuisine on, 36; Japanese cuisine vs., 16; Rosanjin's critique of, 22, 145–146; as symbol of imperialism, 251; UNESCO intangible cultural heritage and, 2, 105
fruit, 213, 218nn33-34, 222, 225–226, 231–233
Fujimori, Alberto, 192
Fujiwara no Asahira, 54
Fujiwara no Koremasa, 54–55
Fujiwara no Tadazane, 57
Fukego (Stories of Lord Fuke), 57
Fukuda Ikuhiro, 244
Fukuoka Masanobu, 61
Fukushima nuclear disaster and 3/11 earthquake, 3, 18, 27, 61, 107, 167–168, 302–303, 308, 315
fusion, 85, 100, 187–189. *See also* Nikkei cuisine
Futari wa ninpu (Kubota Miki), 207

gastrodiplomacy, 99–102, 113, 187
gastronomic booms: in 1980s in Japan, 9–10, 130, 146, 193, 290; Peruvian, 193
Gauntner, John, 86–87
gender, 53, 169, 172–174, 176, 221, 246, 249, 309

Get Jiro, 1
Giannoulis, Elena, 70
giri (social obligation), 24
Giron, Avila, 41
globalization, 8–10, 99–100, 127
Gluck, Carol, 67
Go-shussan!, 207
Gopnik, Adam, 2
"Gourmet Club" ("Bishoku Kurabu," Tanizaki), 139, 265
grains, 320; barley, 7, 43, 46; buckwheat, 67–68; *kiwicha* (amaranth), 194–195; millet, 43, 323–324; quinoa, 194–195. *See also* rice
gyōza dumplings, 15
gyūdon, 134

habitus, 20
Haga Noboru, 19
haiku, 25, 220, 225–229, 232, 236–237
hamo (conger pike eel), 162
Hanley, Susan, 320
Harada, Nobuo, 320
Harajuku, 17–18
Haruo Shirane, 228
Hatanaka Mioko, 305
Hayashi Fumiko, 25, 243–245, 254; *Hokugan butai*, 247–249; *Hōrōki*, 243–247, 254; *Ukigumo*, 249–254
Heian (period), xvii, 21, 48–53, 58–61, 228
Heldke, Lisa, 61
Hello Kitty, 5–6
heritage: cultural, 101, 104–105; Japan's promotion of, 104–105; as part of Kyoto's brand, 23, 156–159; production of, 67; UNESCO intangible cultural, 73, 99–100, 104–105, 118, 134, 154–155, 316
High Moon (Takatsuki Hiroshi), 26, 287–290, 291–292
Higuchi Kiyoyuki, 48, 319
hin'i, 163–164
Hinostroza, Rodolfo, 189
Hokama Yuki, 176
Hokkaido, 243, 247
Holden, T. M. J., 16

Holland, 41
home cooking, Japanese (katei ryōri), 27, 317
hondashi, 190
hooks, bell, 12, 14
Hōrōki (Hayashi), 243–247, 254
Hoshigaoka saryō (restaurant), 139–142, *See also* Kitaōji Rosanjin (Kitaōji Fusajirō)
hospitality, 35, 39, 41. *See also* omotenashi
Hototogisu (journal), 231
hunger, 243, 247
hygiene, 144–145, 209
Hyōgo (prefecture), 66

I Am a Cat (*Wagahai wa neko de aru*, Natsume Sōseki), 72
ichijū sansai (one soup, three dishes), 7
identity: colonialism and, 173; cultural, 113–114; fusion cuisine and, 191–192, 197–198; Japanese gastronomic, 21, 66, 72, 74–76; Japanese national, 221, 242, 248; soba and, 70–72, 75–76; in *Spirited Away*, 284; umami and, 127–131
Ikebukuro Gyoza Stadium, 17
Ikeda Kikunae, 119, 129
Iki no kōzō (The Structure of Iki, Kuki), 71
immigration, 8, 10, 188–189, 192
imperialism; domestic science training and, 176; Japanese, 177–178, 251, 255; luncheon meat and, 172–173, 176–178; US occupation and, 252; Western, 251. *See also* Japanese empire
indigenization, of luncheon meat in Okinawa, 175–182
Indochina, 251, 253–254
Into a Black Sun (Kaikō Takeshi), 261
The Invention of Edo (Gluck), 67
Ioki Hyōtei, 223
Ippudo ramen chain, 4
Iron Chef TV series (*Ryōri no tetsujin*), 16, 35, 147, 305
Isamu Noguchi, 141
Ishida Hikari, 215
Ishige Naomichi, 19, 321
Ishimure Michiko, 306
Ishizuka Sagen, 307
itamae, 190
Itami Jūzō, 16, 72, 147
Ivry, Tsipy, 211
Iwasaki Shin'ya, 68
Iwate, 65
izakaya (pub), 9, 16
Izumo (region), 65

Japan Sake and Shochu Makers Association, 83
Japan Sake Brewers Association, 86
Japan Travel Bureau (JTB), 86, 212
Japanese cuisine: authenticity and, 100–101, 109–110, 169, 196; as blend of cuisines, 134, 322; concept of umami and, 118–119, 123–125; Cool Japan campaign and, 5, 85, 107, 112, 154; craftsmanship and, 161–164; as foil to Western cuisine, 35–39, 46, 102, 126–130, 134, 143–145, 191; ideal vs. actual practices, 27, 134–135; kaiseki cuisine, 158, 163–164; *kaiseki ryōri* and, 99; of Kyoto, 157–158, 161–164, 167–168; Meiji period and, 102; in *Oishinbo*, 60–61; in Peru, 196–197; popularization of, 192; presentation and plating of, 45, 99, 108, 133, 138, 141–142, 147; promotion of, 99–100, 108, 119, 123–125, 164–165, 188, 196; Rosanjin's effect on, 135, 142; sake as part of, 83; seasonality in, 48, 50, 99, 133; soba and, 73–74; soft power and, 106–107; Western influence on, 100–101, 127, 129, *See also* aesthetics; French cuisine; fusion; Nikkei cuisine; umami; UNESCO; washoku
Japanese diet, traditional, 130; pregnancy and, 209–210, 213; in *Spirited Away*, 280; umami and, 129–130; "westernization" of, 9, 130, 323
Japanese empire: collapse of, 242, 250; food and identity of, 242–243, 246; *Hōrōki* as critique of, 244–247. *See also* colonialism
Japanese External Trade Organization (JETRO), 124

344 INDEX

Japanese National Tourism Organization (JNTO), 6, 105, 112
Japanese-Peruvian Association (APJ), 187, 191, 194–195
Japanese Society for Culinary Innovation, 163
Japonisme, 36
Jesuits, 38
Jiro Dreams of Sushi (film), 15, 133
Johnston, Josée, 10, 16

kabuki, 67, 71–72, 105
Kaempfer, Engelbert, 42–43
Kaikan (magazine), 187, 195–196
Kaikō Takeshi, 26, 61, 243, 261–262, 266–268
kaiseki cuisine (*kaiseki ryōri*), 48, 99, 106, 112, 134–135, 139–142, 158, 163–164, See also Japanese cuisine; Kyoto; washoku
kaiseki ryōri, 99, 106, 112. See also Kyoto
kaiten zushi, 9
kamado (stove), 322
Kamakura (city), 139
Kamakura (period), xvii, 59
Kamigata, 70
Kanadehon Chūshingura, 72
Kansai (region), 9, 66, 82, 140, 322
Kantō (region), 9, 322
Karafuto, 243
Kasai Toshiya, 70
kashi, 232
Kawahigashi Hekigotō, 231
Kawaii Monster café, 17
kazoku kokka (family nation-state), 244
Keene, Donald, 233, 237
kelp (*konbu*), 50, 119–120, 126, 162
Kikuchi Yūjirō, 321
Kitaōji Rosanjin (Kitaōji Fusajirō): American appreciation of, 146–147; as artist, 137–138; ceramics and, 137, 140–141; craftsmanship and, 163; culinary nationalism of, 135, 137, 143–146; early life of, 137–138; effect on Japanese cuisine, 135, 142; plating and presentation, 140–141; as restauranteur, 138–142; washoku and, 146

Kitcho Arashiyama (restaurant), 124
kiwicha (amaranth), 194–195
Kiyomi Mikuni, 125
Kobayashi Kazuhiko, 323
Kojiki, 280
Kokin wakashū, 58
Kokon chomonjū (Notable tales of old and new), 59–60
kokutai (national essence), 242
konbini (convenience store), 9
Korea, Republic of, 106, 138
korokke, 134
Kubota Miki, 207
Kuki Shūzō, 71, 75
Kumakura Isao, 19, 119, 316
Kunio Tokuoka, 124
Kurosawa, Tsutomu, 229
Kushner, Barak, 19, 321
Kyoto: as brand, 48, 153–156; craftsmanship as component of brand, 74, 159–165; cuisine (*Kyō ryōri*), 99, 158, 164–165; cultural expression in Kyoto cuisine, 162–163; customers in, 168; as Heian imperial city, 48–49, 153, 155; history/heritage as component of brand, 156–159; Kyoto City, 153; Kyoto prefecture, 153–154; local condition affecting taste of cuisine, 165–168; multiplicity of meanings of, 153; promotion/education in cuisine of, 23, 164–165; soba and, 66, 70; trademarks and, 155
Kyoto International Manga Museum, 288
kyūshoku (school lunches), 108
Kyushu (island), 37

lacquer, 50
Leach, Bernard, 36
Lebesco, Kathleen, 5
literature, 50–53, 55, 58, 60, 221, 243
local food, 307–308
local specialty, 65, 264, 266–267
Lucky Peach, 2
luncheon meat: association with Okinawan culture and, 181–182; introduction of in Okinawa, 174;

Okinawa's indigenization of, 175–182; as part of militarized culture, 172–173; prevalence of in Okinawa, 171–172; US imperial tradition and, 176–177; US military and, 182

mackerel (*saba*), 162
macrobiotics, 144
magazines, pregnancy and, 214–216
maki, 190–191
Mamma Tomosawa Ninpu-chan hen (Tomozawa), 215
Manchuria, 138
manga: *Oishinbo*, 16, 60–61, 138, 147, 305; pregnancy and, 207, 212; soba and, 76; soft power and, 5
manners, 35–39, 46, 77, *See also* etiquette
March 2011, 107, 155, 167, 302–310
Marui seikatsu (Ishida Hikari), 215
Masaoka Shiki, 25, 58, 220–237; appetite of, 25, 222–223; critical writings of, 238n15; on food as treatment, 223–224; food/eating terms and, 235–236; fruit and, 222, 225–226, 231–233; gifts of food and, 224, 232; on inability to chew, 25, 229–230; katakana and, 239n26; Nagatsuka Takashi and, 233–235; as poet, 25, 58, 220–221; poetic form and, 240n56; relationships with men, 221–222, 233–235; sexuality and, 237; women and, 221–222
materialism, 277, 279, 289, *See also* capitalism; consumerism, critique of
Matsuhisa Nobuyuki (Nobu), 4, 189
Matsuoka Toshikatsu, 109
McCracken, Grant, 154
McDonald's, 14, 129–130
meat, in Meiji era, 305
media, Japanese: anime, 5, 110; Cool Japan, 5, 85, 107, 112, 154; *gurume* TV dramas, 16–17; *Iron Chef* TV series (*Ryōri no tetsujin*), 16, 35, 147, 305, *See also* manga
medicine: Chinese, 208–209, 214, 307; midwives, 209–210; pregnancy and, 209–210, 212

meibutsu, 9, 65. *See also* local specialty
Meiji (period), xvii, 101–103, 242, 252–253, 323
memory: collective memory, 60; memory therapy (*kaisō ryōhō*), 231; postwar, 179, 250, 297
Mexican cuisine, 105
Michelin guide and rankings, 2, 16, 81, 86, 106, 114, 124, 133
midwives, 209–210
Mie (prefecture), 66
Minamata disease, 306–307
Minamoto no Toshiyori, 59
mingei (folk art), 39
Ministry of Agriculture, Forestry and Fisheries (MAFF), 6, 105–107, 111–112, 118, 123–124, 296, 304, 316
Ministry of Economy, Trade and Industry (METI), 5
Ministry of Education, 108
Ministry of Foreign Affairs (MOFA), 6, 105–106, 112
miso, 35, 40, 42–43, 45, 59, 190
Miyadai Shinji, 303
Miyasaka Shizuo, 224
Miyazaki Hayao, 26, 61, 273. *See also Spirited Away* (*Sen to Chihiro no kamikakushi*, Miyazaki)
Miyazawa Kenji, 279
Momofuku Ando, 3
Momofuku restaurant, 1
monosodium glutamate (MSG), 119–120. *See also* Ajinomoto; umami
Morisada Mankō (Morisada's sketches), 70
Morisue Yoshiaki, 321
MOS burger, 13
Mount Fuji, 107
Murai Yasuhiko, 321
Murase Tadatarō, 73
Museum of Modern Art (New York), 143

Naccarato, Peter, 5
Nada (region), 82
Nagano (prefecture, region), 65
Nagasaki, 40
Nagatsuka Takashi, 233

Nakai Seibei, 138
Namura Jōhaku, 208
Nara (city and prefecture), 66, 236
Naruse Mikio, 243, 251, 254n3, 256n40
National Museum of Modern Art, 135
National Restaurant Association, 123
nationalism: cultural, 125–127; gourmet, 133; rice as metaphor for, 247. See also culinary nationalism
Natsume Sōseki, 72
Netherlands, 89, 91
A New Star (Kaikō Takeshi), 61, 261–265, 268–270
New Yorker (magazine), 4
NHK (Japan Broadcasting Corporation), 118
nigiri sushi, 76. See also sushi
Nihonjinron, 127–129
Nikkei cuisine: defining, 189–192; emergence of, 188–189; evolution of, 195–198; factors in popularity of, 192–195; promotion of, 188, 196; as representative of Japanese cuisine abroad, 187; restaurants and, 188–189
ninjō (human emotion/desire), 24
Nishiyama Matsunosuke, 68
Nobu restaurant, 4, 189
Noguchi, Isamu, 141
Noma restaurant, Copenhagan, 1, 133
noodles: ramen, 65, 196; soba, 46, 65–77, 166, 197–198; sōmen, 65; udon, 65–66, 68
nostalgia, 26, 67, 269–270, 280, 289, 298, 308
nouvelle cuisine, 2, 35
Nye, Joseph, 107

Obama, Barak, 15
Obon (holiday), 43
Oda Nobunaga, 321
Ohnuki-Tierney, Emiko, 17
Ohsawa, Georges, 144
Oishinbo manga, 16, 60–61, 138, 147, 305
Ōkagami (*The Great Mirror*), 54–55
Okamoto Kanoko, 137
Okamoto Tarō, 137

Okinawa Ichiba (magazine), 178
Okinawa (Ryūkyū): Battle of Okinawa, 173; cookbook images of, 179–181; immigrants from, 188–189, 195, 197–198; indigenization of luncheon meat of, 23, 175–182; introduction of luncheon meat to, 174; Japanese imperialism and, 177–178; prevalence of luncheon meat in, 171–172; US domestic science training in, 176; US military in, 173–174, 179, 182
Olympic Games, 107, 111
omakase (chef's choice), 4
omotenashi (hospitality), 16
omuraisu, 9
Onaga Kimiyo, 177
Onna chōhōki (Namura Jōhaku), 208–209
Ono Jirō, 15, 133
onomatopoeia for food textures, 11–12
organic foods, 10, 53, 89
Organization to Promote Japanese Restaurants Abroad, 123–124
Orientalism, 7, 84
Osaka, 66, 68, 70, 135, 137, 266
Osechi (traditional New Year's meal), 140

Pacific War, 173–175, 250. See also World War II
Paris, 145
Parker, Thomas, 135
pasta, wafū (Japanese style), 14
peasant/farmer cuisine, 320
Peregrinations (Pinto), 36
Peru, 4; aji (Peruvian peppers), 190; emergence of Nikkei cuisine in, 188–189; gastronomic boom in, 193–195; immigration of Chinese to, 188; immigration of Japanese to, 188, 192–193; popularity of Nikkei cuisine and, 192–195; revival of indigenous foods, 194–195
Picasso, Pablo, 137
Pilcher, Jeffery, 135
The Pillow Book, 50, 228
Pinto, Fernão Mendes, 36–38

place brands: craftsmanship as component of brand, 159–165; defining, 5; food safety's effect on, 167–168; history/heritage as component of brand, 156–159; Kyoto as, 48, 153–155, 168–169; local conditions/tastes, 165–168; tourism and, 164; trademarks and, 155

Pleij, Herman, 276

poetry: *chōka*, 230; classical, 48, 228; food/eating terms in, 235–236; food in early, 55–56; haiku, 25, 220, 225–229, 232, 236–237, 306; tanka, 233, 235–237

pōku (pork). *See* luncheon meat

Pom Pom Purin café, 17–18

Ponyo (Miyazaki), 273

Portuguese, 36–38

pregnancy: diet and, 207–216; manuals regarding, 208–210; sweets and, 212–214, 217n20; weight gain and, 210–212, 214–216

quinoa, 194–195

rakugo, 67, 72–73

ramen: as *B-kyū gurume* food, 9, 164–165; disposable food packaging and, 293, 297; history of, 3–4, 321; instant, 15, 217n15; as part of blended Japanese cuisine, 134; in Peru, 196–197; popularity of, 2, 4, 65, 312; ramen shops, 4

Rath, Eric, 19, 134

Redzepi, Rene, 133

Restaurant of Many Orders (Miyazawa), 279

restaurants, affluence of 1960s and 1970s and, 262

Revel, Jean-Francois, 322

rice: cultivation of, 111; at Expo 2015, 111; gastronomic boom of 1980s and, 290; Koos, 43; in literature, 53–55, 57, 59–60; as part of traditional Japanese diet, 36, 39–40, 129–130, 296–297; pregnancy and, 209, 217n11; rejection of imported, 310; rice burgers, 10, 13; in sake, 43–45; as symbol of Japanese nation, 247

Rockefeller Foundation, 143
Rodrigues, Domingos, 38–40
Rodrigues, João, 38
Rosanjin. *See* Kitaōji Rosanjin (Kitaōji Fusajirō)
Russo-Japanese War, 305

sake: *atsukan*, 84; breweries, 82–83, 86; categorization of, 85, 87–89; ginjō, 85–87, 91, 166; *junmai* "pure sake," 21, 82, 88, 92, 166; premodern production of, 44–46; promotion of as Japanese national drink, 21, 83–84

Sake Today (Gauntner), 91
San Francisco, 144
Sand, Jordan, 17
Santo Kyōden, 70
Sasagawa Rinpo, 321
sashimi, 39–40, 312
Satō Masatoshi, 51
Satsuma (domain), 322
Sei Shōnagon, 50–51
senbei rice crackers, 14
sexual assault, 174
Shiga (prefecture), 66
Shimada Akio, 305
Shin Yokohama Ramen Museum, 17
shindō funi, 307
Shinju Mariko, 295
Shinshū (Nagano region), 65
Shinto, 274
Shizuoka (prefecture), 17
Shizuoka Sushi Museum, 17
Sho Hiroko, 180
Shogun (Clavell), 39
shokuiku (food education), 108–109
shōyu, 190
slow food movement, 88–89, 307
Smil, Vaclav, 323
soba, 21, 46, 65–73, 322; yakisoba, 5
Soba Connoisseur (*Soba tsū*, Murase Tadatarō), 73
Soba Encyclopedia (*Soba jiten*, Uehara Rorō), 73
sodium glutamate, 119–120
soft power, 5, 106–107, 109, 242

The Soil (Nagatsuka), 234
Solt, George, 19, 321
soy, 35, 39, 41–43, 45–46, 70
soy sauce (shōyu), 41, 42–43, 188, 190
Special Secrecy Law (*tokutei himitsu hogo hō*), 303
Spirited Away (*Sen to Chihiro no kamikakushi*, Miyazaki): anorexia and bulimia in, 274–275, 278, 282–283; bathhouse as Cockaigne in, 275–277; consumption and, 281–282; as critique of capitalism, 276, 279, 281–282; as critique of consumerism, 277, 279, 284; excrement in, 280–281; Japanese folklore and, 285n1; plotline of, 273–274, 276, 280, 283–284, 286n17; role of food in, 274, 277–280; traditional Japanese values and, 276
staple foods, 321
Stray Notes While Lying on My Back (Shiki), 223, 226–227
sugar, 322. *See also* sweets
Sukibayashi Jirō restaurant, 15
Sunada Toshiko, 290
Suntory company, 14
sushi: boom in West of, 35, 99, 192; as fast food, 68, 76; fusion sushi, 189; history of Japanese cuisine and, 322; Nikkei cuisine and, 190, 192; regional cuisine and, 9; sushi police and, 109–110; in Tibet, 313–314
Sushi Police Washoku (anime), 110
sweet potatoes, 322–323
sweets: allusions to Heian court and, 48; history of Japanese cuisine and, 322; Jiyūgaoka Sweets Forest, 15; pregnancy and, 212–214, 217n20. *See also* confectionary; *kashi*; sugar; *wagashi*

Tachibana no Chikage, 55
Tachibana no Norisue, 59
Tadakoso, 55
Taguchi Randi, 308
Taikaku, 59–60
Taira Tomi, 178

Taishō period, xvii, 140
Takahama Kyoshi, 231
Takatsuki Hiroshi. *See* High Moon (Takatsuki Hiroshi)
Takekuma Yoshitaka, 290, 296
takuan (pickle), 312
The Tale of Genji, 48, 228
Tampopo (film), 16, 35, 72, 147
Tanizaki Jun'ichirō, 139, 265
tea: ceremony, 38, 102, 134, 142, 208; gyokuro, 61, 166; Kyoto Uji, 153, 157, 160–161, 165–167; matcha, 160; Portuguese evaluation of, 36; Western depictions of, 38–39, 42–44
Teiichi Yuki, 135
tempura, 13, 68, 322
teppanyaki, 35, 84, 153
Terumi Aiba, 158
Tibet, 313–316
Timken, Beau, 86
Titsingh, Isaac, 43
tofu, donuts, 10
Tōhoku (region), 61
Tokugawa (period), 207, 208, 214, 216, *See also* Edo period
Tokyo, 66–76, 111, 236, 264, 293, *See also* Edo
Tokyo Electric Company (TEPCO), 303
Tomoko Shimizu, 276
Tomozawa Rie, 215
tonkatsu, 9, 102, 134
Toshiro Konishi, 189
tourism, 7, 27, 65, 67, 100, 112, 153, 164, 182, 193
Toyotomi Hideyoshi, 68
Troisgros Brothers, 36
A True Description of the Mighty Kingdoms of Japan and Siam (Caron), 41
Tsuji Shizuo, 135
Tuck, Robert, 237

Uchi and Uchiko restaurants (Austin, TX), 4
Udon soba bakemono Ōeyama (Udon and Soba, monster of Mount Ōe), 70
Uehara Rorō, 73, 75

Uji shūi monogatari (A Collection of Tales from Uji), 53
umami: chemical basis of, 119–120; culinary nationalism and, 22, 125–127, 130–131; cultural identity and, 127–129; promotion of, 118; promotion of washoku and, 118–119, 123–125; traditional Japanese diet and, 129–130; use of term, 120–123; washoku and, 130
Umami Information Center, 124
Umami Manufacturers Association, 124
umeboshi (pickled plum or apricot), 312
UNESCO: Convention Concerning the Protection of the World Cultural and Natural Heritage, 104; Convention for the Safeguarding of Intangible Cultural Heritage, 104; definition of intangible cultural heritage of, 104–105; French cuisine and, 2, 105; Japanese role in, 104; Mexican cuisine and, 105; recognition of washoku as intangible cultural heritage and, 2, 22, 56, 73–74, 99–100, 105–106, 118, 133–134, 154–155, 315–319; Republic of Korea and, 106; soft power and, 106–107; world heritage sites and, 104, 107
University of the Ryukyus (UR), 175, 180
The Unknown Craftsman (Yanagi Sōetsu), 39
Utsuho monogatari (Tale of the hollow tree), 55

vegetables: corn, 321; daikon, 142; effect of Kyoto conditions on taste of, 165–166; food waste and, 292–293, 295–296; in Kyoto cuisine, 161–162; Kyoto heirloom varieties and, 156–157, 160

vegetarianism, 53, 307
Vincent, Keith, 58

wagashi (Japanese sweets), 102
Wakayama (prefecture), 12, 66
wasabi, 39, 99, 190
washoku: defining, 7, 22, 60–61, 101–104, 187; policing of authenticity of, 109–114; promotion of, 108, 118–119; Rosanjin and, 135, 146; soft power and, 106–107; as term, 101–104; umami and, 130; as UNESCO intangible cultural heritage, 56, 105–106, 118, 133–134, 154–155, 315–319; visual appeal of, 147; World Washoku Challenge, 22, 112. *See also* Japanese cuisine
Watanabe, Minoru, 319
White, Merry, 19
Whole Foods grocery store, 4
World War II, 8, 130, 304, 323. *See also* Pacific War
World Washoku Challenge, 113
Wright, Frank Lloyd, 36
Wu, David, 8

Yamai no zōshi, 55–56
Yamamoto Satomi, 55
Yamato (premodern state), xvii, 102
Yamazaki whiskey, 14
Yanagi Sōetsu, 39
Yayoi (period), xvii, 323
Yomiuri (newspaper), 122
Yoshida Kōzō, 141
yōshoku (Euro-American cuisine), 22, 102–103

Zagat guide, 2
Zen, 133